SYNCOPATIONS

Modern and Contemporary Poetics

SYNCOPATIONS

The Stress of Innovation in Contemporary American Poetry

Jed Rasula

THE UNIVERSITY OF ALABAMA PRESS

Tuscaloosa

Copyright © 2004
The University of Alabama Press
Tuscaloosa, Alabama 35487-0380
Manufactured in the United States of America

Typeface: Perpetua

∞

The paper on which this book is printed meets the minimum requirements of American
National Standard for Information Science–Permanence of Paper for Printed Library
Materials, ANSI Z39.48-1984.

Library of Congress Cataloging-in-Publication Data

Rasula, Jed.
    Syncopations : the stress of innovation in recent American poetry / Jed Rasula.
       p. cm. — (Modern and contemporary poetics)
    Includes bibliographical references and index.
       ISBN 0-8173-1302-8 (alk. paper) — ISBN 0-8173-5030-6 (pbk. : alk. paper)
    1. American poetry—20th century—History and criticism. 2. Experimental poetry,
    American—History and criticism. I. Title. II. Series.
    PS325 .R377 2003
    811'.54—dc21

                                                        2003006259

Contents

Illustrations

Preface

Syncopations hovers midway between being a planned book and a collection of occasional essays. Charles Bernstein had suggested several times over the years that I gather my writings on contemporary poetry into a book. My reluctance to do so resulted in this hybrid. *Syncopations* attempts a conceptual chronicle of the promise of American poetry from 1975 to the present, a promise identified in the subtitle, "the stress of innovation." As it stands, concept exceeded chronicle. While numerous publications contributed to the final result, most of them became thoroughly transformed in the process. "The Catastrophe of Charm" and "Literacy Effects" remained intact in order to serve an indexical role to *The American Poetry Wax Museum* (they were originally written before I thought of writing such a book, and they turned out to bear some premonitions of it years in advance). Apart from bringing the first one up to date, the concluding sequence of homages (to Clayton Eshleman, Ronald Johnson, Robin Blaser, and Nathaniel Mackey) are also much as previously published. Otherwise, the bulk of *Syncopations* has either not appeared in print before, or has been drastically recomposed.

Decades of challenging correspondence and debate with Don Byrd have played a decisive role at every stage in the writings that make up this book. I am also indebted to Bruce Andrews, who patiently read through a large and ungainly preview of *Syncopations;* his incisive suggestions made the present text legible to me. An anonymous reader for the University of Alabama Press also provided challenging and invaluable criticism. Most of the original pieces absorbed into *Syncopations* were written in response to invited talks or publications; and my gratitude for the continuum of initiations goes to Charles Bernstein, Michael Davidson, Clayton Eshleman, Lyn Hejinian, Leland Hickman, Devin Johnston, Hank Lazer, Jean-Jacques Lecercle, Kevin McGuirk, Andrew Rathmann, Jerome Rothenberg, Rod Smith, Barrett Watten, Charles Watts, and Anne Williams. Alan Gilbert was kind enough to send copies of *apex of the M* at a crucial moment. Special mention should be made of my association with Clayton Eshleman's magazine *Sulfur,* which provided a primary context for my work for nearly twenty years. Six pieces published in *Sulfur* are worked into the fabric of *Syncopations.* Other parts of *Syncopations* appeared in *Aerial, Poetics Journal, Contemporary Literature, The University of Toronto Quarterly, Chicago Review, Temblor,* and *The Recovery of the Public World,* edited by Charles Watts and Edward Byrne. A number of the pieces (or portions of them) were initially given at conferences: the Sulfur Conference at Eastern Michigan University; annual conferences of the Modern Language Association; the keynote address for the cultural studies conference "Recycling Narratives" at the University of Toronto; "The Recovery of the Public World" in Vancouver; as well as lectures for the University of Paris–Vincennes, the University of California at San Diego, the University of Waterloo, and the University of Georgia.

Thanks for research assistance go to Andrew Griffin and to the support of the Advisory Research Council of Queen's University. Final revisions benefited by the largesse of the Helen S. Lanier endowment at the University of Georgia, for which I am deeply grateful.

SYNCOPATIONS

Introduction

Now I'm talking about epic
as Voice. and as
disobedience. For
example I have disobeyed his chart, or is it
charter—Your, Yours, Yours.
Your idea of how I'm supposed to write.
                    Alice Notley, *Disobedience*

Syncopations is a partial chronicle of my attentions to contemporary American poetry during the past twenty-five years, designed to resonate in the space between *The American Poetry Wax Museum: Reality Effects, 1940–1990* (1996) and *This Compost: Ecological Imperatives in American Poetry* (2002). There is a thematic thread running through the book—a thread, not a thesis—on the topic of innovation, a term I prefer to the more common application of "experimental" to any work that doesn't appear strictly conformist. Innovation is not altogether volitional; innovation in poetry can be circumstantial. But in an American context suffused with a hunger for Old World monuments, appreciating and even recognizing innovation has been difficult. So while the chapters in *Syncopations* were written between 1986 and 2001, they hearken back to an auspicious year, 1975, when the fruits of innovation were at a peak, yet went unacknowledged. The bounty of 1975, it seems, required a quarter century to meet with comparable abundance. The present profusion is evident in a short list of singular books published in 2001: *The Veil* and *The Pretext* by Rae Armantrout; *Lip Service* by Bruce Andrews; *The Downstream Extremity of the Isle of Swans* and *Louise in Love* by Mary Jo Bang; *With Strings* by Charles Bernstein; *Eunoia* by Christian Bök; *The Mood Embosser* by Louis Cabri; *Radio,*

Radio by Ben Doyle; *The Mercy Seat* by Norman Dubie; *Drafts 1–38, Toll* by Rachel Blau DuPlessis; *The Gauguin Answer Sheet* by Dennis Finnell; *Felt* by Alice Fulton; *Torn Awake* by Forrest Gander; *How to Do Things with Tears* by Allen Grossman; *A Border Comedy* by Lyn Hejinian; *Cascadia* by Brenda Hillman; *Notes on the Possibilities and Attractions of Existence* by Anselm Hollo; *Ring of Fire* by Lisa Jarnot; *Poasis* by Pierre Joris; *Again* by Joanne Kyger; *If in Time* by Ann Lauterbach; *Seven Pages Missing* by Steve McCaffery; *Disobedience* by Alice Notley; *Airs, Waters, Places* by Bin Ramke; *Plot* by Claudia Rankine; *Fox* by Adrienne Rich; *The Weather* by Lisa Robertson; *Nova* by Standard Schaefer; *Earliest Worlds* by Eleni Sikelianos; *Fuck You—Aloha—I Love You* by Juliana Spahr; *Such Rich Hour* and *Oh* by Cole Swensen; *Self and Simulacra* by Liz Waldner; and *To Repel Ghosts* by Kevin Young.[1] The alphabetic order in which I've listed these texts accents their eclecticism, a reminder that traditional points of orientation and affinity have eroded dramatically in recent decades. Half of these authors are women, a fact requiring no special representational effort; many of these books are distinctly innovative, though their authors are not regarded as "experimental"; and as for the publishers—trade, university press, and alternative—there is no evident aesthetic disposition by which one might sort the titles from conservative to radical as a way of determining publisher. Nor do they conform to standardized presentational models:

1. Adding a few titles from 2000 accentuates the variety, further compounding the encouraging portent of things to come: *Your Name Here* by John Ashbery; *Serenade* by Bill Berkson; *Men in the Off Hours* by Anne Carson; *On the Nameways* by Clark Coolidge; *Madame Deluxe* by Tenaya Darlington; *Comp.* by Kevin Davies; *Fidget* by Kenneth Goldsmith; *Swarm* by Jorie Graham; *Musca Domestica* by Christine Hume; *Utopic* by Claudia Keelan; *Talking Dirty to the Gods* by Yusef Komunyakaa; *No Eyes: Lester Young* by David Meltzer; *The Promises of Glass* by Michael Palmer; *For* by Carol Snow; *Isolato* by Larissa Szporluk; *The Architextures* by Nathaniel Tarn; *Marriage, A Sentence* by Anne Waldman; *The Annotated "Here" and Selected Poems* by Marjorie Welish; and *The Tapeworm Foundry* by Darren Wershler-Henry. Several of the poets (here and above) are Canadian, which raises the question of what an "American" poet is, particularly given the reciprocities established since the Tish group in Vancouver welcomed Donald Allen's clan of New American poets in 1963, reaffirmed in the 1980s by the Kootenay School's interaction with language poetry. To acknowledge the consequences and significance of these precedents, the configuration of American poetry 2000–01 can't help but be magnified by the inclusion of Bök, Cabri, Carson, McCaffery, and Robertson in the lists above: their inclusion is a reminder that "Canada" is a necessary inconvenience.

six of the books are "selected poems," yet *Selected Poems* is not a title any of the authors have chosen. Twelve of the books are long poems or sequences, five of which are between two hundred and four hundred pages. Several among the remaining titles have the feel of book-length projects because the poems have such focal consistency. Collectively, these works incarnate Lyn Hejinian's sense that "The daring statement unites us":

A paradox
A parody
The paradise of comedy
The imperative that permits
It says that everything may make do
(*Border Comedy* 211)

The originary scene of my ruminations, 1975, was another matter altogether. To provide some background, the volatility of the sixties had continued into the early seventies; within a short time the war in Vietnam was abandoned, and Nixon had been driven from the White House; Allen Ginsberg's chronicle of the public debacle of the 1960s, *The Fall of America,* was published in 1973; and the next year Gary Snyder's *Turtle Island* appeared—not only a book of poetry, but a pledge of ecological and political allegiance that auspiciously won the Pulitzer Prize. Nineteen seventy-five was a momentous year in American poetry, consolidating the whole postwar period, it seemed, in the following publications: *The Collected Books of Jack Spicer;* the third volume of Charles Olson's *The Maximus Poems;* the final installment of Louis Zukofsky's lifework, *"A"22–23* (*"A"24* having previously appeared); George Oppen's *Collected Poems;* Edward Dorn's *Collected Poems 1956–1974* and his long poem *Gunslinger;* Robert Kelly's even longer poem *The Loom;* and John Ashbery's *Self-Portrait in a Convex Mirror.* The list should suggest that I had great respect for demanding books. There's not a bagatelle in sight. I was also attentive to a number of other books published the same year, like Anne Waldman's *Fast Speaking Woman* and three book-length projects: Charles Reznikoff's *Holocaust,* Nathaniel Tarn's *Lyrics for the Bride of God,* and Paul Blackburn's *The Journals.* The large ethnopoetics conference in Milwaukee that spring helped consolidate a certain tribal aspiration: Tarn and Snyder were prominent; Jerome Rothenberg was at the center of it all (*Poland/1931* had appeared the previous year, and New Directions reprinted the Dial Press selected poems *Poems for the Game of Silence* in 1975); David Antin's sharp intelligence was much in evidence, and his groundbreaking talk poems were being prepared for publication as *Talking at the Boundaries* (1976); Clayton Eshleman didn't attend, but he was part of the clan (*The Gull Wall* was another 1975 title), having provided a primary forum for alternative poetries in *Caterpillar* from 1967 to 1972. It was in *Caterpillar* that I first encountered Ron Silliman, Rae Armantrout, and Michael Palmer. (It would be a few years before I took note of *The Maintains* [1974] and *Polaroid* [1975] by Palmer's friend Clark Coolidge.) There were scintillating books coming out of Canada, like Christopher Dewdney's *Fovea Centralis,* Steve McCaffery's *Ow's Waif,* and periodic installments of an immense poem by bp Nichol called *The Martyrology.* While I didn't see them at the time, by 1975 there were books or chapbooks out by Ron Silliman, Charles Bernstein, Bruce Andrews, Ray DiPalma, Bob Perelman, and Barrett Watten. There are more I could mention, but the point is that the achievement *and* the potential of adventurous poetry were conspicuous. These were bodies of work that said: *Sit up and take stock, Proceed with caution* (and *Be bold and irreverent*). The historical sense they imposed was considerable.

But it was apparently not enough. I can't say I was all that well informed about the poetry establishment in 1975, though I recognized the look of slick but inconsequential books that kept appearing on library and bookstore shelves, invariably published by East Coast trade houses that clearly had bigger fish to fry; their poetry books looked decorative, as if their proper element was a furniture showroom. I was in Indiana, having previously lived in Europe, so I had not developed distinct partisan coordinates. I remember reading A. R. Ammons, Robert Lowell, Edward Dorn, and Robert Duncan with equal enthusiasm. Nineteen seventy-five changed all that, as I naively expected some kind of public celebration of these eye-opening books by Spicer, Zukofsky, and the others. It didn't happen. It was weirdly gratifying when Ashbery's book took the Pulitzer, the National Book Award, *and* the National Book Critics Circle Award. *But—but—but* . . . didn't anyone notice the others, I wondered. "Notice" is too gentle a word; they were scorned with an air of implacable indifference. Nothing promotes theoretical reflection and self-examination like discovering that the poetry you esteem is distasteful to the culture brokers.

In hindsight, 1975 marks the decisive ascendancy of writing degree programs, a world in which Columbia MFA graduate Gregory Orr was the latest wunderkind, *Burning the Empty Nests* having appeared when he was only twenty-five, followed shortly by *Gathering the Bones Together* (1975). The Yale Younger Poets prizewinners of the time were Iowa MFA graduates Michael Ryan (*Threats Instead of Trees*, 1974) and Maura Stanton (*Snow on Snow*, 1975), followed by Carolyn Forché's *Gathering the Tribes* in 1976, a year that saw first books by fellow Iowa alumni Ellen Bryan Voigt (*Claiming Kin*) and David St. John (*Hush*). Another emerging reputation in the workshop world was Dave Smith, casting a wide net with *Mean Rufus Throw Down* (1973), *The Fisherman's Whore* (1974), and *Cumberland Station* (1977). Other 1975 publications include *The House on Marshland* by Louise Glück, *In the Dead of the Night* by Norman Dubie, *Bloodlines* by Charles Wright, and Robert Pinsky's *Sadness and Happiness*. Michael S. Harper was emerging as a black alternative to Don L. Lee and Amiri Baraka. His 1975 title, *Nightmare Begins Responsibility*, was flanked by *Debridement* (1973) and *Images of Kin: New and Selected Poems* (1977). Marilyn Hacker made an impact with *Presentation Piece* (1974, National Book Award 1975) and *Separations* (1976).

The American Poetry Wax Museum can be read as my attempt to make sense of how that perplexing moment came to pass. It is only in retrospect, of course, that these were harbingers of hegemonic forces to come. In general, the world of mid-seventies poetry was dominated by figures of long and secure standing in the establishment, a prizewinning cadre, some of whom were gathering big heads of publishing steam. The septegenarian Robert Penn Warren was suddenly liberated into unprecedented productivity, while Robert Lowell famously published three books in 1973 (*The Dolphin, History,* and *For Lizzie and Harriet*), with a *Selected Poems* appearing the year before his untimely death in 1977. Anne Sexton's suicide was followed by nearly annual posthumous collections (four between 1974 and 1978). The closely set and continuously printed work of A. R. Ammons's *Collected Poems 1951–1971* (1972) filled nearly 400 pages; but hard on its heels came *Sphere* (1974), *Diversifications* (1975), and *The Snow Poems* (1977), doubling the total. James Merrill's Ouija board epic *The Changing Light at Sandover* was furtively premiered in *Divine Comedies* (1976) before swelling to 560 pages by the end of the decade. And what would the seventies have been without the influential regionalism of William Stafford, Richard Hugo, and James Wright? They all published regularly throughout the decade, along with Richard Howard, John Hollander, Irving Feldman, Philip Levine, Audre Lorde, Sandra McPherson, W. S. Merwin, Howard Moss, Adrienne Rich, Mark Strand, Charles Simic, and David Wagoner. Such abundance was not confined to the establishment. Robert Creeley and Denise Levertov published prodigiously; the Black Sparrow poets seemed to be laboring under a productivity quota (Kelly, Eshleman, David Meltzer, and Diane Wakoski—though she had several trade publishers in hand as well); there were some very long poems by Frank Samperi and Theodore Enslin; and of course there was that human rival to the Los Angeles flood basin, Charles Bukowski.

The attention deficit disorder institutionalized in the poetry world is something I have addressed at length in *The American Poetry Wax Museum* and need not reiterate here. (Chapter 5, "Literacy Effects," was a preview of that book, which in 1988 I had no plans to write. *The American Poetry Wax Museum,* written five years later, retained from "Literacy Effects" not only its argument, but its bear-baiting rhetoric in denouncing the routinization of effort and reception that characterized the poetry establishment in the postwar era.) My aspiration was to shame scholars, if not poets themselves, into a more informed approach to contemporary poetry. Even as I wrote the book, however, I sensed that I was writing an epitaph. No doubt the inside moves of careerism are the same as ever—possibly more so[2]—but the bifurcation of the poetry world into square

2. For one thing, there are more prizes. Fiscal realism joins hands with hyperbolic careerism: endowments are established at various presses to guarantee annual publications of poetry, so the books that are published are automatically deemed prizewinners.

versus hip, official versus renegade, metropolitan versus provincial, was rapidly eroding. What will emerge from the disappearance of this routinized choreography of opposing postures, I can't say. Poetry is an art of mimesis, so it's predictable that poets will imitate (or determine to avoid imitating) various practices now under way. The chapters that follow pay homage to some of the more distinctive practitioners of American poetry in the late twentieth century. While I largely dispense with the standard rhetoric of proclaiming them "major" figures, it should be clear that I have taken some care in choosing the poets I write about, and I hope that my ruminations may persuade younger poets, among others, to consider the wealth of precedent all around us.

I

Women, Innovation, and "Improbable Evidence"

Remember the slogan that worked wonders for Bill Clinton's 1992 presidential campaign? "It's the economy, stupid." Substitute *women* for *economy* and you've got the new world of American poetry. This is far and away the most important transformation, and it's one that will continue to erode old protocols and refashion institutions in unforeseeable ways. (The only thing that's predictable, I think, is that the changes will be for the better.) A familiar air of elitist masculine privilege has long dominated institutions like the Academy of American Poets. The old boys network will, in time, subside to mortality; but even before then it faces certain demographic ravages, foremost of which is that publications by women are achieving statistical parity with those by men.[1] The big prizes remain in disequilibrium (it's as if the candidates are all on a Rolodex established by 1975, which industry officials consult to make sure that

---

1. Consider the Iowa Poetry Prize, which publishes two or three books a year. Both 1999 titles were by women, two out of three for 1998. Many of the previous years were split, one each. A more significant pattern can be seen in the National Poetry Series that, until 1994, consistently published at a ratio of three men to two women. From 1994 to 1999, however, seventeen of the twenty-five titles have been by women (three of those years included only one man each year).

Bill and Charles and Mark and Bob and John get equal share in the spoils), and if it weren't for Levertov, Rich, and Josephine Jacobsen, the sum total of major awards to women would be even more paltry than it is. Where a welcome difference is evident is in awards for first and second books, the Walt Whitman and the Lamont (now James Laughlin) Prizes. Seven of the Whitman and six of the Lamont Prizes in the nineties went to women.

The role of women poets in American culture has usually been symptomatic, meaning particularized and exceptional. Emily Dickinson, H. D., Marianne Moore, Laura Riding, Sylvia Plath: each one of a kind, and chasteningly isolate, lost in a sea of men whose work collectively imposed a sense of poetry's tasks and possibilities. Women writers might be unique, but their singularity was rarely held up as exemplary. The postwar period imposed such a strictly masculine ethos on poetry that the careers of important figures like Muriel Rukeyser and May Swenson become case studies in vanishing tracks. For a generation of women who were empowered by the women's liberation movement, as well as in the poetry workshops, the challenge of getting out from under masculine shadows was considerable, but it was not suffered individually. For all the negative consequences of the MFA programs (conformism, careerism, anti-intellectualism), the workshops did end up enfranchising women writers on a large scale. Women constituted 40 of the 104 poets in the omnibus workshop-oriented *Morrow Anthology of Younger American Poets* (1985), and more than half—21 of 37—of Nicholas Christopher's *Under 35: The New Generation of American Poets* (1989).[2] It's not that a statistical ascendancy of women necessarily results in increased variety, though I think that is now verifiably the case. More important is the singularity of

2. Most of the significant anthologies of the 1990s were engaged in partisan politics, concerned to establish the credibility of certain zones of praxis. It is telling that a notable gender disparity prevails in the more vanguard-oriented collections: Paul Hoover's *Postmodern American Poetry* (28 women out of 103 poets, and only 4 of 31 born before 1934), Douglas Messeri's *From the Other Side of the Century* (20 of 81), and Eliot Weinberger's *American Poetry Since 1950* (5 of 35), though Weinberger suggests that "a subsequent selection of the innovators from the post–World War II generations would probably contain a majority of women" (xiii).

invention (the subject of chapter 8, "Experiment as a Claim of the Book"). But there are two significant contributing factors to consider: age and heterodoxy. Heterodoxy is not programmatic and may reflect nothing more than demographics. But insofar as much of the postwar poetry map has been defined by alliances, groups, and movements, it is worth bearing in mind Alice Notley's claim about her own generation of women: "Our achievement has probably been to become ourselves in spite of the movements" (Foster, *Poetry and Poetics* 86).[3]

Age is important because it takes a generation (at least) to overcome a dominant paradigm. Pioneering figures in radical feminism are now seniors, and the baby boomers—first-generation beneficiaries of institutionalized gains attributable to feminism—are middle-aged. In terms of writing, not only are more women being published, but a considerable number of them are older, their work reflecting maturity and experience. Kathleen Fraser's career is a useful index not only because of her own insightful testimony in *Translating the Unspeakable,* but also because her 1997 selected poems, *Il Cuore: The Heart,* reflects the attending pressures of emancipation. She includes only fifteen pages published before she was forty, and the assurance and diversity of her work is most apparent in the past two decades. A real diversity of style and idiom among women writers has only recently become evident on a widespread scale, for particular historical reasons. Fraser recounts various institutions in which she taught from 1969 to 1974: "Women students constituted the majority of writers present, but they seldom spoke unless called upon and, in their writing practice, tended to follow a safe and limited model

3. The critique of "movements" as constraints has been extended to feminism by Steve Evans in his preface to a special issue of *Differences* titled "After Patriarchal Poetry: Feminism and the Contemporary Avant-Garde" (2001): "We know . . . how the feminist poetry that has been institutionalized within women's studies programs and teaching anthologies can be restrictively organized around a normative concept of 'experience' that renders all but the most tentative formal innovations by women inadmissible and anathematizes theoretical reflection on poetic practice (by poets themselves, by their readers) as an overly intellectualized interference with the immediate pleasures afforded by cathartic identification" (i–ii). Evans laments the way such exclusions have resulted in the legacy of "[a]n avant-garde without women, a poetics without poetry, [and] a poetry for which entire registers of experience, innovation, and reflexivity are taboo" (ii).

of prosody learned in earlier classes" (*Translating* 2). The figures who established and gave luster to this model—the low-key personal free-verse lyric of the 1960s—were largely male, and this was the dominant approved style in the workshops as they multiplied through the seventies. It took more than twenty years for women to work themselves free of this laconic idiom, going on to develop heterogeneous writing practices. (A key moment along the way was Anne Waldman's performance text "Fast Speaking Woman," which was indebted to the breath-oriented poetics of Charles Olson and Allen Ginsberg, while pursuing semantic liberation from the discursive and rhetorical protocols of Waldman's male models and peers.) Women readily felt the need to divest themselves of a pregendered mode, while for male poets the beguiling sense of a manner easily adapted to masculine attitudes resulted in a dispiriting acquiescence to a moribund style, and the later books of many of the MFA heroes of 1975 are documents of a generational disaster.

In the polarized atmosphere that prevailed for about twenty-five years (1958–83, say), certain acclaimed figures became moral-aesthetic icons. The reverence with which followers would refer the question of authenticity back to Theodore Roethke or James Wright, cultural authority back to Lowell or Olson, or elegance back to W. H. Auden and James Merrill, now seems the mark of a vanished time. The dominant spirit of opposing camps marked such avowals with a devotional air. With Olson, Lowell, and Ginsberg around (squirming under the shadows of William Carlos Williams, T. S. Eliot, and Ezra Pound), the figure of The Poet was at once glamorous and suffocating. The dominant poets today are less imposing—in part because they are less saddled with associated cultural baggage, but also because that baggage was deeply invested in specific forms of gender empowerment. Many of the most acclaimed and innovative poets now are women (the two facets are often combined), and there seems to be a more genial spirit of cohabitation. Little gladiatorial resolve is at stake, and even the ideological differences of personal background and poetic orientation are muted when one considers the success of Lyn Hejinian and Susan Howe as well as Alice Fulton and Jorie Graham, who now occupy the position of respected elders, having published regularly during the past two decades and built up reputations accordingly.

Plenty of other names (from several generations) could be added—
Barbara Guest, Rosmarie Waldrop, Ann Lauterbach, C. D. Wright, Alice
Notley—but it's interesting how many women began publishing po-
etry only near or after the age of forty (Fanny Howe, Susan Howe, Lyn
Hejinian, Norma Cole, Beverly Dahlen, Rachel Blau DuPlessis, Joan
Retallack, Hannah Weiner).

The phenomenon of the mature woman poet arriving fully achieved
and as if out of nowhere dramatized the appearance of Amy Clampitt
in 1983 with *The Kingfishers*—a phenomenon repeated with Anne Carson. Apart from a Canadian chapbook, Carson burst on the scene with
two big books, *Plainwater* and *Glass, Irony, and God* in 1995, at the age of
forty-five. Three further volumes have confirmed that, unlike Clampitt,
Carson's prodigality is matched by variety. In very short order she has
slipped into place as a defining figure of the new millennium, one of the
"wisdom writer[s]" for Harold Bloom, "in a less-than-fingers-on-one-
hand group of writers" for Susan Sontag (Rehak 38). Such accolades have
resulted in a lavish MacArthur Fellowship and the lucrative Griffin Poetry Prize in Canada. The sudden lionization of Carson, along with the
fact that her books are published by Knopf, would have been evidence of
a setup twenty years ago: a career manufactured for (and by) Manhattan
literati.[4] But the terms of engagement and appraisal have changed. For
one thing, *Glass, Irony, and God* was published by New Directions, with a
preface by Guy Davenport, whose previous attention to poets bore conspicuous marks of partisan affiliation (Pound, Zukofsky, Olson, Jonathan
Williams, Ronald Johnson). But the Carson phenomenon is skewed in
other ways as well, in that she is not launching herself strictly as a poet
(as would formerly have been the case); nor does she aspire to teach
other writers, since she is a classics professor at McGill University in

4. The case of Carson is complicated by the fact that she's Canadian, while her poetry
has been published by New York trade publishers. Curiously, it was not until after she had
been awarded the MacArthur Fellowship that Canadian bookstores and libraries acknowledged her as a Canadian poet. Because she has become such a singularly important figure
in American letters, however, it will be interesting to see whether future anthologists can
resist including her despite her nationality.

Montreal (her originality, in fact, may be traced to her indifference to, or unfamiliarity with, contemporary poetry).

The sudden ascendancy of a middle-aged poet like Anne Carson is not unique—*Harmonium* was published when Wallace Stevens was forty-three; Robert Frost was thirty-nine when his first book appeared—but the modern prototypes for the figure of the poet as (virile) youth are pervasive: Pound, Stephen Crane, T. S. Eliot, e. e. cummings, Langston Hughes, and Laura Riding gave modernism a youthful face, substantiated by the next generation (in England by Auden, George Barker, and Dylan Thomas, followed stateside by Rukeyser, Delmore Schwartz, John Berryman, and Lowell). In the postwar period reputations continued to be made by poets in their twenties: Richard Wilbur, Merwin, Rich, Merrill, Hollander, Plath; and the Beats, too, embodied youth. At the time of the Six Gallery reading in San Francisco in 1955, Ginsberg was still under thirty, Snyder was twenty-five, and Michael McClure was a few weeks shy of twenty-three. (A month later, twenty-year-old Elvis Presley signed a contract with RCA.) The phenomenon of flaming youth was more or less institutionally imposed on the first generation of poets to go through the MFA programs, as published books were necessary for career advancement. The meteor of youth, preternaturally gifted, continues to flare of course (Brenda Shaughnessy, Larissa Szporluk, Jeff Clark, Lisa Lubasch, Tessa Rumsey), but more and more of the "new" poets are actually older. Consider some recent debut volumes: *Delirium* (1995) by Barbara Hamby (b. 1952); *Apology for Want* (1997) by Mary Jo Bang (b. 1946); *The New Intimacy* (1997) by Barbara Cully (b. 1955); *The Bounty* (1997) by Myung Mi Kim (b. 1957); *The Thicket Daybreak* (1997) by Catherine Webster (b. 1944); *Bite Every Sorrow* (1998) by Barbara Ras (b. 1949); *Of Flesh and Spirit* (1998) by Wang Ping (b. 1957); *Hotel Imperium* (1999) by Rachel Loden (b. 1948); *A Taxi to the Flame* (1999) by Vicki Karp (b. 1953)—all at least forty years old.[5] Many poets are now over forty by the time a second book appears: *The Dig* (1992) by Lyn Emanuel

5. Other examples—by older poets whose birth dates I don't know—include *Candy Necklace* (1997) by Cal Bedient, *The Cult of the Right Hand* (1991) by Elaine Cerranova, *The Arrangement of Space* (1991) by Martha Collins, *At the Site of Inside Out* (1997) by Anna Rabinowitz, and *Sister Betty Reads the Whole You* (1998) by Susan Holahan.

(b. 1949); *Trace Elements* (1998) by Barbara Jordan (b. 1949); *For* (2000) by Carol Snow (b. 1949); *Rough Cut* (1997) by Thomas Swiss (b. 1952); *Smokes* by Susan Wheeler (b. 1955); *Transit Authority* (2000) by Tony Sanders (b. 1957); *The Oval Hour* (1999) by Kathleen Peirce (b. 1956); and *After I Was Dead* (1999) by Laura Mullen (b. 1958). Even some of the so-called young poets are publishing first books at an age formerly considered mid-career (e.g. Rich of *Leaflets;* Merwin of *The Moving Target;* Creeley of *For Love*): *Madonna anno domini* (1997) by Joshua Clover (b. 1962); *And Her Soul Out of Nothing* (1997) by Olena Katyiak Davis (b. 1963); *Polyverse* by Lee Ann Brown (b. 1963); *First Worlds* (2001) by Eleni Sikelianos (b. 1965); and *Point and Line* (2000) by Thalia Field (b. 1966). Most striking, though, is the sharp surge of accomplishment evident in a number of poets whose distinctiveness became most evident in the 1990s, including Ann Lauterbach, Marjorie Welish, Norma Cole, C. D. Wright, Forrest Gander, Mark Doty, Brenda Hillman, Dean Young, Donald Revell, Bin Ramke, Stephen Ratcliffe, and Andrew Schelling.

All this is in striking contrast to career patterns a few decades ago. By the time they were forty, poets such as Jerome Rothenberg, Robert Kelly, and Clayton Eshleman were each listing a few dozen books (a number augmented by their work as editors and translators). Mainstream poets had lists less pumped up with chapbooks, but the numbers could still be substantial (Merwin had thirteen titles by the age of forty). In addition, those who rose to prominence in the postwar decade benefited from a relatively less prolific scene. By the time he was forty, Lowell had already appeared in eight major anthologies, as had Merrill by the same age. Others could be found in even more anthologies: Anthony Hecht (11), Richard Wilbur (14), James Wright (10), and W. D. Snodgrass an astonishing seventeen anthology appearances *before* his second book appeared at the age of forty-two. Some opposing poets also fared well, like Gary Snyder, who at forty had been in at least sixteen anthologies. The much discussed "anthology wars" of the 1960s benefited both sides, establishing various rosters that anthologists up to the present have felt obliged to duplicate or honorifically extend by rhetorical enframing. The prolonged *ideological* influence of the arrayed groupings lasted for decades. But to this point there has been only one comparably influential ideological bloc: language poetry.

As with the Beat/Black Mountain predecessors, early publication—along with judicious anthologies of poetry *and* prose—meant that language poetry had a reputation and growing influence well before most of the participants were forty years old. But because of the group identity, these enfants terribles were middle-aged as they came to individual prominence. As a generation, the poets associated with language writing have been publishing books regularly for several decades, so the body of work is now both extensive and documentary. But because of its procedural orientation, language writing is not easily assessed in the normative terms of individual "growth and development." This has the effect of making early works by, say, Bob Perelman and Bruce Andrews look preternaturally "mature." But procedure is not all. By avoiding the alignment of the poem with a private voice and the vicissitudes of personal experience, language writing was energized by its relationship to public discourse. Early critical references to blip culture—to the depthless surfaces of a postmodernism that language poets purportedly reflected with corresponding depthlessness—gave the misleading impression of language poetry as simple transcription. Twenty years later, a documentary propensity is far more evident. By no means, however, has this led to a wholesale acceptance of language poetry or its theories and principles. Anthologists venture only as far as Michael Palmer and Susan Howe; and Ron Silliman's appearance in the Oxford *Anthology of Modern American Poetry* (2000), edited by Cary Nelson, may have more to do with his past affiliation with *Socialist Review* than his role as language poet and theorist. References to language poetry abound, of course, but most remain references only.

Meanwhile, the mirage of an offending doctrine (or a disagreeable practice) persists. This can be jesting, as in David Lehman's *The Daily Mirror: A Journal in Poetry* (2000):

I think I will write a one-line
"Language" poem here it is

it's called "Syntax" and the line
is "Sin tax" (87)

As Lehman's poem indicates, language poetry can now be assumed as a familiar reference, deserving a lighthearted roasting. A more pervasive assumption is that language poetry is passé,[6] or else something to surmount, as proclaimed on the back cover of William Olsen's 1996 book, *Vision of a Storm Cloud:* "William Olsen's newest work is the harbinger of a new wave of American poetry. In moving beyond the 'new formalists' and the 'language poets,' Olsen has crafted poems that are energetic, expansive, and romantic." Whether language poetry is something to be lampooned or overcome, it has at least become habitually cited.

The most revealing response is a poem by Ronald Wallace from *The Uses of Adversity* (1998), which I take to be symptomatic of a widespread resentment usually not ventured in print.

L=A=N=G=U=A=G=E
The poet says that language is an absence,
and a *beautiful absence,* at that. Representation
is an illusion not worth pursuing, a limitation
on the imagination's plate. It makes no sense
to her, she says, mimesis and narration
are out of the question, boring, passé, old-fashioned.
She feels a rancor for the empirical. Abstraction,
disjunction, juxtaposition, and all the other *shuns*

take her fancy. And all the friendly stories
of my childhood pack up and walk out the door,
taking with them their pungent oranges, melons, raspberries,
the sweet fruit salad of the juicy familiar,

6. Or something long gone: "I've read some interesting poems from that domain," Philip Lamantia remarked in 1998, "but I can't see it as a direction, no. And it's been over as a movement for some time now" (Meltzer, *San Francisco Beat* 148).

leaving us with a mouthful of semiotics,
poststructuralism doing its after-dinner tricks. (82)

A fugitive publication during its brief run (1978–82), $L=A=N=G=U=A=G=E$ has long since come to signify something for a considerable number of people who never read it and have probably never even seen a copy. A selection of pieces from the magazine appeared in 1984, and the publication had itself gone out of print by the time the phrase "language poetry" had trickled down into the vocabulary of poets like Wallace, for whom it signifies a critical fashion, an obtuse scholastic ado about nothing. Given the considerable population of MFA graduates and poet-professors in the United States, many may have identified language poetry as the probable cause of critical indifference to their own work. Foremost in Wallace's poem is the contention that language writing abjures the tangible world, seeking solace in the boneyard of abstractions. Andrews and Bernstein, introducing *The L=A=N=G=U=A=G=E Book,* were worried by the persistence of such assumptions way back in 1984: "[T]he idea that writing should (or could) be stripped of reference is as bothersome and confusing as the assumption that the primary function of words is to refer, one-on-one, to an already constructed world of 'things.' Rather, reference, like the body itself, is one of the horizons of language, whose value is to be found in the writing (the world) before which we find ourselves at any moment" (ix). The "bothersome" assumption that words should be compliantly referential clearly encompasses the position taken by Ronald Wallace.

Wallace's poem stakes a strikingly masculinist territorial claim, defending the integrity of personal identity and/as childhood memory, portraying the offending party as a woman—which is to say, an unnatural aggressor. In Wallace's world there is clearly a place for women—as mothers, preparing "the sweet fruit salad of the juicy familiar" in the kitchen. What's most unusual about Wallace's poem is that it dates from 1998, twenty years after the magazine he names in his title was published. Regardless of one's own interest in (or some would say tolerance for) language poetry, it is increasingly untenable to think of the language writers themselves as merely executing further proofs or demonstrations of first principles, comporting, that is, within the boundaries of groupthink. The legacy of language poetry has been disseminated into the environment of poetic innovation at large; and as Wallace's worried poem suggests, there's something about this legacy of innovation and women that go together.

At least Wallace craves satiety, unlike William Logan, whose critical distemper thrives on disavowal. His 1989 review of Michael Palmer's *Sun* for the *New York Times Book Review* qualifies as some pinnacle of obtuseness: "Reading Michael Palmer's poetry is like listening to serial music or slamming your head against a streetlight stanchion—somewhere, you're sure, masochists are lining up to enjoy the very same thing; but for most people the only pleasure it can have is the pleasure of its being over" (*Reputations* 46). "In Palmer's work, language is frequently reduced to its surface gestures, which is fine if you're a gesture and if not, not" (47).[7] In cavalier pronouncements like these, Logan substitutes grumpy posturing for critical discernment, repeating the time-honored gesture with which metropolitan sophisticates dismiss unwanted visitors: the clever rebuke, the archly casual put-down with which Rosencrantz and Guildenstern are sent from the court to their unwitting doom.

One exception to the intemperate rebuke and the offhand dismissal is Lyn Emanuel's cautionary essay "Language Poets, New Formalists, and the Techniquization of Poetry," in which she charges both camps with a dereliction of duty: "Beneath the rhetoric of innovation lies an investment in the status quo," she claims, as they fail to "renovate the ghetto of free verse" and "flee it," instead, "for the subdivisions of technique" (221). Emanuel does not take a populist view, exactly, but she is con-

---

7. This dismissal of Palmer replicates Stein on Pound, though surely Stein would be no more amenable to Logan than Palmer is. Logan's bile extends far beyond language poetry. He likens Creeley's work to "the tedium of diary jotting or the Dictaphone," producing "vacuous ruminations that are those of a man as a chamber decompresses and the oxygen goes out of his head" (*Reputations* 170, 171); and he gazes ruefully on the "cruel tedium" of Ashbery's "vast rhetorical machines, spewing out meaning and non-meaning indifferently" (40). Logan's dyspeptic temperament is touted by Penguin, the publisher of his poetry, in lieu of blurbs. The back cover of *Night Battle* (1999) offers the following: "A brilliant, almost cheerless collection"; "The most hated man in American poetry"; and "William Logan is our Geoffrey Hill: cranky, gifted."

cerned with audience and access. "Language poets and new formalists must move from the issues of art—what is collected, withheld, made special—to considerations of audience, who will be walled out from these technologies, these new museums of language" (220). The precipitous rise of public poetry events such as slams and contests has revealed a massive audience, to be sure, but I doubt this is what Emanuel has in mind. I think what she favors is a greater deliberation when it comes to questions of form; what various formal choices signify to different constituencies; and in the consideration of constituencies, whether one is content to preach to the converted. While her point is well taken, Emanuel's focus on formalism is out of touch with the abiding concerns of the language poets. The blatant politicization of language evident in the work of Bob Perelman, Ron Silliman, or Bruce Andrews is hard to construe as driven by formalist criteria. Silliman's use of the Fibonaci series in *Ketjak* and *Tjanting* was no more formalist than another poet's decisions about line breaks. In both cases they are functional guides to the shaping and patterning of emergent material; but Silliman's books do not enact large-scale rehearsals for the preservation of a fetishized form, whereas those poets who place a primary value on "writing in forms" are doing just that.

The issues that continue to emanate from language poetry are not formal.[8] Formalism is a straw dog. The real dirty word in the American poetry clubhouse is *intellectual*. The fitful absorption of modernism into Anglo-American letters was prelude to a lurking and easily revived anti-intellectualism. Resentful accusations of "difficulty" in poetry, commonly associated with modernism, usually mean that the reader (critic) doesn't want poetry to think. This attitude consigns the poem to a kind of hotel-

8. See John Koethe, whose "Contrary Impulses: The Tension between Poetry and Theory" addressed diverging practices in American poetry with unusual clarity in 1991. Charting a zone divided between workshop personalism and the language poets, with deconstruction as the theoretical burden inducing the most stress for poetry, he advocated "a poetics [that] would neither reject the domain of subjectivity, as deconstruction does, nor try to incorporate it into the domain of the objective, as the poetics of authenticity tries to do" (49). The preoccupation with form evaporates under pressure of such ontological exigencies.

bar, cocktail-hour pianism, a strictly decorative role. It does not pro-
scribe thoughts from the poem, but asks that the thoughts be familiar
enough so as not to disturb the atmosphere—that is, the idle chatter, the
drinks, the flirting. Difficulty returned to poetry with a vengeance in the
context of Black Mountain, but not always in the obvious terms of intellectualism. Creeley's work, for instance, is as accessible as that of Carl
Sandburg on the level of diction and vocabulary; but it renders even the
simplest declarations instances of a moral challenge. It is the singular pluralized in the simplest speech: "As soon as / I speak, I / speaks" (294).
"There is / a silence / to fill" (344). "My face is my own, I thought"
(152). Creeley's is a poetry difficult in its claims, and foremost among its
claims is the thought of simplicity. The work of Olson or Duncan, on the
other hand, is post-modernist; that is, it openly wears its learning, but
doesn't pretend that its enigmas can be solved by tracking down references. The references have integrity; learning is invited, promoted, demanded, but as gymnastic prelude to a performance that doesn't end on
the page, but rather is an initiation to a life on call. You heed the calling
(or not, as the case may be).

A fundamental cause of widespread misconceptions about language
poetry is ignorance of the poetics that gave rise to it, which is all the
more alarming considering its availability. The "New American Poetry"
convened by Donald Allen in 1960 was the immediate provocation. For
those poets who ventured into *that* new world only as far as a dabble of
Ginsberg, a taste of Snyder, a sidelong glance at Frank O'Hara, the theoretical claims of language poetry seem esoteric in the extreme. Another
source behind the intellectualism of language poetry was "theory" in the
scholastic sense. In 1987 the Canadian critic Stephen Scobie asked, with
deliberate provocation, "Wouldn't you agree that the two greatest poets
of the last twenty years have been Roland Barthes and Jacques Derrida?"
(240). Hyperbole aside, Scobie makes a legitimate point, one that takes
us back to 1975. At that point I had read Derrida's *Speech and Phenomena*
but knew nothing about him or the French intellectual scene;[9] so my

---

9. I'd spent much of my undergraduate years studying Heidegger, which led me to the
Northwestern series on phenomenology and existentialism in which *Speech and Phenomenon*
appeared.

interest was piqued when, at the ethnopoetics conference in Milwaukee, I heard David Antin ask another poet if he had read Derrida. It was a time when poets were quick on the draw. Perhaps the first appearance of Foucault in English was in *Io,* Richard Grossinger's journal of poetics, esoterica, and bioregionalism. My own poetry magazine, *Wch Way,* devoted a substantial part of the first two issues (1975) to a discussion of Barthes's *The Pleasure of the Text.*[10] The Canadian journal *Open Letter* was a trove of speculative riches, concentrated in the Toronto Research Group reports of bp Nichol and Steve McCaffery. Coming into a life of poetry at that point, then, entailed a complex mix of work and play, esoteric and exoteric, body and mind. Above all, it meant that nothing could be taken for granted when it came to form *or* content. When Ed Sanders published his manifesto *Investigative Poetry,* the recognition of his claims felt immediate: What other kind was there?

Times change, of course, and the terms of investigation change too. It's understandable if younger poets now feel that further investigation of the formal resources of language as ideological material feels dated; on the other hand, if you acknowledge the ideological parasites language clearly supports, such investigations are always relevant. The ongoing trauma of vanguard innovation—what Paul Mann calls *The Theory-Death of the Avant-Garde*—is pertinent as well; that is, given the capitalist exhortation to constant revolution in the modes of production, how revolutionary is it for artists to replicate such a structure in their media? By

10. *Wch Way* appeared intermittently from 1975 to 1984, coedited first with Ron Barnard and later with Don Byrd (the final two issues were copublished with Jerome Rothenberg's *New Wilderness Letter*). Pointedly bucking magazine trends, *Wch Way* published long poems or larger selections of work by its contributors. A sense of the contents can be gleaned by listing some of the books in which material published in *Wch Way* later appeared: *Empty Words* by John Cage, *Talking at the Boundaries* by David Antin, *Without Music* by Michael Palmer, *Ground Work: Before the War* by Robert Duncan, *Evoba* by Steve McCaffery, *Call Steps* by Kenneth Irby, *My Emily Dickinson* by Susan Howe, *Bedouin Hornbook* by Nathaniel Mackey, *Phantom Anthems* by Robert Grenier, *The Sophist* by Charles Bernstein, *Primer* by Bob Perelman, *Loop* by John Taggart, *Spring Trances in the Control Emerald Night* by Christopher Dewdney, *Solution Passage* by Clark Coolidge, and *Complete Thought* by Barrett Watten, among others. Numerous other writers appeared in *Wch Way,* including Paul Metcalf, Frank Chin, Edward Dorn, Rosmarie Waldrop, Kathleen Fraser, Clayton Eshleman, Will Alexander, Howard Norman, John Clarke, Robert Kelly, Jackson Mac Low, Charles Simic, Michael Davidson, and Charles Stein.

the same token, complacent return to the anachronistic precedent of "tradition" is not a viable alternative. Above all, there's no excuse for not being informed, and this is tantamount to an intellectual avowal. The cultural outlook of Americans tends to vacillate between wide-eyed Euro tourism and chest-thumping affirmations of a jar in Tennessee. This schizoid outlook filters down into stereotyped apparitions in poetry: "A Baroque Wall-Fountain in the Villa Sciarra" (Wilbur) versus "Autumn Begins in Martins Ferry, Ohio" (Wright); between the cosmopolitanism of J. D. McClatchy and the populism of the poetry slam. Such effortless examples of contrariety have been mistaken for variety in surveys and anthologies, as if poets were types of animals to be led onto the ark, two by two.

The world's complexity contests the convenience of such an arrangement. Leslie Scalapino succinctly renders the challenge: "Poetry in this time and nation is doing the work of philosophy—it is writing that is conjecture" (19). The conjectural challenge was a vital concomitant to the New American Poetry: Donald Allen's 1960 anthology had included a forty-page section titled "Statements on Poetics," and the impulse was extended to an entire volume in 1974, *The Poetics of the New American Poetry*.[11] By contrast, the establishment as well as the workshops maintained a superstitious hesitation to engage in the philosophical challenge of *poetics,* preferring to talk about "craft." Another (and maybe the most salutary) consequence of language poetry is that poetics has become an increasingly vigorous feature across the denominational sockets of American poetry. Heather McHugh's *Broken English* (1993), Lyn Hejinian's *The Language of Inquiry* (2000), and Anne Waldman's *Vow to Poetry* (2001) are exemplary records of poetics as vitalizing accompaniment to the writing life. It is also encouraging to see how many compilations have appeared in recent years, including *By Herself: Women Reclaim Poetry,* edited by Molly McQuade (2000); *After Confession: Poetry as Autobiography,* edited by Kate Sontag and David Graham (2001); *We Who Love to be Astonished: Experimental Women's Writing and Performative Poetics,* edited by Laura Hinton and

11. Ron Silliman followed Allen's precedent, rounding out his selection of language poetry in *In the American Tree* (1986) with a portfolio of poetics; Mary Margaret Sloan did likewise in *Moving Borders: Three Decades of Innovative Writing by Women* (1998).

Cynthia Hogue (2002); *American Women Poets in the Twenty-First Century,* edited by Claudia Rankine and Juliana Spahr (2002); and *Telling It Slant: Avant-Garde Poetics of the 1990s,* edited by Mark Wallace and Steven Marks (2002).

A common mistake is to presume that poetics is afterthought, window dressing, postcoital to the ontological drama of the poem itself. In the American context, there's a certain reverence for the posture of superstitious restraint in a poet when it comes to speaking about poetry. For some poets this may well be a psychological necessity, but as a cultural model it perpetuates mystification about agency. A body of poetry, enshrined, may become paralyzing: aloof, authoritative, unapproachable, and mesmerizing. What I most admire in poetry is how it instructs me, and the provenance and methods of instruction are endlessly various. I take Thoreau's precedent seriously, and would abandon even the most beloved Walden of my imagination if I found myself cutting a steady track to the shore from the habit of dipping in its waters. So inebriating is the spell that Olson or Ginsberg, H. D. or Eliot cast over acolytes that some never recover (yet recovery need not imply repudiation). The pieces in *Syncopations* admittedly constitute a kind of advocacy; but advocacy is not finality any more than provisional recommendations for local acts of social justice are prescriptions for utopia. Ralph Waldo Emerson (sounding like a Situationist) entertained the bracing thought that we might ponder the disappearance of literature altogether.[12] He did not mean that it might be crushed out, but that its own powers of transformation, if fully absorbed into the character of the culture, would erode the very institutions that form the context of literature, the background against which the figurations of literary activity are made legible.

A species of heckler's gloat is evident from time to time when pundits

---

12. "Criticism must be transcendental, that is, must consider literature ephemeral & easily entertain the supposition of its entire disappearance" (quoted in Richard Poirier, *Renewal* 27). I take Emerson's notion, in part, as intimation of an expanded (or maybe reclaimed) orality. Given Emerson's acute sense of flux and flow, he was disposed to view texts as frozen moments that might be thawed out. In a fully animated cultural milieu there'd be no need for a text, because every articulation would meet its moment head on, no deferrals necessary. This unimaginable prospect is one in which everyone would be constantly prepared for the sublime utterance.

mention the academic success of mavericks (a.k.a. language poets) like Charles Bernstein, Barrett Watten, Bob Perelman, and Steve McCaffery. (Oddly, the same charges have not been made about Creeley or Snyder, even though their hipster patrimony was more substantive, with far greater risk of seeming compromised by academic affiliation.) But changing circumstances demand more discernment, especially when it comes to the role of institutions. Poetry always has its institutions. A slam is no less *instituting* a scenario than a classroom—both fill up with expectations—and institutions reinforce expectations. Language poetry did not emerge solely as an oppositional enterprise, nor did it aspire to renegade or outsider status; so academic success does not necessarily imply betrayal. Language poetry is most important for backing up the determination of certain poets (by no means restricted to a group of insiders) to disentangle themselves from the prefiguring nets of less visible (but therefore even more dangerous) institutions than academe: the tyranny of the lyrical ego, the breath unit, the anecdote, the scenic moment, and the encumbering paraphernalia of authenticity. Naturally, the institutional success of language poetry means that its own procedural strictures, specific to the hegemonies of 1975, may now seem oppressive to younger poets. But before forgetfulness runs its course, it is imperative that younger poets realize that the very openness of the present milieu is significantly indebted to the Houdini-like routines of their predecessors, engineering an escape from the locked trunks (the noncommunicating vessels) of 1960—the Hall-Pack-Simpson "New Poets" and the Allen "New American Poetry"—as well as the weak detente represented by the workshops.

Language poetry emerged from (and to some degree perpetuated) the bipolar disorder of competing institutions in American poetry, but it seems to have nourished poetic practice in markedly nondenominational ways. This unintended enrichment, handled with care, has the potential to transcend sectarian vexations that have long seemed instinctive to readers; and after all, the liberation of the *reader* was the guiding light of much that was published in $L=A=N=G=U=A=G=E$. Before the aura of theoretical intimidation began to emanate from language poetry, there was an available assumption that you need not *abashedly* point to "human interest" as the plausible rationale for reading a poem. By the same token, if your interest in others is genuine, a poem can be an effective vehicle for making acquaintances. There is a considerable body of poetry (e.g., Rodney Jones) that serves little purpose for me but this: it expresses views and sentiments, it negotiates pieces of fate and ponders the cost of inclination, in ways that offer me some access to all my kin with whom I have "nothing in common" but the fact of kinship. Who doesn't count such distance and dissimilarity as being in the family way? The poetry that enhances my understanding of those who don't think as I do may fall short of the demands I would impose in the terms provided by theoretical sophistication, cultural complexity, or aesthetic gratification. But the measure of dynamics in a culture's poetry is that there *are* more satisfactions, and lessons, than any particular tradition or prospective practice can contain. That's why I admire Ron Silliman's pluck in listing a catalogue of alternates in his introduction to *In the American Tree* (xx–xxi)—a gesture he repeats in his afterword to *The Art of Practice,* edited by Dennis Barone and Peter Ganick: "That more than 160 North American poets are actively and usefully involved in the avant-garde tradition of writing is in itself a stunning thought," he reflects, adding in boldface, "**[W]e in North America are living in a poetic renaissance unparalleled in our history**" (377). This may be the case, though I wouldn't attribute *all* the virtues to the avant-garde.

In the first issue of *Sulfur* (1981), Eliot Weinberger remarked, "One effect of the poetry pandemic has surely been the elimination of exogamous reading. It has become so hectic in one's own longhouse that one rarely has the time or stamina for visits to other clans. Twenty years ago, in the ardent days of the anthology battles, even diehard Beat or Black Mountain partisans could, at the least, recognize the insignia of the opposing troops" (*"Sunrise"* 221). The warning about parochialism in one's reading and associations is perennially relevant, though it should not be taken to imply, as alternative, some vacuous universalism. I concur with Charles Bernstein's exhortation in *A Poetics* that "We have to get over, as in getting over a disease, the idea that we can 'all' speak to one another in the universal voice of poetry" (5). Much as I agree, however, I'm concerned that this can be construed as sanctioning a new parochialism within the heterodox pockets of American poetry. The division of labor is replicated in the disciplinary configuration of universities, and that division is mirrored increasingly in the special interest constituencies in the poetry world. Part of what these *special interests* compel is an assumption of prior consent. This quickly passes over into a covert regulation of taste. If you are keen on the avant-garde, your notice of Mary Jo Salter will be limited to the expected snicker or the rude aside. If *The Simple Truth* (Philip Levine) is your thing, the work of Leslie Scalapino will seem both creepy and beside the point. I'm not suggesting that "we all" must learn from one another or die (to vary Auden's infamously belabored line), but rather that there's a value in overcoming one's own presumptions, particularly presumptions of familiarity with what goes on across the way, in the enemy's camp, the neighbor's backyard, the other guy's poem.

This might sound like an ecumenical recommendation, urging a catholicity of taste that will prove impractical to sustain. After all, the sheer volume of published poetry now exceeds the grasp of even the most fanatical followers. Part of the survival value of a sectarian orientation is pragmatic: you learn to read signs of association (editorial boards of magazines, types of poetry published), you are attracted or repulsed by the names of the blurb writers, you find certain presses reliably invigorating and others predictably bland, and so forth. For almost fifty years the poetry world as a whole constituted a varied but reliable system—so much so that I spent hundreds of pages in *The American Poetry Wax Museum* documenting how the system was established and how inflexible it had become. In astonishingly short order the terms have changed. Traces of the old system will undoubtedly continue to have influence and even prevail in many sectors, but there is now some evidence of salutary transformations. There continues to be a plethora of published poetry (and the space devoted to poetry in bookstores seems to be mushrooming), but it's becoming more and more difficult to use place of publication (journal or book) as a reliable indicator of poetic orientation. Affinities are less binding, not so programmatic.

Small press, university press, and trade publishers no longer signify quite what they used to, and crossovers are more common. Alice Notley, whose work epitomized the range of small press formats for decades, is now a Penguin Poet, as is Anne Waldman. The variety of Cole Swensen's publishers cannot be converted into a familiar record of "progress" from outsider to official status: *New Math* was published by Morrow in 1988 and *Try* by the University of Iowa Press in 1999; between these two, Swensen published three books with alternative presses (*Park* with Floating Island, 1991; *Numen* with Burning Deck, 1995; and *Noon* with Sun and Moon, 1996). Rosmarie Waldrop continues to traverse a similar terrain, as her New Directions titles (1987, 1994, 2000) are evenly interspersed among numerous books representing a veritable roll call of small presses (Tender Buttons, Kelsey Street, Station Hill, Paradigm, Burning Deck, and others). Fanny Howe's books chronicle a smart catalogue of small presses (Telephone, Kelsey Street, The Figures, Alice James, Lost Roads, Littoral, O Books, Reality Street, and Spectacular Diseases), while her *Selected Poems* (2000) was one of the inaugural volumes in the New California Poetry series published by the University of California Press. Younger poets may be beneficiaries of this flexible mingling of alternative and mainstream publishing venues. Liz Waldner's first book, *Homing Devices,* was published by O Books in 1998, followed two years later by *A Point Is That Which Has No Part,* a University of Iowa Press Iowa Poetry Prize recipient. Jena Osman's *The Character* was published by Beacon in 1999, and was recipient of the Barnard New Women Poets Prize. A work like Stacy Doris's *Kildare,* published by Roof in 1994, might easily find a place with a trade publisher now. But lest the borders seem permanently blurred, I would wager that another Roof book, *Free Space Comix* by Brian Kim Stefans (1998), with its dense layering of typographic effects and inside references to vanguard poetry, is *not* crossover material.

The role of university presses in publishing poetry during the past thirty years has been extensive—and extensively lamented, with some justification, since the product was uniformly bland for so long, the poems seeming almost interchangeable from one title to another and from one press to another. That has been changing. Books of unpredictable vintage (along with more readable instances of old vintage) are being published by the university presses of Wesleyan, Wisconsin, Iowa, Illinois, Louisiana, Massachusetts, Georgia, and even the smaller university presses of Colorado, North Texas, Notre Dame, and NYU. The trade publishers tend to be more predictable, although the Barnard New Women Poetry Series published by Beacon is admirably varied in its choices. Having imported a whole contingent of the old Atheneum poets (Merrill, Merwin, Strand, and Hollander), and benefited from Clampitt's ascension, Knopf favors the sleek aestheticism of Mary Jo Salter, Eric Pankey, Laurie Sheck, Deborah Digges, Henri Cole, and Edward Hirsch; but Knopf also publishes Sapphire, as well as those mavericks Anne Carson and Richard Kenney. Otherwise, it is difficult to detect a specific house feel in the poetry issued from the Eastern trade publishers, which manifest no particular distinguishing traits like those I associate with Graywolf, Copper Canyon, or Coffee House, let alone the more avowedly alternative presses like Sun and Moon, O Books, or Roof. But odd mutations are not unprecedented: North Point Press made a memorable debut twenty years ago with titles by Ronald Johnson, Leslie Scalapino, and Michael Palmer, but since its transformation into Counterpoint, Alfred Corn is on the list.

The factors contributing to this ventilation of publishers' poetry options are difficult to assess. That's one reason why I think a plausible contributing feature is the demographic bulge of new women writers. Increased familiarity with language poetry has also played a chastening role. The MFA programs, being housed in universities, could only immunize themselves from intellectual life for so long. Something had to give; and it was conspicuous when academic champions of language poetry began to proliferate throughout the nineties and workshop poets had to make some accommodation to experimental challenges. The careers of Jorie Graham and Donald Revell exemplify the trend. The dominance of John Ashbery has probably also had some impact in convincing other poets that transparency and accessibility are not automatic virtues. In his wake, readerly tolerance for incomprehension has risen (and must account in part for the ascendancy of Irish poet Paul Muldoon). Finally, there has been a gradual admission into poetry of discursiveness (going back to Frank O'Hara and Ted Berrigan, David Antin's talk poems, and C. K. Williams's work after he started using long lines), and this has attenuated the lure of anecdote (or at least rendered it more conspicuous as a *New Yorker* prerogative).

Vindication for innovative poetry has also derived from a most unlikely source, David Lehman's *Best American Poetry* series, in which the following poets have appeared: Rae Armantrout, Charles Bernstein, Mei-Mei Berssenbrugge, Clark Coolidge, Peter Gizzi, Lyn Hejinian, Nathaniel Mackey, Tom Mandel, Laura Moriarty, Haryette Mullen, Alice Notley, Michael Palmer, Maureen Owen, Bob Perelman, Wang Ping, Joan Retallack, and Leslie Scalapino—many of them in several of the annual volumes. The timing helped, as the series was inaugurated in 1988, just when language poetry was gaining visible scholarly acclaim. John Ashbery and Jorie Graham were editors in the first and third year, and their choices were more consciously disposed to experiment than other early editors like Mark Strand and Donald Hall. But consider this: Bob Perelman and Michael Palmer each appeared in three of the first four volumes, and Clark Coolidge twice, as well as single appearances by most of those named above. One should bear in mind that the series emphasizes poems, not poets as such; and even the most experimentally disposed writers produce poems assimilable to a context like the *Best American Poetry* series. At the same time, editors appear not to have been under obligation to favor certain lengths, and the series has included some adventurous longer poems. Despite the emphasis on poems, editorial orientation and personal affiliations clearly emerge in the choices. Strand, Robert Bly, and Hollander are positively clannish in their conservatism, while Charles Simic and James Tate go out of their way to include work by unknown poets. Robert Hass's choices for 2001 field the most diverse array yet. Adrienne Rich proved that an entire volume could be programmatically commandeered (drawing the wrath of Harold Bloom, who, editing a "Best of the Best" tenth anniversary publication, denounced Rich's volume and bypassed it altogether for his own selection).[13]

13. Because of the special focus of the *Best American Poetry* series, of course—not to mention the revolving editorship—it would be misleading to infer significant patterns from inclusions or exclusions. Despite influence and acclaim, Charles Bernstein, Frank Bidart, Lucie Brock-Broido, Mark Doty, Rita Dove, Carolyn Forché, Ann Lauterbach, Bin

Inclusion in a *Best American Poetry* volume provides the poet with some exposure, of course, but the real benefit is brutally pragmatic, providing a juicy line item for a vita or an author's note.[14] The proliferation of prizes and honors is an increasingly pervasive (and invasive) element in the scene. Pushcart Prizes, National Poetry Series, *Best American Poetry,* Guggenheims, plus a half dozen (or more) prizes administered by each of several institutions (Academy of American Poets, the American Academy of Arts and Letters, *Poetry* magazine), not to mention the prizes associated with publishing series (Brittingham Prize, Piper Award, Sandeen Prize, APR/Honickman Prize, etc.)—plenty of prizes, but also plenty of competition, so that even being in the running is a boost. Tory Dent's biographical note in *What Silence Equals* (1993) cites her as a finalist (not winner) in the Yale Younger Poet series, the National Poetry Series, and the Walt Whitman Award (Dent went on to win the James Laughlin Award for *HIV, Mon Amour* in 2000). The proliferation of awards has led to some (slight) diversification in recipients, though none so astonishing as the bestowal of the $100,000 Tanning Prize to Jackson Mac Low by the Academy of American Poets in 1999 (previously awarded to Merwin, Tate, Rich, Hecht, and Ammons).

The fact is that virtually all poetry is now under some kind of institutional supervision. It's as if a few decades back, poets said *Give us some money* and the NEA appeared, with Congress close behind asking for administrative (and eventually moral) accountability. And the universities said *Sure, come on in; we'll stake your share.* Then the poets said *Give us some notoriety,* and the Academy of American Poets and other institutions got to work fetching lump sums from donors to beef up the stockpile of

---

Ramke, Mary Jo Salter, and David Wojahn have each appeared in only one of the fifteen volumes in the *Best American Poetry* series (1988–2001). Nonetheless, the series is hardly exonerated from perpetuating a familiar roster. The list of those with a half dozen or more appearances largely replicates the anthology profile established by the 1960s: Hall, Ashbery, Simic, Hollander, Ammons, Creeley, Graham, Howard, Koch, Merrill, Strand, Tate, Wilbur, and Charles Wright.

14. On the dust jacket of *Felt* (2001): "Alice Fulton's honors include a fellowship from the John D. and Catherine T. MacArthur Foundation. Her work has appeared in six volumes of the *Best American Poetry* series, including *Best of the Best American Poetry*."

awards, and Bill Moyers and Helen Vendler televised it, while Miguel Al-garín and Bob Holman took the sound waves of the Nuyorican Cafe to the airwaves and "a bohemian rhapsody of rap swagger [spread] across the land" (cover copy, *Aloud*). By the end of the 1990s poetry was every-where, showered with prizes, attention, and career opportunities. Even Hollywood personalities started trying to edge in on the glamour. But it was also full of contenders. Now the real challenge for younger poets is how to stake a claim, how to get some attention, without resorting to flamboyant self-abasement (shameless self-advertisement) or falling back on the consolations of the clique.

It's a dilemma made vivid in two recent anthologies of the thirty-something generation: *The New Young American Poets,* edited by Kevin Pru-fer (2000), and *An Anthology of New (American) Poets,* edited by Lisa Jarnot, Leonard Schwartz, and Chris Stroffolino (1998). Both offer about three dozen poets, only one of whom appears in each anthology. Nearly all the poets in both anthologies are graduates of MFA programs, and many (possibly most) also hold other advanced degrees. Prufer's collection might be construed as mainstream, with an introduction by Richard Howard and publication by a university press. The other is published by Talisman, with editor Jarnot declaring that the poets share a "marginali-zation from mainstream literary culture" (1). Insofar as the Talisman po-ets think of themselves as outsiders, it's because they've been trained in those sites (such as Brown, Naropa, Buffalo) where a romance of the out-side has been institutionalized. But Prufer's poets are only "mainstream" in a precarious sense; that is, with a mainstream swollen with contend-ers, their chances for success (national reputation) are very slim. In fact, at this point a pure outsider pedigree might prove more durable in terms of career advancement, and Jarnot's group may have an advantage that formerly belonged to the establishment: they went to the same schools together and have well-developed networking skills. The differences be-tween the two groups are not, in the end, very dramatic (and there's certainly no evidence of lifestyle distinctions like Beats versus Squares in the 1950s). The *look* of the poems is a bit more various in the avowedly vanguard volume, though hardly as eclectic and innovative as Walter Lew's *Premonitions: The Kaya Anthology of New Asian North American Poetry.*

Whatever differences there may be, they are effaced by the format of the anthologies and by the presentational rhetoric that needlessly perpetuates the clannishness of the 1960s "anthology wars."

A real wild card now is the audience. For one thing, audience is no longer identical with readership. The boost in orality provided by the growth of poetry slams has certainly had some spillover effect, creating new readers, but American culture is being drained of literacy skills at a considerable pace. Curiously, this may result in a growing audience for published poetry as the very act of reading becomes more archaic, specialized, attaining a certain antiquarian glamour. There will be increased urgency on the part of readers to identify themselves to one another (and the poetry world may start to resemble gay subculture of the pre-Stonewall era; to say nothing of the fact that so much of American poetry culture always *has been* gay subculture (see *Word of Mouth: An Anthology of Gay American Poetry,* edited by Timothy Liu). A clear symptom is evident on the Internet, which has facilitated contact between special interests of every stripe, not just poetry. Far from promoting a demise of the book, it seems that the growth of the Internet has precipitated a renewal of interest. (On the other hand, it may simply be the case that online chat rooms thrive on topicality, and the books are not being read so much as *sampled.*) The user-friendly marketing strategies of Amazon.com enable shoppers to track associative links based on purchasing patterns. If you like a given poet or a specific title, Amazon will prompt you with a series of covert advertisements by informing you that "other customers who bought *X* also bought *Y.*" This is strictly demographic data uninflected by opinion or critical assessment, though that's available too, since Amazon provides review clippings from a variety of sources and also encourages its users to write their own reviews.[15] The terms of appeal become more

15. Concomitant with the rise of Internet purchasing is an increased burden of instantaneity. Readers' evaluations of books on Amazon.com rarely offer historical context or suggest anything like lineage. If the positive side of this situation is a blurring of nascent boundaries among those writing today, the derelict side of the equation is an obscuring of precedent and, ultimately, an effacement of history. Reading the younger poets of the 1990s, it is difficult to avoid the sense that the new ecumenical spirit goes only so far.

immediate, and more visceral. Consider the enticement on the back cover of *Selfwolf* by Mark Halliday, described as being "like reading e-mail from Whitman's unknown grandson to Pynchon's missing daughter, or vice versa. More readable than Hart Crane, more candid than Jorie Graham, and more up-to-date than Alexander Pope, Mark Halliday is either a new colossus on the scene of post-contemporary American poetry or an infinitesimal blip of male bourgeois anxiety."[16]

Language poetry has cast an enabling shadow of sorts, bearing with it the ghost of Jack Spicer, agent provocateur extraordinaire; but *The Maximus Poems* seems as remote as Doughty's *Dawn in Britain,* while fugitive informants like Gerrit Lansing, Ken Irby, Ronald Johnson, or Robin Blaser might as well have been writing Sanskrit. The festschrift can play a certain resuscitating role. The extraordinary four-day symposium in Vancouver known as "The Recovery of the Public World" (in 1995) was an international gathering of poets and critics in honor of Robin Blaser (some of the proceedings were subsequently published under that title by Talonbooks, edited by Charles Watts and Edward Byrne). On a more diminutive scale is the 150-page portfolio on Ronald Johnson in the premiere issue of *Facture* (edited by Lindsay Hill and Paul Naylor). Such occasions serve as lifelines to essential bodies of work that otherwise float off into the uncharted Atlantic of recent history.

There is, I think, a generational issue contributing to this increased bandwidth of contemporary awareness and a corresponding decrease in historical resonance—synchronic prevailing over diachronic perspective. Coming of age in the 1960s (and earlier) meant being stung to acute historical consciousness. The poetry I have most often written about is work that is "of " that moment in this sense: its demands were large, its terms of access unnervingly demanding. To be confronted with *The Cantos* and *The Maximus Poems* and *"A"* as a teenager, and to determine to read them, was to submit to nothing less than the "negative capability" demanded by Keats. There were no guides; even academic work on *The Cantos* was almost nonexistent. So one's viewfinders were strictly of the world of allied poetries sparked off by the grand examples of Pound, Olson, and Zukofsky. I cannot overstress the pedagogic importance of being an amateur (do-it-yourself) reader of these huge poems.

16. Jacket copy isn't usually so daring. Much of the space is reserved for professional appraisals. Blurbs commonly consolidate tribal views: Creeley and Silliman weigh in for Scalapino's *New Time;* Hollander and Howard for Tony Sanders's *Transit Authority;* Lauterbach and Fraser rally behind *The Human Abstract* by Elizabeth Willis; while Gerald Stern, John Updike, X. J. Kennedy, Stephen Dunn, and Annie Proulx circle around *Picnic, Lightning* by Billy Collins. But there are (again) signs of border crossing in unlikely pairings of blurb contributors to the same book: Edward Hirsch and Marjorie Perloff (John Koethe, *The Constructor*); Richard Howard and Ann Lauterbach (Bin Ramke, *Massacre of the Innocents*); Rita Dove and Dean Young (Olena Kalytiak Davis, *And Her Soul Out of Nothing*);

The terms of appraisal suggested in the blurb for *Selfwolf* provocatively situate poetry in its cultural moment. *Colossus* or *blip*. But the terms are prejudicially disposed to the agora, the marketplace, where the American attention span vacillates wildly between such extremes, and in doing so concede poetry to a permanently subordinate role in the mass media entertainment complex. But there is another order of poetry that goes about its business without the pretense of legislative intervention or cultural dictation; an order of poetry readily acknowledged elsewhere but difficult to see in the United States, where "esoteric" is a bad word, where cultural activity that doesn't suggest a desire for personal prominence is illegible. In the unitary endowment of national culture, merit is always confused with the politics of taste. But the claims staked so insistently by Olson, Duncan, and Blaser, among others, are perpetual reminders of a continuum of language from private resonance to public law. While definitions of poetry may vary, poets do aspire to some finality and integrity of utterance. In any consideration of the art, it's important to distinguish between the literary life versus a life in poetry. In the

---

Forrest Gander and Jane Miller (Tessa Rumsey, *Assembling the Shepard*); Lyn Hejinian and Wayne Koestenbaum (Lisa Lubasch, *How Many More of Them Are You?*); and the trio of Guy Davenport, Jean Valentine, and Gregory Orr (Tom Andrews, *The Hemophiliac's Motorcycle*). Nothing quite compares with the heterogeneous clusters on the back cover of *True North* by Stephanie Strickland (Barbara Guest, John Matthias, Molly Peacock, Maureen Seaton, Marie Ponsot, and N. Katherine Hayles) and *Bag 'o' Diamonds* by Susan Wheeler (David Lehman, Harold Bloom, Barbara Guest, Lyn Emanuel, and Ben Belitt). Amid the proliferation of blurbs, it is worth recalling that Black Sparrow launched a generation of poets without resorting to blurbs. In the heyday of small presses—when "small" meant letterpress—blurbs would have been a desecration. Besides, blurbs were conspicuously associated with the inner sanctum of the poetry establishment. The expansion of poetry presses through NEA funding meant that fledgling presses like The Figures and Roof could afford to have their books printed by the same jobbers (McNaughton and Gunn of Ann Arbor, most famously) as the trade publishers and university presses. Now it's a visual tossup concerning publisher identity, as most books (and not just poetry books) conform to industry standards, and those standards routinely dedicate the back cover of a book to blurbs. Blurbs, like the poetry they appraise, can be an extension of billboard and blip culture; but they can also initiate a fructifying interface between different poetic constituencies, diverging sensibilities, and even become a site of miniature essaying (an idiom perfected by Jorie Graham).

American context there's no more acute instance of the difference I mean than Emily Dickinson, who had no literary life at all, but whose life in poetry is as singular and exponentially imposing as a chunk of radium. This is what bedevils the thought of national culture in America, so much of which is comprised of the work of renegades and misfits. Even someone as eager as Whitman to be the national bard bore no resemblance to what his peers would accept in that role.

The presumption that centrality translates to significance where cultural politics are concerned invariably results in a warped perspective, but it's no less the case that the periphery precipitates its own idolatry (in terms of "avant-garde," "outsiders," "rebels," etc.). In a meticulously orchestrated class culture like that of France, such bipolarities might mean something; but the heterology of American culture has been oversimplified far too long by terms like *Beat* and *Square,* terms instantly absorbed by (if not invented by) Madison Avenue marketing. It's a common mistake for those in the vanguard to assume a comparable solidarity on the part of those who appear to be "mainstream"; but heed the geographical implication here, which recognizes that exigencies of transport (like depth of water and width of channel) promote habits of attention. Corporate "culture" has long since colonized the roadways, and franchises along the interstate highways are symptomatic instances of national enterprise. There's no difficulty transposing this model onto poetry, where franchise operations also prevail along certain channels, places where the stream broadens, allowing a greater volume of traffic. But in our poetic archipelago there are lots of byways and wayside meanders that cannot be thought of as either mainstream or vanguard.

Distinguishing mainstream from avant-garde has some utility, of course; but its utility is limited to institutions. If such a distinction applies to particular works, those works are sadly no more than byproducts of the institutions to which they adhere. That's why I make a point of detaching the work of Bruce Andrews from the (institutional) phenomenon of language poetry; its robust and impetuous character is "vanguard" at the level of somatic encounter, not adjudicated theory. A particularly poignant episode provides some insight into the agon suffered by younger poets in the 1990s as they confronted what seemed a bipolar disorder of literary options. A number of students in the poetics program at SUNY Buffalo (Lew Daly, Alan Gilbert, Kristin Prevallet, and Pam Rehm) initiated a sort of palace revolt with their magazine *apex of the M,* the first three issues opening with lively editorials. The editors denounced the nihilistic mechanism of language-oriented poetry along with the self-help complacency of workshop verse, proposing instead "a radical transparency of language that is ultimately objectless" (*apex* 1: 5). The editors proposed as the goal of their magazine to explore "whether there can be a purely secular form of alterity" (6). Charged with mystical obscurantism, in the second issue they ventured a political program that retained spirituality by amalgamating it to extremity in every register, evidently following the precedent of Georges Bataille's gnostic materialism: "Anguish and the ecstatic, not play and the ironic, are the tears in the fabric of ideology" (*apex* 2: 6). In the end, the editors offered up nothing less than a millennial utopian program, "a reintegration of poetry into the entire range of radical populist traditions, both 'secular' and 'religious': iconoclasm, apocalypse, democracy, tyrannicide, antinomianism, civil disobedience, prophecy, rioting, festival, unionization, communism, prison liberation, libertinism, work-action, ludditism, utopianism, exodus" (*apex* 3: 5). With this, the programmatic side of *apex of the M* became manifestly Rabelaisian. Its flamboyant contradictions and hectoring vivacity was salutary insofar as it reminded readers of the pataphysical ground of poetry in all places and times. As soon as poetry aspires to the social register and the political platform, it loses touch with this groundless ground and becomes Literature. Poetry is fundamentally esoteric, in several senses: it is socially insignificant (although, as symbolical capital, poetry must exist the way gold bars exist in Fort Knox, in a precarious affiliation with currency standards) and therefore represents an uncommon or esoteric enterprise; but it has a long tradition of obscurity and obscurantism, and its legendary affiliations with the muse tradition suggest that poetry is esoteric with respect to mind or psyche as such.

As esoterica, poetry's value is at once inscrutable and beside the point. As public enterprise, on the other hand, poetry is now caught in a conspicuously widening culture gap (or series of gaps). Insofar as it is deeply invested in literacy and in the knowledge criteria of literate culture, poetry is bound to seem antiquated, esoteric, scholastic, and casually intimidating even when it purports a more populist orientation. As an active component in oral culture, poetry is periodically rekindled into prominence, even if only at the level of affective immediacy. There is a third zone, an interface between orality and literacy, that is more emphatically visual in the venues of electronic media. There is obvious potential here for the inauguration of new poetic enterprise, one in which poetry might conceivably rival film. Not a serious rival, maybe, since poetry's investment in the word will limit its semiotic appeal in the long run.

These different theaters of operation have already resulted in serious erosion of the model of a unitary tradition. The enticements of opening up the canon lead to the proverbial can of worms, as incommensurate practices sit side by side in the nonreciprocating terms of one medium or another. The first two volumes in the Library of America anthology of modern poetry, *American Poetry: The Twentieth Century,* offer a case in point. The inclusion of lyrics by Cole Porter, Dorothy Fields, and other Tin Pan Alley composers, as well as an assortment of blues lyrics, confronts the reader with an admirable model of poetic praxis even as it deprives these examples of their full register. (The *Norton Anthology of African American Literature,* by contrast, includes a CD so that readers can be auditors.) By the same token, even large-scale efforts to transport orality into anthologies suffer an attenuation in the transfer; *Poetry Nation,* edited by Regie Cabico and Todd Swift; *Aloud,* edited by Miguel Algarín and Bob Holman; and *The Outlaw Bible of American Poetry,* edited by Alan Kaufman, are precarious monuments.[17] A positive side effect of this misplaced application

17. In a state of total immersion, of course, the work in these anthologies becomes more "readable" as rhetorical contours become normative by the sheer mass of surrounding material. That is, your discrimination as a reader dissolves, allowing some approximation to aural receptivity. I should point out that the orientation of the anthologists is not uniform. Kaufman's *Outlaw Bible* is openly hostile to the status quo: "Outlaw poets relate to the poetic tradition, and to their contemporaries in the Academy, with the bristling wariness of a street hustler getting frisked by a cop. They've seen how excessive veneration for the poetic mainstream has turned the practice of the art today into an ongoing memorial service held by those who want poetry to stay in the closet" (xxvi). While the use of *Bible* in the title is probably intended as taunt, it tips the agenda toward canonical aspirations.

of orality is that the poems in these anthologies disclose the poverty of so much other poetry intended primarily for the page. Also disclosed by the plenitude of anthologies (these and others) is the poverty of the anthology as a means of representing poetic activity. Anthologized certifications too easily submit to the old paternalist hypothesis of a master plan, divine providence applied to human enterprise from above, the canon of idealism (in both senses, as aspiration and as secret code). But poetry is nothing without matter and mutter, utterance and exigence. Its fetishism defines its utopian truth: "the fetish confronts us with the paradox of an unattainable object that satisfies a human need precisely through its being unattainable" (Agamben, *Stanzas* 33).[18]

Innovation does not mean change for the sake of change; experiment does not mean fiddling with a perfectly serviceable tool. Innovation is a necessary response to force of circumstance in which the apparent utility of the medium is insufficient. The myth of the self-sufficiency of the lyric occasion has been a dominant feature of late-twentieth-century American poetry, despite the abundance of long poems, sequences, and proce-

---

Nevertheless, Kaufman's presentation of the poets into such groupings as "Slammers," "Meat Poets," "American Renegades," and so forth, provides an intelligible profile of the "outlaw" stance. Cabico and Swift, on the other hand, avow a fusion (hence their subtitle, "The North American Anthology of Fusion Poetry") of insider and outsider: "We believe it is far too easy and reductive to classify poetry as either written or spoken, for the college or the bar, as slick or slam. In reality, many serious poets—the kind who get published in books like *Best American Poetry* and who teach as professors at universities and win or are nominated for major awards like the Pulitzer or the Governor General's—read or perform their work for audiences, and get their message across, wonderfully" (26). They, too, offer some provocative groupings ("Fusion Bomb," "Pound Unplugged," "Media Byrons"), but the great service of *Poetry Nation* is to present a fully integrated assembly of Canadian and American authors.

    18. Commenting on their pertinence (or impertinence) for us now, Jerome McGann says of Rossetti's paintings that "their fetishism defines their truth" (104). As for Agamben, "Precisely because the fetish is a negation and the sign of an absence, it is not an unrepeatable unique object; on the contrary, it is something infinitely capable of substitution, without any of its successive incarnations succeeding in exhausting the nullity of which it is the symbol" (*Stanzas* 33). Given this model of infinite substitutions, it's clear why Agamben finds in poetry the exemplary form of the fetish.

dures of "disturbance" (in Jack Spicer's sense). The durability of lyric suggests it is a transcendent vehicle, something immune from historical change; yet current practice increasingly betrays a suspicion that there is no such immunity. From a broader perspective, (modern) lyric might be seen as a technical device specific to a historical formation: a means, within print culture, to yoke consciousness to certain subject positions amenable to the systems requirements of modernity. You don't have to blatantly refer this to Michel Foucault's power/knowledge complex, Friedrich Kittler's discourse networks, or some other hypothesis of coercion or self-induced entrapment by the wiles of capital and the byways of psychological sublimation. The point is to suggest that in considering poetry we at least acknowledge the potential of some viral disorder, a set of ascertainable pressures inflecting (and possibly initiating) the very impulse to *be a poet,* to assume a posture that signifies autonomous expression, exalted transport, rapt inwardness inexplicably concretized as utterance, the enigma of a *voice* in *print.*

Recognition of so imposing a circumstance does not entail unilateral response. It is possible to continue writing poetry just as one wears shoes, talks to strangers, or stops at traffic lights. The world compels our attentions in familiarly structured ways, so why develop a hyperbolic focus on just one of the structures and compel it to change? To put it this way, of course, reverts to the tool model: poem as utilitarian artifact, communication device, or broadcast transmitter. As poets have commonly remarked (or complained), poetry makes nothing happen. Is the tool, then, dysfunctional? Might it not be the case that this says something, instead, about functionality, attesting to the scope of functional requirements permeating even the deepest levels of subjectivity? Theodor Adorno said of art as such that it is anarchic, since it harbors the dream in a functionalist society of having no function. Its function is to have no function, and this, he thought, preserved the image of utopia. The issue of innovation, I think, necessarily arises from this prospect. In the face of so many incitements to functionality—*serve and protect*—it takes a tremendous effort to detach the cognitive and affective powers from the herding instinct to belong; to divert these powers along nonremunerative channels; and to focus on the materiality of language as at once

compromised yet happily received, in the precarious poetic labor of re-
convening the world from scratch.

From scratch: the term evokes the "mark of distinction" in G. Spencer
Brown's *Laws of Form,* from which Niklas Luhmann has elaborated a cogent theory of art: "The unity of art resides in that it creates for the sake
of observation and observes for the sake of being observed, and the medium of art consists in the freedom to create medium/form relations"
(*Art as a Social System* 117). The status of the *observer* here is important, for
Luhmann regards art as a perceptual system distinct from a social system. *Communication* is specific to social systems, in his view, so artistic
activity is undertaken primarily without reference to communication.
This is not to say it is antisocial. Even if a poet is pragmatically dedicated
to transmitting a message, the temporal delay involved in preparing an
artifact (poem as message) plunges the activity into a perceptual realm
distinct from the intersubjective circuit of a communications environment. For poets deeply invested in the notion that poetry is vital to this
communications environment, the means are plentifully available to sustain the illusion; the solace of formalism and the vanguard drama of dissidence are equally compliant. But artistic creation is not about living up
to expectations or conforming to models of polite or impolite behavior.
For Luhmann, following Spencer Brown, to create is to make a distinction. "The first step in the making of an artwork leads from the unmarked space into a marked space, and it creates a boundary by crossing
that boundary" (117).

Accordingly, for all genres the medium of art is the sum total of possible ways of crossing form boundaries (distinctions) from within
toward the outside and of discovering fitting indications on the
other side that stimulate further crossings by virtue of their own
boundaries. The medium of art is present in every artwork, yet it
is invisible, since it operates only on the other side—the one not
indicated—as a kind of attractor for further observations. The process of discovery transforms the medium into form. Or else one
fails. In working together, form and medium generate what charac-
terizes successful artworks, namely, *improbable evidence.* (118–19)

By means of the artwork you find yourself on the other side of a boundary you didn't know you crossed until you found yourself on the far side of it. There is no name for that boundary except the name of the work ("Blood Count," "*Le Déjeuner sur l'herbe,*" *A Border Comedy*), and the work itself is evidence of the crossing. But it is *improbable* evidence, because there's no way of stipulating in advance where the work will take you or how the evidence will attest to your crossing. Or if there is—if the poem simply gratifies your expectations—it is a commodity, a calculable return on investment in a commercial environment.

Luhmann's perception that "communication" is somehow alien to art is illuminated by French playwright Valère Novarina. Responding to an interviewer's question, "What is the purpose of literature?" he responds:

> To make the ground less stable. We are surrounded by idols, with landmarks that are false because they are too solid, with wooden gods who do not speak. Literature is not an art of communication. Enough communication! Enough communicators! Before he communicates, man must frequently speak to himself. They want to give us a too uniquely social and utilitarian image of language; they try to reduce us to existing only as communicative beings, always under the other's gaze. But we are, above all, animals who attempt to be reborn by speaking. *(Theater of the Ears* 133)

For Novarina, "speaking" here doesn't mean rational discourse, but it is significant that he uses that verb rather than one more commonly associated with animal vocalization. Virginia Woolf (who pledged allegiance to the body as the final resource of speech, yet whose writing is incessantly intellectual) wondered whether human articulation amounted to anything more than barking. Novarina touches on this double figuration —meaty mentation—in his remark that "language is not in my mind, like a tool that I would borrow in order to think. It is entirely within me: words are our true flesh, completely, much more so than our apparent body" (125). Contemporary violinist and composer Eyvind Kang also evokes the somatic integrity of art (in a passage in which the word "music" might be instructively replaced by "poetry"):

Music isn't dead but held captive. They only allow a peep at music, which is kept prisoner within a parade of falsely glamorized forms. But like a corpse which has been overly made up, the forms are glamorized to the point where music is no longer recognizable.

Why do we perceive the form of music, not its actual flesh? Music is flesh; it is molecules. Forms of music may be depraved or noble, fragile or strong—aren't the passages between them growing unfamiliar? In these ages music suffers like a body whose inner workings have been kept hidden away. (167)

Much published poetry, viewed from the prospect afforded by Novarina and Kang, seems resolutely pitched in claims of reasonableness and self-control, maintaining a polite distance from philosophical rumination as well as from bellowing. Very little may have changed since Whitman's lament that conformism was the measure of his day in the period following the Civil War. The image of Whitman as nurse situates the poet in an environment encompassing all utterance, groans of pain and desperation echoing in the halls of government buildings converted into makeshift hospitals and morgues; and amid these helpless sounds emitted by bodies in torment Whitman goes from bed to bed, talking and listening, writing letters for wounded soldiers, transcribing last wishes: the poet as amanuensis of extremity—handling, with care, *improbable evidence.*

As I've elaborated here, the chances for improbable evidence are improving. Innovation in poetry is less contested (or ignored) now, and this is largely attributable to both the number and variety of women. If there is a danger ahead, it may be in the complacency with which we may come to *expect* singularity from women poets and allow expectation to coerce experience. Routinized innovation is no better than routinized formalism. It is my hope that the auspiciousness of this moment will not be missed: 2001 should be more consequential than 1975, when institutionalized inattention held the field. The sounds that emanate from poetry should come from the stress of innovation, like the creak of rope in a ship's rigging as it attests to a nautical breeze and a breath of fresh air.

Seeing Double

The Grapes of Dysraphism

A word is beside itself

A word twists backward
peeling its skin up over its face

A word looks behind itself
        Michael Palmer, *Sun*

GLOSSING POETRY AND PROSE

In 1973 David Antin consented to do a reading of his work at the San
Francisco Poetry Center, but was reluctant to be identified as a poet:

> i always had mixed feelings about being considered a poet   "if
> robert lowell is a poet i dont want to be a poet   if robert
> frost was a poet i dont want to be a poet   if socrates was a
> poet ill consider it." (*Talking at the Boundaries* 1)

The salient fact about the three figures Antin mentions is that Socrates
talked, engaging people in dialogue, while Lowell and Frost were masters
of "an unnatural language act   going into a closet   so to speak
sitting in a closet in front of a typewriter" (56). As an advocate of direct
address, Antin made himself into an *occasional* poet in the extra-ordinary
sense of that term; his poetry (as public record) consists of transcripts of
specific occasions. Sitting in a closet with a typewriter, as he tenden-
tiously puts it, ensures that "you dont address anyone   what you do

is you sit at the typewriter and you bang out the anticipated in front of the unanticipated." His solution has been to do "talk poems," improvised live, "so in a sense"—as he told another audience—"i prepared to come unprepared to this place" (*Tuning* 85). To anticipate (as writer) is not synonymous with preparing to be unprepared (as speaker); but the results are in fact published, as if the anxiety of unpreparedness generated a keen anticipation for a textual conclusion to an oral event. The kerygmatic implications are dizzying, especially for one who eschews the scriptural claims of poetry for the patently mundane activity of talk. He reconciles the two by declaring a commitment to the present, which in his work bifurcates into two occasions—talking and then typing it up: "you see it would be a great mistake to believe that my love for the present only occurs when im talking   because once ive established my love for the present through my talking i dont give it up   when i'm writing when i'm sitting in front of the typewriter i feel like im sitting in front of a typewriter   and ill be damned if i am going to feel a profound sense of obligation to another moment that now no longer exists" (94).

The peculiarities of public obligation were memorably rendered for me in 1986, when I got an announcement in the mail from the Huntington Library:

POETRY READING
Poet David Antin
Reading his own work

Not only was Antin advertised as "reading," but the card went on to say, "He will discuss his work and answer questions following the reading." And underlined in boldface: LATECOMERS WILL NOT BE ADMITTED. However, I arrived late, had no trouble being admitted, and found Antin doing his customary talk to an audience of what looked like wealthy donors to the library. After about twenty minutes, an elderly man who had been distracting me by his increased fidgeting grabbed his companion, jerked her out of her seat, and lurched to the door, muttering angrily, "You see, *he's not going to read anything!*" Such a conflict of cultural codes was relishing to witness, and it left me wondering whether Antin had insisted that the

Huntington publicist announce a "reading" so he could count on some shock value, or whether the institutional slot for presenting a poet was so imperturbably *the reading* that the wording couldn't be changed without forfeiting the genre altogether. In any case, "it is not the habit of poetry to be open to interruption"; so Antin provisionally defined poetry as "uninterruptible discourse" (*Talking* 23), a definition that brings Bakhtin to mind.

An incisive gesture of dissent arising from totalitarian oppression was Mikhail Bakhtin's condemnation of monoglossia, or the denial of retort. Monoglossia is the authoritarian rule of uninterruptible discourse, a form of political violence applied to the inherently dialogic function of language. As a literary thesis, dialogism was Bakhtin's celebration of the carnivalesque spectacle of popular narratives evolving into a new polyglot medium, the novel. The novel is a rainbow coalition preserving the integrity of irreconcilable voices in a parodic decentralization of ideological dominants (and, yes, this sentence itself is a parodic reminder of the monologic autonomy of Bakhtinian academese). Like Antin, Bakhtin favors the Socratic initiative. The social basis of discourse thoroughly saturates both the lexical and semantic tenor of an exchange. Even in the closet, before the typewriter, "The word, directed toward its object, enters a dialogically agitated and tension-filled environment of alien words, value judgments and accents, weaves in and out of complex interrelationships, merges with some, recoils from others, intersects with yet a third group" (*Dialogic Imagination* 276). A case could be made that the concept of heteroglossia has gained credence precisely because it condenses in a single term those features of rhetoric that have concurrently risen to prominence; namely, process, performance, and contingency.[1]

---

1. The cross-pollination of concepts is a curious matter; the reception of Bakhtin's work in English departments would appear to have been fortuitously prepared by the dominance of James Joyce (second only to Shakespeare in MLA bibliography citations). What better example of heteroglossia than *Ulysses*? At the same time, *Finnegans Wake* either invalidates Bakhtin's views on the novel, or if those views are accepted, disqualifies the *Wake*. As for poetry proper—what better affirmation of monoglossia than Pound's *Cantos,* which transform a polyglot linguistic surface into the rhetorically tendentious voice of the poet himself. However, Pound later acknowledged his work to be the "record of a

Bakhtin always emphasizes the interactive reciprocity of *subjects* rather than the encounter of subject and object.

Bakhtin accuses poetry of repudiating "alien languages . . . the possibility of another vocabulary, another semantics, other syntactic forms and so forth." The poet aspires to possess language, personalize it, using each word "according to its unmediated power to assign meaning (as it were, 'without quotation marks'), that is, as a pure and direct expression of his own intention" (285). Authorial intention merges with the divinatory legacy of the muses to make of poetry "a unitary and singular Ptolemaic world outside of which nothing else exists and nothing else is needed" (286). Does this evoke poetry, or a bedtime story? Bakhtin's reservations about poetry concern its quest for autonomy.[2] Poetry errs in aspiring to be at once universal yet stylistically unique, or individual. Bakhtin sees this as a violation of the heteroglossia found at the heart of social discourse: "In poetry, even discourse about doubts must be cast in a discourse that cannot be doubted" (286).

Example and counterexample can be marshalled to make heteroglossia appear native to poetry and prose alike. In a seamless, rhetorically eloquent analytic prose, Bakhtin argues on behalf of heteroglossia. His comment on a discourse about doubt that cannot itself be doubted is also applicable to the essays in *The Dialogic Imagination*. Monologism is not an efficacious observation about poetry, but a formula for paradox. By em-

---

struggle," and thus "botched" as poetry. Was it then dialogic? Does a bungled attempt at pure poetry inadvertently acquire the merits of heteroglossia? Bakhtin, after all, values the novel precisely for its preservation of struggle, the marks of its occasion. Still, we need to be wary of Bakhtin's intimations that the novel somehow spontaneously assembles unmanageable heterodox impulses into an exemplary cacophonous whole.

2. The dangers of autonomy, however, are exemplified by a social science positivism that Bakhtin periodically drubbed. "Monologism, at its extreme," he wrote in the notes for revising his study of Dostoyevsky, "denies the existence outside itself of another consciousness with equal rights and equal responsibilities, another *I* with equal rights (*thou*). With a monologic approach (in its extreme or pure form) *another person* remains wholly and merely an *object* of consciousness, and not another consciousness. No response is expected from it that could change everything in the world of my consciousness." (*Dostoevsky's Poetics* 292–93) Bakhtin's binary absolutism renders much of this problematic, as always.

phasizing the generic properties of the novel, Bakhtin does not adequately address the monoglossia of prose as such, so he underplays the
distinction between poetry and prose, a distinction he presumes to be in
place by contrasting heteroglossia and monoglossia. Ironically, he makes
a poetic (or monologic) case for the dialogism of the novel, and his own
writing is untouched by the heteroglossia he celebrates. Apparently
Bakhtin did not recognize the irony, as Antin did when he scanned his San
Francisco audience and observed, "[W]e have among us here many great
conversationalists who dont have interruptable discourse or theyre interruptable   with great difficulty   i confess   myself   to shar-
ing some of these characteristics" (*Talking* 23). According to Bakhtin's
schismatic terminology, if it isn't hetero it must be mono.[3] But what is
his genre? Neither poetry nor fiction, is the medium of discursive prose
a third force, an invisible figure that slips between other genres in a confidence game? Prose may be a kind of preaching, as Herman Melville
implies in *The Confidence-Man:* "The other was pleased to find that he had
not, as he feared, been prosing; but would rather not be considered in
the formal light of a preacher" (910).

Etymologically, verse is return, reversion, circulation, recycling, turning back to the beginning again and again; while prose is straight ahead,
progressive, expansive, innovative. But there's more than etymology involved in distinguishing the two. What exactly is prose? In *The Emergence
of Prose* Jeffrey Kittay and Wlad Godzich describe it as a secret agent—

---

3. Bakhtin's writing erupts with neologisms, which deflect the stylistic tendency of
prose to become monologic. So much attention has been paid to the evolution and/or
consistency of Bakhtin's ideas that it seems to have escaped anyone's attention to read the
performative values of his text—which I can't, not knowing Russian. In translation Bakhtin
appears to be uniformly and consistently "Bakhtinian." There is a very curious observation
Tzvetan Todorov makes to the effect that Bakhtin's ideas about psychoanalysis "remain absolutely unchanged" over a fifty-year period (*Bakhtin* 96). What more astonishing record of
monologism could there be? Despite my critique of his generic definitions here, I value
Bakhtin for what Todorov calls his philosophical anthropology, or his equation of a disequilibrium that *humanizes* humans. Todorov's formulation is admirable: "Whoever wants to preserve himself, loses himself; internally we are all boundaries; and in 'being' (*être*) we should
read: the other (*autre*)" (97).

even a double agent—occupying all the discursive positions simultaneously, not by actually being there and filling the positions, but by forming
the ground against which all discursive situations are figured. The point
is easy to see if we simply think of the now customary designation of
poetry as a special configuration of speech, whereas prose, as Molière's
Jourdain realized, is what everybody speaks without knowing it. Prose,
like ideology, is so pervasive that people cease to remark its omnipres-
ence. It's there like air, invisibly encasing everything: "It does not participate, does not get its hands dirty, cannot be put into quotes. Among all
the discourse it contains, it takes the position that it is just holding them
together, it is just what there is. The prose of the world" (126).[4] Prose,
then, is the average, the nondescript, the unremarkable—a pedestrian
hubbub that gives rise to heteroglossia.

I am not prepared to equate heteroglossia with what Kittay and Godzich call prose; it's enough to remark on their proximity (which, I should
add, goes unremarked in *The Emergence of Prose*). Bakhtin celebrates the
plebian vigor of the quotidian, but at the same time he wants to secure
recognition for the artistic innovations of the novel. Bakhtin succeeds in
making his case for heteroglossia because of his binary model: regardless
of whether we believe poetry culpable as he describes it, or adopt his
convictions about the novel, the concept of heteroglossia is assured success because it readily flips back and forth to either side of the equation.
It answers to our needs, whatever they are. Take the business of the quotation marks: Bakhtin says poetry evades quotation marks, while the dialogic novel puts everything in quotation marks (not just reported verbal
exchanges). Kittay and Godzich argue that prose cannot be put into quotation marks; it thrives by being beyond excerpt or report. Heteroglossia

4. "Prose" so defined by Kittay and Godzich resembles perception in Maurice Merleau-
Ponty's late account in "The Intertwining—The Chiasm." The perceptual gaze—which is
not scopic in the Lacanian sense, but a fleshly attending—offers us "things we could not
dream of seeing 'all naked' because the gaze itself envelops them, clothes them with its own
flesh." Merleau-Ponty goes on to ask, "How does it happen that my look, enveloping them,
does not hide them, and, finally, that, veiling them, it unveils them?" (131) Likewise, prose
reveals the world by the thoroughness with which it covers and overcomes it—the living
body disclosed by its flailings in the gunnysack.

vanishes into the stylistic traces of its erasure, where it is exhibited as "text." Prose, that phantom accessory, emits an eerie glow from deep within the text, for it is the unframed enframer admiring its own likeness in the frameless mirror of its dialogic reflection, exulting in the image of itself bearing the mask of a gratified other.

The intrigue of Kittay and Godzich's work is how it enables us to ponder prose in its emergent phase, before it had become an invisible background, when medieval jongleurs found themselves at wit's end when called upon to give prose synopses of their epics. Lacking the mnemonic stability of oral versification, the sense of the whole threatened to crumble. The ability to recount a sequence of episodes divorced from their metrical support was a challenge to the jongleurs, as confounding for them as it would be for us to recite a book of *Paradise Lost* instead of summarizing it. The process of conversion for the jongleurs was laborious and could not be willed any more than one can look at the familiar psychological schemata of the rabbit/duck, the old/young woman, or the ascending/descending stairs of M. C. Escher and choose to see one, then the other, merely by deciding to do so. The components of interpretation and symbolization require of text and context the customary apparatus of figure and ground. The problem is which is which; and if each term of any pair may be eligible as both figure and ground, how is the apparition to be arranged so that one precedes the other in a determinate sequence?

HOMOPHONIC SEAMS

Prose and poetry, text and context, words and things: Can these common pairs be seen in terms of a figure/ground dialectic? Do such terms comprise a mutually constitutive equilibrium? Is it language that originates and sustains the world? Or is language a manifold of conceptual horizons repeatedly ruptured by, and at odds with, an intrusive world? "In prose you start with the world and find the words to match; in poetry you start with the words and find the world in them." As quoted, I hesitate to give a source, since the citation is technically deficient. Here it is again:

That is, in prose you start with the world
and find the words to match; in poetry you start
with the words and find the world in them.

An attractive generic distinction is that both positions seem tactical, contingent, optional. They are complementary rather than antithetical. Unlike Bakhtin's poem/novel distinction, neither term here negates the other, and in fact they mutually preserve one another in a systole-diastole coupling.

The manner in which I first cited this formulation would have cleanly converted it into the *syndrome* of my own discourse here. By rendering it prose, my voice could have talked through it as if the quotation marks were not there (which is often the function of quotations anyway, to exercise a pleasurable ventriloquism, a continuity masquerading as difference). By making a pledge of accuracy and preserving the line breaks, on the other hand, the "world" (of my intentions, my priorities, my p[r]ose) is less securely confluent with the extract; its difference is dramatized, the alterity of its genus exhibited. The line breaks *intensify* the exhibit, making "on display" more showy, palpably coercive even, than the unobtrusive addition of tiny hash marks around the same words interlineated as prose embedded in my prose could have done. As indented poetic quote, the fluency is not securely mine.

Whose fluency is it? Only three lines were cited, and anyone without access to the book from which they're drawn has no way of knowing what they manifestly *are*. Lines of a poem, obviously; but how big is the poem? "That is," with which the citation begins, would seem to indicate a larger context, an argument that connects the distinction between poetry and prose with something preceding it. Thinking of the broader context as a geometric volume (like the Newtonian orb of Eve's dream in *Paradise Lost*), let's take a step back for an expanded view:

Poem, chrome. "I
don't like the way you think":
a mind is a terrible thing to spend.

That is, in prose you start with the world
and find the words to match; in poetry you start
with the words and find the world in them.

"Poem" coupled with its near-homonym "chrome" looks like an abridged sentence. However, it might be read as a rendition of a sentence from a language, like Chinese, that doesn't use the copula, in which case it is a complete sentence. If so, this may be a poem in the Poundian lineage. Ezra Pound's development of the ideogrammic method was derived from Ernest Fenollosa's essay on "The Chinese Written Character as a Medium for Poetry," in which he states unequivocally:

> The moment we use the copula, the moment we express subjective inclusions, poetry evaporates. The more concretely and vividly we express the interactions of things the better the poetry. We need in poetry thousands of active words, each doing its utmost to show forth the motive and vital forces. We can not exhibit the wealth of nature by mere summation, by the piling of sentences. Poetic thought works by suggestion, crowding maximum meaning into the single phrase pregnant, charged, and luminous from within. (28)

"Poem, chrome" exhibits the condensation of the Chinese written character, positing equivalence by immediate juxtaposition. What is being made equivalent? Is a poem like chrome and, if so, how? Does the poem reflect things like a polished hubcap?

But what about the intervening reproach: "I / don't like the way you think"? Is this a rebuttal of ideogrammic method? In the poem, it's in quotes. What do the quotation marks signify? A speaking voice? Another's voice? An *other* voice, as in another position? A conceptual indirection? A colon, which is a surrogate copula, carries the quoted statement forward to the next line. There is certainly a conceptual equivalence between "I don't like the way you think" and "a mind is a terrible thing to spend." But is this equivalence, this balance, viable when the two statements are not dressed in the same apparel of punctuation? Several mechanisms of transference are set in motion by this asymmetry, drawing the otherwise complementary statements into a web of dystopic asymmetries such as thought/statement, conscious/unconscious, intention/expression, spoken/written, voiced/unvoiced, marked/unmarked, and so on. Both statements are, in different ways, marked. But if marked, are the markings parallel?

The reason for the quotation marks is ambivalent. Is there a corresponding ambivalence in the allusion? Such equivalence might be established by identifying the allusion as twofold, referring not only to the adage about wasting the mind, but to Wordsworth's lines, "getting and spending / We lay waste our powers." Above all, how would we describe the pursuit of ambiguity here? Does this dilation of multiple reference draw us further into the text, where we lose sight of the ongoing syntactic flow in a hall of mirrorlike allusions (as illusions), or does it draw us out of the text to a world of stable references, fixed contours of signification that plant us squarely before such verifiable notions as "Fenollosa" and "Wordsworth," "colloquial truisms" and "Chinese written characters"? There is a further complication: the variation of the familiar truism "a mind is a terrible thing to waste." Maybe the substitution of *spend* for *waste* is a covert nod to blind Milton considering how his light was "spent." And Milton himself may well have known that phallocratic regimes sustain themselves through seminal expenditure, outside of which one is merely *spent*. The tally of carnal expenses goes back in antiquity to fantasies of seminal matter forged in the (male) brain. To say a mind is a terrible thing to *spend* is to concede that something's always going to be wasted (people "get wasted" on drugs and drink), so the real concern is the destination of the expenditure, the economy within which it circulates. Economy—from Greek words for inhabiting, managing—is how the expenses are accounted for. So circulations of the song constitute a household labor. A homework assignment might reasonably include terminological distinctions like debit and credit, trash and compost—maybe even prose and poetry.

The segment of the poem exposed so far has exhibited a notable parallelism, culminating in the exemplary symmetrical construction juxtaposing poetry and prose. The second citation given above, however, began with one of the terms but did not include the other, which in fact precedes it in the actual sequence:

> Prose,
> pose—relentless
> furrier.
> Poem, chrome. "I
> don't like the way you think":
> a mind is a terrible thing to spend.
> That is, in prose you start with the world
> and find the words to match; in poetry you start
> with the words and find the world in them. "Bring
> soup in—very hot."

The system of equivalences seems expanded in this account. The farther we wander up the axiological field of the text from the initial citation, the more clearly we are immersed in a play on words, an economy of homophonic equivalents. But are these "general equivalents" in the symbolic economy of philosophical idealism, in which "The phallus is the general equivalent of objects, and the father is the general equivalent of subjects, in the same way that gold is the general equivalent of products" (Goux 24)? Do homophonic equivalents disclose a symbolic economy like that given in Goux's handy summary? Do they have the consistency of conventional pairs like fire and water, man and woman, innocence and experience, left and right, being and nothingness? Or does the convention consist in the schism rather than in the terms set into motion? Some perspective is needed, some relief from the tick-tock opiate of binaries.

It is tempting to use the distinction between poetry and prose as a reference point and step back from it in a series of interpretive frames, each time quoting more of the poem (encasing it in farther

What is this text, after all, in the most verifiable material sense? It is a photograph, for that's how typesetting is done now. The printed text in the book from which I've been quoting is a photograph,

reaches of prose), and each time omitting nothing of what has been quoted already, until in the end the entire poem would be given intact—subsumed, as it were, in a single quotation. It would be a series of reverse blow-ups, in other words, as though the initial three lines of the poem were just tiny grains of a photograph, and if we stepped back and took in more lines (more grains) they would fall into resolution as an image. You may be justifiably dubious that this method (or any method) could finally produce a synoptic *image* in place of the para-tactic succession of actual words and grammatical units. It would probably be confusing if I were to ask you what a given poem looks like, because we're not accus-tomed to viewing poems from a distance. The shape of a poem emerges, subliminally, amid the concrete registration of optical scanning as we process its alpha-betic display into "sense." That subliminal image then constitutes recognizable features contribut-ing to the feel of the text, even if you never give it a thought (shown a page of *The Ring and the Book* and a page of *Rock-Drill* from across the room, you would not

but this is already a simplification. It's actually a photograph of a photograph. The typesetter proc-esses the text by keyboard and code into a computer file; this file, this digital template of the text, is then reactivated in a sepa-rate procedure involving a rapidly spinning disc, which is a piece of film filled with images of the let-ters of the alphabet, in bold and italic, and so forth: a palette of fonts. The computer code in-structs a projector to beam light through this disc (this photograph of an alphabet) in a determined order, exposing a sheet of photo-graphic paper to a precise combi-nation of letters, yielding at the designated size a string of words, such as "in prose you start with the world." This paper is then extracted from the machine in a lightproof aluminum tube and developed by means of the usual chemical baths. What emerges from the solution, soaked and gleaming and clipped by clothes-pins to a line to dry, is the text. To be precise: a photograph of the text. Later, in layout, this photo-graph is cut into sections and pasted onto graphics boards and sent to a print shop, where the images (pages of text) are photo-

confuse Robert Browning with Pound). While successive sentences are paratactic, they are grammatically sufficient in themselves to produce meanings. But what of the homophonic parataxis in the lines quoted so far? This poem is not nonsense, or if it is, it's a choreography of discernable senses into a cumulative non-(or anti-) sense. Still, it seems unlikely to resolve itself photographically into an image (mental or ocular). Even Pound, that ardent proponent of the ideogram, left a "rag bag" of snapshots and musical cues, phanopoeia and melopoeia, all mixed up together in what he called a "vortex" in preference to an "image." Even a pictorially framed poem like Frost's "Stopping By Woods on a Snowy Evening" might dissolve into controversy as readers differ on whether or not the woods are deciduous.

Christopher Collins thinks literacy trains us to dissolve the image: "Literary interpretation has therefore come to be considered a means by which images, the particular perceptlike representations evoked by language and scanned by the inner eye, are either sequestered from or assimilated into abstract-propositional

graphed again. From these photographs master plates are produced from which the actual pages of the physical book, the commodity, are printed. What circulates, then, as the poem, is the photograph of a photograph, itself composed of projections from a prior photograph of letters of the alphabet. (Plato would double over . . .) Where is that legendary "text itself" in this slipstream of transitive images? Do all these repetitions of a primary image degrade or obscure it? Do I squint at the poem and confess I can't quite make it out?—or, if I can't, is it because of some flaw in the economy of reproduction?

I would like to say *Let me show you the poem,* and hand you a wet, slippery thing. I would like to say *Step back, take another look.* Hanging from clothespins on a line is the entire poem across the room, all thirty-five inches of it, hanging on a continuous strip of photographic paper still moist from the chemical wash. I would like to offer you the use of a (quarter-a-view) telescope of the sort you find at historical overlooks, so you could train your gaze on this semantic vehicle, selectively focusing on different segments of discourse; once these obstacles to thematic clarity are dealt with, the entire text can be translated into nonimaginal, categorical prose" (2). This procedure of "critical interpretation" is distinct from "enactive interpretation." In the enactive mode we recognize that texts "are notated scripts composed to be played by readers and that, though scripted in a public code, these works are performed on a private, inner stage." Enactive hermeneutics is generally resisted, Collins argues, because iconophobia conflates image-making with transgression.[5] We

5. There are also intimations of *regression* in iconophobia, insofar as phonocentric scripts are fantasized as a more developed mode of writing. W. J. T. Mitchell's outline of the relation between word and image is helpful: "The history of culture is in part the story of a protracted struggle for dominance between pictorial and linguistic signs, each claiming for itself certain proprietary rights on a 'nature' to which only it has access." "Among the most interesting and complex versions of this struggle is what might be called the relationship of subversion, in which language or imagery looks into its own heart and finds lurking there its opposite number. One version of this relation has haunted the philosophy of language since the rise of empiricism, the suspicion that beneath words, beneath ideas, the ultimate reference in the mind is the image, the im-

the distant text. It would have been nice to withhold the name of the author, the title of the poem, and other bibliographic data until, in a process of stepping back over and over again to attain more and more comprehensive views of the context, the ground against which this poem figures, that information would simply emerge into view as natural protuberances on a landscape, segments of billboard parade along the route (like the old Burma Shave ads). To use the initial citation of a few lines as a pivot from which to step back and attain progressively larger views would be to engage the Emersonian vision of circles; nothing would please me more. We might, by such procedure, wander so far afield we could inadvertently stumble on Eve recounting her dream to Adam, in some point of space-time at which the sonic boom of biblical exegesis is just now belatedly arriving.

Reading involves the sense of sight. And yet, by *seeing* more of this poem, "Dysraphism"—as for instance across the room, apprehending its total length—we can read less of it. From the distance of an arm span a text in twelve-

pacify the iconographic threat by transposing it into that neutral (prose) register called "meaning." The images, then—dart-gunned, stunned, and finally stuffed— stand in docile array in the exhibit our imperial attention secures for them.

Iconophobia is not simply a fear of images, but a fear of the contaminating agency that unwanted images represent.[6] There are other sources of somatic alarm. Consider phonophobia, a term that might be defined as "protection against rhymes." The

---

pression of outward experience printed, painted, or reflected in the surface of consciousness" (43). What's arresting in Mitchell's account is the suggestion of an uncanny slippage between one sense and another, between one medium of accounting and the next, such that the perceptual occasion is itself split into a contest of faculties. The seams, in other words, are not boundaries between discrete events; rather, their weave intrudes distractingly right across any "middle" and infects every "center" with insecurity.

6. Claude Gandelman, in *Reading Pictures, Viewing Texts,* offers a variety of tableaux suggestive of such contamination— including flaying, mapping, and peeling —in which the scopic drive intensifies in order to ward off other threats. In Gandelman's view, seeing is a kind of touching; so in order to inspect the trauma of sight, we should also investigate the haptic dimension.

point type passes out of legibility. To sustain this masquerade of a close reading, I want to insist on the functionality of scale, SIZE. The poem at hand is a massive impediment to the easy assurance of the transcendental ego. To arrive at an author function in the present tense requires some expeditionary maneuvering. We will get there, but we're not there yet, any more than he or she is here now, supervising our progress.

Literacy turns us all into animals. In the presence of the written word, we become the birds who flock down to Zeuxis's legendary painting to pluck its depicted grapes. To read is to nibble the fruits of representation, to concede the priority of delusion. To read is to conclude that the senses can only be satisfied by illusory means. The delectable poison of a doubled language—binding ear and eye, word and thing, in a continuous loop—allows us to "taste at the root of the tongue the unreal of what is real" (Stevens, *Collected Poems*).[a] Interpretation is a

---

a. "Poetry is a mechanism that demechanizes man and his relation with things," Odysseus Elytis writes. "The poet reaches the point where he goes into partnership with his own contradiction" (Ivask 30).

reading process would short-circuit if we were to attribute semantic value to rhymes as such, however inviting it is to unspool obvious implications. Yeats's "The Secret Rose," for example, concludes: "Surely thine hour has come, thy great wind blows, / Far-off, most secret, and inviolate Rose?" The rhyme here is semantically rich, suggesting a *blown rose*. On the other hand, the opening rhymes of the poem have no semantic consequence: "Far-off, most secret, and inviolate Rose, / Enfold me in my hour of hours; where those / Who sought thee . . . "The use of rhyme, then, functions as a merely occasional invitation to semantic significance, because the task of attributing semantic value to *all* homophones is too demanding. Iconophobia is a fear of images, plural, the figure of one image being shadowed by some dark counterpart. So rhymes and puns play in the shadows, ominously, like "tick tock."[7] *Tick*

predator in this zone between real and unreal, perception and illusion, confidence and doubt. The text, in its material manifestation, is the photo of a photo. Likewise, Zeuxis's grapes can be thought of as the grapes of grapes. Interpretation purports to put us in touch with—while seeking the shortest distance between—the words of words. The principle is one of recursion. Whatever *is* recurs, and its recurrence effectively prohibits us from distinguishing priority, or authenticity (Derrida's rule of iteration).

I quoted the line by Stevens from the third impression (1966) of the *Collected Poems* published by Faber and Faber in London (1955). The entire volume is identical to the original American edition published by Alfred A. Knopf. That is, pagination and typography are the same, along with the floral and geometric patterns separating the poems. There is little here to trouble us about questions of authenticity, correct text, and so on. My text, third impression of a secondary issue though it is, has a status equal to that of any current edition. Is this a conundrum, relating to the issue of mass media

---

7. "The fact that we call the second of the two related sounds *tock* is evidence that we use fictions to enable the end to confer organization and form on the temporal structure. The interval between the two sounds, between *tick* and *tock* is now

tick is redundant; *tick tock* is ominous. *Tick tock* in a mechanism is
mundane; *tick tock* in a narrative is
numinous. But what about tocks
that disrupt poems like a nervous
tic? Are the relentless homonyms
of "Dysraphism" (the poem by
Charles Bernstein I've been sub-
jecting to a conceptual striptease)
toxic?

Phonophobia stipulates a binar-
istic resolution: meaningful or
not, pertinent or impertinent.[8]

---

charged with significant duration" (Kermode 45).

8. And since readers are never omnis-
cient, noticed or unnoticed. For instance,
in "The Voice of the Shuttle," Geoffrey
Hartman uses a Dickinson poem to illustrate how "Human life, like a poetical figure, is an indeterminate middle between
overspecified poles always threatening to
collapse" (348). In his subtle reading of the
poem, however, Hartman neglects to notice a crucial homophonic pun in—of all
places—the middle stanza:

> Our pace took sudden awe —
> Our feet — reluctant — lead —
> Before — were Cities — but Be-
> tween —
> The Forest of the Dead —

The first stanza gives us the image of an
"odd Fork in Being's Road," so we're prepared to hear, in this afterlife, of feet being
reluctantly *led.* "Lead" gives us the present

reproduction and Walter Benjamin's speculations on decline of
the aura? When I read Stevens's
poems from my edition, I experience no loss of aura (unless I
think of the limited Cummington
Press editions as unique and salutary, since it makes sense to affili-
ate Stevens's work with objets
d'art of the printer's trade). I am
confident that the words are the
right words in the right order
(a book is not a box—there's no
settlement during shipping). But
consider this: the words appear to
be *the right size.* What is "the right
size" of a word? In print, readabil-
ity or legibility is the requisite
scale. But then, billboards are legible too.

What would a Wallace Stevens
poem mean if it were encountered on a billboard, with every
letter six feet tall? What would
"Credences of Summer" be in the
medium of skywriting? These
questions are peculiarly appropriate to Stevens, for whom the
world appears massively textual-
ized anyway; the epistemic rever-
ies of a Stevens poem are often
derived from attempts to adjust
different cosmic codes to a common denominator, so that a global

Having started with Bakhtin's distinction between the novel and the poem, then shifting to a related distinction between poetry and prose, we now arrive at the cognitive paradox of figure-

script continuity can be achieved at last.[b] Stevens's poetic enterprise is pursued exclusively within the conventional field of the published book; the type size of the *Collected Poems* approximates that of the pica typewriter, and while the brevity of book pages sometimes requires Stevens's lines to be run over, the poems generally fit the scale. The same cannot be said for the work of many other poets. Anyone who has seen the Three Mountains Press edition of Pound's *Cantos I-XVI,* with its monumental initial capitals and robust typography, might regard the New Directions and Faber editions as an attenuation of the text. The open spread of Stéphane Mallarmé's *Un Coup de dès,* along with the composition-by-field of Charles Olson and Robert Duncan, has left a challenging record of how central the issue of dimension is—hardly to be relegated to a designer's whim, or the conceptual realm of what

---

tense of the verb, but the rhyme with "Dead" changes it from verb to noun. This is a sumptuous and characteristic Dickinson pun. It's a moment of acute foreboding, of both seeing and wanting not to see, being "Between" in the "Forest of the Dead" yet wanting to be beyond in the celestial City. Spooked volition is masterfully condensed into that one word, "lead," as it dilates between time present and past (and future eternal), but also settles into inert metal. Most amazing is the fact that the word "Dead" is, in effect, rhymed with a word that isn't even there, "led." Hartman, as I mentioned, doesn't notice any of this. His inattention propagates in a curious way in Garrett Stewart's *Reading Voices: Literature and the Phonotext.*

Stewart draws significantly from "The Voice of the Shuttle" as well as from Hartman's *Saving the Text.* After discussing Hartman at length, and then explaining the way "Gods wounds" etymologically devolved to "zounds" (which Stewart calls "a rhyme with—and virtual echo of—the sound of the word 'sounds' itself"), he concludes: "By such contraction and displacement, such *coupure,* the archetypal wound is made flesh in read writing" (141). It's as if the mortal slapstick of Dickinson's rhyme continues even here (and still unremarked): not only does "read" echo *dead* and *lead,* but it homophonically conceals/reveals "red," the color of a flesh wound.

b. In the final collection, *The Rock,* the world is porous to any alphabet, any representation, any thought, from "The Poem that Took the Place of a Mountain" to the aquatic undertone of the eponymous rock as "the drowsy motion of the river R" ("An Old Man Asleep").

ground resolution, as in the familiar rabbit/duck diagram. The
specific anxiety in "Dysraphism" is
induced by the presence of motivated rhymes and homonyms,
which are (or are not) semantically consequential. The problem
is not one of similarity, like twins
who can be named with confidence only by their parents.
Rather, the rabbit is visible at the
expense of the duck and vice versa.
We can't see (nor adequately conceive) both at once. So this poem
sets off a homophonic ringing in
the ears, which is at the same
time iconographic; together they
make a synaesthetic blur(t). But is
it prose or poetry that's doing the
posing? Which is the poseur? Will
the real poem please stand up
(as they used to say on *What's
My Line*)? The poem is distracted
(posed) and deflected (in chrome)
by its own analogies. The acoustic
analogies, being homophonic
puns, keep baiting attention with
a feverish consistency. The homophones permeate everything, and
consciousness is the tar baby.

What we are considering here
is the condition of twoness, dou-
blings, and duplicity. As it happens, the speaking animal is also a
sexed animal, and sexual dimor-

text editors call "incidentals." In
the expanded field of Olson's
typographic specifications, the
pages of *The Maximus Poems* are
8½ x 11 inches. There are poems
in that volume as brief as one or
two lines, yet their position on the
page clearly involves a habitation
of the surrounding space. (That
is, the poems are not all lined up
at a conventional drop point from
the top of the page, as in most
books of poetry.) What status
does the empty space have for any
consideration of Olson's text? Is
the space part of the text? When
scholars cite a poem in couplets,
the blank lines between couplets
are represented as part of the quotation. We could say, to be precise, that the interlineated blank
spaces are quoted along with the
couplets. But what protocol is
available for the citation of an
Olson poem such as "veda upanishad edda than"? The four words
quoted here are all four of the
words of the poem, and in the
proper order; but is the poem
constituted solely of words? How
much of the poem is constituted
by blank space? And how much
blank space should I include with
the cited text? Lacking a page the
size of Olson's, quotation is,

phism has ominous implications for language.[9] Twoness may be a convenient bifurcation anatomically, but a debacle for transcendental yearnings. Every word,

9. Obviously, I'm indebted to Lacan's formulation of lack, "the central defect around which the dialectic of the advent of the subject to his own being in the relation to the Other turns—by the fact that the subject depends on the signifier and that the signifier is first of all in the field of the Other" (*Fundamental Concepts* 204–05). The complexities of Lacan's exposition are more subtle than my account; however, I am not writing psychology but making an analogy. I'm skeptical about "Lacanian" readings of texts as if they were people, so the anatomy of symbolic economies pursued by Goux seems to me a preferable way of engaging the same issues without having to (pretend to) transpose complex psychoanalytic maneuvers onto texts— and I would define a text, in this light, as *a mind that does not think back,* however thoroughly it seems to have *anticipated* any thoughts about it a reader might have. Goux contrasts "materialism" (related to *mater*) with "paterialism" or idealism. The difference between the sexes is symbolic of the symbolic, he suggests, and the "paterialist ideology of conception [is] *the archaeological sexual core of idealism as the conception of conception*" (225, Goux's emphasis). Paterialism copies materialist reproduction and then declares the copy to be the original, the archetype. This much, at any rate, is sufficient to underscore my point above, that sexual difference is symbolic panic.

strictly, impossible. One can approximate, but approximating the conceptual value of blank space puts us squarely in the paradoxical position of producing something out of nothing. What Stevens's snow man says, of "Nothing that is not there and the nothing that is," is offered by Olson not as a propositional enigma, but as a structural ambiguity of the text itself, the text given as sheer unquantifiable space. The difference is that enacted by a Zen koan or a particle physics experiment; which is to say, Stevens and Olson are complementary—engaged in complementarity—in ways that their sociological status as "poets" only confuses.

Interpretation is logocentric. Stevens is eminently interpretable because his words refer to other words, and the syntagmatic chain of grammatical association effectively stipulates a "scale" within which every word achieves its resonance. Stevens's poems are examples of perfect recursion. Whether I read "The Snow Man" in the Norton anthology, in the standard editions (*Collected Poems* or in Holly Stevens's *The Palm at the End of the Mind*), or quoted in a scholarly article, it always mas-

every one, is two; every sign is duplicitous. The human propensity for symbolization projects signification as such into the split or rift between divergent signs. The Blakean affirmation of contraries continues the Empedoclean insistence on conjunction and division, eros and strife. Consciousness can never be pure, central, autonomous, or complete, because it derives (through language and nurture) from others. Self-consciousness turns you into your own doppelgänger:

> but here you are. Transient
>   cathexis, Doppler
> angst. And then a light comes
>   on
> in everybody's head. "So I
> think that somewhere we
> ought to make the
>   point that it's really
> a team approach." Riddled
> with riot. What
> knows not scansion admits
> expansion: tea leaves
> decoy
> for the grosser fortune—
>   the slush
> of afternoon, the morning's
> replay.
>   Prose,
> pose—relentless

querades as itself. The birds of my mind submit to their customary feeding frenzy on Stevens's grapes.[c] I bring up Olson to suggest that not all poetry is logocentric. What's more, the complicity between interpretation and logocentrism is a useful indicator of why there are so many interpreters of Stevens, so few of Olson. The issue here is not aesthetic evaluation, but epistemological recognition, and Stevens's poems court a familiar epistemé.[d]

c. Stevens was not unmindful of the grapes:

> It was when I said,
> "There is no such thing as the truth,"
> That the grapes seemed fatter.
> The fox ran out of his hole.

This same poem, "On the Road Home," continues its reverie of nested testimonies to (what else?) language: "It was when I said, / 'Words are not forms of a single word. / In the sum of the parts, there are only the parts. / The world must be measured by eye.'"

d. *The Maximus Poems* constitutes a singular resistance to the prevailing epistemé of ennui and dispossession. Olson loved to cite the Heraclitean tenet that man is estranged from that which is most familiar, and the Maximus figure is designed in part to reclaim a kind of Viconian giant in the revealed amplitude of the body in its spatial and temporal extensions. Olson's trip-

furrier.

Poem, chrome.

Enlightenment—the luminous bulb in the cranium—needs a "team approach." Prose and poetry are the Romulus and Remus of Roma, the "doublends jined" that Joyce, in another urban tale of amour, dubbed Shem and Shaun, penman and postman. There is no end of "Doppler angst" in either poetic scansion or prose expansion. Lights going off in heads is a cartoon image, befitting a 'toon poem. Its tunes, its *melopoeia,* are hummed in shamelessly conspicuous ways ("Reality is always greener / when you haven't seen her" and "pompous. / Pump ass!" are a few of the viewfinders, the acoustic apertures, through which we pass on our way to the rhyme of *expansion* with *scansion,* en route to prose/pose and poem/chrome).

Following the customary paths of exegesis, one would set about explaining this poem in terms of precedents, elaborating the extortionary metaphysics of presence by which tradition reasserts itself in the seemingly innocent antics of lyrical behavior. The "light [that] comes on / in everybody's

The overwhelming priority of interpretation—in its logocentric intimacy—is to locate *the word of the word.* If we take the patristic decision to interpret to be that of clarifying the message of prophetic textuality, the literal words —letter by letter—are never regarded as the true or intended words. The literal words are the accidental, incidental, and excremental material by means of

---

tych *typos-topos-tropos* reflects his involvement in the drama of force: the informing disfiguration of the material world. What Gilles Deleuze says in the conclusion of his book on Proust is applicable to Olson's epistemé: "Philosophy is like the expression of a Universal Mind which is in agreement with itself in order to determine explicit and communicable significations [but] truths remain arbitrary and abstract, so long as they are based on the good will of thinking." As Deleuze goes on to say, "philosophy, like friendship, is ignorant of the dark regions in which are elaborated the effective forces which act on thought, the determinations which *force* us to think. . . . The truths of philosophy are lacking in necessity and the mark of necessity. As a matter of fact, the truth is not revealed, it is betrayed; it is not communicated, it is interpreted; it is not willed, it is involuntary" (*Proust* 160). Deleuze of course was a philosopher. Leave it to a litterateur like Roberto Calasso to add pungency to the thought: "Literature grows like the grass between the heavy gray paving stones of thought" (*Literature and the Gods* 183).

head" could, by such method, be regarded as the trace of poetic lineage. Specifically, Robert Duncan's famous "Poem Beginning With a Line by Pindar" begins with the line *"The light foot hears you and the brightness begins."* Duncan puns fleetness of foot into electromagnetic illumination. The link between Duncan and the text at hand may appear tenuous; but Marjorie Perloff actually resorts to Tennyson's "Charge of the Light Brigade" in discussing this passage (*Poetic License* 27). It's even plausible that Byron the Bulb (from *Gravity's Rainbow*) is gleaming nearby. As it happens, the poem itself provides numerous echoes of a more explicit nature. Homer, Chaucer, Robert Creeley, Gertrude Stein, and Wallace Stevens are all evoked.[10] By such markers as

which the true words can be discerned: the actual words are insufficiently mental and therefore require more words, more images, other cadences. (The paradox in this is that an *increase* in modes of materialization is driven by the aspiration to idealize.[e]) The words of the text are always optimally rendered by the formula "in other words." In other words, to read this text we need a different set of words. Not a mathematical set, but a stage set, a theatrical tableaux.

The covert thespianism of critical protocol takes many forms, adopts many disguises. The problem is that some of the costumes are from different scripts, as if the interpreter were trying to act two parts at once. The paradox of interpretation is that it aspires to see both figure and ground simultaneously. The aspiration of the

---

10. "Best / of the spoils: gargoyles" (Homer); "The pillar's tale: a windowbox onto society" (Chaucer). "Extension is never more than a form of content" inverts Creeley's dictum that form is never more than an extension of content. The "tea leaves" in "morning's replay" reprises Stevens's "Sunday Morning"—without coffee and oranges. Gertrude Stein is named in the text. John F. Kennedy is parodied ("'If you don't keep up / with culture, culture will keep up / with you.'") and even talk show host Geraldo Rivera flick-

e. The paradox is nicely put by Charles Gould in Joseph Conrad's *Nostromo*: "things seem to be worth nothing by what they are in themselves. I begin to believe that the only solid thing about them is the spiritual value which everyone discovers in his own form of activity" (318). Another character observes with exasperation that "Those Englishmen live on illusions which somehow or other help them to get a firm hold of the substance" (239).

these allusions to predecessors, "Dysraphism" intimates its own form as a recursive pattern of inheritance.

The enigmatic title of Bernstein's poem merits a footnote by the author, the purpose of which seems less to clarify the unusual term than to ponder poetic applications.

"Dysraphism" is a word used by specialists in congenital disease to mean a dysfunctional fusion of embryonic parts—a birth defect. . . . *Raph* literally means "seam," so dysraphism is mis-seam-

ers at the edges: "Heraldically defamed." Finally, the poet himself is implicated in that the title of his book of essays appears enjambed as "*Content's / dream.*" Discussing another poem by Bernstein, Christopher Beach notes that "If such a poem . . . is largely intertextual, it is participating in an intertext of which the individual source texts have become difficult or impossible to determine; thus, it is one much closer in kind to the universal text of Barthes or the discursive formations of Foucault than to the deliberately structured intertextual matrix of Pound or Olson" (248). Michael Davidson ("Discourse in Poetry") has also discussed Bernstein's work as an exception to Bakhtin's declarations about the monoglossia of poetry.

critic is to be the recording angel, accessing the text in its entirety without losing the details. (Hypertext theory is now working out the details; a staging of *The Waste Land,* for instance, could give you a split-screen parallel of Eliot's own data base—no longer mere "allusions"—so the initial reception would more closely approximate the cultured purview that relishes the text in the aura of its debts, or what Joyce called "stolentelling" [*Finnegans Wake* 424]). A double vision is desired, but desired in a state of binocular resolution. Two, apprehended simultaneously, must merge into a legible figure, *one.* This may be the symmetrical unity of form and content, or it may blend psychological disposition with ideological outlook; but whatever it is, its "success" inheres in its calculated squaring of fact with fantasy, signified with signifier. Like an arithmetic problem, the figures must add up. Textual explications rarely concede insolubles; at most we get an admission of partiality. Exegesis strives for clarification and summation. The point of an "overview" is to behold without equivocation, to subordinate the

ing—a prosodic device! But it has the punch of being the same root as rhapsody (*rhaph*)—or in Skeat's —"one who strings (lit. stitches) songs together, a reciter of epic poetry," cf. "ode" etc. (*Sophist* 44)

The epic poet, reciting the adventures of Odysseus, not only stitches songs together, but tells of a world where nothing is what it seems, where the boundaries or seams of heaven, earth, and underworld are continually crossed over and restitched by the hero, who survives all these trespasses by semantic wile, calling himself "Outis," the seme of "Noman." As that other "O," Charles of Gloucester, contemplating his "Neolithic / neighbors" in *The Maximus Poems* declares: "I prefer my boundary of / land literally adjacent & adjoining mid Mesozoic at / the place of the parting of the seams of *all* the Earth" (Olson, 549).

Odysseus is a latecomer in the epic that bears his name, not appearing directly until Book V. The epic opens on Olympus, with the gods reflecting on human duplicity:

fuzziness and disturbance, the exigent noise of the system, so that the *big picture* comes through. This is the cartoon version of things: learning to see through the dots, the residual materialistic phantom of the medium, whether that consists of sound waves, light waves, electric frequency, smeared pigment, or inks variously poured, rubbed, drawn, dragged, stamped, spattered, and imprinted.

To think of a written text as replicable in another medium is to either exalt or debase it. A note on the fridge reminding you to get milk has limited textual value, however efficacious its message. *Ulysses* on the other hand, though it might "remind" you of some nagging obligation, persists beyond your encounter with it, independent and aloof. There's a certain magic involved. To obtain a quart of milk from a scrap of paper with some graphite clinging to it is quite a feat, but it doesn't compare with the wizardry of Homeric Greek appearing in a "Dublin" conjured into English from the vantage of Trieste, Zurich, and Paris. The "big picture" of *Ulysses* is in fact a crib, so there's little to be gained by reading

Greed and folly
double the suffering in the
    lot of man.
See how Aigísthos, for his
    double portion,
stole Agamémnon's wife
    and killed the soldier
on his homecoming day.
(Homer, *The Odyssey* Book I,
lines 33–37)

This leads to Athena's wistful reflection that Odysseus's redoubled
suffering is not due to greed and
folly, but to the vengeance of
Poseidon. Odysseus is subject to
all manner of double inflictions.
He suffers endless homesickness,
but this malaise is in sharp contrast to the paradisal circumstance of his trysts with Kirke and
Kalypso. He is even granted a con-
ditional immortality as long as he
remains on Kalypso's island. Eventually, Kalypso is persuaded to aid
Odysseus's homeward quest with
a helping gust of wind (Book V,
line 268).

Bernstein's "Dysraphism"
opens with an oblique evocation
of Homer's intrepid sea(m)-man:

Did a wind come just as you
    got up or were
you protecting me from it? I

Joyce's work for its plot. We persist with it for the *dots*. The dots
plot an itinerary of reverie; the
words are succubi feeding off a
reader's incalculably personal associations and competence. Yet
why shouldn't hermeneutics factor in readerly *incompetence*—
more openly, I mean, than gesturing toward some "horizon of
interpretation"? Critical mastery
is actually predicated on omnis-
cience. But even the most diligent
student skims over some obscure
reference. How many readers of
Four Quartets stop to look up "har-
uspicate"? How secure does the
Poundian feel about being able to
identify the ideogram *"ching ming"*?
Does the Elizabethan scholar re-
verberate like a tuning fork with
Shakespeare's debts to Raphael
Holinshed?

The text ceases to be "itself"
the moment I begin to read it. I
am answerable to what I absorb
through reading, but *rereading* is
more patently indicative of the
scope of my desires. The fascination with the text is how it becomes *me,* how it constitutes—
through what *are* worth calling
dialogic means—the transitory
monologic moments when what I
find before me accords with what

felt the abridgement
of imperatives, the wave of
    detours, the sabre-
rattling of inversion. *All lit
up and no place to go.* Blinded
    by avenue and filled with
adjacency. Arch or arched at.

The question with which the
poem opens might be thought
of as Odysseus's ironic jibe at
Kalypso.[11] But given the rampant
homophony throughout "Dysraphism," "wind" invites its twin,
the verb *to wind up,* which is both
to "end up" (as Odysseus has,
at the *beginning* of his epic, in
Kalypso's clutches) and to *begin,*
to get started. The pitcher, wind-
ing up for the pitch, grips the
seams (trying not to get caught using pitch or some other illegal
stickum); just as the poet, wound
up with homophonic semes, uses
words that are not what they
seem. Quite apart from ancestral
provocations (Homer, Pound,

I feel within, behind, or around
me. In other words, to the degree
that there is interest there are
dividends: I split apart into pieces
that talk, and include in that collo-
quy even this textual counterpart
that is patently not me or mine.
The textual other inhabits me
through a circulatory system, and
it beats. But isn't this just flagrant
subjectification? Or is it interpretation?

I'm talking about detours, and
detours create value.[f] To read, no
less than to hear, is to concede the
mobilization of language to another voice; but listening interpel-
lates its own tacit voicing into the
occasion. Value is created both
ways, as the voice of another displaces my own initiative, and as
my own yearning to participate

11. In the Homeric text the hero is immediately suspicious of the goddess' sudden inclination to set him free, which is in-
timated here in the "sabre- / rattling of
inversion." On the other hand, Bernstein
is a New Yorker, so maybe the opening is
an homage to Boreas, who protected
Megalopolis from Spartan invasion.

f. "Metaphors, symptoms, signs, representations: it is always through replacement that values are created. Replacing
what is forbidden, what is lacking, what is
hidden or lost, what is damaged, in short,
replacing with something equivalent what
is not itself, in person, presentable. . . .
Now the notion of value, whether for exchange, compensation, indemnification,
purchasing, or repurchasing, is implied in
every replacement. Whether this exchange
involves comparison, substitution, supple-
mentation—or translation and representation—value enters into it" (Goux 9).

Stein), the opening question of "Dysraphism" deliberates on origin, succession, simultaneity, causality, and synchronicity: the very issues pertinent to any consideration of interpretation's path from word to world. Is the wind—the *pneuma,* the breath-potency of speech—latent but unrecognized, or is it nonexistent? Smile or gas? Continuous or discontinuous? Particle or wave? There is a "wave of detours" linked in some way with the blinding avenues that leave one "filled with / adjacency"; detour and adjacency emphasize the poem's parataxis. Its parts are not logically sequential, but they are rhetorically efficient. The opening lines deploy, in swift succession, the rhetorical functions of metonymy, metaphor, and irony (as abridgement, detour, and inversion). The syntagmatic procedures of the text itself (of which parataxis is the hyperbolic manifestation) favor "adjacency." Even the explanatory note that enthuses over the fortuitousness of the term "Dysraphism" (serving the poet much as Hegel's celebration of the term "Aufhebung" served, he said, a philosophy intent on taking its cues from the

dislodges the text, misreads, forgets, deviates. The cumulative motion of exchange is a deposit: I leave tracks where I've gone, so to think of the "text" is to see it soiled with passage, accompanied by a compost heap of marginalia. Likewise, consciousness of self is susceptible to trails, lines, deposits from textual visitors. As Whitman says at the end of "Song of Myself": "look for me under your boot-soles."

In its aspiration to encapsulate or reduce the bulk of the text, to discern its core or essence, interpretation ends up adding more to the accumulating mass (a prospect thematized, by the way, in Ashbery's "Self-Portrait in a Convex Mirror"). This approach commonly supposes that a given text is a bluff, a front for some other secret or ulterior operation; it presumes that its words are really *other words.* To be literate is to be immunized against the material order that intercedes between mind and text. To be literate is to see through the text but not *see* the text.

Compounding the problem is a long-standing split between exegesis and textual editing. The text

elation of language itself)[12] offers up the title as a paradigm discovered by syntagmatic means: in Dorland's standard medical dictionary *dysraphia* is preceded by *dysprosody,* "disturbance of stress, pitch, and rhythm of speech."

The dysraphic spectacle summoned up in "Dysraphism" is a disturbance of speech, a patchwork quilt of stitched rhapsodic stutter aspiring to cumulative epic import. An epic legacy of reflection is at stake: the epic unification of vision with idea, surface reflectance with the blaze of revealed identity. Achilles's shield and Odysseus's scar are icons of an ocular disposition to certify an order of events as a visual array, which come to fruition in the ceaseless scrutiny of the visible by Aeneas, whom Virgil introduces

12. Hegel found it "remarkable that a language should have come to use one and the same word for two opposite determinations. It is a joy for speculative thought to find words which in themselves have a speculative meaning" (*Science of Logic,* 1: 119–20). Semantic duplicity gives rise to jubilation, as Hegel detects in the "speculative" spirit of language an iridescence in which the rolling gait of the dialectic is crystallized, or shines forth, disclosing the cortical array of thought as a prism.

editor's job is to clean up the text, to make its potential intrusions disappear in the act of reading. This is the source of misconceptions about reading, for the scholar always dissolves the details into the whole, whereas for the interested reader the whole is just as likely to be resolved into the detail, the familiar feature that makes the whole accessible and memorable. The plot of *Jude the Obscure* can fade away over time, while the memory of Little Father Time's mordant suicide note remains vivid. The note becomes a synechdoche of the novel itself. The interpretive urge would create value by exchanging one text (the literary work) for another (the critical commentary) in a metaphorical substitution. But the attempt produces metonymic supplements, or augmentations of the "original." This is because the original is subject to change. How? Because readers change, and the original is enacted only in the reader.

Think of the reader as a monitor attached to a VCR. The text itself is the videocassette, but it is transmitted by mechanical means. There may be a tracking problem

as reflecting on the sack of Troy, narrating the fall, but with interruptions: "He broke off / To feast his eyes and mind on a mere image, / Sighing often, cheeks grown wet with tears, / To see again" (*Aeneid* 20). To see again the glories preceding defeat, but also to see the defeat. Imagine his tears, pooled into a well of archetypal Western topoi: to read *The Aeneid* is to gaze down on our own reflected faces. Robert Duncan offered a reading of such an image to Norman O. Brown ("Nobby") in a letter, quoting from his own poem then commenting on it:

> Thirst not
> The Well is full.
> Do not trouble the water.)

> But it is our calling to trouble the water, Nobby. And needs all the (most happily) inspirations of our imagination or (most unhappily) cunning of our art to obey the "Do not trouble the water" to mean troubling the water. . . . I am the more acutely aware of the *trouble* troubling the water brings and I know no

(faulty text editing), or there may be a deficiency in the monitor (typeface, cracked spine, text defaced by somebody's crude underlining), so the resolution of the image is not what the producers "intended." The technical apparatus that brings you the text in the first place also intercedes in the textualizing process. The text is never separable from the page it's printed on without exhaustive labors, flight preparations, which don't actually launch it into a pure noetic space so much as they reduce the ambient noise of that space below the threshold of audibility (the seatbelt sign blinks off and you're free to move about the cabin). We need to conceive of value outside the simple framework of the clean text and the totalizing interpretation. The metonymic supplement that our attention ceaselessly adds to the object of attention is itself a source of value; hence the Jewish exegetical supplementarity of the Midrash. Anything said with reference to something else adds to it. We know the production through its reproduction, and we know through our own reproduction that production never ceases.

We are now supposedly im-

strength in that trouble except faith and most important that it is as we know it
is *blind*. ("Homage to
Robert Duncan," 11–12)

As Homer was said to be blind.
And Tiresias. "To see again" is also
to see doubly, to see with the wisdom of hindsight, but as if for the
first time.

To posit a complete image beyond, below, despite the ripples,
takes faith, blind faith. Troubled
water: disturbed speech. Dysraphism is a disturbance of speech that
reveals speech to have already
been disturbing. As in the Greek
and Latin epics, "Dysraphism" is a
saga of misadventures, but at the
level of homophony and pun. So
there will be "No identification,
only / restitution." The face reflected in "Dysraphism"'s chrome
will never be yours (the unabated
parataxis mops away simple reflection). Nor do the face and the
prospect of reflection ever with-
draw the allure. "There is never
annul-/ ment, only abridgment."[13]

13. The nonidentity of the very term
is instructive as well, since "abridgement"
of the poem's second line loses its "e"
here, three pages later: intention or accident? Poet or typesetter?

mersed in a system of reproduc-
tions that proliferate without
originals. An original is conceivable only through a plenitude of
copies. It might even be the case
that the sense of plenitude attributable to *origin* is itself a byproduct of reproductive heterology.
The multitude of copies suggests
a generative potency in some
source or center. But the trace
elements of mnemonic systems
(in the mind or on the page) invariably occlude what they would
represent, finally opening out on
what David Farrell Krell calls "the
verge," where memories do not
retrieve anything from the past
but simulate a double performance of "mirth and mourning"
(9). Even the meaning of *memory*
is forgotten: "The sense of memory was so broad as to encompass
both death and love: *hē mnēmē* is
remembrance in general but also
a record, memorial, or tomb;
mnaomai means to turn one's
mind to a thing but also to woo
and to solicit favor" (2). I like this
exhortation to court the past,
make love to our own vanished
moments, to rub vitality back
into them through the bellows of
remembrance. This memorial re-
suscitation is not funerary, but a

Never a dull moment, for it's garbled in transmission, yet somehow preserved, elated, lifted up. The poem's appearance is illusory: "*All lit up and no / place to go.*" Sibilants, fricatives, and dentals keep discharging their energies into a surface that may not "go," though it won't go away: "get lost" the text snarls at the reader, who already is. "Sometimes something / sunders" in the culminating lines of the poem that sweep Homer, Virgil, Shelley, and Chairman Mao along in a rapid paratactic transit of the vernacular:

> Dominion demands distrac-
>   tion—the circus
> ponies of the slaughter
>   home. Braced
> by harmony, bludgeoned by decoration
> the dream surgeon hobbles three steps over, two
> steps beside. "In those days you didn't have to
> shout to come off as expressive." One by one
> the clay feet are sanded, the sorrows remanded.
> *A fleet of ferries, forever merry.*
> Show folks know that what the fighting man wants
> is to win the war and come home.

means of incubation. Origin is seeded in every moment; it's not a matter of negotiating long detours through intervening obstacles, but of literally collecting our wits from attachment to distraction by all the *allures* so that the originary pregnancy of the present is recollected.[g] Remembrance entails expression, or pressing the juices out of the fruit of whatever's at hand. Proust's memory is contingent on a cookie, and the vast amplitude of his book constitutes the memory of appetite.

g. The concept of "allures" is from Hindu poetics by way of René Daumal: "In poetry, that which corresponds to the concept of 'rhythm' is not metrical form, limited to sounds, but 'allures' which regulate the complex course of sounds and meanings, images and emotions" (13).

Slaughterhouse becomes "home," two steps back are "beside," and the *ferries*, not the *fairies*, are merry. Everything seems susceptible to slippage; reading succumbs to the manic energy of association, so to ascribe classical allusions and submerged references to "Dysraphism" is no more (im)plausible than to link the author's initials, C.B., with a CB radio and suggest that the text is a broadcast, in Jack Spicer's sense of the poet as transmitter of Martian chatter.

Are we finally on the way to anything in such a poem—*unterwegs zur Sprache*? The text proceeds paratactically, and most of the phrasal units are enjambed. The semantic progress is a kind of descent, then, which suggests a mode of revelation. Is this therefore a prophetic text? Is it an impermeable form, resolutely hermetic, unyielding? Does it "say" anything at all? It is, I would suggest, autointerpretive; every word, each and every one, is a secret agent of two. Its duplicity is an open secret, a purloined letter. Whatever it says behind your back is manifestly right under your nose, maybe on the tip of your tongue:

> If you mix with him you're mixing
> with a metaphor. "It's
> a realistic package, it's a
> negotiable package, it's
> not a final package." Glibness
> of the overall, maybe: there is always something dripping through.
> We seem to be retreading the same tire
> over and over, with no additional traction. Here
> are some additional panes—optional. Very busy
> by now reorganizing and actually, oddly, added
> into fractionation ratio, as you might say. Or just
> hitting against, back to everybody.
> Reality is always greener
> when you haven't seen her.
> Anyway just to go on and be where you weren't or couldn't be
> before—steps, windows, ramps. To let
> all that other not so much dissolve as
> blend into an horizon of distraction, distension
> pursued as homing ground
> (a place to bar the leaks). Say,
> vaccination of cobalt emissaries pregnant with bivalent
> exasperation, protruding with inert material. I

can't but sway, hopeful in my way. Perhaps
portend, tarry. The galoshes are, e.g.,
gone; but you are here. Transient cathexis, Doppler
angst. And then a light comes on
in everybody's head.

The epistemological task of the reader—here made more conspicuous
than in "Skunk Hour" or "The Old Cumberland Beggar"—is how to seg-
regate illumination from cartoon, how to keep the transformative vision
from looking as patently artificial and intrusive as the balloon over Dick
Tracy's head, and "To let / all that other not so much dissolve as / blend
into an horizon of distraction, distension / pursued as homing ground /
(a place to bar the leaks)." This is a poem that makes it futile to separate
matter from manner, thesis from synthesis, content from form. The cartoon sublime—in which Bernstein is preceded by Ashbery—is a way of
dramatizing the disjunctions glossed over by suppositions about the unity
of the work of art.

"Dysraphism" (poem and concept) raises a question: Is the medium
debased by the message it transmits, or is it rather that the message decays in the channel that transmits it? Does Bernstein's work sully the
genre of poetry? Do its flippant parataxis and homophony make it novelistic, in Bakhtin's terms? Or is this a nonpoem, a box of goods damaged
in transit? If poetic genres are still coming through loud and clear, is
"Dysraphism" simply a decayed message, a broadcast tattered by static?
Noise in the channel is called "parasite" in French. The parasites chatter
away, adding their own litter to the transmitted message, static that bumps
a phoneme so that "prose" becomes "pose." (Is prose really needed to
pose the poem's questions?)

The internal combustion pressures of the text—viewed as heat—
make the intratextual domain an excitable region: Mallarmé enthused
over the Book at about the same time the automobile (which would shortly
embody Futurism for F. T. Marinetti) was being engineered. Octavio Paz
describes the vista opened up for these hustling engines of autonomy:
"Language now occupies the place once occupied by the gods or some
other external entity or outward reality. The poem does not refer to any-

thing outside itself; what a word refers to is another word. The meaning does not reside outside the poem but within it, not in what the words say, but in what *they say to each other*" (4). In a similar vein, John Stuart Mill, discriminating poetry from rhetoric, suggested that "eloquence is *heard,* poetry is *over*heard . . . Poetry is feeling confessing itself to itself" (539). The implication is that the poem is a society, with its own back alleys and trade secrets and gossip columns and police blotter, so our attention as readers is both voyeuristic and civic. But not quite, according to Paz, for "Media are not what signify; society is what signifies, and what it signifies is *us,* in and through these media" (158). There are messages, and there are also systems checks (like the test pattern on off-hours television channels). In "Dysraphism," the authorial specter of human agency is subject to a radical reversal, a solarization, such that the speaker is the channel itself and the "channel" is what used be called the author.

Chatter clears the channel, as if what mattered was not the semantic repertoire, but the steady roll of consonants and vowels, like bowling balls down the lane, knocking away the thicket of parasites that clog the portal. "The great human repertoire of muttering and murmuring gives irreducible tonal evidence of *someone* there," as Richard Poirier puts it, and this is as essential a message as any other (*Poetry* 154). It is also the primary semiotic activity of animals, and "Like that of talking birds, the object of our communication is to communicate communication" (Paz 159). Unlike the test signal that blatantly declares "THIS STATION IS NOT BROADCASTING AT THIS TIME," human sociality means that communication is not divisible according to a digital on/off pattern. Every word performs a double function, perpetuating its own form (its singularity, which earns it a discrete entry in the dictionary) while at the same time playing a subordinate role in a lexical event that is less easily replicable. In the lexical event, words are "replicants," and the poet plays the role of Deckard in *Blade Runner,* who falls for the creature he's supposed to "retire" (i.e., terminate). The words of a poem—those replicants—are not just signs, not just androids and semantic workers, but passional volitions. The propositional *meaning* of words is generally written in invisible ink on a sheet of glass; no matter how many times you view the world through it, it doesn't arrest your vision until, in poetry, breath fogs the glass and language suddenly appears. Once you focus on transparency, you notice it has *another side*. You can go through it, and also get behind it. To do so (outside the analogy of a pane of glass or a piece of paper) is to hear what Bakhtin meant by dialogism: the word is not simply the word of the other, but the other's word moving in reverse, as it were, toward you through the familiar terrain of your own words. Words are not borders *of* the real, but boundaries *in* the real. The truly dialogic word is not the perfect complement to one's own, but its uncanny host. Heteroglossia helps preserve the integrity of words as habitations, and discourse as shelter. The word, thoughtlessly preserved in countless habitual uses, suddenly flutters away from habit into orbit.

The social character of the nonsemantic (embodied in the insistent title of William Carlos Williams's magazine, *Contact*) is what motivated Bakhtin to emphasize the dialogic countenance of the word as such: "The word wants to be heard, understood, responded to, and again to respond to the response, and so forth *ad infinitum*. It enters into a dialogue that does not have a *semantic* end" (*Speech Genres* 127). Striving to be understood is a momentary aspiration; but as Bakhtin suggests, the interlocutors are themselves transitory features of an ongoing *pulsation of the word*. So it is not surprising to find, in his final work, a distinction between the transient discursive episode and an "infinite and unfinalized dialogue in which no meaning dies," transcending not only the bounds of human life —"Everything organic is drawn into life in the process of exchange"— but even the organic as such: "Nothing is absolutely dead: every meaning will have its homecoming festival. The problem of *great time*" (169, 170). Dialogism is extra-human; it even appears to be microbial. The archaic energy of exchange persists throughout the chain of creation, sometimes settling into semantic oases that stabilize relations (like conversational or sexual partners), but sustains itself overall by an ongoing exfoliation of chatter throughout the medium. "Meaning," then, is a temporary rest or skip, the accentual downbeat, a syncope in the festive tempo of "great time."

From the perspective of great time, whatever seems to be the case ("the world" according to Wittgenstein) exposes the seams of saying so. The poet of "Dysraphism" may appear to be throwing us knuckleballs; if so, it's because of the way he grips the seams. The words of "Dysraphism" trick us into nibbling their literal sense, and like the birds that flock to Zeuxis's painting expecting grapes, we are surprised by the sign instead, and forced to recognize that we don't mean "literal" literally. This galumphing hayride has been crammed with quoted goodies, and footnoted innuendos too—but doubling what? I began with a citation in prose, one that distinguished prose (starting with the world and finding the words to match) from poetry (starting with the words and finding the world in them). The prose quote was a masquerade,

> so the same words
> were repeated
> in three lines,

lines which donate seams (line breaks) to the text. The words alone are deficient; you can no more "start" with them than you can decide to have been born yesterday. *Starting* is fortuitous and inscrutable, so instead of hearing the word as synonymous with beginning, I hear in it *shock*. You *start up* in your seat as you begin to doze off; the synapses fire, jerking your hand, and the brain stutters, flushing images across your closed eyes. Whatever seems to be the case is a stress point, a fault line where, in a lucid interval, you might grip the seams of world grinding on world.

PARADISE GLOSS'D

A psychology of the seam: "The psychological rule says that when an inner situation is not made conscious, it happens outside, as fate. That is to say, when the individual remains undivided and does not become conscious of his inner opposite, the world must perforce act out the conflict and be torn into opposing halves" (Jung 71).

Interpretation of texts is not so different from quantum mechanics. We still strive to locate its position (relative to generic coordinates), its mass (displacement of cognitive space), and its velocity (momentum in the sociocultural plane). Niels Bohr's Copenhagen Interpretation stipulates a *domain of suitable reference,* which is that of the observer ('s scale,

dimension of the observer's milieu and points of reference: the Copenhagen Interpretation attests to the terrific mobility of psychological *projection*). Each time we seek knowledge of something "in itself" we learn something, instead, about the desire to make reference to "things in themselves." That is, we learn something if we take the position of the Copenhagen Interpretation; otherwise, we learn the caustic lessons of skepticism and feel ourselves to be the dupes of experiments conducted not by us, but *on* us, by mindless forces outside our control; and what better definition could the skeptic desire of a "thing in itself" but a mindless force outside our control?

Adam and Eve in Paradise live in bliss, which is a state sufficient to their means, commensurate with their powers and their will, and above all predicated on that contentment that enables them to "know to know no more" (Milton IV: 775). All creation is given over to their use and satisfaction of their needs but for one conspicuous tempting thing, the Tree of Knowledge. If everything in Paradise signifies satisfaction, the tree signifies the surfeit of satisfaction: satisfaction satisfied, carnal knowledge elevated or enhanced by suprasensory knowledge. In Milton's blissful bower, the happy couple appear to be perfect Lockean dupes, beguiled by the primal blank of their own minds to revel in a cornucopia provided by the senses. The interdiction regarding the tree is, strangely, God's own satanic provocation (the original temptation); without such prohibition they would never have known there was anything missing, anything else to be known. What *Paradise Lost* offers in its account of the Fall is the prospect of complicity between narration and interpretation, God and Satan, adequacy and surplus.

Interpretation is born of Eve, or rather borne on and by her, almost in spite of her. Eve is subjected to that peculiar interpretive conceit, "we," prevalent in academic discourse, a doubled or multiplied person laboring under one canopy of skin. She is extracted from Adam, "formd flesh of thy flesh" she tells him, "And without whom am to no end, my Guide / and Head" (IV: 441–43). Thinking Adam's head her own, she is mesmerized by the wonder of her own face reflected in a pool. But she has seen something else in the water, the amniotic murmurings of which, as it issues from a cave into a liquid plain, first arouses her to consciousness. "I thither went / With unexperienc't thought," she tells Adam, and peers into the water to find "A Shape within the watry gleam appeerd / Bending to look on me" (IV: 456–57, 461–62). Now, this unexperienced thought does not enable Eve to recognize the reflective properties of water or even the category of the person. It is just a tantalizing apparition impressing itself on her nearly blank slate. But a voice, a superconsciousness, intervenes, predicating self-awareness as an agency of the Other:

> there I had fixt
> Mine eyes till now, and pin'd with vain desire,
> Had not a voice thus warnd me, What thou seest,
> What there thou seest fair Creature is thy self,
> With thee it came and goes: but follow me,
> And I will bring thee where no shadow staies
> Thy coming, and thy soft imbraces, hee
> Whose image thou art. (IV: 465–72)

Before the interdiction of knowledge, then, comes the intervention of interpretation, as Eve is led from adoration of her reflected image to a prospective adoration of that which she herself reflects (her maker). She is a breaker in a circuit, and the issue of interpretation hovers over the extent to which she needs to know this. (Later, reincarnated as Oedipa Maas, Eve's interpretive dilemma will be: "*Shall I project a world?*" [Pynchon 82]). Sanctioned knowledge permits her to know herself through the medium of Adam, which is to say, through the elaborate mediation of the law and the syntagmatic chain of being. The law of Eden says to her, in the words of the Stephen Stills song, "If you can't be with the one you love, love the one you're with." Eve is then led off to consort with Adam in a "meek surrender" of her "submissive Charms" (Milton IV: 494, 498). Eve's fate is to be mate, matrix, matter, or clay to Adam's architectural will, weave of his desire; *mater,* mother and other in one, but one that always turns out to be two—duplicitously so, in Adam's view.

I want to turn to a hermeneutic distinction between understanding and explanation in order to clarify the interpretive milieu established for Eve by divine meddling in her epistemological reverie. In Paul Ricoeur's exposition, "explanation is not primary but secondary in relation to understanding" (10). Understanding cannot be broken down or decomposed (it is proximate to revelation); but it can be supplemented, and explanation is the supplement. "Understanding is . . . the nonmethodical moment that, in the sciences of interpretation, combines with the methodical moment of explanation. This moment precedes, accompanies, concludes, and thus *envelops* explanation. Explanation, in turn, *develops* understanding analytically" (142). Clearly what happens to Eve is that prior to any possible development of understanding, she is given an explanation. Her understanding is expected to conform to the explanation.

The description of Eve's mirror stage and submission to Adam is immediately followed by the indignant response of that voyeuristic witness, Satan. Satan's interpretive frenzy, as well as his downfall, can be charged to the intentional fallacy as he speculates what God intended by this conjugal arrangement. Eve is, in the vocabulary of grifters, a "mark," set up for a take or a fall. In this instance, she is to be the unwitting beneficiary of patristic exegesis. The interpretive task of the Church Fathers was to mediate between literal and doctrinal meanings. This was eventually elaborated in Dante's quaternity of literal, allegorical (typological), moral (tropological), and spiritual (anagogical) meanings in the Letter to Can Grande. Eve is not burdened with such discriminations, but she is conveniently positioned between expositors of the literal and the doctrinal persuasion, Satan and Adam. Satan comes to her in a dream—but we know, via narrative voice-over, that he was not so much *in* the dream but was the very author of the dream, perched "like a Toad, close at the eare of *Eve;* / Assaying by his Devilish art to reach / The Organs of her Fancie" (Milton IV: 800–02). The substance of Satan's oneiric intervention is a variant of Comus's great speech about the "full and unwithdrawing hand" of Nature's bounties, in which "Beauty is natures coyn, must not be hoorded" (Milton, "Comus," lines 711, 739). Eve's divine inclinations are encouraged as befitting so lofty and beautiful a creature. In the dream she smells the savor of the fruit as Satan bites into it, and also experiences the vertigo of ascent, beholding in those pre-aeronautical days the spectacle of "Earth outstretcht immense" (Milton V: 88). Interpretation here is to be understood in the performative sense, as Eve narrates (and represents) her dream to Adam the next morning. Contributing to Freud's theory of the dream as the satisfaction of a wish is the recognition that the preconscious wish is for sleep, and dreams protect sleep.[14] Appropriately, Eve's final dream sensation is one of falling asleep (Milton V: 90–93).

Eve falls asleep inside her own dream. She is possessed of the vertigo of a prohibited ascension and *passes out* at the moment of the most acute overview, when Satan flies her to the zenith of the stratosphere. The dream is traumatic. Freud went to great lengths to convince his peers that dreams are just what the word says they are (in German the link is even closer, between "Traum" and "Trauma"). Appropriately, the tautological condition is perpetrated by the dream content in Eve's case; not only is her dream traumatic, but its function in protecting her sleep succeeds when she dreams—at the instant of maximal exposure to transgression—that she is falling asleep. This is the perfect autointerpretive experience, the song that sings itself. It is a serpentine occasion, but distinctly non-biblical inasmuch as Eve is positioned inside an ouroboric loop. As in so many Hindu dreams of the sort chronicled by Wendy Doniger O'Flaherty in *Dreams, Illusions, and Other Realities,* Eve's is a dream that elaborates the paradox of dreaming a dream, of sleep inside sleep, where any seemingly final condition is but a flickering intimation of the unverifiability of all conditions. Consciousness is ineluctably *nested.* Each inner fact is encircled by an outer fact, which is in turn rendered inner by another outer, and so on.[15]

Eve tells her dream to Adam, and the very telling is a therapeutic solution of its residues; it is tamed in the telling by being reinserted into its ouroboric circuit. In other words, Eve's is a literal interpretation, as in the "interpretation" of a song in performance. The dream is replicated word for word, not paraphrased (she is, after all, not approximating the

---

14. In *The Intrepretation of Dreams,* VII:D, Freud even goes so far as to maintain that dreams arousing us from sleep still contribute to the function of protecting sleep. This sort of "protection" by annihilation appears to be an early intimation of the death drive.

15. My debt to Emerson is obvious, but the reference to Hindu sources acknowledges Emerson's own debt. "All is riddle, and the key to a riddle is another riddle. There are as many pillows of illusion as flakes in a snow-storm. We wake from one dream into another dream" (1117).

phantasmagoria we usually confront in telling our dreams, but—unaware of it herself—repeating Satan's whispered script). In the context of *Paradise Lost* this is a satanic interpretation, much as in patristic exegesis the scriptures were not to be taken literally, for that was to give credence to the fallible and superfluous, succumbing to the peril of satanic innuendo. As author of Eve's dream, Satan wants her to take the dream literally as a code of instructions for devouring the forbidden fruit. Satan miscalculates, of course, for the dream is not a template for action, but a tautological loop that will chase its own tale in endless hyperactivity, one that by its very structure as a closed circuit permits neither modification or application. It is a script that says, at the end, "Return to the beginning." What is satanic, then, is not literalism as such, but a category error: the replication on one logical plane of a set of instructions that have proven efficient on another logical plane. The instruction operative in Eve's dream is a perfect illustration of the coding of the dream work in general, which is "Keep sleeping." But satanic interpretation, presuming sleep to be a dormant state of receptivity in which one stores up plans for waking action, fantasizes the dream as a precondition for what will be enacted in a waking state. In other words, it is not literal at all, but interjectional, or typological, like the hypnotic cues implanted by the Communists in John Frankenheimer's film *The Manchurian Candidate*—or, less flamboyantly but no less effectively, by ideological interpellation.

Satan implants dream instructions as prescriptions for waking behavior, while Adam behaves as an interpreter proper, the one whose reading of the dream follows in the mode of explanation. He is patristically disposed to interpret the doctrinal rather than the literal aspect of the dream. After noting that since Eve is chaste the dream cannot have derived from any evil source, Adam goes on to elaborate the medieval doctrine of the soul's faculties:

> But know that in the Soule
> Are many lesser Faculties that serve
> Reason as chief; among these Fansie next

> Her office holds; of all external things,
> Which the five watchful Senses represent,
> She forms Imaginations, Aerie shapes,
> Which Reason joining or disjoining, frames
> All what we affirm or what deny, and call
> Our knowledge or opinion; then retires
> Into her privat Cell when Nature rests.
> Oft in her absence mimic Fansie wakes
> To imitate her; but misjoining shapes,
> Wilde work produces oft, and most in dreams,
> Ill matching words and deeds long past or late. (V: 100–13)

Since "mimic Fansie" is an inferior faculty, one cannot submit to the dream in its literal sense unless one falls prey to one's own inferior functions. Doctrinally stated, temptation comes from within, not from without.

The title of Adam's mode of interpreting would be "Paradise Gloss'd." The Edenic ideology of incorruptability sustains him through the next phase of his interpretation:

> Evil into the mind of God or Man
> May come and go, so unapprov'd, and leave
> No spot or blame behind: Which gives me hope
> That what in sleep thou didst abhorr to dream,
> Waking thou never wilt consent to do. (V: 117–21)

Adam is expressing the hope here that the dream is a secondary residue, incapable of generating action. The dream explains a prior stress or stimulus; the dream is itself *already* an explanation. For Adam, explanation is secondary, but, curiously, this understanding of the dream is advanced by way of explanation.

To delve into the manner in which Eve gets inserted in the competing tautologies of Satan and Adam, consider Eve's dream as ouroboric—she dreams she falls asleep—which can be depicted as a circle:

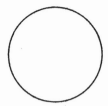

In the interpretive matrix that unfolds between Satan's script and Adam's matinal retrospection, this simple circle assumes another form:

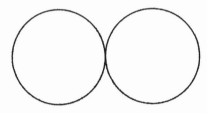

The infinite circle of the ouroborous expands into the mathematical sign for infinity. Eve is positioned at the juncture, the point at which each tautology flips over to its obverse. She is the image of structural coupling held *in potentia* between contrasting models of interpretation: hermeneutic and phenomenological, figurative and literal, predictive and reflective. She is also assigned a patriarchal role as symbol or token in exchanges between men, a servomechanism of the engines that affirm their identities *as* a rule of interpretation. She is the *relay* of an autointerpretive matrix that simulates a surrogate otherness for those two great solipsists, Satan and Adam. As the requisite matrix of interpretation, Eve is the unconscious receptacle of the Word: she is the text that talks but does not *talk back*. She embodies patriarchy's fetish, text-as-woman, the function of which is to be pregnant with mute significance.

Ricoeur again: "Psychoanalysis, as a *talk-cure,* is based on this very hypothesis, that of the primary proximity between desire and speech. And since speech is heard before it is uttered, the shortest path from the self to itself lies in the speech of the other, which leads me across the open space of signs" (16). Eve, accordingly, hears God's voice telling her she is looking at her own reflection in the water, and she hears this before she has any chance to address the image herself, or know it *as* (if) herself. The voice that preaches self-consciousness is the voice of the Other, the Big O. To return to the self, then, involves tracking an utterance back to the interruption of reverie. Self-absorption—poised in dialectical contemplation of itself experiencing its own nature doubled in the world—is intercepted by another voice. "Getting back to the basics," where self-consciousness is concerned, means mastering the hypodermic dose of introjected otherness. Long before cinema, long before Rimbaud, there is Eve, called upon to demonstrate "Je *est un autre.*"

The voice of a patriarchal god displaces and replaces Eve's own voice as a prosthetic supplement. We can hear in Freud's famous dictum, "*Wo es war, soll ich werden*" (Where it [Id] is, there I will be), the conduit to identity being formed by channeling self into object, bodily member into prosthesis. The divine prerogative of prosthetic insertion simulates a lack on Eve's part, perhaps the very "lack" presumed by Freud himself as the basis of female sexuality. Eve's trauma derives from two sources: one is the satanic whisper, the pre-text of her dream, the other is a divine supplement, as she is instructed to identify consciousness of self with the voice of the Other, whether satanic or divine. She is outfitted with a cognitive dildo (crafted by a divine manufacturer, no less), a master phallo-prosthesis. All of this is designed to preserve her purity, secure her chastity: prosthesis signifies a celibate anatomy, incorruptable matter.

What is the basis of this phallic autocracy? The first danger, the sure path to sin, is for Eve to look at her own reflected image and find in it an Other. The phallic injunction says to Eve, in effect, you may inspect this image all you like, but you will never find the phallus, nor any transcendental signifier. She must discover the phallus elsewhere, since the phallus is inexorably appointed undersecretary to his master's voice. She must stand at alert like the quizzical dog at the bell of the gramophone horn. Eve must be spliced to the tape-loop of phallic certainty: interpretation is the straight gate, the rigid semiconductor, direct path from self to Self.[16]

16. This condensed account could be expanded by a review of ancient doctrines of consciousness as *seminal* in nature. The phallic legacy, prior to its elaborate symbolization

I want to return now to Ricoeur's suggestion that identity is contingent on the first encounter with speech, which is developmentally the speech of the Other (*l'Autre* in French, in which Lacan finds the apex portal of the Alphabet). The most direct access to the self, then, is through the Other. The implication is that the self is invariably *interpreted* or translated by relay through another's speech; but why must interpretation cleave to the "shortest path"? There are different sorts of abbreviation; a path is not self-evident any more than a self is. Furthermore, the most literal model of interpretation—interpretation as performance—establishes an indexical relation to the text: to interpret, simply repeat every word. Allegorical, moral, and anagogic modes of interpretation, on the other hand, presume that the shortest path to the meaning of a word is by way of other words. "In other words . . . " This is the routine of explanation; whereas the literalist/performative mode is the route of understanding, literally "standing under," donning the mask, repeating the formula. Both are schemes of magic: manipulation by homeopathic repetition, or manipulation by allopathic inversion.

The problem of interpretation is a conflict about frames, a procedural dispute, a methodological controversy about the legitimation of borders and limits. What is the frame of reference? What is a text, and what is a context? How much context belongs *with* the text to make the *con-*, or make the text a "con"? There's a confidence game involved: the context is whatever we feel confident the text can be absorbed or *taken in* by. You fall in love with the poetry and end up living with the prose.

That is, in prose you start with the world
and find the words to match; in poetry you start
with the words and find the world in them.

---

in myth and ritual, is initially a physiological fantasy that imagines the male head filled with seminal fluid, supporting thought in a sort of amniotic bath and traveling down the spine, where it is secreted in procreation (cf. LaBarre). Consequently, the link between "conceiving" and "conception" in acts of thought as well as in biological reproduction is manifestly phallological. The near homonym with *fallacy* is striking.

3
News and Noise

Poetry and Distortion

Davy Crockett had a literary style. Rather than blow his squirrel to bits he'd strike the tree just under its belly so that the concussion would stun it.

William Carlos Williams, "The Great American Novel"

Friedrich Schiller's distinction between the sentimental poet and the naive poet, while two centuries old, still provides serviceable parameters for considering contemporary practices. The *naive* poet embodies a fusion of form with content, an unproblematic union with nature, bestowing on the reader a gratifying sense of totality. Such a model has often been called "classical." But Schiller sensed that something else was in the air, a tendency in poetry to forgo a pristine alliance with the way things are. So he had to admit that the naive poet "completes his task, but the task itself is a limited one" (234). While it hadn't quite arrived, Schiller glimpsed the alternative: Romantic longing, an insatiable yearning for the infinite that would transfigure the face of poetry. It sounds counterintuitive to accept Schiller's term *sentimental,* his name for an agitation at the heart of poetry's enterprise that would catapult it from one accomplishment to another without settling for any finality. In English Romanticism, the naive perspective is embodied in Keats's Grecian urn, its union of beauty and truth prompting the affirmation "that is all / Ye know on earth, and all ye need to know." The sentimental is found in Samuel Taylor Coleridge's "Dejection: An Ode," when he ruefully concedes, "I may not hope from outward forms to win / The passion and the life, whose fountains are within" (lines 45–46). By 1983 the two had been instructively merged by Steve McCaffery: "to ground yourself in words always lean against your reading / and balance on the weight of what you don't know" (*Seven Pages* 222).

At the end of the twentieth century—in the wake of poets like César Vallejo and Paul Celan—Schiller's sentimental poet would seem to prevail. That may be the case, yet the intuitive sense of the poem most dominant in American culture remains "naive." Readers continue to be hungry for poems in which "the sign completely disappears in what is signified" (191), a characteristic of the naive according to Schiller. Robert Bly once published an anthology of poems affirming the ecstatic immediacy of the cosmos in the everyday, calling it *News of the Universe.* In the intervening decades, with the ascendancy of John Ashbery and the language poets, a certain tolerance for cognitive dissonance has inflected the American poetry scene; readers find it less objectionable when the sign not only fails to achieve union with what it signifies, but is also openly set adrift amid a swarm of other signifiers. We seem to have passed from naive to sentimental, from news of the universe to noise of the universe. But do these apparently contrasting terms define an unbridgeable gap? Do noise and news refer to the same universe?

Don Byrd once characterized public readings of poetry as producing little more than "a meaning glow," a view diagnostically linking poetry with network television programming. Most poems, like most television episodes, bear a simple message: they say that the transmitter and the receiver work, that the channel is intact. In doing so, they perform a strictly maintenance function on the equipment. Only rarely do we sense the pertinent disruption of information as unrefined *material,* richly plural, aggravatingly unmanageable, challenging the uniform scale of all those modular poetry chips out there, chattering away the mantra of *I-Me-Mine.* Those who think of poetry as a socially convenient site for self-disclosure may be participating in a larger tide of social narcissism; and in this respect poetry stands in a precarious relation to the social sector, where its most enduring contribution is not to "art," but to the bureaucratic database lampooned by W. H. Auden in "The Unknown Citizen." The testimony of poetry substantiates the statistical accountancy of the body politic, its temper and distemper. Just as polling organizations "sample" the public for the pulse of its momentary mood and deejays "sample" old records, poets "sample" their private sentiments. The accessibility of testimonial verse is a choral byproduct, as one poet's childhood vacation blurs chromatically into another's equally generic memories. The ethnic rainbow of poets concluding the *Norton Anthology of American Literature,* as critics have complained, speak uniformly in the low-key lyric realism of the first-person singular, the diction as well as the sensibilities being indistinguishable but for local details. With aesthetic issues in disrepute in recent decades in the academy, poems have become vulnerable to appropriation strictly for their representational content, and at that level they have proven to be uncompetitive in a milieu dominated by prose fiction.

The parameters of "content" in such circumstances can be seen in a different light if you think of the social environment itself as a triumph of systems engineering. Poetry is no longer written in bucolic settings where the creative imagination finds aesthetic resonance in "Nature." Quite the contrary; poetry now has to suffer the diffusion of the matrix, the network, the database, the code; it has to endure in the very temper of language a rapid modulation of signal to noise and noise to signal in order to keep pace with the infusions of freshness and novelty that now, as always, have made the vernacular amenable to poetry. The challenge of the vernacular has enabled Victor Hernandez Cruz and Maurice Kilwein Guevara, among others, to work in a bilingual idiom. Others, such as Albert Goldbarth, handle commercial product brand names as vernacular joysticks of poetic adventure (in *Popular Culture*) and conjure up, in the idiom of an encyclopedic flâneur, the cosmological apparitions of *Heaven and Earth* and a revival of the American fascination with hieroglyphics in *Adventures in Ancient Egypt.* But the vernacular is a precarious solution, inasmuch as the normative verbal postures of American life have developed into the stupefying minimalism of "whatever."[1]

---

1. Still, is it possible to regard this meltdown of vocabulary as a style of resistance? And if so, resistance to what? Is minimalism in vocabulary and syntax an attempt to recover semantic depth on some devotional plane of altered receptivity?

Despite (or because of) this gesture of beneficence and antique opportunity, the traditional rhetorical resource of *eloquentia* has grown rather
wan. John Ashbery, whose work is often linked with the high sublime, is
consistent in his supplications to camp. In his case, the convolutions of a
rhetorically supple syntax coupled with a conceptual free-fall—in which
one reads poem after poem with only the haziest sense of what it might
be "about" (or so a certain critical consensus has it)—resolve to consistency at the level of style. It is by way of a largely unexamined notion of
"style" that Ashbery's work has most often met with approval. Yet style,
however conceived, can be an obstacle to apprehending the condition of
not understanding to which the poems actively contribute. One critic observes: "By repeatedly acting out his desires in a formulaic language, Ashbery accomplishes neither vision nor ironic distance"—familiar terms
from the protocols of the New Critics. "But he does accomplish a sense
of community, a shared nostalgia for meaning" (Costello 514). *Nostalgia
for meaning:* best if shared, apparently. As Ashbery's career has advanced,
a sense of shared disorientation has emerged as a value: "the natural noise
of now" (Bayley 3). At least the term "noise" begins to engage the issue;
and another critic explicitly links Ashbery to information theory: "his poetry derives informational complexity by parasiting, adding bits of noise
to, the messages of ordinary language" (Kevorkian 471). Where modernist poets *cited* predecessors in collaged parataxis, Ashbery *parasites* by
mingling his own chatter with the austere idiom of his sublime hosts. The
jargon of information theory may not provide the most accurate vocabulary for estimating Ashbery's achievement, but it does offer a precise way
of measuring the milieu, the language of the tribe, in which Ashbery has
risen to such strange prominence. However you characterize his poetry,
the result will not be far from Daniel Cottom's observation that it provides "a coherence as precisely unnamable as it is presumptively familiar
and vital to whatever it is we call communication" (165)—an assessment
rendering Ashbery cousin to Beckett. Ashbery himself, early in his career,
confessed an attraction to Gertrude Stein's work in comparable terms,
her *Stanzas in Meditation* striking him as obedient to "some rhythmic impulse at the heart of all happening"—an impulse so pervasively insinuating "one feels that if one were to close the book one would shortly re-

encounter the Stanzas in life, under another guise" ("Impossible" 252). The easy interchange Ashbery envisions here between the esoteric text and the exoteric dimension of daily life is symptomatic of his own body of work, especially as its audacious obscurities are made familiar, if not more accessible, by the profusion of idiomatic expressions and common parlance in which they are couched.

Despite its frequent evocation of a Saturday matinee adventure, its allusions to comic-strip antics, and its glamorized innuendo of that epic archetype, the quest, Ashbery's work is strikingly intransitive. "A Wave" might be his definitive title, suggesting a frothy agitation that goes nowhere and subsides into inevitable iteration. Momentum becomes undertow. Ashbery has been consistently committed to the intransitivity inaugurated for poetry by Mallarmé. Who gives us a better sense than Ashbery of what it feels like to be stuck on the page, spinning one's semantic wheels and throwing up a sublime detritus of colorful muck? Even the allegorical corolla that hovers over Ashbery's poems intimates a fondness for staying (albeit in Hotel Lautréamont) instead of straying; lingering, not getting on; the antic sports of Gogo and Didi waiting for Godot rather than the open highway of the Beats. In Ashbery's world, familiarity prevails over novelty.

There are corresponding effects evident in certain other poets, involving another equilibrium: news and noise. While the phenomenon called language poetry that emerged in the 1970s did not actually speak in terms of, or even address, information theory, this theoretical lacuna did not impede the actual *practice* of a poetry that, more than any other in recent times, solicits an interpretive vocabulary inimical to the prevailing discourse of academe as well as to the metropolitan discourse (rapidly fading) of poetry and poetics. Language poetry has been approached from an orientation decidedly concerned with the performative and the constative rather than the thematic or the personal—understandably so, given the improbability of assimilating most language poetry to the expressive gesture of a determinate personality. The performative has been of evident relevance largely *because* certain language poets have toyed with the self-expressive gesture. That they have done so in order to undercut a complacency they resist in workshop verse as well as in the deluxe products of Official Verse Culture does not, for all that, efface the person from poetic center stage. Who might have predicted, in 1978, that Charles Bernstein would write some of the most autobiographically dialogic work of his generation? Or that Lyn Hejinian's *My Life* would sell more than ten thousand copies, its title and autobiographical structure making it marketable far beyond any demand for its formalist experiment? Or that Ron Silliman's epic ABC series would rival Allen Ginsberg's travelogues as a voice-over for their time?

When considering those cybernetic quanta, news and noise, a resiliently "abstract" variety of language poetry seems more pertinent than the work of Hejinian, Silliman, Bernstein, and others who have received more critical attention. In Bruce Andrews and Clark Coolidge we have careers of a procedural insistence and intensity that lays direct claim to the threshold across which noise and news riff and rap.[2] This work that superficially resembles nonsense, it turns out, is intimately allied with strong moral and aesthetic principles. Amid the conceptual upheavals traceable like seismic faults in the landscape of contemporary poetry, an omnibus such as Coolidge's *Solution Passage* comes across as the real boy actually crying wolf—or in his obliquity, "What's it come to but a striped boy shouting 'Mica'" (21). Coolidge's obliquities have an affinity with the operatic constellations Bruce Andrews conjures from the debris of New York's blaring verbal convulsiveness; and together they represent an extremity of verse practice disclosing *that* extremity as vital to any consideration of the American demotic as presently constituted in the hyper- and interstices of our mass-mediated attention span.

SOLUTION PASSAGE

Poetry is information
A remumblery
I project
Louis Cabri, *The Mood Embosser*

2. For a thoughtful treatment of issues related to signal and noise—in the more visual medium of Robert Grenier's handwritten multicolored palimpsests—see Bob Perelman, *The Marginalization of Poetry.*

"Meaning, and the constellation of mental attitudes that exhibit it, are manufactured products. The raw material is information" (Dretske vii). The universe is packed with information, most of which is inaccessible to us without the aid of high-powered microscopes or radio telescopes. "In the beginning was information. The word came later." That is, a word is a selective refinement of information, a javelin hurled at meaning. "Meaning is generated by the way information is coded" (248).[3] We can experience information without adducing meaning, just as we can gauge the tenor of a conversation in a strange language without understanding a word. Normally, in fact, the brain actively suppresses information to avoid overstimulation. This is how *meaning* is induced to appear. The danger of meaning is that it becomes addictive: the redundancy of the fix, the expected result. Fred I. Dretske suggests that information be regarded as "semantically relevant" but distinct from meaning as such (46). In other words, the greater the access to the variety of information available, the better off we are—so long as we can abstain from bestowing *habitual* meanings, or opportunistically colonizing information to soak up a meaning glow.

Clark Coolidge's *Solution Passage* is a book that aggressively engages one of the central issues of information theory, that of entropy or disorder. Claude Shannon of Bell Laboratories launched information theory in the late 1940s in order to demonstrate mathematically (and thereby technologically) that messages could persist in the midst of haphazard noise or disorder. The primary mechanical problem underlying clear transmission in media like radio, television, and telephone is how to send a message so it survives the residual noise in the channel used to convey it. How can you distinguish information from noise? An illustration: a glass of water is entropic. That is, its contents are uniform; each molecule is indistinguishable from any other. Add an ice cube and a singularity has arisen: everything in the glass is still H^2O, but there's now something to talk about, a distinction to be made. Ice is information, while the

---

3. As any reader of *The Cantos* can attest, Pound sought to generate meaning by transfiguring information, liberating it from customary contexts into the rehabilitating sanction of his poem, conceived as a synthetic and absorbent pinnacle of cross-cultural awareness.

water it's in is noise. When the ice melts, it's all noise (or all information, but all of which is inaccessible *as* information). Language is comparable: a random list of words is noise, but a phrase—not even a complete sentence—is an eruption of singularity. *Information* in its broad, cosmic sense is raw material, an indistinguishable mass. It's noise, it's randomness, it's what presents itself as inherently meaningless, chaotic. It is entropic.

In 1949 Warren Weaver suggested as evidence of entropy in language the phrase "Constantinople fishing nasty pink" (Shannon and Weaver 102). Compare this with "molasses arrow stunt boiler"—a typical line from *The Maintains;* compare it, for that matter, with most of Coolidge's early work.

of   about

since   dot

(*Space* 80)

These four words may as well be random, since they convey little more than any other four words. In fact, the geometric design by which the words form a square may be more significant than the words themselves. In another poem from *Space,* it doesn't seem to matter if more words are added:

my from even or mate   dents while live   ham this so
    them hemp   first last some dome   main there fire
walls so bill   dwindle sent said mint   crew dent
    of unless   was with to it   took at else
vanilla shall straw   down told   apart din frill be
    grow vans stock   seem roll ale   not not than pins

(*Space* 47)

This text lacks the glue, the 50 percent redundancy of which English is calculated to consist; so "reading" it is more like scanning the horizon for signs of sentient activity, biosemiotic and zoosemiotic traces.

Normally, half the words we use are not chosen freely, but rather comply with the structural (statistically regulative) requirements of the language. For messages to persist in the midst of noise, it is necessary to encode the message with redundancy. Meaning is consolidated when the same point is made over and over (or when the coding itself reinforces a particular meaning—coding being a labor of syntax). Coolidge started off by forgoing redundancy altogether: *Space, The Maintains,* and *Polaroid* document the challenge of finding "a syntax in the dictionary" (Foster, *Postmodern Poetry* 21). *Quartz Hearts, American Ones,* and *Own Face* offer determined forays into sentence and phrase that can be accomplished only by means of redundancy. *Solution Passage* boldly presses the issue to the juncture between noise and meaning, entropy and message, and the effect is uncannily like being present at that unimaginable distant threshold where sounds blended into patterned articulation and we became homo sapiens because of words.

Perched at that seam where noise threatens any message, Coolidge's poems stand out with unforgettable singularity as ripples of order, transitorily charged with sudden unsolicited evidence of life itself. Working on the edge like this is not achieved alone. Summoning missing information is something that sender and receiver conspire on together, as when a bluesman appeals to his audience, "Help me, help me now." Coolidge's omissions are an invitation: "Still these omissions have their balance . . . / Will what you mean to follow see me through" (*Solution Passage* 78). There is always the sense that noise and disorder are inherent in the channel. "Sometimes the words will not mean / what they must mean to others to me" (115). Not only do meanings bump and grind, mix and clash; writing makes its own noise. Where most poets try to exorcise that noise, Coolidge abets it.

> the finches are sprouting with their
> metal spring rain songs. And the drench penciling
> down you hear, if not only the hiss high pure pitch
> of the inner ear. (161)

The inner ear has its own residual noise, which even the most precise attention to fine-tuning will not abolish. "The mot juste / is not a puncture sealer" (224).

It can be tempting to think of the "pure pitch" of the inner ear, like the humming of a telephone wire in a spring shower, as the sibilant rustle of language as such, the "murmur" that ripples with such evident gratification for Blanchot, Foucault, Barthes—"a vast auditory fabric in which the semantic apparatus would be made unreal; the phonic, metric, vocal signifier would be deployed in all its sumptuosity, without a sign ever becoming detached from it (ever naturalizing this pure layer of delectation), but also," adds Barthes here, "without meaning being brutally dismissed, dogmatically foreclosed, in short castrated" (*Rustle* 77). In a related vision from *S/Z,* he speaks of literature as "an intentional cacography" (9), its cacophonously diagrammatic embellishments of plain sense conceived in the "deliberate 'static'" of connotation, which introduces a "countercommunication" to the denotative. But to persist in so crisply Gallic a hypothesis is to risk assimilating noise to the order of news—not news that stays news, but news that's no news. What Coolidge's work presents is presentiment as such, wobbling on the axis of newsy noise or noisy news. I have introduced the vocabulary of information theory here in order to keep at bay the sirens of sense-making with their dangerous promise of semantic finality. The relation of signal to noise is as reciprocal as that between figure and ground in a visual field. The sign, as C. S. Peirce says, is a sign *for* someone; the act of recognition constitutes it in its singularity; its singularity is what sets it apart and, in doing so, also discloses the mass or background, the fathomless density that accompanies the singular. For information theory, the only way to distinguish information from noise is by quantitative means: information is that which survives the residual noise of a communications medium, like the image that surmounts the ambient fuzz of televisual "snow," the song or voice battling for equity with static in a radio broadcast.

Quantitative considerations arise in the case of Coolidge as well. *Solution Passage* is a large book—in fact, I can think of no precedent for a four-hundred-page collection of a poet's work selected from a mere three or four years—but the axiom holds true, statistically *and* conceptually. *Solution Passage* does contain more information—however you define it—than the usual eighty-page poetry book. How much is enough?[4] Coolidge's work, through that semantic puzzle that makes his phrasing congruent with Weaver's "Constantinople fishing nasty pink," renders the issue of bulk relevant again, because it impinges on the statistical issues of communication. The ideology of poetry as concise, unmediated transmission is impugned by a book that irreverently transcribes as much noise as it does "meaning." But this is no idle slap in the face of public taste: Coolidge charts a poetic practice that has notable affinities with action painting and bop prosody in which identity persists, albeit as manifold, repetitive, entropic. "I have no slant on my self but these hearty / interminable dicings" (111).

Coolidge ultimately draws more from that open-road hipster exaltation of "whether I want to or write" (104) than from any modular constructivist poetics.[5] *Solution Passage* makes credible again the notion that

4. The question is loaded, of course, and should be retracted at once. It implies that poems are tricks and that all you need of them is enough to get the drift, the hook, the angle. As if a poet were a card shark. But it is rare to be *materially* confronted with the prospect of sheer poetic bulk. Coolidge's *ethos* has its derivations in jazz at least as much as from any literary source, and in jazz playing, time *is* the medium; the sculptural potential of its enactment is indistinguishable from the exigence of cooperative inspiration and stamina. To feel when Coolidge is *on*, you have to get with it as a reader (and close reading won't get you there). Still, there are pragmatic approaches. One way into *Solution Passage* is to read Coolidge's portrait/encounters with historical figures, of which there are many that move with the critical concision and exacting inspiration of Mina Loy's great precedents in her poems on Joyce, Brancusi, and Wyndham Lewis. See "Homage to Melville," "The Century That Breaks" (Picasso), "A Chimney for Max Jacob," "Lights of Things an Autumn" (Yves Tanguy), "Pauses Covered with Looks" (Wallace Stevens), "Portrait Distracted" (Hitler), "After Beckett," and "The Cubists," along with the three that grapple with Rilke (116, 126, 190).

5. Note the word substitution in "whether I want to or write"—where *write* substitutes for *not*. This is salient not only of Coolidge's practice, but also of Jack Spicer's. Spicer used such substitutions (*died* for *said, and so far* for *and so forth*) to engage the dilemma that "words / Turn mysteriously against those who use them" [125]). In Spicer's case, the most powerful and poetically resonant examples of words turning against their users are the deictic markers (here and there, this and that, the pronouns, etc.), words that are in fact designed for maximum adaptability to a speaker's needs, but that conform to *any* speaker's needs, neutralizing in the process the singularity of personal identity.

poetry be read with the same stamina applied to prose. No aesthetic of the *mot juste* can disguise the realities of process, heat, and abundant cumulative formations (the redundancy that informs). Coolidge is clearly a poet of process (in exactly the senses applied during the 1960s—the issue is not, despite all claims to the contrary, yet expired). For him, there is no rewriting as such, no recourse but to "crack a further page of the strapping vein bulk manual / and thrive back in, and dine" (98). Coolidge goes back through Jack Kerouac not only for a basis in spontaneous improvisatory writing, but also to draw on jazz. His "Note on Bop" can be read as an *ars poetica,* and his citation of drummer Elvin Jones summarily dispenses with the issue of bulk: " 'The length of my solos doesn't mean anything. When I go on for so long, I am looking for the right way to get out. Sometimes the door goes right by and I don't see it, so I have to wait until it comes around again. Sometimes it doesn't come around at all for a long long time' " (*Now It's Jazz* 95). Where most poems propagate themselves by means of formal structure, those in *Solution Passage* are best experienced like jazz solos: primary evidence of decisions made on the spur of the moment, each moment looping through others in an organic vortex of sheer duration or "improvisational momentum," as Coolidge calls it in an interview (Foster, *Postmodern Poetry* 25). In "Note on Bop" the crucial issue is how to grab hold and ride the impulse: "the shaping of the always initial impact becomes the highest of enveloping tasks" (*Now It's Jazz* 93). There is no line, no beginning, immune from the stress of its enveloping task. Coolidge's are poems "composed of the empty space of the first thought the second thought erased."

The traditional bebop practice based on standard pop song structure is a bit misleading as to the nature of Coolidge's debt to the music. His writing seems closer to the precedent of free jazz (of the mid-1960s, when Coolidge began to publish)[6] and work backward in time, to the

---

6. The music I have in mind as bearing some resemblance to Coolidge's poetic strategies is mainly associated with the Chicago AACM (Association for the Advancement of Creative Musicians) and recorded on the Nessa and Delmark labels, such as *People in Sorrow* by the Art Ensemble of Chicago, Joseph Jarman's *Song For,* Muhal Richard Abrams's *Levels and Degrees of Light,* and Roscoe Mitchell's *Sound* and *Congliptious.* But to be clear, Coolidge's own musical orientation predates exposure to these figures, most of whom are younger than he is.

point in *Solution Passage* where if the choruses as such aren't evident, the lyrical organization seems intent on some kind of *return* to first principles ("enveloping task"). The longest poem in *Solution Passage* is "Of What The Music To Me," and a host of overt and veiled references to jazz run through many of the poems. But the issue is not to forward a jazz seman- tic. Coolidge's poems consist of very specific language events, making them remote from any mode of writing "about." Consider "rolling my hands to a flash of theme / in ascension" (61); this could easily be read as what the hands of the poet do in writing, rolling themes toward the ascendancy of the inspiration. But Coolidge happens to be a drummer, likely to have played along with the recording of John Coltrane's epochal 1965 disc *Ascension*. As a phrase, "rolling my hands to a flash of theme / in ascension" communicates evocatively whether you know this or not. If you do, you can see how the line has been encoded as it were with a kind of redundancy, two messages packed into one. Later in *Solution Passage* a use of the capital letter *A* accentuates the impact—"in Ascension the bits come therming down" (374)—a line that takes us back to infor- mation theory, which derives the notion of entropy from thermodynam- ics. The bits that heat up in Coltrane are "bits" also in the technical sense of binary units, irreducible elements of information encoded in ones and zeros. *Ascension* remains a high point of "Free particle jazz" (373), evi- dence of "Ecstasy impossible to be memorized" (289, referring actu- ally to Ornette Coleman). The heat of the moment in poetry or music is always charged with multiplicity (think of Whitman with his multi- tudes), however solitary its enactment may appear. A line like "Nobody knows the numeral troubles I shine" (216) is a switchboard of contending phrases; the blues line "Nobody knows the troubles I've seen" merges with the gospel "trouble in mind" to make the line. And no matter what record executives (or literary critics) may think, "Nobody's mind is re- issued" (375).

These tailspinning inventions in Coolidge's poems do not make for easy reading. (*Light*, yes, in the sense of levity; his humor is sly but per- vasive.) To read them aloud is not only to be reminded of the jazz link, but also to be confronted directly with the rhythmic persuasions that or- ganize the poems' dynamics. The perceptual apparatus is lyric but not particularly imagistic, that overworked vein—

The Memory of Seeing, who can tell just how
tainted it is with invention. And the
uncontrollable solders of intention that tend to leak. (287)

(Note the precision, easily misread—it's *solders,* not *soldiers.*) Coolidge is
nonetheless "A graduate of world enough and tongue" (195)—not entirely disaffiliated from the lyrical persuasions of Wordsworth—and it
comes across most pertinently when the poems are read aloud. To render
audible a poem from *Solution Passage* is to linger at the threshold of poetic
chiaroscuro and begin to discern voices coming out of the dark.

Solution Passage is a book that thoroughly saturates (contaminates) the
space of the lyric in American verse practice, preempting the homespun
self-conscious awkward intensities of an A. R. Ammons (to cite a characteristic exponent of all that Coolidge erodes—although Ammons's
dedication to the poem as daily practice merits other points of comparison). The lyrical struggle is chronicled in three encounters with Rainer
Maria Rilke, the most insistent voice behind the poem-as-song (enlarged
to Being in Rilke's "*Gesang ist Dasein*"). Coolidge manages to retain his
own ear's persuasions—informed as ever with the spunky sweetness of
jazz—while admitting to the contagions of Rilke's ontological plan-
gency:

> The fear of death is like a wheel in the brain
> whirling wider with no road to express.
> And here and there by the weed a puff of sex. (116)

The full impact is best seen in an encounter that brings to mind the legendary cutting sessions in jazz (which reportedly drove the young Charlie
Parker to tears):

> Rilke, give me your paw.
> And we will ladder our pain across pointless vasts
> striking each other like Dumbs to the Head.
> There is no light in Kafka, there is no mass to you.
> You light but do not heat the Dense, or do you
> hate? In a turret above your neighboring

countess's farm you switch an arm as if
a broom across the page, and return to
the blinding squares an initial and a date.
You and I a vow primed to meet
the Language meshed enough to hold
what veers but nears.
You will not bear. I will not wait. (190)

Coolidge's preference is for heat, not light: for language, being entropic, is always collapsing in on itself, creating as much confusion and darkness as clarity. What Rilke "will not bear" is precisely that birthing of prodigious density Coolidge seems intent on throughout *Solution Passage,* best exemplified by "the unceasing teem of that top cymbal" that he claims as a basis for his lines, the earmark of bop drumming, a surging hiss like breakers along a sandy beach.

Coolidge's poems are in fact so densely written that *all* the words feel like nouns. The space is crammed, but the lines are clean. The model is more Picasso than Rilke: "I want to develop great cracks / in my solid like Picasso" (140)—cracks through which whatever light there is comes streaming through, seminally, sexually. "The body (her) at last from all angles at once / (Picasso had it)"—enabling "Everything that could ever / be written in a single sudden hand gesture" (198). A sexual mudra, rather than a text, might be the result.[7] The process is irreverent with regard to the channel (the conventions of the lyric poem) but full of respect for the continuity of the act:

> Writing *is* a prayer for
> always it starts at the portal lockless to me at last leads
> to the mystery of everything that has always been written. (25)

Coolidge's relentless materialization is sustained through a complete avoidance of terminology associated with modern idealisms such as semi-

7. Consider Coolidge's *The Book of During* (1991), a single poem of forty-four sections in 240 pages. Because of its explicitly sexual content, it enables the reader to chart with some precision the balance of information and entropy outlined above.

otics, structuralism, Marxism, or archetypal psychology. His Yankee distrust of jargon makes for a serviceable poetics that *as* a poetics can be articulated only in terms of the concrete practices of jazz drummers in "A Note on Bop." No generalities, no categories, just a proliferation of discrete phenomena. No ideological toehold to allow you to race ahead in a Coolidge poem, gasping with the pleasure of anticipated unity (compare anything in *Solution Passage* with a Robert Bly poem). There is nothing here that proposes to guide your life; the sensory inertia is all yours to grasp and move as you can. The poems are evidence of a separate life, lived elsewhere, dense with "not knowledge but embrace. / The heat of luck in proximity. / The ponder" (137).

Solution Passage is scrupulously exasperating on both the macro- and the microscopic levels. Like Williams, Olson, and Spicer, Coolidge has left creases in the smooth fabric of American poetry that cannot be disregarded, even if your goal is just to iron them out. The issue of proportionate scale launched with *Solution Passage* (if not before, in *The Maintains* and *Polaroid*) has grown even more pressing with subsequent publications. Although there are subtle procedural differences and divergences of texture from one project to another, the sheer bounty of Coolidge publications since 1986 imposes on prospective readers the news and noise distinction I have broached so far in terms of poetic diction. From the enlarged prospect of a "career," which is where canonical considerations come into view, the business of picking and choosing is confounded almost at the outset by the panoramic possibilities at hand. Apart from *Solution Passage* and its successor, *Sound as Thought* (1990)—and the relatively short earlier collections *Space* and *Own Face*—Coolidge's other books are presented as integral structures, long poems or sets ("set" in precisely the sense of a jazz set in a nightclub). *The Crystal Text* (1986), *Mesh* (1988), *At Egypt* (1988), *Odes of Roba* (1991), *The Book of During* (1991), *The ROVA Improvisations* (1994), *Registers (People in All)* (1994), *Keys to the Caverns* (1995), *Alien Tatters* (2000) and *On the Nameways* (2000) amount to well over 1,000 pages of material—added to which the 650 pages of *Solution Passage* and *Sound as Thought,* not to mention the fifteen titles published between 1966 and 1982, inexorably press the question of how much is enough. The issue of bulk seems less invasive when

the career at hand participates in a familiar domestic drama of self-
development; but in the case of Coolidge the criteria become curiously
personal rather than public. That is, by virtue of so many freestanding
integral book-projects, Coolidge's oeuvre does induce in the reader the
role of surrogate anthologist. To read Coolidge is more like being engaged in an endurance test or a stark physical challenge. In the jazz repertoire the recordings of Cecil Taylor, Steve Lacy, Anthony Braxton, and
David Murray represent a comparable capaciousness. Coolidge's long-
standing debt to jazz is made most explicit with *The ROVA Improvisations,*
a book that actively solicits comparison with musical "sets," the first consisting of poems written while listening to recordings by the saxophone
group Rova, the second consisting of improvisations on the first set of
poems. With work arising from such patently performative commitment
the issue of "payoff" is beside the point;[8] nor do the aesthetic parameters of career highs and lows seem relevant. In the presence of a new
work by Clark Coolidge, one is moved to respond to it in its entirety as
either news or noise—a distinction imposed by the work as a reader's
prerogative.

Despite the enticing sense made available by a collection like *Solution
Passage,* which one might read with an eye to culling the "best" of it for
some further occasion, Coolidge has shown little interest in abetting (let
alone perpetuating) such an impulse. As with the work of Bruce Andrews, to which I'll turn in a moment, this seemingly inscrutable gesture
reconvenes poetic practice altogether beyond the coordinates sedulously
maintained by arbiters of taste. This does not exempt us from considering the pertinence of such a gesture for the future of poetry; in fact, it
can't be ignored without tacitly consigning poetry to the status of an evolutionary cul de sac. Coolidge's perturbations have not raised much con-
sternation in the poetry "scene," as it's called; yet in the end I suspect
they will not be a cosmetic wrinkle, but a deeper seismic rupture, suitable to the torments of the Age of Information, alert, answerable, and
mortal—"an open else":

8. David Meltzer catches the drift: "it's the work of getting it right / in a moment /
no cornball monument / just a statement of who where / when it was what" (*No Eyes* 148).

Would you have us start before the Morse?
Tapping within skin on a room, as the air war
laws above all our sectioned flare.
Stone before the mirror? Face before dark?
Raise a fist and make a finger of it point?
These creases are questions, the chamber clad
the cartridge, locked as mackerel.
In the sky a hair, ladder as a thigh
and as kept, stroke without purchase
slicing through to past us. (192)

BRUCE ANDREWS AND THE LIMIT-WORK

There has been surprisingly little application to literature of the concept
of *strange attractors,* a term used in physics and mathematics for certain
types of chaos dynamics. There are three kinds of attractors: fixed point,
limit cycle, and strange attractors. A *fixed point attractor* is best exemplified by a physical force, like a magnet, that predictably stabilizes energy.
An example is a guitar string, the vibrations of which diminish in a reliable manner to a fixed point, which is the taut, motionless, silent wire.
A *limit cycle attractor* is a periodic oscillation, like the orbit of the moon
around the earth, or like the variation of tropes upon a set theme in the
conventional lyric. A *strange attractor,* as its name implies, is unpredictable. Strange attractors are found in situations of turbulence; or, rather,
strange attractors precipitate a catastrophic conversion of stability to
"chaos" or pure energy. The pertinence of these models for literature is
obvious: the literary work is a deft blending together of an authorial fixed
point (a vibratory energy that is sustained for a while and finally dissipates) with the limit cycle of a genre (the periodic recursion of form, of
generic traits). The combination of these two forces provides an endlessly
gratifying sensory appeal, along with the formal cognitive model to explain or interpret the apparitions. When literary works were comfortably
confined to fixed point and limit cycle systems, readers rarely had to
confront the chaotic, let alone that paradoxical state of the *reliably chaotic*
strange attractor. But the strange attractor has become more familiar in

the twentieth century, where it is recognizable in the vanguard gesture of confrontation: Hugo Ball's sound poems at Cabaret Voltaire; Marcel Duchamp's urinal, signed "R. Mutt"; Merret Oppenheim's fur-lined tea-cup; or, less conspicuously but no less influentially, Kandinsky's leap into abstraction and Henry Cowell's piano "clusters."

Roland Barthes once spoke of the "limit-work" within an author's oeuvre, "a singular, disconcerting text which constitutes at once the se-cret and the caricature of their creation."[9] The body of work Bruce An-drews has published since 1973 suggests a different application of the principle of the limit-work. Within a nation's literature there are au-thors whose writing in its entirety constitutes the limit-work of a given genre. Andrews may be the paradigmatic instance of American poetry at its limit. When he was starting out in the late 1960s, American po-etry was huddled so resolutely around the middle axis of the corn belt that it was difficult even to calculate what the limits would look like apart from a few fringe cases: Charles Bukowski's beery *noli me tangere;* the stark minimalism of Aram Saroyan; the prairie orgasm declamations of Lenore Kandel or Michael McClure; Ed Dorn's hip epic high; and Ed Sanders's yearbook-doodle Hellenism. But did any of this work con-stitute an extremity? Coolidge and Saroyan obviously anticipated the language-centered strategies that led to Andrews's work, among others. But their influence is symptomatic of post-sixties poetry in general; limit-works (at least in the United States) tend to provoke imitators and even schools. What distinguishes Bruce Andrews is that his work is anti-thetical to any possible school or group, however much it may have con-tributed to making the group visible in the first place. Bruce Andrews is a one-man heterodoxy. If language poetry signifies a limit in the field of American poetry, Andrews is probably fated to represent a limit within (or of) language poetry, which makes him the limit of the limit. Curi-ously, the very limit he signifies is incalculable within the paradigm of the limit. His unlimited semiosis is proximate to (if possessed of an entirely

9. Barthes attributes the phrase "limit-work" to another critic, Thibaudet, but reserves his own use of it to evoke the realm of intertextuality where a work as such is no longer efficacious. See "From Work to Text," *Rustle of Language,* 58.

different sensibility) Emerson's wonderful remark that "In the transmission of the heavenly waters, every hose fits every hydrant" (676). So I can only say that Andrews outruns limits, overflows into the *extremities*.

Andrews's is the only body of poetry I know that can be compared in its energetic occupation of space with the subway graffiti, "wild style" of the 1970s. David Antin used to say that if Socrates was a poet, then he didn't mind being a poet, but if Robert Lowell was a poet, forget it. By the same formula, if Phase II, Superkool, Slave, Slug, Mono, Doc, and Lee of Fab 5 were poets, Andrews is a poet. To liken Andrews, on the strength of the identifying trait "poet," to Dave Smith or Sharon Olds is to be grotesquely disoriented. Not that any of Andrews's readers would make that mistake. The distinction is between those who aspire to the diplomatic corps of National Verse Culture, and those, like Andrews, who don't. That Andrews, Ron Silliman, Bob Perelman, and others are rigorously committed to the linguistic inspection of the American state, its polis both vernacular and doctrinal, marginalizes them on ideological grounds; and the brand of "experimentalism" marks them as even further removed from the mainstream expectation of accessibility (or noise-free "communication," as if the dicta of Scientology constituted the prerequisite attitude for the aspiring poet, whose goal is to be officially certified as "clear"). In other words, an ideology of the simple, the transparent, the heartfelt, precludes recognition of those values as themselves ideologically infused.

Like Andrews, the borderline poet exemplifies by sheer pressure of that liminal interface a complexity destined to look like obscurity to those at the center. Any avant-garde activity is of course potentially a first exploration; but unless the terrain is subsequently inhabited, there is no reason to accredit an avant-garde with reconnaissance as such. The only calculable effect of avant-garde or border positions is in what the perimeter illuminates about the already known. This, it seems to me, is sufficient reason to take note of the work of Bruce Andrews. His is a fundamentally *hermetic* poetry, not in the sense of obscure or private, but rather as the substantiation of boundaries, the setting out of *herms*. In Andrews's case these herms are vernacular precipitates of American English. Andrews renders the familiar strange; those transparent check-

points, those words, through which we pass all day as we pass them
through our mouths and fingertips and ears, are made palpably and aggressively mutant in his choreographies ("A choreographing of use, and
forms of use. The *texts* are use-valued into *works*" [*Paradise* 262]). Dance
approaches chora as public space; chorus—our core illuminated by being reflected back to us from a distance. Andrews's work displays the viral
accessing of the mind by a linguistic dissemination that continually exceeds our abilities to standardize it. Consequently, the swarm of words
is heteroglossic; but Bakhtin's term is overapplied elsewhere, so how else
to nominate Andrews's work?—Excrementitious? Carnalanguage? Poems as heat-seeking cybervores? It doesn't matter, really, but why tag a
poet like a vaccinated dog?

Yet a problem persists about the status of language in this *most* language-
oriented of language poets. The frequently non- and even antireferential
function of words in Andrews oddly resists making the work seem thin,
evanescent, like French poetry in the mode of Mallarmé. It's rather as if
all the signifieds were somehow packed densely into the text with the
signifiers, but not sorted out, aligned, or itemized. Not "motivated"—
but not de- or unmotivated either. Andrews sustains the abstract values
of nonreferentiality while retaining all of the concreteness commonly associated with reference. He begins to show us how the signifier is incar-
nated; how words are like the pointed finger that fails to direct the dog's
eye but arouses the dog's nose. In Andrews's poems the sensuous is not
rapturous or lyrically atmospheric, but thoroughly plastic and physical.
In an explanatory statement in his early book *Edge,* he stresses the importance of "sound, texture, rhythm, space and silence" as brought together in "edges, discreteness, fragments, collision." What he proposes
to do by scrapping the grammatical framework is to exponentially maximize the play of the edges. Of course, insofar as we are disposed to read
in syntactic units rather than word by word, it is the collisions rather than
the discreteness that we notice. But Andrews's work is predicated on the
assumption that grammar is hardwired into the cortex: we'll inexorably
make sense of something, and to recognize it as senseless is not to re-
nounce it, but to recognize its obliquity. What his scattershot page-burst
sensibility addresses is that extremity where words can no longer be con-

soled by the security blanket of syntax; where the proper name leers improper advances; where the mercurochrome of conviviality stands revealed, ideologically, as a psychotic pyramid scheme; where structure and logical hierarchy fabricate a binge-and-purge cycle replicated in every speech act.

The raw carnival procession of words in Andrews's work shows us how utterly isolate and bereft words have become. Not that he says this—the work blares it out sufficiently—but his poems are coagulations of need and desire, "personal" in the way infrared photography registers heat. Andrews's poetry is language solarized. The quality of semantic reversal, or the apparent revoking of meaning, may be discerned instead as opportunities for conviviality in renewed and reframed association: metonymy as community. This was not necessarily evident in the early work; but Andrews has explored, along with Coolidge, a sensibility emerging from minimalism as it convenes on the agora. Unlike the performative reverberations of Jackson Mac Low, where we are invited to attune ourselves to a futuristic animation of words as pure gestures (as in *The Pronouns*), or where as in John Cage a Buddhist "no mind" seems to entail "no body" as well, Andrews yearns for an animal congregation. Andrews's biomorphic wordiness actually resembles McClure's *Ghost Tantras* more than it does anything by Barrett Watten, say, or Susan Howe.

Andrews's work rigorously deploys words as *flaunted* differences— differences that are not resolved, as is customarily the case, into the rhetorical flow of the sentence and into the stratification of meaning as hierarchy. Reading Andrews, we learn to savor the words as characters, almost as individual as people anarchically thrown together in fraught circumstance, helplessly revealed in their difference. When Andrews begins to introduce extensive phrasal units into his poems, in *Wobbling,* the effect is vertiginous, as we sense the fragility of syntactic bonds and are led to surmise the comparable perils of social "order." Later, such long poems as "I Guess Work the Time Up" and "Confidence Trick" mark a threshold of political abrasiveness in which the phrases appear as so many jostling coagulants, unleashed in a rhetorical hemorrhage:

Bass or percussive bass; wacked out nationality—I don t know why you guys are talking about complete sentences, he shoot up

anything; come around the store sometime—Survivors will be
exiled—Our libertarian (elliptical optimism): I don t play with *your*
pencils—And it wasn t no theory's asterisk, plain characters, rasta
devil dogs President-elect; hard debt trap objects—New new, cir-
cus of death bride narcotic life dread line dud dumdum dominion
—With technically challenging subjects (*Give Em Enough Rope* 178)

Andrews modulates and shuffles voices, attitudes, pronouncements,
takes, come-ons, and styles of verbal display that have a vernacular range
and precision poets rarely attempt. The reader is compelled to make
sense of the text as if it were a fluid public scene rather than the porten-
tous expression of a controlling personality. Andrews's work displays a
cunning resistance to the lure of authority—particularly as it basks in the
structural stability of grammar—and invites the reader to resist as well,
in the companionable mode of participation. Readerly contribution to
such work is mandated at every moment by the text; and, again, this
distinguishes Andrews's work from the performative orientation of his
predecessors. His poetics rarely seems the fossil record of what might
have been; rather, it is the brusque insistence on what is bearing down
on us, from present, past, and future alike.

I began by positioning Andrews at a periphery. It is possible now to
reconsider the model. At the center we have, however vitiated, a poetry
of image. The poetry of image, allied with a mystique of the personal (as
opposed to the "deep image" of Jerome Rothenberg and Robert Kelly in
1961), is standard workshop issue. The image structure of the poems,
percolated through a private sensibility, yields an aromatic associative
brew. The liability of such work is its compulsive filtration system; the
person—*persona:* mask—is the anchor as well as the filter. For these poems to work, the concept of the person has to be determined in advance,
in ways that by comparison make formal metrics seem the very paradigm
of free verse. The fundamental estrangement Andrews introduces to
American poetry is a withholding of the person, an abandonment of that
psychic anatomy on display ever since *Life Studies* and *Dream Songs,* Sexton
and Plath, made poetry synonymous with confession.

In the conventions of personality-lyricism, images awaken deep associations that lead to childhood, life crisis, spiritual transport, or emo-

tional slippage. By contrast, what Andrews has achieved is to retain the sense (pioneered by Whitman) of person as adjacent, circumambient, social. Instead of any confrontation with a repressed Other, there is a polymorphous field of others who come and go the way real people do, as potencies, agents, forces, not personalities at all except insofar as they flaunt their phrasal masks. The abrasions and contusions of interpersonal encounter float free of their customary romance or trauma. Bereft of the identifying traits through which the person assumes poetic centrality, the human dimension in Andrews's poetry is concentrated in inflections of speech. The words have to do *all* the work. The language is never ejected on liftoff. (There is no liftoff; there is, instead, coming and going of the sort Deleuze and Guattari appraise in *A Thousand Plateaus*—derived from Whitman's idiomatic gift to American poetry, which he called "indirection.") "The entire culture is characterized as generating a text that proposes its signification at all points in an aggressive and disturbing manner," Barrett Watten writes of Andrews's work. "All the energy with which these referential bullets are deflected by the subject is returned to the culture at large with a curse" (159).[10] The curse, of course, consists

---

10. Watten's treatment of Andrews initially appears to be little more than a transitional moment in his book, prelude to a discussion of "desiring machines" in Deleuze and Guattari, which in turn leads to an evocation of cultural totality as a "machine made out of words" in William Carlos Williams's notable phrase from *The Wedge*. "Possibly Andrews's machine is closer to the Sex Machine of James Brown than to the cubist Jeep imagined by Williams. The machine imagined by Andrews is not a metaphor," Watten crucially adds, "its limits are those of the entire culture, in which the dispersed subject is enmeshed" (160). In the "total syntax" of Watten's title, a holographic propensity is at work, so even a single paragraph (the two pages on Andrews are one paragraph) can recapitulate the whole project—just as the culture embraces the idiosyncratic profile of the individual in an ironic recapitulation of Whitman's aspirations as (Emersonian) "divine literatus." Watten discloses an awkward feature of Andrews's poetic stance: it permits no outside, yet this prohibition is not grounded in any personal assertion or argument. Bob Perelman's take on Andrews (ten years later) is more openly anxious, advancing a critique of Andrews's "politics" (as "either literary or improbable"), but offering no alternative. "While Andrews's attack on all identity (except that of writer-as- demystifier-of-all-subject-positions) leaves only a narrow margin for readers," Perelman writes, "nevertheless, the harshness of his attempts to write beyond race, class, and gender should not endorse a retreat to more normative genres and content. The political impossibilities of the present are impossible to escape"

of the culture's own haphazard froth and spray, the garbage through which its verbal prow cleaves, which Andrews's poetic salutations repackage with the implicit directive *Return to Sender.*

Eradication of a vertical dimension—high/low, rise/fall—discloses the immense pressures of adjacency words must bear. Parataxis and metonymy are not merely stylistic traits and rhetorical tactics, but traces of political discord and accord as well. As Andrews has noted, the abandonment of depth (or denotative reference) does not necessarily render the remaining surface reassuring (*Paradise* 83). Quite the contrary—a surface without depth, like denotation without connotation, is profoundly disturbing. Andrews's meticulous attention to the corrosives and sublimates of surfaces and edges has rendered the very concept of transparency troubling, even menacing. The menace is the monstrous, the open display of a mutation interior to the word as such, the "radium of the word," as Mina Loy called it. "The material intelligibility of material. Nearly only the strange makes sense," adds Andrews (*Paradise* 262). To which I'll add Paul Valéry: "A man is but an observation post in a wilderness of strangeness. We should speak of 'the strange' as we speak of space and time" (*Analects* 291). To demonstrate the usages of words is to disclose the monster that animates them. After the fixed-point cycles of words, and the limit cycles of genres and texts, we come to the *strange attractor* animating our festive chaosmos.

Andrews's poetry is emphatically antiliterary. It cannot be read in any customary sense, because it will not conform to the presentational apparatus of textual norms. One might compare the high-energy display of Andrews's poetry to the pianistic pyrotechnics of Cecil Taylor, or certain

---

(*Marginalization* 108). Such a conclusion, as it happens, converges with Andrews's own expression of the quandary in 1988 when, responding to audience questions after his presentation "Poetry as Explanation, Poetry as Praxis," he posed the dilemma in the form of a question: "Do you emphasize the underlying principles and total, controlling devices within this overall social machinery, or do you emphasize the openness and the pluralism of the situation?" (*Paradise* 60). Andrews's practice has increasingly disclosed these alternatives as inseparable and thus evidence of a false dichotomy. The semantic raw material, being drawn from radically different social constituencies and milieu, energize the sense of pluralistic openness; while the seamless rapid-fire caterwaul of his syntactic replay of such materials just as effortlessly recapitulates the arbitration of totalizing devices of control.

extremities of performance art, rather than to the work of other poets. However, since Andrews has chosen to frame his writing as poetry, and has contextualized that writing within a poetry community partly of his own making (as coeditor, with Charles Bernstein, of the influential magazine $L=A=N=G=U=A=G=E$), the challenge is clearly to understand the poetic relevance of the limits Andrews proposes. To use Barthes's words, his work is not "the secret and the caricature" of American verse practice—or not quite. In its implacable insistence on noise and in its open verbal aggression, however, it sets the secret in motion; and in doing so threatens, as no other work has, the moment of genteel self-censure that makes poetry The Right Stuff for blurb writers and metropolitan taste-makers. With inimitable explicitness, Andrews himself provides the perfect rebuke: "I am your problem" (*I Don't Have Any Paper* 108)—the voice of a strange, a *stranger,* attractor.

PARTS AND WHOLES AND ALBERT GOLDBARTH

"The parts need not *refer* to a whole; they can implicate a whole by implicating its constitutive processes," Bruce Andrews contends in a proposition that would realign the balance of news and noise (*Paradise* 81). The conventional supposition is that the details may remain murky while the big picture either illuminates or confers an emergent semantic shadow over them. But Andrews's poetry practices an inversion; the details, phrase by phrase, are familiar enough, but what's confounding is how they add up. The issue of reciprocity between part and whole is hardly new, and in the American context it has been thoroughly fretted by Walt Whitman to begin with. "The problem presented to the New World," Whitman remarks in "Democratic Vistas," "is, under permanent law and order, and after preserving cohesion, (ensemble-Individuality,) at all hazards, to vitalize man's free play of special Personalism" (987). The jostling of parts amid the whole is evident even in Whitman's syntax here, demonstrating the imposing quality of the demand.

"Shall a man lose himself in countless masses of adjustments," asks Whitman (986). In *Leaves of Grass* the issue takes the following form: Which "whole" is it that constitutes the vital background against which the prodigious tumble of poems coheres? What is the destiny ordained for the individual poems by the poet's relentless shaping and packing and repackaging of one book, *Leaves of Grass*? Who is finally found or kerygmatically proclaimed during the nine incarnations of *Leaves* with their masses of adjustments? In his introduction to a facsimile reprint, Roy Harvey Pearce celebrates the 1860 edition for its "beautifully wrought sequence" exemplifying an "archetypal autobiography" Whitman subsequently abandoned for an injudicious recourse to "prophecy" (xlvii). Whether or not one agrees that prophecy is the inferior term, the 1860 book charts a vastly different allocation of its resources than the more familiar "deathbed" configuration of 1891.[11] The question is: Which edition contains the most information? Which is it that maximizes its news, compared with which the others precipitate noise? The answers will vary, of course, because poetry is temperamental, not mental. Its "information" is not unilateral, but consists of moods and dispositions, kinks of momentary receptivity and the encompassing swells of a lifespan. (Take a look at some old favorite anthology or book of poems you haven't looked at in a while, and consider whether the checkmarked or dog-eared poems mean anything to you now.) Some readers of Whitman em-

---

11. There is, among other things, a title sequence, "Leaves of Grass," in twenty-four numbered sections, the first of which is what we now know as "As I Ebb'd with the Ocean of Life," and the fourth and ninth parts consisting of what became, respectively, "This Compost" and "There Was a Child Went Forth." The telluric magnetism set off by these poems in such motivated proximity constitutes a veritable geological event that is quite expunged from later editions. Confronting the catastrophe of Civil War, Whitman's sense of his poetic calling changed, and all subsequent editions reflect his growing determination to conflate the Union with some intuited manifest destiny of his own book. We could say that his aesthetic criteria changed with time and under pressure of public events; but it might be more apposite to note that Whitman's sense of the balance of noise and news underwent a mutation. We might even say that his sense of destiny dictated a more programmatic than poetic profile, and that the explicit "adhesiveness" (I use the term in the phrenological sense Whitman favored) of the 1860 edition has to do with a principle of social order that extends with ease from part to whole, such that every line of every poem renegotiates in its own terms the proportion of noise it will bear. Later editions work by a procedure of certification, section titles delegating a collective responsibility in which the poems participate by proxy (much like Congress). It is a system in which noise is either banished or thematized into submission by selective evocations like the war portraiture of "Drum Taps," the elegies for Lincoln, and in which the self-doubt of "As I Ebb'd" and "Out of the Cradle" is confined to—and muted within—the parenthetical showcase of "Sea Drift" with its nautical theme.

brace the sustained squalor of the 1860 edition, pitched at an intensity close to megalomania, as if the poet imagined his book might somehow divert a war (and Whitman's most afflicted heir, Ezra Pound, was smitten by precisely that supposition seventy-five years later). Others prefer the tidiness of the 1892 edition, every poem given a title and the book as a whole divided into thirteen sections (a numerical echo of the last supper?).

Is it the case that Whitman's—and for that matter, anybody's—poems enter the curriculum because "they are convenient examples // of the supreme functioning of one and many in an organization of / coopera-tion and subordination" (Ammons 315)? To be fair to Ammons, his is a pro forma concession to common sense at the end of his "Essay on Poetics," which is an *essay* in Montaigne's sense, an attempt to saunter through and round about a topic. Charles Bernstein's "Artifice of Absorption" is a similar "essay," though it resides in the book *A Poetics,* otherwise formatted as prose. In which of these two pieces—"Essay on Poetics" and "Artifice of Absorption"—do the line breaks count more? Does it depend on the presentational context? What about the line breaks in Alexander Pope's "Essay on Criticism," Karl Shapiro's *Essay on Rime,* or Bob Perelman's "The Marginalization of Poetry"?

And what
                    difference would it make
                                        if I asked this question
            in William Carlos
                        Williams' step-
                                    down hoof-probing line?

Someone might object to the aura of formalism behind the question and say it makes no difference at all: meaning is meaning. But how does meaning get here, there, anywhere, if not through embodying convey-ances? What *is* a body, with its organs and skin and bones—form or con-tent? Chemically regarded, a human body constitutes a unique form, a singularity, while the content is continuous with the hydrocarbons con-stituting the atmosphere of the planetary surface, which has no difficulty reabsorbing the chemical constituents of the body after death. Nor does a dictionary have to struggle to absorb the words of a language. So how do we distinguish form from content, news from noise?

Albert Goldbarth pitches the question in a slightly different key: "[W]ho are we to say to the supplicants thronging at various niches and altars: this mouth is an oracle, this one not?" (*Gods* 106). The answer is that they all are; it's just a matter of sequencing.

> When I drive this wheaten vastity, I see how life is space
> enough for each of us to segue through a programmed range
> of consecutive selves, some less than what we'd wish for, some
> so seemingly "other" we shiver in our passage. And that Shiva
> the Destroyer, and Shiva the Dancer of Life, are one—is just
> a mythic hyperstatement of whatever robot/tobor me-*du-jour*
> we carry confusingly into the lives of those we love (see
> Paramount's 1958 *I Married a Monster from Outer Space*).
>
> (Goldbarth, *Adventures* 44)

The masks of self correlate to the masks of others only in their prodigality, not through any one-on-one or heart-to-heart ("we're born instinctively knowing / an enemy awaits us, and the world provides it a series of faces / keyed to match our ageing understandings" [*Adventures* 43]); and the ever present model of prodigality is the tower of fecal industry that lifts the aspiring mortal heavenward on its tide of deposits (*Comings Back* 63).[12] One vision of Goldbarth's poetic alter ego might be the "young street artist [who] snapped, began a dance somewhere between / kabuki and epilepsy," is incarcerated in an asylum, where one day his keepers "find he's written SHIT / with his own, across the rec room wall in letters two-feet tall, / it being his only possession and, to that extent, the whole / of his increasing need to individuate himself"

---

12. The seventeen-page poem in question is "Letter to Tony"—"suitable for presentation as a gift"—prefaced by this toxic epigraph: "On August 23 gas-masked workmen spent two days cleaning out a three-bedroom apartment that its residents turned into a garbage dump with two-feet deep human excrement . . . Cleghorn told authorities the apartment's condition resulted from 'personal tragedy.'—The Chicago *Daily News*" (Goldbarth, *Comings Back* 51).

(*Marriage* 59). In the compendium of anatomical propriety, blood and feces and urine and snot and menses and other effluvia have the social status of noise, but the medical status of news. Those performance artists who have dallied in, preserved and framed, or otherwise made art in hyperbolic magnification of organic events, are situated right at this juncture where we can witness a "catastrophic" leap from one category to another, from shame to praise, debasement to exaltation or vice versa (see *Rubbish Theory* by Michael Thompson). These are not just bravura performances by cultural renegades, but acts of deep mimicry.

What is the model for a radical traversal of opposing states of being? —a god, of course.

The Gods
—the unimaginable patterns in the atoms of stars
and nervous systems—need to be imagined; we
provide them Masks: Ahura Mazda, Mithra, Jehovah, sometimes
sculpting lesser masks for *these* Masks

(*Gods* 104)

Now our miseries,
our formerly pennyante and shameful miseries, are bridges
to their likeness in the lives of the grand; the pain we bore,
intolerably huge but hidden in us, now, at last, is paid
its proper magnification. I return to Dickens
with clarified vision.

(*Gods* 86)

Traditional astrology proposed an active labor of parallelism and analogy, homology and tropism—*as above, so below*—and this sidereal arrangement gives Goldbarth two titles: *Heaven and Earth: A Cosmology* and *Across the Layers*. The former collection opens with a poem on the discovery of radio astronomy when a Bell Telephone investigation into the source of static in car radios revealed its origin in a persistent hiss transmitted from the Milky Way.

The universe
wants to talk to us, I'm sure of that,
it wants to and it does,
though we perceive it as the white talc
over thumb-plump purple grapes,
as the shakos of dust below the bed,
the umber fronds of rust up a bumper.

(*Gods* 101)

The voluble cosmos wants to talk, and it does, but its voices come and go; messages fray; names contort in the great digestive apparatus that is language;

The Volks grows close as a skullcap.
Forty hours—by 11 p.m. near Chittenango
we lose Brooks Benton's voice, and static
scratches like a rat to be let from the radio.

(*Original Light* 61)

The cultural chaff from some vast interstellar threshing flakes down through the known universe in (as) bits of light and heat, dense pledges of a curatorial imagination. The news that emerges from such fallout not only deserves but also thrives on its precipitating parasitical noise. Joyce cram-packed *Ulysses* and *Finnegans Wake* with an enlivening congestion, rendering sacred homage to the profane; and this approach has been most sedulously carried forward in celebrations of the effluvia of American popular culture—the schlock panoply of Woolworth's in Don Byrd's epic *The Great Dimestore Centennial* and in Goldbarth's panoramic ogles. "And thus did Alka make war on Pain, and / (here the script breaks off) // The battle is daily waged, the cosmic battle / of Order versus Entropy"—"an iffy stability with the spit of stars" (*Gods* 116, 119).

"Of composts
shall the Muse disdain to sing?" James Grainger

simply asks: *The Sugar-Cane, a Poem,*
his 18th-century verse treatise
on efficiently running Jamaican sugar plantations.

(*Gods* 107)

"Compost" is a winsome paradigm for industrial junk and personal debris, but it suggests the scale of value to which Goldbarth's catalogue rhetoric refers.

Chicago may be an unnamed setting for many of his poems, but the locale is as plausibly Duckburg, populated by a stellar cast including Leonardo da Vinci; Newton; Rembrandt; Bruegel; Hobbes; Cellini; Giotto; John Dee; Hokusai; Winckelmann; Degas; Klee; Thoreau; Dickens (Goldbarth's most likely candidate for patron saint, if not P. T. Barnum); Tu Fu; Edward Hopper; Houdini; van Gogh; Judy Collins; D. W. Griffith; Ben Jonson; Cheyenne Bodie (the 1950s television character); Ernst Haeckel; Rod Serling; "Frankenstein" director James Whale; Edgar Rice Burroughs; Nicolas Flamel, the alchemist; William Harvey; botanist John Bartram; the Shakespeare forger William Henry Ireland; not to mention a polyglot gaggle of gods like Anubis, Poseidon, Loki, and Vishnu, among whom Rapunzel and Bullwinkle may find hospitable inclusion. Albert or "Albie" Goldbarth is a frequent persona, as are his parents and Grandma Nettie.

> These are our modern mythological figures, avatars of Another Plane: Smokey the Bear; Elsie the Cow; Mr. Clean; Snap, Crackle and Pop; the talking Kool-Aid Pitcher; Speedy Alka-Seltzer. These are the icons, like it or not, of Cleveland and Pocatello and Philly and Jacksonville. And under their trademarked, tutelary scrutiny, with the cultic theme-music and slogans appropriate unto each, the organizing rituals of our American days take place. (*Gods* 105–06)

It's to be expected that we will encounter a Captain Comet Secret Decoder Ring and a Sky Commando Photomatic Code-o-graph Badge in a book called *Popular Culture* (25, 27)—which includes a visit to a party-

gag warehouse and a glimpse at the World Trade Center of the Aluminum
Siding Queen of 1957 (63)—but *Popular Culture* also includes "The Quest
for the Source of the Nile." This is only sensible, of course, for what
would pop culture be without Stanley and Livingston, Hope and Crosby,
or the Three Stooges bumbling into the inner sanctum of a pyramid?
Conversely, an establishment called Bubba's Lawn Ornaments puts in an
appearance in a poem ostensibly on "Sumerian Votive Figurines" (*Gods*
4)—an appearance no less incredible than Little Orphan Annie in a poem
about Wordsworth and Coleridge in *Adventures in Ancient Egypt* (59). The
karmic and the comic are twins, just like Goldbarth says they are (*Gods*
114). The University of Texas Special Collections Library offers up such
disconcerting wonders as John Masefield's teddy bear, "Bruno"; Carson
McCullers's nightgown; and Compton Mackenzie's "rubber toilet cush-
ion and kilt" (*Arts and Sciences* 31). Goldbarth has the feverish sensibility
of the novelty hound, so even the most implausible references probably lead to real places, like the Vent Haven Museum in Fort Mitchell,
Kentucky, with its collection of five hundred ventriloquist's dummies
(*Original Light* 41). The art of animating the inanimate, dusting off detritus and making it strut and croon, is this poet's driving ambition. His
poetic mentors are not poets at all, but the "Golden Voices: Pinto Col-
vig (Goofy), Clarence / ('Ducky') Nash" of Disney studio animation
(*Arts and Sciences* 70). "Mr. Goodbuy, Mr. Goodwrench, and Mr. Good-
meat each is the potent genius of his domain, and has it bad (I mean the
spasmic cardiac pitterpat of sexual yearning) for Penni Wise, and Cora
Gated, and Bar-B-Cutie, and maybe even the bluesy chanteuse for The
California Raisins" (*Gods* 109). Wading in the slosh of cultural fallout,
Goldbarth's radioactive discernment ekes Lucas Cranach out of a chut-
ney contest.

> And so
> we seek each other out, samurai and Nefertiti,
> suffragette and Elvis clone—partners, in the knowledge that
> the taste between the legs is news from home.
>
> (*Beyond* 43)

If the phantom double of Bruce Andrews's poems are word lists, and Clark Coolidge's doubles are shivers of randomness, Albert Goldbarth's phantom shadow is the essay. *Great Topics of the World,* one of his books of essays, could serve equally well as the title of a collection of poems, and apart from their prose appearance the essays differ little in tone and theme and diction from the poetry. Donald Finkel's blurb for *Heaven and Earth* could apply to any of Goldbarth's books: "He straddles the ages, one foot on the big bang and the other on last Saturday." His poems are ecumenical; thematically, they exemplify the condition proclaimed by Friedrich Schlegel, who in the wake of the French revolution called poetry "republican speech: a speech which is its own law and end unto itself, and in which all the parts are free citizens and have the right to vote" (*Philosophical Fragments* 8 [Critical Fragments #65]).

Bruce Andrews's profusions display the great jostle of phrase, making a Manahatta of meta-Whitmanian brag and bluster; just as Coolidge draws down the enchanted sizzle of pell-mell bop prosody. Goldbarth's catalogues and promenades rival Whitman's. He shares with Andrews a hefty word hoard of the vernacular; and in both poets a vehemence of expression is the result, though the means and ends diverge. Goldbarth, unlike Andrews, tells stories—he even tells jokes—yet he also tends to lamentation, his kaddish multiplied across numerous poems and large sequences like "Ancient Egypt/Fannie Goldbarth" (*Adventures* 77–109). One of his more poignant registers of loss is for words as they pass out of common usage:

> That afternoon, I worked on my Holmes poem:
> words, even the words, were disappearing—all
> those "dear" "quaint" Victorian commonplaces
> sloughing off the surface of the mother tongue.
> *Landau* clattered by for the last time. *Brougham*
> followed close behind. These carriages
> vanished on a far rise, leaving only their horses,
> bewildered a moment, lightened of the load, then grazing.
> They'd never return to an *ostler,* never again.
>
> (*Popular Culture* 15)

Goldbarth dedicates himself to preserving the residues, the phantom sensations and the concrete litter of the ages. His poetry is an immense calculus, something rivaling the combinatorial diagrams of Athanasius Kircher or Juan Caramuel de Lobkowitz. His material need not be classical or historical, though it often is. The comic books and pulp fiction genres exercise comparable background pressure and yield a steady static of foreground details. "You close those books"—the sci-fi portals to an "Else Dimension"—"and set-scenes from the real Earth / we're born on gleam like keys to converse worlds" (*Popular Culture* 29). I hear these keys in both a masonic sense and a musical sense; Goldbarth is the kazoo-wielding chronicler of American hermetica, the deep mystery of astrological stars transfigured into the kitsch glamour of human stardom.

Such profusion of themes and means prompts a testimonial agony:

By now—how many poems do we need
to read, before we'll admit one thing
says another? that even the hummingbird skull,
the cigarette paper, the thumping cranberry heart
in the caked-over runt of the letter,
says another?

(*Gods* 112–13)

You could also ask how many poems need to be written. After all, Goldbarth's productivity is commensurate with that of Andrews and Coolidge. In the 1990s alone his books amounted to nearly a thousand pages. He is the Zola of fin de siècle American poetry, but with a sense of humor. Goldbarth's encyclopedism, being avowedly cultish and kitschy, would seem to have the built-in advantage of not taking itself too seriously. But the constant undertone of some imminent, if never solemnly transacted, mourning rite implicates the work in a posture of earnestness that sends out mixed signals. The mixture is of course American, and Goldbarth might well claim to be merely documenting whatever the culture provides. So much for "content." The form of Goldbarth's poems is recognizably anecdotal, in a loose free verse amenable to the prevailing workshop models of the past thirty years. But the scale of the poems—as sequences, as long poems, and as organized into thematized books—sets Goldbarth's work apart, far enough apart, in fact, to make company with Andrews and Coolidge. For the element common to all three, despite considerable differences, is the *practice* of poetry as performance; the embrace of the poem as an ad hoc site of improvisatory energies, a site of convenient provisionality in which the elation of momentum prevails over any residual sense of consoling form. Goldbarth begs (and begets) consolations, but as part of the performance. His cloying sentimentalities are no less performative than the borscht-belt peppiness of Charles Bernstein. If Andrews is a kind of Cecil Taylor of American poetry, and Coolidge is an Ornette Coleman, Goldbarth might be compared to Chet Baker. Pretty boy Chet recorded too much, did too much smack, was sometimes embarrassing when he sang (yet moving, too), but he knew the repertoire and had a sound all his own.

POETRY AND DISTORTION

Confronting (I set aside the question of actually *reading*) thousands of pages by Coolidge, Andrews, and Goldbarth, one has to consider strategies of approach. The issue of size—sheer bulk and length—surpasses the cases at hand. It's useful to return to a symptomatic preoccupation of American poets in the 1960s: the long poem. It now takes a special effort to imagine a moment when *The Cantos, "A,"* and *The Maximus Poems* were still under way. But the specter of the long poem was not limited to the life-spanning aspirations of Pound, Zukofsky, or Olson. Williams's *Paterson* emerged as a comparatively succinct project, and Jack Spicer weaned himself of individual poems in order to compose "books," even though most of them were short. If John Berryman's *Dream Songs* took awhile to accumulate, it had less to do with the nature of the project than the poet's personal traumas. Despite the jackhammer punch of confessionalism, the truly symptomatic poetic phenomenon of the 1960s was "process," marking an aspiration most commonly associated with long poems and sequences. Poets frequently published sections of ongoing projects without intimating any telos or conceivable end point. Robert Duncan's "Passages," Robin Blaser's "Image Nations," Gary Snyder's "Mountains and Rivers Without End," and Diane Wakoski's "Greed" were typical. The atmosphere of the ongoing was so prevalent that even a narrative project like Dorn's *Gunslinger* seemed another of those open-ended works as its installments appeared. Theodore Enslin published more long poems than anyone, though the epistemological character of *Forms, Synthesis,* and *Ranger* made them hard to distinguish from journals. From 1965 to 1972 John Cage published installments of "Diary: How to Improve the World (You Will Only Make Matters Worse)" (in *A Year from Monday* and *M*), and Paul Blackburn's *Journals* concretized a tacit link between the long poem and the personal diary. Process as ethos was most ardently manifested in Clayton Eshleman's magazine *Caterpillar,* in which portions of Blackburn's "Journals" appeared while he was still alive, along with regular chunks of Enslin's *Synthesis* and Kelly's *Loom.* Works in *Caterpillar* often bore the prefix "from," an honorary marker, in that context, for a poem made coextensive with a life. Eshleman (with coeditor Robert Kelly) favored long poems complete as such (especially by the editors, Kenneth Irby, and Thomas Meyer) in addition to the many ongoing works excerpted in *Caterpillar* like Armand Schwerner's *Tablets,* Blaser's *Holy Forest,* Jackson Mac Low's *Light Poems,* Daphne Marlatt's *Rings,* George Quasha's *Somapoetics,* as well as colossal projects by Frank Samperi, George Stanley, and others.

In many respects, the counterculture complex in poetry was most potently concentrated in the work of Robert Kelly, whose prodigality daunted readers long before he turned forty (a point Guy Davenport made as early as 1974 in *Vort*). Kelly published nearly two dozen titles in the 1960s, and while some were pamphlets, many were two hundred pages or more, including several long poems or sequences: *Weeks* (1966), *Axon Dendron Tree* (1967), *Songs I–XXX* (1968) and *The Common Shore* (1969). *The Loom* (1975), a four-hundred-page drama of alchemical narratives— while by no means the last of Kelly's long poems—culminated the sixties surge and remains one of the unheralded treasures of its time. Kelly's legendary productivity presaged the issue I've raised with respect to Coolidge, Andrews, and Goldbarth, inasmuch as increased exposure exposes one to the futility of being selective. Kelly's notebooks (now in the Poetry/Rare Books Library at SUNY Buffalo) reveal a facility best compared to a professional musician: some performances may be transcendent, but the everyday musicianship reveals effortless proficiency. In a (classical) pianist of that magnitude, of course, one can be selective and go for the Scarlatti, Ravel, or whichever composer you prefer, confident in the musician's ability to deliver. But what is the equivalent with a poet? Kelly's work has often deployed theme and variations in its approach to topics, so it may (however loosely) be accessed in terms of ostensible subjects. But that hardly sets the work apart from normal collections of lyric poetry. The reader, browsing, will commonly read a poem because of its title, especially when it serves unabashedly as a framing device. Confronting the amassed waveform of Kelly's career, how do you choose what to read? And is it a genuine choice if it's confined to what happens to be in print?

The question goes to the heart of what constitutes a career and the shape of an oeuvre. To what extent is "prominence" in the poetry world simply a reflection of packaging? In *The American Poetry Wax Museum* I offered data indicating how anthologies perpetuate certain career patterns, but there is surely more to it than that. If poetry is "news that stays news" (in Pound's famous definition), how is this news distinguishable from the market noise of careerism? The phenomenon of the selected poems commonly plays a focusing role in most cases, and it's hardly beside the point that such volumes tend to be issued by trade publishers. This association, in turn, consolidates the legitimating role played by those publishers, lending credence to the assumption that only significant poets deserve a gathering of selected works. Some get the chance to offer their selections to the public gaze several times.[13] In addition, *Selected Poems* seems to be a neutral title, but it's not; it is a well-worn generic portal through which

13. Examples include selected poems by Galway Kinnell (1982, 2000), Mark Strand (1980, 1990), Robert Lowell (1965, 1976), Robert Bly (1986, 1999), and Kenneth Koch (1985, 1991, 1994). Some careers proliferate compilations of selected poems: Robert Penn Warren (1944, 1966, 1976, 1985, and posthumously in 2001), Adrienne Rich (1967, 1974, and the Gelpi edited reader 1975, revised 1993), Creeley (1976, 1991, and various compilations limited to a decade, not to mention the 1982 *Collected Poems*), and Ammons (1968, 1977, 1986, a *Selected Longer Poems* in 1980 and *Really Short Poems* in 1990; Ammons also had, somewhat uniquely, a mid-career *Collected* in 1972).

preselected "major" poets pass on the way to Parnassus. In its own way, a collection of selected poems singles out as news a specific body of work, tacitly reducing the books from which those poems are selected to noise. Poets from the vanguard side of the tracks, when given the chance to issue a book of selected works, commonly find another title: *Ten to One* by Bob Perelman, *Desire* by David Bromige, *The Name Encanyoned River* by Clayton Eshleman, *Red Actions* by Robert Kelly, *Lion Bridge* by Michael Palmer, *Thirsting for Peace in a Raging Century* by Edward Sanders, *If In Time* by Ann Lauterbach, *The Annotated "Here"* by Marjorie Welish, *Il Cuore: The Heart* by Kathleen Fraser, *Notes on the Possibilities and Attractions of Existence* by Anselm Hollo, *The Veil* by Rae Armantrout. Jorie Graham's mid-career move to align herself with the vanguard was signaled in her resistance to the generic "selected poems," choosing *The Dream of the Unified Field* instead. But in keeping with my data from *The American Poetry Wax Museum,* the lion's share of simple brand-name "selected poems" (by trade publishers one and all) go to a host of routinely anthologized figures (Harold Moss, Robert Pack, Karl Shapiro, Daryl Hine, Donald Justice, James Schuyler, John Frederick Nims, Richard Howard, Richard Hugo, Louis Simpson, Stanley Kunitz, W. D. Snodgrass, Maxine Kumin, Marilyn Hacker, John Wood, William Matthews, Linda Pastan, Rita Dove, and more). The term Selected Poems, in this context, transmits a generically processed code as readily as top 40 AM radio.

Estimating the balance of news and noise is difficult in generic settings.[14] The force of institutionalized habit is symptomatically rendered by the phrase "watching TV," which names a generic activity effortlessly prevailing over any specific content. For some time now, "reading poetry" (and—for many it's often the same thing—*being a poet*) has been a comparably generic marker. The *generic* here means complete effacement of the distinction between news and noise; an amalgamation of the terms into *newnoise* or *nonuisance*. But the enduring charge and challenge of po-

14. As Marshall McLuhan recognized, *all* settings are rendered generic by new technologies: "In the electric age there are far too many clichés available for retrieval. The paradoxical result is the end of garbage or of 'rag-and-bone' shops. As we tend to extend consciousness itself by the new technology, we probe all, and scrap all, in a deluge of fragments of cultures for creativity" (158–59).

etry need not be reduced to "news" and "noise." I have deployed them here as a way of raising questions about borders (identifying, maintaining, patrolling, leaking, trespassing) in a graduated series of distinctions between poetry and nonpoetry, mainstream and renegade, sense and nonsense, accessible and inaccessible. The use of "noise" here has been restricted to its role in information theory. But there is another, more common sense of the term, with more decisive social implications. In *Noise: The Political Economy of Music,* Jacques Attali suggests that "change is inscribed in noise faster than it transforms society" (5). As a result, noises are *"prophetic* because they create new orders, unstable and changing" (19). "Music makes mutations audible" (4), so "the utility of music is not to create order, but to make people believe in its existence and universal value, in its impossibility outside of exchange" (57). Drawing on René Girard's theories of ritual sacrifice as social baptism, Attali designates two principles: "First, that *noise is violence:* it disturbs" and "Second, that *music is a channelization of noise,* and therefore a simulacrum of the sacrifice. It is thus a sublimation, an exacerbation of the imaginary, at the same time as the creation of social order and political integration" (26). "The game of music thus resembles the game of power: monopolize the right to violence; provoke anxiety and then provide a feeling of security; provoke disorder and then propose order; create a problem in order to solve it" (28). Such a "game" extends beyond music to all the arts. Attali's perspective *naturalizes* noise to the domain of music, even though his broader aspiration is to examine social structure as a regulator of stability and change. To extend the concept of noise to language (where, it's important to add, it should not be confused with *nonsense),* means encountering something like the innermost alchemy of the word as Hugo Ball glimpsed it through his tin-man costume in the liturgical buffoonery of Cabaret Voltaire.

If, like Attali, we concede that noise is prior to music—noise understood simply as the profusion of worldly sounds—then music *models* the organization of noise into possible social harmonies. But the paradigm is not readily transferred to language. Literature is not "music" to the "noise" of language. If anything, literature reminds language that noise might be a destiny: "Rather than attempting to reduce noise to a minimum, literary communication *assumes* its noise as a constitutive factor of itself" (Paulson 83). Literature "opens up a kind of foreign language within language, which is neither another language nor a rediscovered patois, but a becoming-other of language, a minorization of this major language, a delirium that carries it off" (Deleuze, *Essays* 5). It might usefully be called an *unmaking* that *recomposes the real*. Of course, there is always an order of literature content with the notion that it "contributes" something to society, that it's a cultural "activity," and the poets who aspire to this kind of social service distrust noise. It's no accident that they emphasize the "music" of verse, for they know the purpose of music is to banish noise. But there are others whose sense, construed as senseless, makes a noise in which the joy has yet to be savored.

Much as the appeal to music is a tradition in poetic theory, it is also a willed impediment, an ingratiating superstition, a covert pledge to the involuntary inscribed in the legacy of the muses (see Rasula, "Poetry's Voice-Over"). The association between the lyre and celestial harmony is ancient, and the music of the spheres is memorably both subject and object of Dante's *Commedia*. Bruce Andrews's *Lip Service* recapitulates Dante's *Paradiso* in an idiom that puts considerable stress on the assumption of continuity between celestial order and the profusion of human tongues. As the title makes patent, there is an inevitable sophistry involved when negotiating the leap between human and cosmic spheres of reference. The noisy surface of *Lip Service* demands a rational awakening —an awakening to *ratio* as root of "reason"—not a mystical assent.[15] In this respect, Andrews, seemingly dedicated to recapitulating social speech in the image of cacophony, joins hands with David Antin (Socratic inquirer). What Antin attempts in his talk poems is to disencumber himself of the accumulated baggage of poetic precedence and expectation so that he can maximize his critical faculties. Antin has a predecessor (unlikely as it may seem) in Matthew Arnold, who concludes *Culture and Anarchy* with an homage to Antin's hero: "in his own breast does not every

15. Lyn Hejinian cites a dictum by Tolstoy that applies here: "If the complex life of many people takes place entirely on the level of the unconscious, then it's as if this life had never been" (*Language* 346).

man carry about with him a possible Socrates," evident in the "power of a disinterested play of consciousness upon his stock notions and habits" (299). In his 1864 essay "The Function of Criticism at the Present Time," Arnold famously advocates "a free play of the mind on all subjects which it touches" as a necessary precondition—in fact, the very ground—of poetry: "the creation of a modern poet, to be worth much, implies a great critical effort behind it" (142, 134). Arnold had used the occasion of his inaugural lecture as Professor of Poetry at Oxford in 1857 to make much the same point. Lionel Trilling offers a handy clarification of Arnold's aims: "Criticism is not what poetry *is;* it is what poetry *does*" (196).

David Antin, the language poets, and Matthew Arnold come together in affirming the characteristic activity of the Enlightenment: critical inquiry (Lyn Hejinian's book of essays renders homage in its title, *The Language of Inquiry*), which was in turn an extension of scientific investigation. In order to concretize the modern prospect of poetry defamiliarized, consider an image from that legacy: Robert Hooke's illustration of the microscopic view of a period from *Micrographia* (1665). The familiar punctuation mark, so enlarged, struck Hooke as a radical challenge to the semantic stability it was presumed to serve. Rather than incarnating a Euclidean value, it seemed to Hooke a "*smutty daubing*" or "a great splatch of *London* dirt." Hooke looks into the microscope at the hitherto stable realm of grammatical order, only to find it teeming with microbial animation. Just as Hooke, confronted with his "splatch," wonders what a period really is, we might say that modern poetry has been defamiliarized as if under a microscope, leaving readers wondering what poetry is. Poetry used to be smoothly rounded, but poems now flicker into mutation like Hooke's period. Poetry is no longer strictly defined by precedent. Classical criteria, transmitted through humanism, retained an architectonics of scale that precoded poetic performance. Elegy, pastoral, ode, and satire served as vehicles of proportional human value, ceaselessly reaffirming and reinscribing thoughts and feelings in a framework of reiterations. And while they continue to be evident—and revisiting the treasure house of examples is indisputably nourishing—they also seem anachronistic, out of step with that critical spirit Arnold held to be the touchstone of the modern temperament. (Poetic formalism is

Figure 1. Robert Hooke,
Microsopic Enlargement of a Period,
from *Micrographia* (1665)

a bit like keeping a bale of hay in your garage to remind you of the horse-power that preceded automobiles.)

Abandoning traditional forms, modern poetry has grown fond of devices, procedural strategies, and modes of investigation that are misleadingly (but commonly) called "experimental." A salutary example is Ron Silliman's poem "Sunset Debris," thirty pages long, which consists entirely of questions.

> When is revision not cowardice? What is it about green eyes? Do you want to be clinical? . . . Does that smile signify tension? If my skull is large, are my ears small? Who does not dream fondly of the days when one could eat hot dogs for breakfast? . . . What are white male vibes? (*Age of Huts* 23)

"Under certain conditions any language event can be poetry," Silliman proposes. "The question thus becomes one of what are these conditions" (49).

Silliman's question implicitly evokes Wallace Stevens's poem "Of Modern Poetry":

> The poem of the mind in the act of finding
> What will suffice. It has not always had
> To find: the scene was set; it repeated what
> Was in the script
> > (*Palm at the End of the Mind* 174)

In Stevens's scenario, modern poetry is unscripted poetry: poetry lacking, or at odds with, *prescription;* that is, the relation to precedence changes. But if tradition is no longer so invested in repetition, in reinscribing familiar pretexts into new texts, then how do we recognize "what will suffice"?

Imagine that the modern poet, trying to find what will suffice, is spooked by stage fright, but with this interesting twist: there is no longer any stage. So the stage fright is not performance anxiety, but refers instead to the absence of the stage itself, lack of a presentational frame (and therefore a species of the uncanny, the *unhoused*). As Stevens says, it didn't used to be this way, "the scene was set" and the poem repeated a prepared script. Historically, we can specify settings and transactions in a network of patronage, performance, commemoration, homage. Eventually poems accumulate into a body of available public sentiment, collected in anthologies like *The Beauties of Poetry Displayed* (1757, an approach that continues to be the dominant means of purveying poetry), and poetry plays an increasingly decorative role as a source of epigraphs for novels, bezels of wisdom and consolation in speeches and sermons, and transcribed in commonplace books. Poets achieve provisional notoriety as public figures, culminating in the consolatory institution of the poet laureate. But consider the fate of one poet laureate in an acoustic corollary to Hooke's microscopic period: on the CD accompanying *The Norton Anthology of English Literature* you can listen to Tennyson reciting "The Charge of the Light Brigade"—or almost. I suggest we hear this momentous recording as a juncture or fault line. The barely audible voice of the poet laureate marks the terminus of a vanishing tradition. It's as if his voice inches partway into our modernity and then disappears like an arctic explorer shrouded in blizzard snow. What we get instead is an explosion of sound intrinsic to the medium itself, the technical sputter of a nascent technology.

These sounds make a claim, and pose a question: What if, in listening to this recording, we were to identify the poetry in the static rather than in the voice? And if someone were to produce sheer sound, rigorously formalized but with no attempt to make sense, would it be poetry? It's a question pertinent to the grand "Sonata in Urlauten" by German Da-

daist Kurt Schwitters. This "Sonata in Primal Sounds" is fastidiously organized and in its own way fulfills any requirement that a poem exhibit
formal integrity. Being primarily a visual artist, Schwitters was more
prepared than most poets to confront the issue of form uncompromised
by content. "The only essential thing is giving form," he maintained. "Because the material is unessential, I use any material the picture demands"
(215). With respect to abstract poetry, Schwitters said the point was not
to "create meaning but rather a worldfeeling" (213). This is realized in an
exemplary way by his Ur-Sonata. The "worldfeeling" it transmits is one
we might call *starting from scratch*.

Starting from scratch means starting with noise, inessentiality, uncertainty; in poetry it means—following the critical spirit of experimental
science—adopting propositional rather than performative expectations.
What would it mean to acknowledge noise as integral to the production of poetry? Speaking of Caribbean Nation Language, Barbados poet
Kamau Brathwaite insists that noise is a "decorative energy" that is "unnecessary but without which not enough" (53). Nathaniel Mackey speaks
of an analogous condition in the "creaking of the word" of the West African Dogon people, "the noise upon which the word is based, the discrepant foundation of all coherence and articulation" (19). By its creak the
word announces its creative impairment, the paradoxical endowment of
a disfiguration, an enabling deviation from the norms of semantic destiny.
It *must* creak—like the rope in the rigging of a ship; its noises celebrate
obscure enlivening forces. Words have "not merely a power to inform,
but also to form and to deform" (Lecercle 118), and this deformation is
not a lapse or loss, but incitement to further creation, a seismic jolt that
is at once ontological threat and poetic opportunity.

Noise is a volatile term that may be made more amenable by turning
to Robert Frost, who called poetry "a sort of extravagance, in many
ways. It's something that people wonder about. What's the need of it?
And the answer is, no need—not particularly" (902). Frost is cunning,
so his "not particularly" is not quite what it seems. If he were pressed, he
might add that poetry in general serves no purpose, but that a particular
poem is a necessary extravagance. "There's always this element of extravagance," he says later on. "It's like snapping the whip: Are you there?

Are you still on?" (907). Extravagance is Frost's model of the poetic event as such: "That's the height of it all, in whatever you do: 'bet your sweet life,' you know" (910). Frost is distinctly Emersonian in his paradoxical insistence that poetry is at once vital and unnecessary. You could also say that, like Georges Bataille, he regards art as superfluous, while maintaining that superfluity is the principle of life. Common to Emerson, Frost, and Bataille is a refusal to separate message from noise, insight from accident, utility from excess.

To review how we got to this point: Wallace Stevens set the stage by noting that for modern poetry there is no stage. Modern poetry is therefore an act of the mind finding what will suffice—specifically (following Matthew Arnold) a free play of the mind. The critical spirit, responding to the sheer multitude of claims on its attention, can no longer localize poetry in the unilateral model of a tradition (if Robert Lowell was a poet, no deal, says Antin, but if Socrates was a poet, I'll consider it). Tradition is a way of conserving message and insight; it is a model of utility; but tradition is deeply invested in repetition and redundancy, shutting out noise, accident, excess. Any system needs to be revitalized periodically, but a fresh input of energy brings the risk of incorporating the alien. Put simply, innovation always looks like distortion, viewed from inside a tradition. This is because a tradition operates by means of performative criteria, whereas innovation is propositional, and primary among its propositions is a critique of first principles. This critique can masquerade as childish questions with invasive consequences: Does a poem have to rhyme? Must a novel tell a story? Should a picture replicate appearances? Do we have to put up with this? From within the tradition, such impertinent questions have pestilential consequences—that is, until the consequences become the tradition.

But now we come to the most perplexing thing of all: a tradition marks the essential, yet it has been composed all along by a steady accretion of the inessential. (I'm not far from Frost's whip crack, betting your sweet life on what you don't need.) The challenge we face in sympathetically apprehending both concepts—art as requisite, and art as accidental or incidental—would have appeared to Theodor Adorno as proof that instrumental reasoning and commercialism have alienated us from our

most unique endowment, which is a cultural reserve of vitality not dedicated in advance to specific application. Adorno took to heart Kant's notion of spectatorial disinterest, though on political rather than cognitive
grounds. Opposing the invariable market appeal to the instrumental or
interest-laden perspective, Adorno valued arts for their valuelessness,
their ability to signify and inhabit a space we might accurately call "invaluable" if that were not already taken to mean affordable only for
the wealthy. For Adorno, art resists absorption into the market logic of
equivalence in exchange. Art, "the *imago* of the unexchangeable," he says,
"makes us believe there are things in the world that are not for exchange.
On behalf of the unexchangeable, art must awaken a critical consciousness toward the world of exchangeable things" (123). "Art, in effect, must
escape from this sort of teleology" because "[t]he idea of a destination or
final end is a covert form of social control" (356–57). Therefore, "If any
social function can be ascribed to art at all, it is the function to have no
function" (322).

It is instructive to place Adorno in immediate proximity to a contemporary with whom he is never linked, Gertrude Stein, who said, "A
master-piece has essentially not to be necessary. It has to be that is it has
to exist but it does not have to be necessary it is not in response to necessity as action is because the minute it is necessary it has in it no
possibility of going on" (86). Rather than looking for a causal relation
between culture and society, then, it makes more sense to think of literature and the arts as arenas within which the very notion of efficacy—
along with freedom—is puzzled over, tested, engaged, amplified, and
necessarily left unresolved. This is not to say there is any lack of resolve
on the part of individual artists; but nearly everything valued as art in
the West (since the Enlightenment, at least) has acquired that status, not
because it clearly satisfies a function, but because, given a nexus of possible functions, it equivocates between them in such a way as to suggest
and even demonstrate the value of deviation, vagrancy, and unexpected
pilgrimage.

The point can be illustrated by way of a work so well known that much
of the history of modern poetry has been written as if to stabilize its
vagrancy, to make its noises sound purposive, and to make its impact

seem somehow intrinsic to the tradition, an inevitable evolutionary step. *The Waste Land* is described as "the definitive cultural statement of its time" (in *The Norton Anthology of American Literature*), and "the prototype of the 'modern' in poetry" (by David Perkins in his *History of Modern Poetry* [512]). Its impact on Anglo-American letters is well known. But Eliot's poem became a global guide to the underworld. By 1939 it had been translated into French, German, Italian, Czech, Swedish, Russian, Urdu, and Hebrew. Alternative Spanish translations had appeared in Mexico and in Catalunya; and readers of Greek and Japanese also had two translations to choose from. Many of these translations were important literary events in their own right, undertaken by figures like the great humanist scholars Ernst Robert Curtius and Mario Praz, and major poets like George Seferis, Gunnar Ekelöf, and Junzaburo Nishikawa. (In Tokyo a group of Japanese poets called themselves "Arechi," or Waste Land.) Like Piranesi, Eliot made ruins attractive, and *The Waste Land* served as a prototype for countless poems on a similar scale, poems of catastrophe, commemoration. I am thinking here of works like *The "Thrush"* (1947) by the Greek poet George Seferis, *Alturas de Macchu Picchu* (1950) by Chilean Pablo Neruda, *A Night with Hamlet* (1949–56, 1962) by the Czech poet Vladimir Holan, and *A Mölna Elegy* (1960) by the Swede Gunnar Ekelöf. *The Waste Land* is suitably defamiliarized in this company, a context that attests to a different poem than the one we know all too well. And it is a context inadequately evoked by a familiar term like "influence."

Reorienting ourselves to the dynamics of literary interaction, we might as well stick with Eliot. Unlike traditional models of tradition, in which each new contribution appears at the end of the process as its most recent realization, Eliot offers a model of spatial reciprocity: "what happens when a new work of art is created is something that happens simultaneously to all the works of art which preceded it" (*Selected Essays* 15). The past is far from fixed; in fact, it's like jelly in the hands of the present. The past is a mutation of the present. By making simultaneity the measure of tradition, Eliot envisions the latest text reanimating all the other texts at once, so they all speak in thunderous cacophony. How can anyone be heard in the din?—and will it ever subside? Eliot evokes for me the image of a tree full of crows who all start yammering at once when a new crow lands on the tree. What's useful is that Eliot dispels any sense that a tradition is an orderly arrangement, with unambiguous transmission along noise-free channels. Eliot's sense of simultaneity is accurate to the diffusion of *The Waste Land,* as it happens. In each of the other languages to which it migrated, there were local traditions, local channels of literary transmission to which poets were tuned in, listening to the familiar sounds. *The Waste Land* was not something they heard in their traditions, nor could it have been something they were listening for. They didn't hear it so much as overhear it.

Consider the discomfort imposed on readers by the epistolary frame of *The Birthday Letters,* the fact that these poem-letters by Ted Hughes are addressed to his estranged wife, Sylvia Plath, a reader who, long dead, cannot read. This readerly discomfort corresponds to the famous formula by John Stuart Mill, who said that while "eloquence is *heard,* poetry is *overheard*" (Adams 553). Generalized, Mills's definition implies that readers of poetry are privy to unwarranted disclosures. It also suggests something about the transmission of messages in general. To overhear something implies imperfect grasp (as of context or reference), and it suggests the potential for atmospheric distortion (the listener is not ideally situated to hear well). The latter situation is made explicit in John Ashbery's poem "Litany," which is printed in parallel columns and, if performed, read by two voices simultaneously. You can read only one column at a time, though you might sneak glances at the other. You can listen to only one voice, but you can *overhear* the other in snatches. Ashbery's work in general takes advantage of the fact that, in the posture of overhearing, you can be compulsively fascinated by what you don't understand, or imperfectly grasp. Ashbery's readers in turn learn to accommodate themselves to a high threshold of noise.

Ever since *Self-Portrait in a Convex Mirror* was published in 1975, Ashbery has been discussed as a contributor to a putative lineage from Milton through the Romantics to Yeats and Stevens, an assumption that obscures too much, symptomatic as it is of a common view of literature as a succession of titans. But fellowship in poetry is too diffuse for the formula. One troubling aspect is that the only eligible figures tend to be those whose books are in print. In 1983 I published an article chronicling the extent to which works by modernist women were out of print, and I asked my readers to imagine a modernism in which works by men had been subject to comparable waywardness in transmission. In the intervening years, thankfully, much of the work of H. D., Gertrude Stein, Laura Riding, Mary Butts, and Mina Loy has been reprinted. But it was precisely during the long period of their neglect when masculine modernism was canonized, so even the work of "recovery" often had to work within the predetermined agenda of making women fit into masculine tradition. What impact would it have on our sense of modernism, I wonder, if Marianne Moore's 1924 book *Observations* had been continuously available, with its extravagant index? A salutary instance of generic supplement, Moore's index adds an antiphonal complexity to her poems, and in the process magnifies the investigative protocols latent in the book's title. The index links her practice—otherwise too readily dismissed as idiosyncratic—to a specific discursive horizon.

Another problem with the titanic lineage, to call it that, is the way it obscures cross-pollinations and affiliations between poetry and other arts, as well as between English and foreign poets. In fact, John Ashbery's derivations are as much French as English, and his poetic orientation is immeasurably clarified by his predecessor Blaise Cendrars, who exultantly declared: "The windows of my poetry are wide open onto the boulevards and its shop windows" (58, "*Les fenêtres de ma poésie sont grand'ouvertes sur les Boulevards et dans ses vitrines*"). Throw open those windows and you get lively distractions, noises, movement, and color. You get a parade rather than a quest. You get Ashbery, not Hart Crane II. Ashbery's work (like David Antin's "talk poems"; Ron Silliman's "Sunset Debris"; not to mention Coolidge, Andrews, and Goldbarth) forces the issue of whether we are prepared to deal with poetry as a medium open to challenges commensurate with the vicissitudes of everyday life. By which I mean we now recognize that a woman who shaves her head is still a woman, and a man who wears an earring is still a man; but are we capable of recognizing comparable dislocations *in poetry*? It is also a moot question, because poetry is changing whether we are ready or not. What's more, poetry has been under an exorbitant pressure to change for two centuries now, and reviewing this pressure will bring me to a conclusion.

Consider this, from the German philosopher Hegel:

> Poetry is . . . the universal art of the mind, which has become essentially free, and which is not fettered in its realization to an externally sensuous material, but which is creatively active in the space and time belonging to the inner world of ideas and emotion. Yet it is precisely in this its highest phase, that art terminates, by transcending itself; it is just here that it deserts the medium of a harmonious presentation of mind in sensuous shape and passes from the poetry of imaginative idea into the prose of thought. (Adams 545)

With respect to the Hegelian passage from the poetry of imaginative idea to the prose of thought, it may not be necessary to go as far afield from conventional practice as Antin's talk poems. If we follow Hegel from "the poetry of imaginative idea into the prose of thought," who's to say where we'll end up? Consider the immensity of pressure exerted on all writing by the novel, the one uniquely modern genre. At a certain degree of development and refinement, the novel offers an exorbitant unremitting rebuke to poets, resounding in the very titles of certain novels— *Moby-Dick; The Making of Americans; Ulysses; To the Lighthouse* and *The Waves; Nightwood; Absalom, Absalom!; Finnegans Wake; The Death of Virgil; Under the Volcano;* and *Gravity's Rainbow,* to say nothing of Proust, Beckett, or Henry James. Nor is it simply a byproduct of their poetry that so many have contributed to that unique intergenre of novels or novelistic books by poets: Rilke's *Notebooks of Malte Laurids Brigge, The Great American Novel* by William Carlos Williams, *The Enormous Room* by e. e. cummings, André Breton's *Nadja,* Laura Riding's *Progress of Stories,* and Nathaniel Mackey's ongoing epistolary fiction, *From a Broken Bottle Traces of Perfume Still Emanate.*

In this context it should be borne in mind that the dream of exact expression, "*le mot juste*," originated as a novelist's concern with Flaubert, which—by way of Henry James—prompted Imagism. Ezra Pound reproached his peers (and himself) when he said that poetry should be as well written as prose. It is also worth recalling James's enthusiasm for Arnold, adopting his "free play of the mind" as the ineluctable potential of the novel as literary genre. And this raises a final question: What is the fate of poetry in a world dominated by novels (and, in media spin-offs, novelistic entertainment)? There is clearly a persistent strain within poetry to preserve generic integrity; and while I admire many practitioners in this idiom (tacit members of the Society for Creative Anachronism), they are engaged in performance, and their performance seems not to have proceeded even as far as Stevens in recognizing that the theater has long since been dismantled. The other tendency in poetry, which I have called propositional, is concerned not with integrity but with elasticity. A blurring of genre is inevitable from this perspective, though this is hardly recent. T. S. Eliot, for instance, reviewing *Ulysses* in 1923, suggested that it was not a novel "because the novel is a form which will no longer serve" ("*Ulysses*" 372). It would be convenient if Joyce had simultaneously reviewed *The Waste Land* and made the same remark about poetry. But the temporal simultaneity of *Ulysses* and *The Waste Land* is the best proclamation of the advent of a condition theorized more than a century earlier in Germany, concerning some ultimate elastic literary form, a Mischgedicht or mixed-genre not specific to poetry or novel or drama or philosophy, but something to which they all contribute and in which they partake. German Romantic poet Novalis calls true criticism "the ability to create the product to be critiqued" (Seyhan 82), to which a corollary by Friedrich Schlegel applies: "it is really only possible to speak about poesy with poesy" ("Dialogue on Poesy" 181). There is no place of immunity from this prospect. "Philosophy poeticises and poetry philosophises," Schlegel writes elsewhere (Bowie 53). I admire such extravagant elasticity: it alleviates every genre of the burden of performative criteria—especially as such criteria stipulate generic compliance—emphasizing instead a propositional and investigative horizon.

In *The Life of Poetry* (1949), Muriel Rukeyser offers a holistic vision of the horizon:

We know that the relationships in poetry are clearer when we think in terms of a dynamic system, whose tendencies toward equilibrium, and even toward entropy, are the same as other systems' . . .

We know that poetry is not isolated here, any more than any phenomena can be isolated. Now again we see that all is unbegun.

The only danger is in not going far enough. . . .

For this is the world of light and change: the real world; and the reality of the artist is the reality of the witnesses. (201–02)

We are still approaching this horizon fifty years later, still tentative in the face of its news of the unbegun.

4

The Catastrophe of Charm

Is cadence then
the opposite of decadence?
Baudelaire would not think so.
                    Elaine Equi, *Decoy*

"Essentially an integrated circuit is a very complex silicon photograph. . . . But our silicon photograph doesn't just represent something—the pattern of light with which it was irradiated—it really, efficaciously, does what it is a photograph of. In a sense it is a miraculous picture, like that of Our Lady of Guadalupe or Czestochowa or the Shroud of Turin. It not only represents, but does; it is not just information, but reality; it is not just a piece of knowledge, but a piece of being; it is not just epistemology but ontology" (*Natural Classicism* 208). This passage from "Such Stuff as Dreams: Technology and the Future of the Imagination" is characteristic of Frederick Turner's notable attempt to cross-fertilize aesthetics with technology. This essay, along with "The Neural Lyre: Poetic Meter, The Brain, and Time," "Reading as Performance," and four others brought together in *Natural Classicism* mount an argument for a recovery of the "deep lexicon and syntax of human artistic nature" (281). "To put it aphoristically: we have a nature: that nature is cultural: that culture is classical" (222). There is no Ur-nature that precedes culture: "All nature is second nature" (215). Turner sees the transmission of cultural information as the central human genetic task; art is a "cosmogenetic activity" of making—by "making up"—a world. This is *aisthesis,* the Aristotelian term grounding aesthetics in biology. But Turner adds a twist. He is a spokesman for a panhuman culture based on the biological restraints of the organism, yet he's also an enthusiast of microchip technologies as evolutionary augmentation of the species. This technological progressivism is compromised by his theory of *kalogenetics,* his term for value-creation unfolding through the ages in "a super-temporal conversation with the human community" (162). The phrasing reminds me of the "great conversation" paradigm of the Great Books program of the Cold War era—education on the installment plan as self-improvement. Turner's injunctions, too, suggest a kind of United Nations of aesthetic guidelines. He envisions a repatriation of melody in music, representation in art, and metrically strict oral recitation in poetry. Turner is convinced that these features are literally, genetically, the innate program of being human; to tamper with them is a corollary of drug abuse damage to the central nervous system. What this ends up being, in practical terms, is a global rehabilitation of the old humanism, slightly retooled to modify its sexism and racism (anthropologist Victor Turner was his father, which is the only way I can account for his otherwise inexplicable ethnographic liberalism).

Turner's kalogenetic program spreads out concentrically by a series of equations. He insists on a clearly defined beginning, middle, and end as constitutive of "the grammar of human art": to violate this is to abort the "endorphin reward," to spurn the natural opiate of the brain. Drawing on research suggesting a neurochemical similarity between trance states and the effect of poetic meter on the neocortex, Turner arrives at an ecological dictum: consciousness *is* iambic pentameter (31). Holding "rhythmic repetition as a psychic technology" (181), he hammers home his argument for the primacy of the oral tradition: "Thus at the heart of human artistic performance we find an archaic genetic armature of mammalian/primate ritual" (111).

There is much in the imaginative vigor of Turner's book that brings to mind Olson's speculations in the "Chiasma" lectures, or ethologist Paul Shepard's ruminations on human culture as biological resonance in *The Tender Carnivore and the Sacred Game.* What's disarming about Turner is that he obstinately refuses to acknowledge the actual aesthetic counterparts of the technological environment of the integrated circuit. He enthuses, "We live once again in a world of runes and icons, efficacious and full of virtue; a world in which the distinction between how we know and what we know, statement and referent, meaning and object, has begun to break down" (209). "The new electronic technology is by its nature playful, decentralizing, individualizing, and pluralist" (210). But constantly distracted by his pet bogeys ("modernists" and "deconstructionists"), Turner overlooks the fact that these are the very forces that have been instrumental in breaking down the distinction between the *what* and the *how* of knowing. So, forgoing a potential alliance, Turner castigates a modernism hell-bent on the senseless exaltation of aleatory license. He warns that "the random is the most complete of tyrannies" (223), but doesn't realize this is precisely what modernist poetics took care to respond to, as a historical condition prompted by the unprecedented barbarity of technologized war, postwar, and interwar. Claiming a pedigree for modernism that it never had, Turner's impulse is to clamp a lid on this cauldron of perceived moral poison: "The rules must be followed, or the freedom, the limitlessness, the generativeness, will not come about. And those rules include not only the grammar of language, but also the classical laws of harmony, melody, color, proportion, poetic meter, narrative, rhythm, and balance" (222).[1]

---

1. Turner's orientation reflects his participation in the reactionary wing of American verse formalism that achieved some notoriety in the 1980s—a "new formalism" little more than parochialism masquerading as universality. For more subtle considerations of the cultural significance of metrics, see Allen Grossman, *The Long Schoolroom* (1997) and Roberto Calasso, *Literature and the Gods* (2001). Calasso addresses the enigmatic continuity of metrics from the Vedas to the present, favoring a modern (Baudelairean) view that "meter is no longer a mere function of language, but rather the contrary: language comes into being as a function of meter. It is only thanks to meter that we have style. And only thanks to style that we have literature" (137). Lest this sound like a formalist stricture, Calasso adds, "Whether easy to recognize or not, rhythm is always the underlying power that governs the word" (137). In his view, then, the gift of modernism is its power to reawaken us to deeper rhythms than formal metrics can acknowledge, rhythms he traces back to Vedic emphasis on the *syllable* as the sign of a conjunction between human breath and the gods— the gods, in fact, being nothing other than the wonder of breath itself.

Allen Grossman understands measure as a moral issue and, as such, not to be confined to metrical aesthetics. "We live between the productive violence of representation as poetry and the destructive violence of representation as history," he argues (38). Grossman

It is dismaying to ponder a claim that the human central nervous system is programmed, worldwide, to obey these laws. Or are they rules? Does Turner aspire to legislate what he purports to merely describe? The difference between laws and rules is usefully gleaned by Jean Baudrillard: "A rule can be perfectly arbitrary in its enunciation, but it is much more unbreakable than the 'law,' which can be transgressed. You can do anything with the law. With the rule, on the other hand, either you play or you don't play" (*Forget Foucault* 92). Where Turner silently turns his laws into rules (and in universalizing them approaches a near Stalinist puritanism regarding what art should and should not be and do), Baudrillard sees that poetry's *rules* are of its own making, and that poetry is dangerous because it does have rules rather than laws (or judgments).

> Forms that are beyond judgment have a much greater power of fascination, but they are for that same reason terribly dangerous for any order whatsoever. They can no longer be controlled. At any given moment a category or a form stops representing itself, it no longer enters the stage of representation, it no longer functions according to its end . . . In the language of poetry we are familiar with those sequences in which things seem to take place without continuity, without consequence, without mediation. Language is always an order of seduction to the extent that it is a mutant order. If you suppose continuous, progressive, linear order then it is still based on a mutational "superstructure." The words of a poem are of that order. They do not go through the meaning. One word calls forth another in a catastrophe of charm. (94)

When Turner tentatively concedes that " 'Art' itself implies artifice, even wiles and charms" (32), he is clearly unprepared to move on to the "catastrophe of charm."

---

is prepared, then, to understand modernism as "the revolution that broke the canon of the poetic line [in order] to get the violence out of representation" (176); but he contends that such revolution was corollary to the long historical process of secularization, and that modernism and postmodernism unwittingly disabled the primordial power of poetry's "productive violence." "Thus we have withdrawn from *the great business of poetry, which is to keep the story that we tell from being true*" (177).

If Turner is a neo-humanist, fashionably applying some cybernetics eyeliner and sociobiology rouge, Baudrillard is a theory-terrorist, exacting ransom from concepts taken hostage, fashioning a death's head no less imposing in its anamorphic freakishness than that cylindrical skull floating in the foreground of Hans Holbein's painting "The Ambassadors." Rather than affirming a panhuman culture, Baudrillard recognizes that the society of the spectacle makes us all "living specimens." Following Elias Canetti, Baudrillard sees that this condition effectively impounds history in a deep freeze. "Without even being conscious of the change, we suddenly left reality behind. . . . History isn't over, it is in a state of simulation, like a body that's kept in a state of hibernation" (68).

In contemporary culture, selected packages of historical residue are thawed, microwaved, and served up in media replays, retreads, reruns. This cryogenic state of suspended animation recycled through liquefaction tosses up a continual spatter of data on the various windshields and screens of mediated consciousness. This "ecstasy of communication" is mordantly depicted by Baudrillard as an obscenity in which "the imminent promiscuity of networks" discharges a "pornography of information and communication" through a helplessly enthralled humanoid residue, glued to the screen, the *monitor.* Baudrillard is willing to speculate on every aspect of contemporary life as a condition of terrorism. The social demand that we all constitute ourselves as subjects, for instance, can be seen as a state-sponsored form of blackmail. Subjectivity is quality control for lifelong hostages.

With Baudrillard's acerbic observations in mind, it's easier to recognize what a tremendously cheery naïveté Turner brings to his assessment of the contemporary scene: "Information is the means of production," he writes, "and there is now no way of plugging the leaking joints where the public can feed on the rich flow of free information" (211). Such attitudes are relentlessly exposed by Baudrillard, who plaintively laments that "none of our societies knows how to manage its mourning for the real" (*Simulations* 46). Invariably, as "We sacrificed culture for the chassis" (Andrews, *Enough Rope* 175), howls of discontent were heard. But *mourning* is a term that carries the weight of recuperation; and dealing with the consequences of the lapse of history, subjectivity, and other cumbersome species of representation is now a burden directly taken up by some few poets, here and there.

"Government has failed. No power is invested in the PUBLIC trust. All politics, therefore, is terrorism—the actions of individuals on behalf of private interests, in the name of the people" (Byrd 56). Baudrillard's lugubrious ruminations give way here to Don Byrd's "CALL FOR A GEN-ERAL STRIKE" in *The Great Dimestore Centennial:* "In the middle of the seventeenth century, human beings began to replicate themselves at an unprecedented rate. We may be running out of time and space. The world we have engineered—in order to accommodate the numbers—is a vast artifice, our truest work of art, and we inhabit it completely. It has no OUTSIDE" (56). "Poetry cannot solve these problems," he adds, "but nothing LESS than poetry can solve them" (57). The catastrophe of charm that is poetry cannot afford the pretense of contributing to those aesthetic strongholds where canonical aspirants putter on in a toxic twilight of self-absorption. All the available surplus information inflates us, bloats us, and turns us at last into empty receptacles. We inhabit a cultural bulimia (or it inhabits us). A survival strategy begins with a gargantuan appetite; parsimonious sampling is no longer possible. "We are transistors" (89). In this vast epidermal leotard of electrical transmission that we think of, archaically, as "communication," public affairs and the "public trust" are nothing but text, pure text.

The text is cancer,
and the architecture of feedback deletion
unclear. (64)

—which is to say, homeostatic self-regulation is ontogenetically provided in living bodies. We sweat to relieve ourselves in the heat; but what is textual sweating? How much is enough? What is autopoiesis?

A work like Byrd's *Dimestore* is, in its self-diagnosis, "a work not of art, / an act of hygiene" (123). The circuitry scrubs itself. The text (invariably a microprocessor of other texts) reiterates a single, thaumaturgical question: "How long does it take for an information cancer / to pass through a population?" (152). The nature of the cancer, meanwhile, is unclear. Is consciousness eroded by it? Is the elimination of history one of its gambits? Is social life a media event, subjugated to the law of the instant replay? Is it the unprecedented scale of available information that we are stricken with, or is it the aleatory manner in which it spreads like gossip? "The Truth is rumors / which pass through language / as weather passes through the sky" (150).

Byrd's *Dimestore* is an unnervingly cyborgian production, in Donna Haraway's terms: "Biological organisms have become biotic systems, communications devices like others. There is no fundamental, ontological separation in our formal knowledge of machine and organism, of technical and organic" (97). Yet behind Byrd's switching operations there is a mammalian presence, both in the Ozark colloquialisms and in the dime-store countertop regalia that litters the text—the "MASTER" and "SLAVE" monogram pillows, for instance. But this humanly fallible script clamors for a reader to intercede, rearrange sequences, insert new data, and update hypotheses. Byrd's modular poetics are indebted not to aesthetics, but to word processing. One reads the poem in readiness to respond to cues like DELETE, FIND, BLOCK EDIT, RELOCATE and various other STRING COMMANDS. The book is nothing less than a manifesto for a new art, though its medium is inadequate to what it presages. It shouldn't be a book at all, but a floppy disk or CD-ROM. Composed of seven "Books" patterned on the proverbial wonders of the world, Byrd's text is an information ode ticking off in its titles the lapsed origin-stories of the age of the book: "The Book of the Garden," "The Book of the Father," "The Book of the Dead," and "The Dead Don't Have Books." Despite feedback loops and the computational power of Byrd's poem, it retains the puritan claw marks of the Wonder-Working Providence in coining the neologism *whomans,* a deliriously poised provocation of man and woman, shuffled into a genetic interrogative, masquerading as a noun.

A useful complement to Byrd's *Dimestore* is Bruce Andrews's *Give Em Enough Rope* (the title an homage to the second album by British punk rock group The Clash). While lacking Byrd's aphoristic clarities and contextual explicitness, Andrews's poetry is more fully charged with enraptured futurity. It's a book that instantaneously reduces most poetry to obsolescence in its chillingly efficient demonstration of *implosion,* Baudrillard's term for the collapse of opposing categories within a differential system.[2] In Andrews's book the public is imploded in the private, while subjectivity is imploded in language. The six long poems appear to be a bricolage of linguistic spare parts: a "scripture hologram" (28), "cognitive dissonance figleaf" (29), "Heterophonic portamento" (49), the procedural motto of which is "Make noise, be seen, desultory info chameleon" (144). "Treat me like a labor unit," the text—or *can* it be "the poet"?—says.

To readers gone punchy on TV-dinner poetry (anchored in pronoun, circling like a Ferris wheel around the subject/predicate axle, its cozy image-buckets dangling from different heights, with the familiar old carnival pipe organ noodling in the metrical background), Andrews's work will seem a piling up of soulless words, as cacophonous as Hopkins's sprung rhythm verses that Bridges feared to publish until the barbarous Moderns held the field. Andrews's polyethnic urbanized brawling style feeds off resistance with the intuition of a loan shark: "Direct victim half the society, body is what you ('HEY baby') end up talking about all the present reduced to a showcase for the ego" (168). Andrews does in fact deploy language in a state of undress, denuded of reference-as-reassurance, but reinvested with a potent referentiality *as* or *in* the vertigo of the phrase ("I don't know why you guys are talking about complete sentences" [178]). Protosyntactic chunks like "Key hypnosis nipple leadership; mystery tout" (164) are the common denominator. Yet even this paratactic approach is assaulted in "Swaps Ego," where all the words are capitalized, atomized, isolate:

Another Darkness Librarian Fluent Beau Pepper
       Gargle Crow Omen Conundrum

Parataxis Burst
Pit No Factor Bleed Blending Fashion Ever
       WORDS WASTE VARIETY (125)

---

2. Taking his cue from Marshall McLuhan, Baudrillard holds that the message is imploded in the medium, the medium in the real, and the concept of the social is imploded in the "silent majority" of the masses. See *In the Shadow of the Silent Majorities*.

Despite these distancing tactics, the sequential placement of words tends to bunch phrasal units together, proof of reading's gravity, left to right.

Language in the integrated circuit comes in sporadic bursts anyway, and Andrews's rich pixels jolt the recognition that the phrase *is* the new public unit of the cybernetic caucus. The texture of the writing in *Give Em Enough Rope* is clotted and sutured and in its vocal surges constitutes a *menstruum universale* of information. "While society / stutters in the prompter's box" (13)—"Narcissism is like not seeing that there can't be a private language if the body is a social—Guerrilla means everyone has the tools to do is invent a dictionary" (163). Person and personality stand revealed as a legion of spare parts: "Most Ambitious Self Hearing Lack Of Deep / Someone" (103). These are "the switching operations in which the subject gets lost," according to Baudrillard (*Forget Foucault* 77), the sullen response of the masses to the extortionary social demand to *be* a subject—to get subjective (colloquially: *get down* or, in the paradoxical command: "Be natural"). "Can we implode in the real with charm? Without going all the way to suicide, we continually play on the process of disappearance in our relations to others. Not by making our selves scarce, but by challenging the other to make us reappear" (129).

If we take Andrews's poetry as a challenge "to the other to make us reappear," the final piece in *Rope* ("Confidence Trick") reconstitutes the pronoun *us* in the expanded headroom of a fervently political evocation:

> Equality demands no less; history begins with old man crying, logic you know, airplay your fingertips is not freedom—The disintegrating slop situation on outlaw; read it in the voodoo prospectus, keep trying death squads paid for by our *Christianity* radiation taxes to that human rights clone improves because there are so few rebels left to kill, like iron filings—Polkadot mentality you capsulize it with a commemorative stamp, slunk down in the heroic mode for comfort, Belfast, Capetown, compose loonee tunes that could be written in the mind by institutional simpletons. (153)

There is no workman's comp for being a citizen in a technocracy, no public maintenance apparatus when "men have become the tools of their tools" as Thoreau put it. We are all integers in a data management system from which no text is immune, and in which our own bodies are nothing but text. The compelling case for poetry on the order of *The Great Dimestore Centennial* and *Give Em Enough Rope* is that such work unfolds in the unfathomable struggles of life today—and not a moment too soon. While most current writing obeys one simple law—"Stake thru heart kills most vampirish tendencies of audience" (Andrews, *Give Em Enough* 50) and is addressed to people for whom "history is a leaky ball-point, / fouling the pocket" (Byrd 98)—Byrd and Andrews have elected a barbaric medium that registers the trauma of public life as its own somatic physique. These are works that reveal the mutant gasmask visage gradually defining the contours of the human face. No longer is this the invasion, but the *siege* of the body snatchers. Byrd and Andrews have responded on a scale adequate to the magnitude of the alarm, and their books are singular (if isolate) refutations of George Oppen's disturbing forecast: "We will produce no sane man again" (186).

5
Literacy Effects

Handling the Fiction, Nursing the Wounds

1. There is a ludicrous complaint I've heard poets make for as long as I can remember: "If only poetry didn't have to compete with TV." What is it that makes this fantasy so durable? With a little reflection, those who make this comparison would be hard put to claim that a permanent electrical outage would send droves of people to poetry as an alternative form of entertainment. A more cogent point of comparison would rephrase Pound's dictum about poetry being as well written as prose: poetry should be at least as well written as a network television episode. What is misleading about aspirations by poets to compete with television programming is the corollary that poetry is an entertainment medium. There was a time when poetry was read as bite-sized moral edification; but the moral was gone long before TV encapsulated the edification into the half-hour sitcom and the hour-long dramatic series.

This was originally delivered as a talk for the *Sulfur* Conference at Eastern Michigan University, March 26, 1988. Writing it with no thought of publication, I did not retain page references for all the citations. While the force of its critique of mainstream poetry has been blunted by developments in the 1990s (as outlined in Chapter One), I have let the text stand unrevised as the polemical index to a moment worth documenting (not least because the moment is not over).

The real issue posed by the spectacle of the mass captive audience for TV programming is trivialized by confusing it with poetry. By way of immediate, harrowing contrast, consider this, written by René Char while fighting the Nazis in the Resistance: "Between reality and its report, there is your life which magnifies reality, and this Nazi abasement which ruins its report" (#126). Although, as Eliot Weinberger reminded me, it doesn't bear comparison with the Nazi abasement, television's competition is not with poetry, but with *bios* as such—lived human time; somatic beings not destroyed, but prosthetized by their prostheses. If we want to discover how the report (the concussive sound) of poetry is "ruined," we'll have to look elsewhere.

2. Poetry reviewing generally makes no attempt to contextualize poetry (in relation even to other art institutions, let alone the life of a community or a group). A poetry review is typically a book report on an isolate, self-indulgent moment of pleasurable introspection. As such, the only prospective reader of poetry is a consumer, who is then simply making a generic choice. This amounts to a massive corrosion of the language of value as it might be applied not only to poetry, but also to "cultural literacy."

Poetry solicited for the ideology of privacy adheres to the following principles: (1) it must demonstrate a restraint of the stimulations or aggressions that inhere in charged or intense language; (2) it must display fidelity to the poet's personal life; (3) this fidelity, this "being true to life," must affirm a communal sufficiency (marked as "the voice that is great within us"); (4) but (paradoxically) it must be an innocuous artifact and in no way seek to challenge its status as private concern of a handful of consumers.

The ideology of privacy stipulates that, like any consumer product, poetry should be another tool for social disengagement, a leisurely interest, a hobby. *Consumption* was a euphemism for a nineteenth-century "wasting disease"; now it's the preferred lifestyle of the "stable subject" (though the *stable* subject is more accurately a genetically engineered domestic animal). It's no longer a matter of "meeting the world halfway"; there's no such thing as privacy—privacy has been deleted. Leisure time is now archaic. What is now called leisure or free time is instead a differently calibrated sort of duty, the zone of bricolage in which we cut and snip and sort and paste our attentions, so we become prosthetic supplements to the total-body effect of the media, the coherent and pervasive final report that drifts along just out the door. It is, as Marx forecast, a later stage of the system that produces objects for the subject; now, more than ever, a subject must be produced for the object. (Think of how readily we adapt ourselves like mobile components to VCR, phone answering machine, compact disc, personal computer.) So there is a predominance of first-person singular, home movie poetry, poetry busy displaying adaptable subjectivity in its prosthetic habitat.

3. Let's call this first-person singular poetry hegemony (even when it says "we" it really means more of *my me mine*) *PSI,* for Poetry Systems Incorporated, a subsidiary of data management systems. It *is* a business; its business is producing "the self." (This is not only a commodity, it's a specialty item. We know this because it had to be imported, in the glossy parlance of "subjectivity.") In the subjectivity market, you can't just get it anywhere. Only certain venues offer it, and PSI product is one of the venues. (Notice, though, that all the predominant pedagogic and information sources will generalize PSI product to, simply, "poetry.") How can you identify PSI product? It's as easy as subscribing to any of the roster of magazines hawked by College Subscription Service, as easy as joining the Book of the Month Club, or getting cable TV. PSI product is available in any chain bookstore. Your local midsize community library will stock nothing but PSI poetry (often that's all your university library will have as well). The *New York Times Book Review* is its corporate newsletter (or increasingly *was*—poetry now beginning to evaporate altogether as a literary concern in that organ). Or you can read the critics, whose examination of the scope of contemporary poetry is so routinely unadventurous that it amounts to in-house PSI publicity copy—slick appraisals to be printed in glossy brochures (as if poetry were ever that marketable), or living out the half-life of the excerpted blurb.

4. But poetry also persists by other means. Alvin Rosenfeld, a scholar of holocaust literature, wrote: "A manuscript written secretly and at the

daily risk of life in the Warsaw ghetto; buried in milk tins or transmitted through the ghetto walls at the last moment; finally transmitted to us— such a manuscript begins to carry with it the aura of a holy text. Surely we do not take it in our hands and read it as we do those books that reach us through the normal channels of composition and publication. But how *do* we read it?" I want to stay in the vicinity of this question. But first, what exactly are the "normal channels" Rosenfeld refers to? Obviously he means the simple expedience of publication. But publication is never so simple or expedient as we might believe, thinking of normal channels. Publication is simply one part of a much larger social process, which is the *segregation of access to significant symbols.* A normal channel in this culture is a television channel—and I don't mean this as a pun. Newspapers, magazines, films, recordings, radio, PSI product—all normal channels. What is a reader (a viewer, a listener) for the publishing media that constitutes normal channels? A reader is a digit, a statistical guarantor of the precise scale of another kind of beast known as "the audience." To compete with TV is to yearn for an unknown and ultimately *captive* audience.

5. "Normal channels," then, are the dominant channels. Dominant channels mean channels that dominate the attention of the unknown audience.[1] Stanley Aronowitz: "mass art [is] one-way communication [which] takes on the character of domination" (*False Promises*). Dominant channels are operated by media entrepreneurs who deploy a product in a medium in order to get the attention of an audience—the hook inside the bait of entertainment. This marketing angle regards the unknown audience as accessible only in captivity. The audience is transported invisibly and electronically as statistical integers in the contractual bargaining agreement between network and advertiser.

You've heard of the Nielsen families; these nonelectable officials are,

1. The "unknown public" was envisioned by novelist Wilkie Collins (*The Moonstone* and *The Woman in White*) as "now waiting to be taught the difference between a good book and a bad. It is probably a question of time only." Writing in the high noon of Victorian optimism, Collins imagined that this unknown audience "must obey the universal law of progress and must, sooner or later, learn to discriminate" (191). It's later than he ever would have thought possible.

in effect, your congressional delegates in a national literacy forum, determining what goods and services everyone has access to by means of "normal channels." Recently the networks have threatened legal retaliation against the Nielsen agency because its new method of eliciting viewing information from the statistical sample showed a massive overall decline in the size of the audience for network television. The new Nielsen system required each individual in the family to enter a personal code when watching a program so that they could be demographically identified. The network claim that a significant number of people didn't oblige, whether true or not, reflects a telling hesitation on the part of network top brass to know who they're addressing. It is dictatorship by managerial style—though the style outlasts the individuals whose "taste" and "discrimination" constitute it. As long as an audience can be *targeted* demographically (product X for baby boomers) then the statistical sampling methods are OK; but when the sampling procedure allows (or requires) too much intervention or interference on the part of individual audience members, then something must be wrong. (Horror of horrors—maybe the ten-year-old girl switching on the TV and not punching in her code name is refusing to produce herself as a subject for that object.)

The implicit injunction to the captive audience (name, rank, and serial number) is to concede volition to the broadcast medium in exchange for the privilege of "participating" in the statistical process; just another episode in the lifelong miniseries of political abstinence: "the renunciation of the question of political right through the private pursuit of well-being" (O'Neill 89). This is the participation mystique of an industrial-communications society. It is also a residual sort of mind-cure theology. Donald Meyer, writing on the positive thinking cults of the nineteenth century: "Mind-cure theology was purely expressive. That is, it was the immediate projection of uninspected wish" (81)—an impeccable description, as well, of commercial advertising, in which a product is projected into the virtual psychological space where wishes congregate. Wishful thinking, in Meyer's analysis, is a contradiction in terms: "The wish for plenty was not the wish to have one's wishes fulfilled; it was the wish not to have to wish wishes of one's own at all" (207). Wishful thinking is that studiously orchestrated set of tactics of disavowal known as "keeping the faith." The only literacy requirement for normal channels is faith. The distinction between poetry and TV can be usefully revised by way of David Jones's qualification: "It must be understood that art as such is heaven—it has outflanked the fall—it is analogous not to faith but to charity" (164).

6. Am I actually saying that mind-cure theology is alive and well, that normal channels like PSI poetry product (prime, canners, and utility grades, following Ed Dorn [80]) are massive sedatives, alleviating us from the burden of having to wish our own wishes?

It's not quite so simply dominant. Mind-cure theology is not finally connected with literacy, but with numeracy. As Ian Hacking suggests, numeracy precedes literacy ("Biopower"). (Numeracy is the ability to relish and manipulate number symbols discursively. Sports broadcasting is numerate, not literate; David Letterman's top-ten lists and Harper's Index are numeracies shading over into literacy.) Mind-cure theology is historically linked with another nineteenth-century vogue known as "moral science" (information about and control of the moral tenor of a population). What used to be known as moral science is now called "statistics." Mind-cure theology and the science of statistics are both means of sampling the (then "unknown") audience, to take its moral pulse. It's written into the Constitution, which stipulates census taking as a duty. With that, we're committed to numeracy, at the expense of literacy. "Moral science" has long been fully democratized in the sense of being spread around through government agencies and private sector alike. Through the courts, by means of taxes, public works, welfare, education, and the feedback facilities of entrepreneurial "normal channels," a census is continually being taken.

7. The unknown audience is not so unknown now; captivity breeds familiarity. The normal channels have asked us to identify ourselves, and we have. Eagerly. *What's your name?*— Evelyn. *And what do you do, Evelyn?*— I'm a legal secretary. *And where are you from?* Tallahassee, Florida. . . . — My name is Everett, and I'm a systems analyst from Kalamazoo. . . . This rudimentary scenario is played out all day long on TV sets and talk

radio throughout the land. We have become very adept at being informants, in the strict ethnographic sense of the term. We tell the moral
scientists whatever they want to know. We are actively recruited all the
time for information about ourselves. Not truly different information—
nothing that would single out any of us as being positively unique—but
for the information that makes us typical. In this light, PSI poets have
simply been more gregarious and forthcoming than most, as moral science informants. (Although, as Charles Bernstein points out, they are a
bit more culpable in that they are directly involved in designing the parameters of the questionnaire.)

8. Being an informant is intrinsically a bid for entitlement. Making oneself heard, speaking up for others, buffing up qualifications. Qualifications for what?—for the benefits forthcoming from colonial administrative practices. The inexorable bankrolling effect of cumulative statistics
is something we all feel burdened by, as witnesses and as participants or
informants. My social security number, like my credit rating, is of more
significance to more people than anything I will ever write; that is, it
connects more readily than poetry to an available public medium (demographics and other tabulations of group dynamics); it contributes incessantly and functionally to an ongoing story—a story the nation is con-
scripted to produce, as if contractually. We're all *under contract.*

Consequently, many people feel positively chosen, elected, to bear
witness in the mode of the informant. It's a means of entitlement. Consider as illustration the matter of Love Canal residents on the issue of
chromosome damage due to dioxin contamination of groundwaters: in
1980 the New York State Health Commissioner stated categorically that
these afflicted Love Canal residents were "not qualified" to hold an opinion regarding their own health. Since the authorities wouldn't listen, the
residents took their stories to the press, which was willing to entitle
them as informants. This is what I call a "literacy effect" (poaching on
Roland Barthes's "reality effect"). The literacy effect is a last resort when
normal channels of transmission make a commitment to *moral science* as
statistical equation, when representative sampling and standard deviation become operational norms, along with diagnostic testing and meth-

ods for calculating probabilities, and when the *unknown audience* can be positively identified only insofar as it is a captive audience.

9. What is literacy? Literacy is the guidance, supervision and correction of literate *comprehension,* per se; how we're comprehensive, how we come to understand that even though we don't know everything, whatever we know composes a totality. I like the word *comprehension,* as it bifurcates into "understanding" on the one hand and "encompassing" on the other. The literacy effect propagated through normal channels guarantees that these two distinct capacities of comprehension will *not* be brought together. Two illustrations, parables:

• Literacy effect #1: Once a code of the masterpiece prevails in the arts, the colorful and exotic in travel, and the spectacular in nature, then the most perfunctory *sign* of the thing suffices as a mark of authenticity. Artworks become sample delegates of the durable institutional category Art (just as prose comes to represent the institution of literacy as such, alphabetic competence).
• Literacy effect #2: The establishment of a "proper" or innate domain of literature (with its classics as universal emblems of an omnipotent literacy, with its various subdivisions into genre, mode, and style) is the exercise of self-inflicted literacy as in "self-inflicted wound." To attend to something because a normal channel retails it as a masterpiece (a *must read* for snobs) is to be a victim of one's own intelligence—*self-inflicted literacy.*

10. Obviously, these literacy effects might just as well be called "canon effects." The canon, like any bureaucratically administered organization, takes its directives from licensed operators. The formal and legal requirements for operating canonical mechanisms are analogous to those for obtaining an aviator's license. Next time you read Ashbery, listen for the sonic traces of disconnection and detachment as a living body is made to endure the stress of "rehabilitation" within the canon. The canon is something that needs living human subjects as recreational ammunition under the big top, under the watchful eyes of licensed operators.

Think of the canon as the Elks Club, or better yet the Pentagon, a supervisory body enacting its custodianship of the canon of war ("peace" not being an operable term in Pentagon jargon, which prefers to speak of "permanent prehostility"). Or think of it as a natural history museum with its dioramas. Ever notice how in such exhibits the stuffed animals don't have bullet holes? The essence of the canon (the natural history diorama, the anthology of masterpieces with its "perfect specimens") is to eliminate the bullet holes, to efface any trace of how the critter was bagged.

11. In the institutional double bind of the canon—with its normal or normative channels, its administrative homeorhesis or supervised pathways of change, with its informants and its licensed operators—the arts are taken as work done now but for the benefit of "posterity." The arts are the happy side, the upscale heritage we pass along to our progeny to counterbalance their interest payments on the national debt. Are the arts a subsidiary necrology? Muzak for eternity? It's hard to persist in doubt and uncertainty; hard to conceive an order outside canons and masterpieces, but not because of the old model of an entrenched bastion of privilege, a stronghold of conservatism resisting change. The canon is a mechanism for managing change, while stage-managing the theatrical milieu of "permanence." At stake in the issue of things canonical is the constitution and distribution of cultural capital; and this involves "the relation between the means of literary production and the institutions of social reproduction within which speakers succeed or fail to speak for themselves" (Guillory 521). Do we speak for the same, or speak for change? The issue itself is not stable. It oscillates. The literacy effect is simply the directive to classify canonically.

12. Homeorhesis is the term coined by biologist C. H. Waddington to mean "ensuring the continuation of a given type of change" (105). A multinational corporate head: "For several years we thought we had to manage a crisis and find a new equilibrium; we now know that this idea is incorrect, and that change has to be permanent." If this corporate chief had read *The Communist Manifesto,* he would have had this clearly spelled out for him in the phrase "constant revolution in the modes of produc-

tion." Change has to be permanent. This makes capitalism sound like the purest of Heraclitean perceptions. No wonder the "poetry of the market-place" is so alluring.

Some scholars of comparative literature have lately drawn the same conclusions. Wlad Godzich and Jeffrey Kittay: "Prose is much more heraclitean [than poetry], it begins with change and seeks only to find ways of managing it" (197). In the late Middle Ages and the rise of the vernacular throughout Europe, prose emerged as the faceless, charac-terless inner constitution of writing, as such, something so intrinsically unformed it could adapt itself to the changes. Unlike verse, prose was not a genre and brought with it no generic impediment. As Godzich and Kittay explain, the oral tradition of the jongleurs (a verse-dominant nor-mal channel) handled change by investing the singer with custodianship of his materials. He could play on the cultural changes as they occurred, by working within the mastery of vernacular components, which, being oral, were flexible. But the dissolution of the Holy Roman Empire, and the gradual separatism of emerging nation-states, required means of le-gitimation not contingent on nomadic sophists—which the jongleurs were becoming (singers for hire). These changes required documents that could embody difference without seeming to impose their own ritual legacies on the new material. "The move to documentary truth acknowledges the impossibility of containing time and its changes but manages to locate a form of preserving identity within it, namely an un-changing piece of paper" (xviii).

Now, before it appears I'm too far off the track—just to remind you, the issue is one of change, which is the dominant fact of Western civili-zation for a thousand years. ("What does not change / is the will to change.") And the language of change is prose. The concern of prose is "finding ways of managing change"; it is intrinsically administrative, but eventually bureaucratic. Anything that holds its ground, which appears to resist change, is subject to the reconstructive surgery of disciplinary measures (punitive as well as scholastic). "In order to know . . . one has to occupy fleetingly a fragile position for the purposes of knowing. Such positions and purposes are precisely what disciplines specify. By contrast, he who simply 'inhabits' is now but a native informant. His perspectives are not positionally constructed for purposes of knowledge, and thus they demand interpretation, demand to be themselves juxtaposed, over-laid, put in perspective" (*Emergence* 202).

These are the procedures I've evoked as "The American Poetry Wax Museum." Poetry, not positionally (institutionally) constructed for the purposes of knowledge, is subject to intervention by administrative jurisdiction (or critical interpretation). Entertainment is administratively prose; that is, administered by licensed operators, colonial officials, custodians of what William Burroughs calls "the wad," or what in Rastafarian argot is "the shitstem."

13. Now, this has all been a detour to emphasize that "normal channels" are prose channels. Prose is the expedient medium of access to any information. Like Molière's Mr. Jourdain, we talk in prose without knowing it. We're inside prose; it's all around us. We engage specific genres in order to get a grip on this otherwise unmarked surrounding medium. And of course it's no surprise that the predominant media are prose—fiction, scripts, essays, journalism, history—all prose.

Poetry necessarily operates from inside prose—a fact well enough known by the mid–nineteenth century and the advent of the "prose poem." There's no getting out of prose. Bruno Latour has described how Pasteur successfully marketed his vaccination against the anthrax bacillus by making the "natural" environment of the barnyard into a sort of field version of his laboratory. If the conditions of the laboratory are adopted by farmers, the threat of anthrax can be monitored and controlled. This is how it is with prose; prose is, as it were, the hygienic laboratory that makes the whole world over in its own image. Prose can provide immunity from unwanted microparasites because it is itself the dominant macroparasite. Prose is the universal lab that simulates the literacy effect. So the issue is no longer one of genre, personal preference, talent, genius, any of that—all of which are performative, all which haplessly fall prey to the administrative judiciousness of prose. The issue, in other words, is not one of *writing.* The issue is *(w)reading.*

14. *Do you read me—over and out* (or *over and over*). "Read" in this sentence is an injunction to decode, cybernetically, a binary message; always

binary, it will say yes/no, past/present, in/out, male/female, nature/ culture, negative/positive, normal/deviant, manifest/latent, figure/ ground, passive/active, form/content. Simple alphabetic literacy accommodates methods for choosing between binary configurations like these.

I prefer to seek alliance with any practice of writing that refuses to treat binary elements or dual possibilities as injunctions to choose. So I hear Virginia Woolf's savoring of the "man womanly" and the "woman manly" in *A Room of One's Own* as a kindred perception (108). To abide with both elements of a seemingly incompatible equation is to enact a poetics. This is what I call (and spell) *wreading, or how poetics exceeds its poetry.* This is the writing we read toward. It is an increasingly threatened, unstable, dimly acknowledged respirator, this poem or other scrap of text that appears like the writing Woolf imagines written in chalk on the pavement and instantly rubbed out by the heedless crowds surging over it. How do we read such writing?—writing that comes to us already vanishing, already obsolete, lacking expedience as textbook, classic, masterpiece, map, skyline, history, brochure, or guided audio tour. How to read beyond the gastronomic literacy of any writing that can be predigested, suitable for *Reader's Digest.* How to read beyond Gastronomic Literacy Effects with their additives and preservatives, their trouble-free convenience packages—PSI Poetry and the enriched-flour vocabulary of opportunistic appraisal that attends it, with its litanies of "the poet" and "the poem," and always, trailing helplessly along behind, that native informant, "the self."

15. This has been the most auspicious place, this continent, to undertake such a wreading. From Emily Dickinson—if not from the earliest explorer's diaries—with her comprehension of just how ample the tight spaces inside words, between words, could be.

> Publication—is the Auction
> Of the Mind of Man—
> Poverty—be justifying
> For so foul a thing

Possibly—but We—would rather
From Our Garret go
White—Unto the White Creator—
Than invest—our Snow (#709)

—think of Stevens's snow man, compounding the nothing that is not there with the nothing that is.

To place the person in the text as a wreader is to endow the work with mobility—to take it up off that "unchanging piece of paper" by making the fictive certainty of the paper itself palpable, viable, active. To read is to experience time as strangeness itself, in which you come to reckon with the spatial mystery of a voiceless speech and a bodiless embodiment. "To not finally know whether I am reading or writing" (Coolidge, "From Notebooks" 180). As poets we largely devote our efforts to sculpting this space, this difference, into a habitat. A respiratory cavern, a shelter for wreading—with a "w." (Respiration is to wreading what inspiration is to writing.) Wallace Stevens is so compelling because his nearly exclusive concern is what it feels like to breathe, to stretch out, to fabulate in the sensorium of such environs as "the drowsy motion of the river R." It's not surprising that Stevens—as avatar of the supreme fiction—should be the favored poet in an academic milieu that has bitten off more than it could chew with deconstruction and its relentless (juggling-without-net) demonstrations of the fictive layering of all reality effects.[2]

What's alarming is the neglect of parallel homegrown strategies proposing to take up an active role in handling the fiction—the tradition that passes from Pound's ideograms through composition by field, Olson's proprioceptive "resistance" a heartbeat away from negative capability,

2. Deconstruction was displaced by other academic fixations soon after the above was written. Wallace Stevens's eminence, while it has not diminished, is no longer used to sanction anti-Pound (or Poundian) sentiment. Stevens's turns of phrase, however, continue to supply scholars with titles for books and articles, Michael Davidson's *Ghostlier Demarcations* (1997) being the most recent. The rotund sonorities, the prosodic opulence, of Stevens's lines have proven irresistible for authors looking for titles: *The Voice That Is Great Within Us; Part of Nature, Part of Us; The Rage to Order; Mythologies of Self; The Shaken Realist;* and *The Sovereign Ghost* are all quarried like marble from the Stevens Parthenon.

Kerouac's bop prosody, Rothenberg's symposium of the whole, Silliman's new sentence, and much more. What do we make of the conspira-
torial public ignorance of so ardent a legacy, this poetics that addresses
the artifice of absorption that surrounds us, dispelling the reality effects
and the literacy effects in order to grasp the fictive certainty that, as
Duncan put it, "the real has just those boundaries we are willing to
imagine"?—and further, that in the vacuous pressure cooker of the postmodern (the Baudrillardean snow blindness of hyperreal simulacra),
"The task now is to imagine the real" (Robert Jay Lifton). That, in fact,
the imagination has *real work* (à la Gary Snyder) to do.

16. Normal channels, prose channels, are the media of compliance. They
are the means by which the unknown audience consents to captivity by
testing positive to a numeracy syndrome, agreeing to a certain effacement in order to personally typify some statistical groundswell. In this
sense, to go native now means that the entire culture has surrendered to
its own colonization. The milk tin passed through ghetto walls is easy to
see, like Char's "Nazi abasement." More difficult to see—and this is the
necessary literacy, this recognition—is any act of real testimony in the
midst of so many testimonials (PSI documents of compliancy with canonical administrative procedures). What is it that distinguishes testimony from the testimonial? The difference is heralded in Peter Sloterdijk's complaint that "No one talks anymore of a *love* of wisdom. There
is no longer any knowledge whose friend (*philos*) one would be. It does
not occur to us to love the kind of knowledge we have" (xxvi). Testimony
is knowledge for which this has occurred, in which the eros of befriend-
ing what we know is intact, for as it's written in *Finnegans Wake,* "we ought
really to rest thankful that at this deleteful hour of dungflies dawning we
have even a written on with dried ink scrap of paper at all to show for
ourselves" (118).

6

Ethnopoetics and the Pathology of Modernism

What does it mean for a society to embrace, as its cultural *mythos,* a body of work that celebrates collapse, decay, attrition, and malaise? To pose the question is to evoke the *pathology of modernism.* Unless we're certain that modernism is in fact a lapsed moment suitable for enshrinement, we should enquire what it is in "modern," and "ism," that can clarify *language in pain*—the pathos of logos. Modernism has been our conceptual self-image for nearly a century. The stories that attest to the pedigree of modernism are as familiar as biblical commonplaces were to our ancestors. Our Noahs, Jacobs, Davids, Ruths, and Sauls go by other names: Picasso, Schoenberg, Eliot, Woolf, Wittgenstein. So prodigious is the web of modernist generations that it could easily rival the biblical genealogies, and all the names would still be familiar. This very familiarity, however, is a stigma; and the routinized tale of modernism—deploying the buzzwords *crisis, breakup, revolution, avant-garde*—excites a romantic nostalgia for confrontation between a righteous avant-garde and gullible philistines. Long before there were signs of scholarly revisionism, the salutary provocation of ethnopoetics was scratching a phantom itch on the canonically truncated body of modernism; and in doing so, ethnopoetics was dedicated to recovering a dormant pathic sensibility that preserves a more pressing sense of modernism than the mere recovery of forgotten writers.

Modernism remains indubitably *present* for us inasmuch as our cultural institutions are devoted to the display of modernist art and reciting the modernist story. The customary institutional recitation presents modernism as a compensatory mechanism, an outlet for social stress, hygienic release of fetid air. However, the rise of hegemonic disciplines in the humanities may be an institutional compensation for the aggravated assault of modernism. If modernism is the diagnostic term for a certain affliction, this is not unrelated to the fact that modernism was historically contemporaneous with the social division of intellectual labor. The professionalization of the humanities and social sciences was undertaken by members of the same generations that included Pablo Picasso, Igor Stravinsky, Ernest Hemingway, and a proverbial cast of thousands. The demarcation of fields of study in academia is precisely parallel to the erosion of classical aesthetics and concomitant "breakup" of the arts.

The first-person plural that has laid claim to modernism has submerged and anaesthetized it in "a weird ether of forgotten dismemberments" (Ashbery, *Houseboat Days* 6), a catalogue of sturdy masterpieces certifying modernism as "our" culture; *our* being precisely a canonical prerogative. But a truly historicized and pluralized modernism—taking race, gender and class into account, as well as the international creolization of cultural idioms outside the urban centers of official modernism —bears little resemblance to what the voice-over has been telling us all along.[1] Belated recognition of the "ethnographic surrealism" of Michel Leiris; the renegade Russian Cubo-Futurist, primitivist utopian Velimir Khlebnikov; the multifaceted and unaffiliated black American writer Zora Neale Hurston; the lesbian cenacle of Nathalie Barney in Paris; not to mention the group of immigrant poets of New York writing in Yiddish,

---

1. The most succinct and sobering assessment is by Cary Nelson: "we have forgotten that the restricted and depoliticized canon of modernism is effectively our discipline's testimony before HUAC" (68). There is now a veritable tide of scholarship amounting to an institutional prescription for corrective lenses. The founding of the journal *Modernism/Modernity* and the establishment of the Modernist Studies Association reflect this decisive transformation.

indicate how provocative and unresolved modernism really is as a site in which competing claims of cultural authority have been staged. As soon as we concede the implausibility of any totalizing narrative, modernism can be recognized as a diaspora. Ethnopoetics provides an opportunity to regain an essential *incoherence* of modernism, to reappraise it in light of its fragility, its fugitive testimonials, and its carnally jubilant incantations.

This requires that we recognize in modernism not some passé revolt in aesthetics, but a continuing cultural practice akin to what Michel de Certeau calls heterology or heteronomy. "Heteronomy is at the same time the stimulus and what is inadmissible. It is a wound in rationalism" (*Heterologies* 177). Out of this wound in rationalism pour a host of phantom sensations attesting to mutilation. Peter Sloterdijk refers to a "Zeitschmerz," a temporal pain, gaping from exposed wounds (xxxvi). To those "open wounds" designated by Sloterdijk (Nietzsche, Freud, Adorno, Heidegger) we could add many others (Bataille, Pound, Loy, Celan), but the point is not to establish a list of alternatives to the status quo, nor to canonize (as in a surgical theater) the gaping wounds of modernism, for that would simply reinforce the customary interpretive procedures that *handle* cries of anguish as so much raw material for a thematic exhibition, arranging awesomely lifelike figures in a wax museum tableau.

Liberation theologist Enrique Dussel elucidates the cost of canonical ambitions: "modern European philosophy, even before the *ego cogito* but certainly from then on, situated all men and all cultures—and with them their women and children—within its own boundaries as manipulable tools, instruments. Ontology understood them as interpretable beings, as known ideas, as mediations of internal possibilities within the horizon of the comprehension of Being" (3). In Dussel's account, Eurocentric history is itself a canonical mode of production that hierarchically disposes humans from top to bottom and center to periphery, distinguishing those empowered to speak from those bereft of speech. Ironically, canonical figures are certifiably mute by virtue of having spoken "for us all." They can no longer speak for (or defend) themselves, as the force of their signification is redirected toward a central chronicle, a supreme fiction. "Being is," Dussel asserts, whereas "beings are what are seen and controlled" (6). In an even more pithy formulation he writes that "Before the *ego cogito* there is an *ego conquiro*" (3)—to which we can append Aimé Césaire's "Vomito Negro" to accentuate what it is to have one's peripheralized existence consist of bilious retchings, redemptive only insofar as they affirm the centrality of the empire of Being. Yet, through the pellucid medium of ethnopoetic modernism—in which all voices bear the reproach of those refusing disembodiment—Césaire can partake of tropic sagacities even alongside the canonical eminence (and tropical slumming) of Wallace Stevens, affirming contingency and defilement as actual locations of life:

> The imperfect is our paradise.
> Note that, in this bitterness, delight,
> Since the imperfect is so hot in us,
> Lies in flawed words and stubborn sounds.
> (*Palm at the End of the Mind* 158)

Stevens's delight in flawed words and stubborn sounds strives toward William Carlos Williams's reckoning that "Only the poem / only the made poem, to get said what must / be said . . . sticks / in our throats" (*Collected Poems* 274). In Emerson's estimation of what sticks: "Every word was once a poem. Every new relation is a new word. Also, we use defects and deformities to a sacred purpose, so expressing our sense that the evils of the world are such only to the evil eye. In the old mythology, mythologists observe, defects are ascribed to divine natures, as lameness to Vulcan, blindness to Cupid, and the like, to signify exuberances" (455). The imperative of such exuberance: to stand in front of Raphael's Madonna in the Sistine Chapel and recover its ugliness as Gertrude Stein suggested (Jameson, *Ideologies* 180). This is an exemplary modernist aspiration. At the same time, it's difficult to conceive of a more pertinent characterization of modernism than as an attempt to reclaim in mythology a "use of defects and deformities to a sacred purpose," as

Emerson put it. What else is enacted in "Bambla Jolifanta"—Hugo Ball's celebrated Dada sound poem—but a deformity made to *signify exuberances*?

In the canonical order, by contrast, the authors become prosthetic supplements subordinate to a kind of social register of the arts, or "representative samples" of raw material, the experimental possibilities of which are consigned to the lab. "Eliot" and "Woolf" become brand names in a recipe; and their own proper names are attended by the perennial quotation-mark flutter mouthing its prosthetic appropriations. But why restrict citation to the evidentiary status of a court of law? What else is the judicious use of citation but a *controlled frenzy* of gratitude at finding something worth recycling? Our scholarly modes of address are inaugurated and sustained by a principle of aphorism. We don't reprint our sources at great length, verbatim, as in antiquity. We dismember them in an alert arousal of physiographic attentiveness, then serve them up in pieces. These pieces are aphorisms, or made into aphorisms by abridgment. "Aphorism is exaggeration, or grotesque," writes Norman O. Brown (*Love's Body* 187). "Only the exaggerations are true," he adds, affirming Emerson's dictum that "Exaggeration is in the course of things. Nature sends no creature, no man into the world, without adding a small excess of his proper quality . . . a slight generosity, a drop too much" (Emerson 549). By means of selective quotation we labor at a piecemeal truth, preserving bits of prior texts as homeopathic doses administered to our own work. Carving a text like meat into a pretext serves to heighten the veracity of each piece, swelling it into imaginative consequence. In cultural matters, the canon serves to conceal or deflect the carnal aspect of citation as a culinary medium, foreclosing on its carnivalesque potential. Because so much writing—whether scholastic, journalistic, or even creative—enacts a pretense of thought without passion, images without imagination, evaluation without values, and perception without embodiment, we can extract a redolent principle: a discourse that does not signify or clothe its exuberances does not admit its flaws and deformities. By refusing to admit imperfection as part of its body, the supposition of perfection and certainty expels it; once expelled, the deformity forms an encompassing environment, a container within which the entire exposition proceeds in the confidence that the flaw or limp or stutter or scar is no longer part of itself and therefore no longer relevant. The scar is thereby swollen like a balloon, forming a skin around a discourse that pretends to have no skin in order to deny its scar. It hides its exuberances in the vocabulary of assessment, evaluation—the calculus of the reasonable, seeking clandestine gains behind a mask of neutered objectivity.

The preceding account might serve as allegory of the career of the term "modernism." It certainly applies to the Cold War neutralization of the modernist avant-garde (cf. Rasula, *American Poetry Wax Museum,* ch. 2). But in this instance it's a way of drawing attention to ethnopoetics, a decidedly exuberant discourse on modernism that has never had any trouble declaring its deformities. Ethnopoetics has retained an agonistic stance from the outset. It began as Jerome Rothenberg's partisan attempt to draw attention to certain registers of cross-cultural performance and poetic practice, and it has shown no danger of being recuperated to institutional compliance. There have been two ethnopoetics conferences— at the University of Wisconsin in Milwaukee (1975) and the University of Southern California (1983)—both of them notable for the open contestation, on the part of the participants, of the goals and prospects of ethnopoetics. The conferences assembled disbelievers and opponents in proportion equal to (maybe even exceeding) adherents. Energizing and often fractious disputes were the order of the day. It is equally characteristic that *Technicians of the Sacred,* Rothenberg's anthology that constituted a founding document of ethnopoetics has retained its *agon* through two editions. *Technicians of the Sacred* is unique among compilations of world poetry because of its insistence on the primacy of the poetics of its own (rather than its source) language. The initial aim of 1968—dramatically reinforced in the second edition, 1985—was unwavering: to demonstrate by concrete example that the modern poet's quest for the sacred paralleled quests in other societies, and further, that the "techniques of ecstasy," *being* technical, could constitute a poetics.

In *Symposium of the Whole,* Rothenberg (with wife, Diane) writes, "It is our contention . . . that the most experimental and future-directed side of Romantic and modern poetry, both in the Western world and increasingly outside it, has been the most significantly connected with the attempt to define an ethnopoetics" (xii). One might imagine the initiating impulse for *Technicians* in Rothenberg's recognition of a similarity between the clipped lines of a Creeley poem and the nineteenth-century anthropologist Frances Densmore's method of translating Sioux chants such that each English line represented a single word (often multifaceted, compound) of the original. I don't know whether this was an actual provocation, but it's indicative of Rothenberg's polymathic and transcultural orientation. He notes, for instance, that pidgins and creoles were classed as "marginal languages" and maintains that "this 'marginality' may bring them closer to the languages of our own poetries" (*Technicians* 608). He also cites Bakhtin's attraction to Rabelais's work with its "undestroyable unofficial nature" (602). The concern in both instances is to stress the marginality of the "primitive" as well as the contemporary poet, and to suggest that their margins are mutual.

The originality of *Technicians* is clear enough, but there *are* precedents, and rather than gloss over the traces, Rothenberg makes a show of hailing his "forefathers." Primary among these is Tristan Tzara, hero of much of Rothenberg's poetry (e.g. "That Dada Strain"), but also an early compiler of tribal poetry in *Poèmes nègres* (albeit not published in his lifetime). Blaise Cendrars put together an *Anthologie nègre* (1921), setting a precedent for the 1958 French collection edited by Roger Caillois and Jean-Clarrence Lambert, *Trésor de la poèsie universelle,* which led, in turn, to Willard Trask's two-volume English compendium, *The Unwritten Song,* in the 1960s. C. M. Bowra's *Primitive Song* was another provocation, as were the riches buried away in the nineteenth-century reports of the Bureau of American Ethnology. It was this path, more than any other, that led Rothenberg to the anthropologists, from Paul Radin and Bronislaw Malinowski to his own contemporaries Stanley Diamond, Victor Turner, and others. The one remaining—and crucial—element in the background that spurred Rothenberg's interest in non-Western poetries came directly from the American modernist line from Pound to Olson and Duncan.[2]

---

2. The editorial affiliations are so abundantly in evidence throughout the commentaries that anyone leafing through that section of *Technicians* is bound to be struck by the blatant

Rothenberg cites the case of Australian aborigines who borrow entire poems verbatim from languages unknown to them, to be used for performance—performance *as* interaction with sheer alterity. The texts in *Technician* are not divested of their contexts as thoroughly as this, by any means. But in general, texts taken down in print from oral performance are prone to perversion and betrayal by misguided ideologies of "the text," "the primitive," and so forth. Rothenberg's own decision to group his selected texts in one location without any contextualization at all (other than place of origin) emphasizes his Western aesthetic orientation with its bias toward artistic autonomy and purity.

Consider the Seri "Song of the Winds" (226):

Another mouth is smooth and slippery
and hard, like ice.
He stands erect with his arms outstretched
and from each finger there comes a wind.

---

partisanship. A smattering of foreign poets is invoked, decidedly modernist (Antonin Artaud, Aimé Césaire, Pablo Neruda, André Breton, Vicente Huidobro, Tristan Tzara, Hugo Ball). The American poets proffered as amplification of Rothenberg's tribal poetries constitute the main push, and evoke sectarian affiliations of their own: McClure, Mac Low, Antin, Schwerner, Pound, Whitman, Ginsberg, Snyder, Waldman, Wakoski, Sanders, Baraka, Duncan, Creeley, Oppen, Blackburn, and Levertov are all represented by complete poems or very substantial citations. The American poets' works are generally put to good and accurate use in the commentaries, so the specific list of names shouldn't be troubling, reflecting as it does the editor's affiliations with poets of his own generation. Rothenberg might be charged with practicing the same sort of ethnocentric raids on "primitivism" as his modernist predecessors; but I think the deployment of his peers in *Technicians* served just the opposite cause, putting on display the generational predisposition of certain American poets as the necessary ground in which any ostensible "recovery" might occur. By refusing the mantle of objectivity, Rothenberg energized poetry as a different sort of *evidence* altogether.

As it turned out, some of the American poetry was cut in the second edition, which benefits most particularly from much bolstering of the actual ethnological content, both in the text and in the commentaries. Between the first and second editions, Rothenberg was able to work extensively with a number of poet-translators trained in ethnography, including Dennis Tedlock, Howard Norman, David Guss, Judith Gleason, A. K. Ramanujan, Ulli Beier, Kofi Awoonor, and David McAllester. Valuable as the attention to contemporary poets' work in the commentaries was, the lasting achievement is Rothenberg's felicitous use of ethnographic data to amass a veritable *ars poetica.*

First he blows the White Wind
then he blows the Red Wind
then he blows the Blue Wind.
And from his little finger
he blows the Black Wind,
which is stronger than them all.

The White Wind comes from the north
and is very hot.

This happens to be one of the instances in which the book's Commentaries offer nothing about the context. For all I know, in Seri culture these colors may be primary figures of some cosmological configuration of order and disorder, or good and evil. In this case, as in many others, the tacit intent of *Technicians* is to demonstrate the play of language in the quest for the sacred; we are invited to read "Song of the Winds" for its verbal felicities, its atmospheric charm, not as anthropological evidence. Curiously, then, it is in the Commentaries that the sense of creative flux is most vigorously preserved, as if the contending voices from disparate cultures—arguing about the magic and power of words—were still vociferously making their claims, while the poems by themselves tend to recede into anonymity (and, worse, uniformity). The nearly two hundred pages of Commentaries clamor for attention, constituting a full third of the book; as such, it's the size of many entire volumes of poetics. These are not idle notes, but the real substance of *Technicians of the Sacred*.

The Commentaries offer some guidance to the ethnographic contours informing the poems, as well as the relevance of contemporary poetry to the issues that arise. The inevitable point of reference is shamanism. Rothenberg says of the shaman that his "techniques-of-the-sacred made him, more than the modern poet, supreme physician and custodian of the soul" (491). He emphasizes the affinity of shamanism with Rimbaud's "systematic derangement of the senses," but adds, significantly, that this derangement is "not for its own sake but toward the possibility of sight & order" (487). This is an essential discrimination, because the spice of Rimbaud's pronouncement—repeated again and again by subsequent poets—is its overt antagonism to society, whereas in any culture employing shamanism a systematic derangement of the senses is explicitly socialized, directed toward the good of the community.

The point of engagement thus invoked is, for poets, nothing other than language, the code of signals, the fabric of signification. There is a direct analogy between the code (body or text) broken or violated—again, systematic derangement—within a context of utility and comprehensibility. Rothenberg's concept of "total translation" attends not only to semantics, but also to "word distortions, meaningless syllables, music, style of performance, etc." (551). In tribal societies visionary experience is often pursued by the use of language as innate psychosomatic hallucinogen. The hunt for peyote by Mexico's Huichol Indians makes it explicit; there, the journey to the high desert in search of the psychotropic substance is accompanied by a mutation of all speech functions into their opposites, so that a deer may be called a cat, something beautiful spoken of as ugly, and coming really means going. "Through language, then, as much as peyote, the shaman changes the desert into a flowering world" (554). This is one instance among a great many cited in Rothenberg's Commentaries exemplifying the "law of metamorphosis in thought & word" (544), which is as central to tribal cultures as it is to the poetics of Pound, Césaire, the Surrealists, and others.

Language usage, vitally energized, collapses the distinction between natural and social order. For the Dogon of West Africa, "humans speak a 'language' which is at the same time the elementary substance of which the earth is made. This perception of a 'universe where each blade of grass, each little fly is a carrier of a word' . . . is the expression of a genuine poetics" (534). For the Baiga of India, "An image of an object is regarded not only as vivid in itself but as capable of the most powerful associations with other images. The object can, as it were, exist not only as itself but also as the other objects which it resembles" (578). Much to the point here is the recent push in American poetry to recognize in language itself a domain of attachments and associations energized as self-inhering and not strictly subordinate to referential function.

Despite the instrumental role Rothenberg played in putting poets in touch with one another who would constitute the primary figures in language poetry (attested to by Ron Silliman in his introduction to *In the American Tree*), his own orientation has been oral and oracular in the Olsonian sense. So the poetics of the Netsilik Eskimos, for instance, come to seem a vital clarification of projective verse:

> Orpingalik . . . called this song "my breath" because (he said) "it is just as necessary for me to sing as it is to breathe." (The Netsilik word *anerca* is used in fact to mean both "breath" & "poetry.") The breath, which is all the more visible where he came from (in the language of the Netsilik shamans, e.g., a living person is "someone smoke surrounds"), becomes the physical projection of the process of thought, etc., that goes on inside a man. Orpingalik's extraordinary definition of poetry—"songs are thoughts sung out with the breath" . . . describes an order of composition something like "projective verse." (*Technicians* 563)

The traces of projective verse are further amplified by an observation on the implied poetics of the *I Ching:* "Thought of this kind, when applied to the field-of-the-poem, defines that field both in primitive/archaic & in much modern poetry: that whatever falls within the same space determines the meaning of that space" (567). As a single concise statement of a functional poetics, this is as broadly applicable as any we're likely to see. It fits Pound's *Cantos,* Robert Duncan's "Passages," Robert Grenier's *Cambridge M'ass,* and Susan Howe's *Singularities* equally well.

As Norman O. Brown sagely claims, "There is no breakthrough without breakage. A struggle with an angel, which leaves us scarred, or lame" (*Love's Body* 185–86). I have tried to indicate something of the impediments that disclose the breakthrough implicit in Rothenberg's assimilation of tribal poetries into an American poetics following (not "post-") modernism. Rather than assault the prevailing literary institutions directly, Rothenberg has cunningly sought to import so much from outside that the inside would end up outside as well, all dancing in concord in "a place of first permission" (Duncan 7). Or, in another phrase by Duncan that Rothenberg favors, a "symposium of the whole." Yet, confronting this impossible ambition, Rothenberg has remained acutely aware of the provisionality of every effort, less concerned to achieve "the whole" than to muster a symposium in the old platonic (erotic) sense: a banquet of aspirations. His revisionary work, always challenging the old canon, has sought not to replace it with another one, but to overcome its drone with carnival heckles, so that not only "a new past was . . . being fashioned in the process [but] many new pasts" (*Poems for the Millennium* 2). The whole is not an apparitional epiphenomenon of putative parts, but a craving akin to the enigmatic sexuality of children, Rilke noted (76). Rothenberg (and Joris, as coeditor of the two-volume *Poems for the Millennium*, Rothenberg's most explicit attempt to remap modernist poetry) would probably concur with Heather McHugh's insistence that "poetry is not exposition. It *is* the place that suffers inscription. It bears the mark or scar of what was seen and what was grasped" (2).[3]

In attending to all the open sores of mutilation, the disturbing mutter of words, the interjected *mu* that Jane Ellen Harrison proposed as the performative matrix germinating myths (*muthos*),[4] do canonical labors matter?

> These are the old tasks.
> You've heard them before.

---

3. Further, "All poetry is fragment: it is shaped by its breakages, at every turn. It is the very art of turnings, toward the white frame of the page, toward the unsung, toward the vacancy made visible, that wordlessness in which our words are couched" (McHugh 75). To this might be added the following from Louise Glück: "It seems to me that what is wanted, in art, is to harness the power of the unfinished. All earthly experience is partial. Not simply because it is subjective, but because that which we do not know, of the universe, of mortality, is so much more vast than that which we do know. What is unfinished or has been destroyed participates in these mysteries. The problem is to make a whole that does not forfeit this power" (74).

4. "Possibly the first *mūthos* was simply the interjectional utterance *mū;* but it is easy to see how rapid the development would be from interjection to narrative. Each step in the ritual action is shadowed as it were by a fresh interjection, till the whole combines into a consecutive tale" (Harrison 330).

> They must be impossible.   Psyche
> must despair, be brought to her
>
> > insect instructor
> > (Duncan 65)

To recover modernism is to suffer a plague of insect instructors, the blizzard of details that blur and finally erase the fallacious image of a completed project held too long. To really recover modernism is to help modernism *recover,* like waking up after a stupor; and it deserves as accompanying apparition a singularly noncanonical tale (told only once in antiquity, by Apuleius) of the carnal relations of Eros and Psyche, a tale telling us that the mind is a beautiful girl and the body a beautiful boy, and that together they partake of a romance in their discovery that they are truly made for each other.

Eros and Psyche are figures struggling to awaken to their life together, and this struggle entails nothing less than a rift in the canonical order of Parnassus. In the end, despite trial and torment, mutilation and affliction, Eros and Psyche are permitted to live together without having to bear the burden of canonical offspring. Their mating makes a gift to mortals, instead, named Voluptas. It's a story bearing an insight relevant to exuberant flesh: beneath the institutional agon of concept, system, and wager, there is a sedimentation of erotic trust in which whatever we would know agitates us physically, arousing need, stirring desire. Psyche's knowledge of her lover is constrained by the stricture of darkness; blindly, she is immersed in the delights of love felt as phantom sensations. She scalds Eros when she reduces her knowledge to single vision like Newton's sleep, wanting verification of his identity. It's a familiar story: seeking confirmation of ourselves in our amours, it is the body, the erotic body of knowing feelings, that is most elusive. This is why *names* are more eligible components of canonical order than actual living, intrusively volatile, bodies.

In fact, the body is unimaginable. This is what I take Philippe Sollers to mean when he says, "The body is what the idea of 'man' does not manage to destroy. . . . The body is that in us that is always 'more' than us, that kills its own representation in us and kills us silently" (116). To actually recognize the body in a nonobjectifying way is to experience imaginative fatigue. The body is an *encompassing fiction*—fictive, not false; which is to say, unimaginable. The unimaginable makes sense only with reference to what can be imagined. This holds true for imagining the body; it is a thoroughly organic and inescapable continuity attesting to a continual lapse of imagination on my part, insofar as I am literally unable to conceive of the bodily totality that I in fact *am*. My body, acknowledged as living companion to all my certainties and uncertainties, perennially awaits my return—as if I had ever left. One comes back to the Ithaca (or "Bloom Cottage . . . Flowerville" [Joyce, *Ulysses* 698]) of the body as a homecoming, in which it takes a prodigious feat of imagination to render the facts of duration and continuity palpable. And when the return is made, it is never syllogistic or rhetorical skill that compels the recognition scene, but a flaw or scar that testifies, beyond any doubt, to the veracity of incarnation.

7

Every Day Another Vanguard

"Every day is avant-garde."
Adja Yunkers in Marek Bartelik, *To Invent a Garden*

How do we balance the exceptional, held up as a value, with the norm, especially when the normative seems compromised by statistical mediocrity? What is the relationship between individual volition and the collective when norms are byproducts of mass media? These two questions are facets of a single problem that periodically erupts in American culture—the mood swing that oscillates between high and low, intelligence and stupidity, exaggerated respect for the unique combined with routine embrace of the mundane.[1] The coupling of such apparently opposing terms has been a feature of American art from Whitman to Warhol, with the balance tending against elitism and in favor of—what, exactly? Populism? Which one? Among many, there is the Depression-era populism of the left; a youth-oriented populism of Beat culture and sixties counterculture; and, most notably in the long-range perspective, the populism associated with ethnicity, a singular legacy of which is African American music. But even jazz had its avant-garde—first in the musical secession of bebop complexity, and later brandished in the titles of such

---

1. For a useful discussion of the precarious role of intellect in poetry, see Kevin McGuirk, "Poetry and 'Stupidity': Beats to L=A=N=G=U=A=G=E."

albums as *Looking Ahead* (Cecil Taylor); *Tomorrow Is the Question* (Ornette Coleman); *One Step Beyond* (Jackie McLean); or, unabashedly, *The Avant-Garde* (John Coltrane and Don Cherry). Apart from the Black Arts Movement, the avant-garde has rarely been linked to populism, even when (as in the case of Dada) it's been resolutely anti-elitist. In an American context, despite cultural institutions like the Museum of Modern Art that have served as authoritative agencies of assimilation, "avant-garde" has non-American connotations. The American intelligentsia, trained simultaneously by high culture and mass media, operates with a conflicted sense of allegiance; and, in turn, any residual model of avant-garde bifurcates into incommensurable occasions.[2] Finally, the vanguard is not an elective position, but a zone of intersecting recognitions, a zone that accommodates Elvis Presley as readily as Jackson Pollock—a zone, that is, nearly indistinguishable from fashion. And what kind of avant-garde is *that*?

BURNING OFF DISCURSIVE TOXINS

A provocative primer in considering this dilemma is Paul Mann's *The Theory-Death of the Avant-Garde*. At a mere 145 pages, it appears to be a book of exceptional concision; but appearances are deceptive, since it's written in a holographic manner in which the theses are distributed uniformly throughout the text, the whole book replicated in miniature in each primary unit. On occasion, Mann refers to his method as anamorphic (12, 51), which is not incompatible with a holographic approach. By "anamorphic" he means a reading that grotesquely accentuates one site (the avant-garde) in order to make legible a broader phenomenon, which is the containment of dissidence. The advantage of this anamorphic/holographic approach is its redundancy in the information-

---

2. These occasions are exacerbated by conflicting signals in an American cultural milieu permeated by commercialism. The challenge, as Charles Altieri describes it: "in order not to be identified with 'mere' modernist aestheticism, contemporary aspirants to avant-garde status have to stress their social agendas, yet they cannot pursue those social agendas as directly as did the early avant-garde because in our culture, shock value is clearly a force manipulated by the established economy" (632).

theoretic sense; it is coded to survive the noise of inattention and distraction. What appears in one section will be reiterated (in a different anamorphic staging) in another. It runs the risk of redundancy, of course, in that the reader may well feel inclined to desist when the method of recycling is recognized. But Mann has not cynically provided more than is necessary to pander to the slow learner. The method is intrinsic to the thesis in a way that may not become apparent until the end. The "theory-death" of the title has been rehearsed continuously since the inception of the avant-garde, in Mann's view, and he in turn rehearses this point in the participatory symmetry of a repetition compulsion. It is a book that replicates its thesis in act as well as argument; its writing is congruent with the diagnosis it offers. I have put off indicating what the thesis is, because it will seem distractingly brief, and absurdly familiar (its unoriginality affirming Rosalind Krauss's thesis in "The Originality of the Avant-Garde" that the vanguard dream of originality is always compromised by the power of simulacra). The ultimate implication of holographic method is that the whole book may be derived from a single proposition. Fittingly, the candidates that exemplify the proposition are legion (every reader will mark different salient assertions, but all readers will arrive at the same location). My choice reflects my particular appetite for metaphor: "in culture every exit is a revolving door" (107).

"The avant-garde is not the victim of recuperation but its agent, its proper technology," Mann begins a chapter titled "The Germ of Consent," adding, "this formula . . . has begun to take on a sort of banner tone here, as if it were already reaching out of the text to inscribe itself on a dust jacket" (92). Here, as throughout, he is alert to the potential of germinating a concession in his own text, consenting to the inevitability of recuperation. Dangerously close to having written the last word on the avant-garde, Mann is distressed by his awareness that even the last word is a point of departure for a renewed series of comments, a soap or sitcom of the ongoing saga of "the death of the avant-garde" perpetually reinscribed in each new theory; the vanguard floating in a preservative solution as in a pathology exhibit, in "a state of discursive supersaturation in which advanced art comes to exist only in a kind of suspended animation," and this discourse is itself "lost in hypnotic fixation on images of its own containment" (33).[3] The arrested gaze is most likely that of the media junkie, in whom the hominid legacy of hand-eye coordination has culminated in the digital manipulation of remote control buttons, feasting on the televisual menu of appetites engineered in advance of any primal desire. The vanguard, Mann seems to suggest, is an unwitting (and at times witless) subcontractor in the construction site of new technologies of containment. "The avant-garde is *launched* by the bourgeoisie and is locked in a decaying orbit around it"; "to be avant-garde is already to be bourgeois precisely by one's commitment to innovation"; "the contradiction encompassed by resistance and accommodation [is] the avant-garde's most basic structure and driving force" (81, 68, 9).

Mann's treatment of the avant-garde as a technology finds a useful corollary in Paul Virilio's suggestion that beside every museum of industry there should be a museum of accidents (33). The guidebook for such museums (which would also gratify the vanguard compulsion to fetishize difference) could be *The Atrocity Exhibition* by J. G. Ballard. This would reinforce the view that technology *is* pathology—with Jayne Mansfield's severed head and JFK's brain as metonymically salient icons of the auto industry—while also accentuating Mann's basic preoccupation: "The avant-garde's historical agony is grounded in the brutal paradox of an opposition that sustains what it opposes precisely by opposing it" (11). The vocabulary of ritual violence speaks to the paradox that vanguard aggression is outfoxed by rival brutalities. But there is a further outrage. After 150 years of bourgeois repossession of the vehicles of the avant-garde, one has to wonder to what extent this has rendered art complicit, and whether the avant-garde is a vanguard in name only, "a processed opposition" (86). Citing Burroughs's dictum that the most successful police state needs no police, Mann wearily concedes: "For us, the avant-garde is its avant-guardian" (76). The traditional bourgeois recuperation

3. This prognosis may be applicable as well to the saga of deconstruction, particularly during the brief exhilaration that it bore in its wake at Yale—as in Geoffrey Hartman's euphoric proclamations that the artificial membrane separating theory from literature had dissolved, and that an egalitarian array of commentaries was all that the eye could see in every direction. The site of this Bastille rhetoric has since shifted to hypertext and the Internet.

of the avant-garde has become a mode of production, a "precuperation" (140).

At this point it's best to review Mann's thesis in terms of its nomenclature: recuperation, resistance, and colonization. RECUPERATION: "Recuperation is the syntax of cultural discourse, its elementary propositional form. It is the spectacle of the internalization of margins, the revelation of the effective complicity of opposition" (15). This is the elementary form of a double bind vexing the traditional avant-garde, giving rise to a corollary thesis on RESISTANCE: "The avant-garde is . . . the official narrative of the futility of resistance, the futility of the anti itself" (88). Or, in Gregory Lukow's formulation: " 'Dissent no longer needs to be neutralized. It is part of the act of submission' " (*Theory-Death* 118). In the Derridean phrase that probably has broader application than any other, the "anti" is *always already* recuperated to the "pro"; the dialectic makes it so. "[T]o act against bourgeois culture on any level is also to act in its name [because it is] a dialectical system that relies on internal oppositions in order to sustain and advance itself. Modern culture can only progress by a kind of internalized violence; it must continually attack itself in order to survive and prosper" (11). The precise term for this is *endocolonization,* exemplified in collage, which "juxtaposes fragmented and discontinuous signs in order to develop a syntax for normalizing their contradictions," and is thus by analogy "a program for encoding the marginal without eliminating its utility as margin" (106). As for COLONIZATION:

> The avant-garde colonizes the extra-aesthetic, the extra-cultural, the extradiscursive; as always, advanced art is not only recuperated but is itself a recuperative function. An internalized exterior: precisely the figure of the colony.
>
> The end of the avant-garde is the reorganization of cultural space. The culture industry uses its vanguard to remap the foreign as a margin, a site comprehensible only in relation to itself. (78–79)

By this route Mann discerns—but fails to pursue—the real force of the military thinking from which the term "avant-garde" derives.

In *Pure War,* Paul Virilio argues that a congenital underdevelopment of a nation's resources is the direct consequence of a perpetual escalation of the stakes of "preparedness" for war (92–95). Mann appears not to have included Virilio in his conceptual lexicon;[4] nor does Virilio, for that matter, concern himself with the avant-garde; but to link the avant-garde with colonial depredations, as Mann does, is implicitly to trace an isomorphic resonance between artistic and military vanguards. We might fruitfully consider, for instance, that symbiotic juncture of 1848, when the incipient vanguard (in the person of Baudelaire) takes to the streets in civil discord. The rites of a coercive nationalism, undertaken in a spirit of postrevolutionary paranoia, consolidate the bourgeoisie, which in turn becomes chief target of artistic insolence (or its variant, aesthetic disavowal of worldliness). A more fully historicized thesis than Mann attempts might consider the bourgeoisie not simply as an emergent socioeconomic class enfranchised shortly before the avant-garde arose to protest its ascendancy, but rather as that class consolidated by nation-states mobilizing for "pure war." Such a thesis would have to study the early penetration of the armaments industry into modes of industrial production; and it would be imperative to recognize that "industry" has been virtually synonymous with militarization. This would compel recognition that the continuity of the avant-garde may well be dependent on a continuum of historical dominants, a series of wars: 1870, 1914, 1935, 1939, 1964, and 1991. The avant-garde, in this light, would be a *mutinous* revolt; but the source of the mutiny might arise from a premonition of

4. The (unmentioned) Ur-text for Mann's work is "The Invasion of the Body Snatchers." As theoretical provenance, Foucault's concept of regulatory discourse is discernable; Adorno is a sort of silent partner (elucidating the complicity of revolutionary ideology in the art world with capitalist economies); but the official patron is Baudrillard. Baudrillard is not much cited (Mann has resisted his epigrammatic style almost completely), but those familiar with Baudrillard's work will see him lurking just below the surface throughout. In the end this tactic functions as an implicit critique, since the relatively constrained application of Baudrillard to the avant-garde reveals by contrast the futility that often accompanies a reading of Baudrillard himself, as if he were needlessly disposed to generalize his fastidious observation of particulars (as in the books on America) into amorphous theses about "hyperreality," "seduction," and "the simulacrum."

the civilian populace unwittingly recruited (in an ongoing lifelong draft) for military ends.

The preceding fantasy of another book to stand in the place of *The Theory-Death of the Avant-Garde* is just that, a fantasy. It is also an honorary gesture, since Mann's own fantasia is what provoked it. What remains to be considered is the liability (and the potential gain) of a procedure that resists historicizing the avant-garde. Mann glosses over the distinctions between several terms: "bourgeois," "culture industry," "cultural discourse," and "capitalism" (all of which are at times subsumed into his own variant, "the white economy"). This blurring has the cumulative effect of suggesting a broader application of his thesis than is warranted by the relatively confined scope of the historical avant-garde. Such a thesis finds in the vanguard a synecdoche for any form of disgruntlement, unrest, disavowal, transgression, subversion, or opposition. Mann's dilemma is that of the intelligentsia in general: what to do with one's vigilance. He sees the discursive proliferation of subject positions, of stakes in arguments, as an insect swarm, a pestilence of subintelligent compliance with a totalizing system of staged oppositions. "How can one avoid being nothing more than an ideological drone of some pro or some con, or what is probably worse, of some illusion of autonomy from them?" (18). From this perspective, to take a particular stand (compliance or resistance, inside or outside, etc.) is to nestle into that position as a security blanket, a consoling sanctuary, a "saving illusion" in Joseph Conrad's sense. Is Mann, then, merely replaying the ultimate high cultural modernist gambit, seeking shelter from the storm of rank particulars?

By generalizing an unhistoricized avant-garde, Mann effectively conflates it with late capitalism as such; yet, because he often speaks pointedly to the struggles of the historical avant-garde, we are invited to fudge terminological contours and, in effect, think of even nineteenth-century moments as episodes in late capitalism. Of course, if mercantile economies of the late Middle Ages are seen as a nascent form of capitalism, then capitalism is clearly "late" by the time of the industrial revolution. In any case, it's impossible to surmise from Mann's text what thesis of the rise of capitalism he subscribes to. The same is true for "culture industry," a concept associated with Theodor Adorno and Max Horkheimer but that Mann applies without rigorous adherence to their precepts. Possibly Mann is an adherent of Samuel Johnson's credo about numbering the streaks of the tulip; and maybe he would avow the cogency of Melville's question in "Billy Budd": "Who in the rainbow can draw the line where the violet tint ends and the orange tint begins? Distinctly we see the difference of the colors, but where exactly does the one first blendingly enter into the other?" (1407). What is forfeited by Mann's procedure is the faculty of rainbow discriminations. However, the unyielding insistence on generalities, along with the holographic form of exposition, suggests that Mann is sensitive to Melville's question and has deliberately pursued a dehistoricized thesis.

Why, then, does Mann discuss the avant-garde in such broad strokes? The answer (implicit in his title) is that *the* (historical) avant-garde is not his topic at all. This book is finally a critique of criticism, of discourse, of theory's stage management of a chimera, "the avant-garde," as a "theory-death." "The death of the avant-garde," then, "is the n-state of the recuperation of its critical potential by a narrative of failure" (40). Discourse is regenerated by each petit mal, each microexpiration of vanguard opposition, each minute reminder of the failure of the revolution. To say that the avant-garde is the agent of recuperation, "its proper technology," turns out not to mean that the avant-garde *is* the recuperation as such, since what's really being recuperated is an anemic state of discourse that requires the avant-garde in the same way television networks need audience-boosting programs for the rating sweeps week. The episode called "The Death of the Avant-Garde" is a favorite rerun, a hardy perennial like *I Love Lucy*. "The triumph of death-theory," Mann suggests, is when the avant-garde is "remembered and reiterated precisely as history, as story, narrative, lesson, text—to be retained as left behind" (40). To narrate a failure suggests an unassailable narrator; to narrate a tale of death is to perpetrate the image of oneself as a survivor. And so it is that "theory-death" vindicates theory.

Theory proceeds in its postmortem on the avant-garde by collectivizing individual deaths into a mortuary effect—just as, after a transport disaster, the specific bodies are cumulatively folded into an epitaph on "the passengers." The obtuse generality of the label *avant-garde* is not one of Mann's own devising, but rather an inherited aspect of his subject, which is what the discursive economy does with each and every vanguard provocation.[5] Mann's thesis is that "avant-garde" has served as the *routine* term for denominating resistance, insubordination, opposition, dissent, and that by generalizing many distinct varieties of dissent under the rubric "avant-garde," this discourse has been able to categorically neutralize all of them by demonstrating the ineffectuality of any one of them. Mann thereby brings up the cost of such generalizations, awakening the need for a radical particularism, whereby Marinetti or Tzara can no longer function effectively as synecdoches for "the avant-garde." As one who has always been enthralled by the particulars of avant-garde scenes but also intuitively felt the generic designation to be unsavory, I am grateful for Mann's deliberations. What, then, to make of his own unremitting use of the very generalities exposed by his thesis? Is he suggesting that *all* discourse, no matter how self-aware or how informed of the constraints of "the white economy," is helplessly complicit? The short answer (and as Mann makes clear, there is no other): *yes.* Is the situation as grim as all that? Is there no remaining outsider position from which to defiantly launch, even if in utter futility, a projectile into the breadbasket of bourgeois self-assurance?

Mann follows Baudrillard in suggesting a discursive implosion. "One of our theses: the death of the avant-garde is its most subversive stage": "when recuperation is so generalized . . . the dialectical machinery supporting the institution collapses under its own incorporated weight" (74, 119).[6] He acknowledges that "The present critical project has been en-

---

5. The lack of an index emphasizes the point that there is no information content to the book; that its value is polemical rather than documentary. But of course this also exposes *Theory-Death* to the charge of complicity with the dominant discursive economy. Mann openly allows the charge, but less openly tries to sabotage that discourse.

6. We see the symptoms of such internal collapse in the soap opera of political correctness and multiculturalism, where the new right saw subversion permeating American society, while the left-leaning intelligentsia saw a culture hibernating in the hegemonic blanket of Gulf War patriotism. That both charges were accurate confirms Mann's thesis about generalized recuperation. The culture *is* permeated with patriotism *and* subversion, but what Mann (with Baudrillard, Foucault, and scores of other theorists) sees as an ongoing agony is that the extremes are not actually engaged in any contest. There is either a

gaged most of all in order to comprehend that strange critical state" in which "criticism is not an adversary force but rather a means by which culture discovers its contradictions so that it can accommodate them to itself" (118). It's misleading to call it a "critical" state, since it is patently the cultural context of a generation, or now several, manipulated into an idolatry of the oppositional by images from popular culture. Mann's book is fully internal to the prevailing discourse itself, working out its rules and internal logic. So, as he fails to account for historic differentiation in the role of the avant-garde during the past century, he also neglects the sociological implications of his observation that it is "a means by which capitalism continually adjusted itself to changes in the conditions of change itself" (120). This could be applied to the colonization of youth, and to target marketing in general. The explosion of youth culture during the Cold War disclosed a generational xenophobia that has powered the economy ever since. Population segments become the unwitting vanguard of the syndrome by which the margin is recuperated as the oncoming wave of the next thing to be internalized, and by means of which the collective hallucination of a "permanent growth" economy can be sustained. In turn, adversary forces have helplessly served as a spur to further growth, if only because the avant-garde has accustomed us to the model of a disavowal that can be capitalized on.

The avant-garde exposes, at its own expense, the remorseless appetite of the bourgeoisie (or late capitalism, culture industry, etc.), its

---

preaching to the converted or else an unyielding confrontation (as on the streets in front of abortion clinics). Social change thus falls into the chasm between unanimity and discord in a purely aleatory way. Consequently, that segment of the population traditionally prepared for administrative and leadership roles in the dissemination of ideas and values, the liberal humanists, find themselves masters of a forum that no longer exists (or has been exiled to the storage room in a museum). Those of us trained in the legacy of philosophical counterpoint and rhetorical ingenuity, whose sensibilities have been indexed by education to an itinerary of salient cultural moments (in art, architecture, music, literature), have literally no one to talk to but ourselves. In the hectic proliferation of various jargons of authenticity and professionalism, the arts have failed to adjust to the scale of disenfranchisement and neutralization that the demotic idiom of the middle now represents; we (artists, academics, etc.) have not figured out, for instance, how to sidestep the technical regalia and say, with the clarity of the dentist pointing to a tooth on the X ray, it has to come out.

rapacious cannibalizing of otherness and concomitant self-colonization. The appetite of capital is in turn replicated by the industry of commentary and meta-commentary, so there is little difference between the frenzy of the press corps and academic discord, inciting the lugubrious spectacle of a "masocriticism endlessly postulating its own torment," "an interminable discourse of termination" (19, 115). Mann's is itself an exemplary demonstration of masocriticism. What else is the holographic style but a way of masochistically revisiting the same trauma center again and again? What does Mann intend by participating in, and perpetuating, a discursive momentum that he clearly sees expended in futility (or worse, in complicity with what it would oppose)? His sentiments may be guided by Baudrillard, who reads a certain sullen resistance on the part of the masses' refusal to vote, for instance, not as indifference, but as silent scorn for the stakes of the game. Mann recites a normative protocol in his conviction that the system will finally be overcome by the giddiness with which it processes and recuperates every possible position and v(o)ice. "It might be that the last task of theory is to exhaust itself, to push its terms until they disintegrate or, as Baudrillard would say, 'implode': 'my way is to make ideas appear, but as soon as they appear I try to make them disappear'" (19). Eventually (such is the hope) we stop paying attention to the fates of individual ideas and begin to see the larger picture, which is a cycle of appearance-disappearance, opposition-recuperation, perturbation-resolution—a cycle that reconfirms the priority of its own holomovement (the expectoration of global capital) with every display of a normalized exception. The tradition of informed critique, Mann wants to say, has long since become a tradition most effective in demonstrating its own cancellation, or its own eventual accommodation to the hegemonic norms of a dominant culture. Even the most exhilarating acts of critical repudiation—and this is why the avant-garde is an exemplary case—are primarily excitations local to the grotesque and shameless body of capital, or they are the moments that *circulate,* since circulation as such *is* the holomovement of global capital. (Flânerie is just another name for window shopping.) As any current spectacle demonstrates (and is in turn the demonstration of prior demonstrations), it makes no difference whether sales are motivated by enthusiasm or anxiety, need or negligence; if it sells it sells, and discourse cannot resist a tautology. "One must therefore proceed in the certainty that . . . criticism no longer speaks the voice of alterity, or speaks it only in order to cancel what is always left of it . . . [and] that if difference must be discovered it is precisely a difference from us" (145).

The logical conclusion of Mann's views on the contamination of critical discourse is the necessity of abandoning its venues. He withholds the full disclosure of this aspect of his thesis until the final pages of the book, so one is tempted to read the end as an act of disappearance, a repudiation eloquently resonating in the silence or aftermath of *The Theory-Death of the Avant-Garde*. (But then, Mann troublingly resurfaced in the pages of *Contemporary Literature* reviewing further episodes of the avant-garde,[7] which suggests that an interminable discourse on termination is not so easily disavowed for one whose sensibility and training have been nurtured for precisely such tasks.) We are left with the implication that the traditional avant-garde must once more lead the way, and that exemplary nonproductive acts of disappearance will be pioneered by artists, notwithstanding his charge that "Without exception art that calls itself art, that is registered as art, that circulates within art contexts can never again pose as anything but systems-maintenance" (143). Mann doesn't expect staged repudiations, melodramatic scenarios in which the artist says, in effect, *I despise you all and will no longer give you the satisfaction of opposing me (or siding with me): I no longer play the game.* Nor will it be a Duchampian withdrawal without any accompanying theatrics or denunciation. Instead, what is required is to have never entered the lists in the first place. "What one must imagine is an unprecedented silence, exile, and cunning. . . . Not a critical theater in which to represent oneself but a hidden struggle to dismantle in oneself, in one's network, the entire theatrical apparatus. A fast for burning off discursive toxins" (144). The artist, setting the pace for critics, disappears like Conchis in John Fowles's *The Magus* or Slothrop in Thomas Pynchon's *Gravity's Rainbow*.

The idea is salutary, but that is its liability. It must be asked whether Mann has tipped his hand here, whether even a reference to such acts

7. Mann, "A Poetics of Its Own Occasion."

of nonparticipation risks recuperating them—whether my mention of them here, as it were, seconds the motion Mann makes, and the two of us comply with the logic of containment. Yet here the deficit of the unhistoricized approach bobs up again, for Mann is describing something that may indeed have its own subterranean legacies, its own shadow realm of unincorporated invisibility. I'm thinking of the hermetic tradition documented by Frances Yates. Without attempting to address, let alone settle, the question of whether such a tradition persists today, the very prospect that it may is sufficient to throw the concept of the avant-garde into a certain prominent relief; for the avant-garde has always been (and here I intend a totalizing statement that might, for once, be supported by all the available particulars) conspicuously public, antihermetic, in fact. Overt. The avant-garde serves Mann quite precisely for his larger task of repudiating the recuperative maintenance procedures of critical theory, because it is the very image of what is public and conspicuous. That such capitalist issues as marketing strategy arise in the discussion of the avant-garde makes perfect sense, since the vanguard enters into symbiosis with capital not only in its pursuit of novelty, but also in its insistent comportment in the public arena, an arena (and a public) thoroughly striated with the cargo cult of capital.[8]

The intersection of art and market seems inevitably to contaminate not so much the art as the mode of attention it solicits. The absorption of Art Brut into the gallery/museum network is the subject of Allen Weiss's *Shattered Forms: Art Brut, Phantasms, Modernism.* Like Mann, Weiss is troubled by doubts about "whether any difference, once expressed and examined, can maintain its otherness" (4). Insofar as "The museum remains the site of universalization via representation and the determination of values: spiritual, intellectual, economic, and otherwise," Art Brut risks becoming Art Benign as it enters the museological assembly. "Indeed," Weiss adds, "an insidious tactic of cultural appropriation is to give what is most free and most subversive the highest value in order to neu-

8. The historical avant-garde wasn't in a position to assess the pervasiveness of capital as such. The various sites of Dada, for instance, were impoverished beyond any comparison with American venues of artistic practice.

tralize its practical efficacy" (52). Unlike so many cultural critics of the 1980s-90s, Weiss did not take postmodernism to be liberatory, attributing to it instead a baseless "universalization" arrived at "not through rationalized metaphysics but through international capital": "Postmodernist aesthetics inaugurated the cognitive preconditions for the appropriation and commercialization of all that is marginal, be it within or without our culture" (57). Weiss, like Mann, is horrified by standard procedures of appropriation whereby the radical is rendered exemplary. But unlike Mann, his theorizing is strictly subordinated to a documentary avocation. Weiss is a dedicated chronicler of the alien frontiers opened up by Valère Novarina's proposition that "all words are scars of the spirit" (105), a prospect realized in the "electroprosthetic resurrection[s]" of such radio art as Artaud's "*Pour en finir avec le jugement de dieu*" and Gregory Whitehead's "Oral or Anal," works that strive toward the realization that "It is only when our entire body becomes a mouth that we can truly speak" (114).

The most valuable aspect of *Shattered Forms* is Weiss's adherence to the proposition that "aesthetic alterity is always to be found within ourselves, and must be cultivated" (3). Too insistent a preoccupation with the market syndrome of recuperation, as in Mann's case, can lead to the assumption that the deepest drive of the arts is to be chastened and then repatriated to the bosom of the Oedipal family. It presumes that the "shattered forms" of radical alterity are stages in a pursuit of wholeness, disjecta of a self-recuperation that prefigure social venues of recuperation (canon, curriculum, and marketplace). Weiss, on the other hand, is willing to entertain the prospect that the arts may be driven by the desire to escape that cycle; that certain artists may be in search of a protective disordering, not a consoling order. (Houston Baker's thesis comes to mind—in *Modernism and the Harlem Renaissance*—of African American literature oscillating between a "mastery of form" and a "deformation of mastery.") The art of forgetting thus becomes as crucial as the art of memory, if not more so; and this art proceeds not by obliteration and deficit, but by proliferation and excess, in which memory is overrun by a monstrous ubiquity of fractured codes, shattered forms, and the squalor of material plenitude. What is required is a commitment to a nondialectical materialism Deleuze calls "a realism of deformation, as opposed to the idealism of transformation" (quoted in Weiss, 47).

American academic discourse of the 1990s became immersed in an almost convulsive celebration of margins and marginality and the empowerment of traditionally dispossessed subjects. These books by Mann and Weiss—along with Nathaniel Mackey's *Discrepant Engagement*—served as opportune (if little attended) warnings about the confident assumption of benefits supposedly available at the center, up on the pedestal, and in other sites of legitimation—sites *also* of a long-standing bourgeois requisition of the alien for the theatrical display of its own tolerance. The term "avant-garde" should be retired (with dignity, not ignominiously expelled—although as Mann indicates, the *tradition* of such expulsions is by now an embarrassment). The resources of estrangement and the protective disordering that "avant-garde" once designated now need to be disencumbered of that label and of any other (like "postmodern"), since the diagnostic task of the labeling impulse has long served as a preemptive strike. Any public activity gets labeled soon enough, but only the most naive or nostalgic can now imagine that avant-garde is anything but a designer label for momentarily fashionable mindware. So how do we talk about the events that would really challenge us now? I would side with Mann: confide only in those you trust, be cagey, circumspect, disarming, and don't go mouthing off about subversion if you really want it to work.

TENACITY, OR THE PURSUIT OF THE ORDINARY

The actual order of things is precisely what "popular" tactics turn to their own ends, without any illusion that it will change any time soon. Though elsewhere it is exploited by a dominant power or simply denied by an ideological discourse, here order is *tricked* by an art. Into the institution to be served are thus insinuated styles of social exchange, technical invention, and moral resistance; that is, an economy of the "*gift*" (generosities for which one expects a return), an esthetics of "*tricks*" (artists' operations) and an ethics of *tenacity* (countless ways

of refusing to accord the established order the status of a law, a meaning, or a fatality).

Michel de Certeau, Practice of Everyday Life

Michel de Certeau's thesis of *arts de faire* and the tactics of wiggle room
in subordinate social spaces, along with Situationist strategies of *detourne-
ment* or rerouting, have become pervasive and influential even when
they have not been read. A case in point is *Wittgenstein's Ladder*, in which
Marjorie Perloff does not purport to survey or assess the contemporary
theoretical landscape, even as Wittgenstein is made out to be an avatar of
the following concepts: contingency, the everyday, cultural production,
serial form, praxis as value, and destabilizing of the centered subject.
Perloff's success prompts certain questions: Is the theoretical environment of academe so pervasive that its issues insinuate themselves into any
responsible scholar's work, even when not specifically evoked by way of
theoretical charter? Or might it be that the university environment is
especially porous to issues of public concern, so that even a scrupulously
close reader and literary historian like Perloff—whose work is generally
uninflected by political rhetoric—will come to the conclusion (in this
case quoted from the artist Joseph Kosuth) that " 'Ethics and aesthetics
are one' " (*Ladder* 242)?

Like Perloff's other books, *Wittgenstein's Ladder* provides a web of affiliations, a network swelling to potential dynasty. Here the radiant cluster
of her vortex consists of Ludwig Wittgenstein, Gertrude Stein, Samuel
Beckett, Ingeborg Bachmann, Thomas Bernhard, Robert Creeley, Ron
Silliman, Lyn Hejinian, Rosmarie Waldrop, and Joseph Kosuth; and she
antithetically demotes Bertrand Russell, F. T. Marinetti, Stanley Fish, and
Jean-François Lyotard (whose relevance to her project, however, she
misconstrues). Certain omissions appear obvious, given the subtitle,
"Poetic Language and the Strangeness of the Ordinary": James Joyce,
Harold Pinter, and Frank O'Hara (whose absence is particularly striking,
given that Perloff once published a monograph on his poetry). Less conspicuous in omission is the poetry of Leslie Scalapino, Norman Fisher,
and Charles Stein, among others, which would contribute an instructive

Buddhist orientation to the problem of the decentered subject, a topic Hejinian's work is forced to signify by itself. Another lacuna is Don Byrd's major study *The Poetics of the Common Knowledge* (1994), which not only makes pragmatic and enlightening use of the same coordinates from Wittgenstein, but elaborately addresses *as a poetics* the philosophical consequences of "the strangeness of the ordinary," and does so in the context of the lineage of dissident American poetry that Perloff favors. Byrd's book, no less than Perloff's, can be seen as a prolonged scrutiny of Wittgenstein's speculation, "Why do I not satisfy myself that I have two feet when I want to get up from a chair? There is no why. I simply don't. This is how I act" (*Ladder* 114).

Perloff's approach to Wittgenstein is an extension of her long-standing interest in modernism (*The Futurist Moment* and *The Poetics of Indeterminacy* being most salient): "Wittgenstein comes to us as the ultimate modernist outsider, the changeling who never stops reinventing himself" (*Ladder* 7). Her reading of the *Tractatus* as a war book is audacious and convincing. The persuasiveness of her readings of specific texts, along with her documentation of dozens of works "written under the sign of Wittgenstein" (6), would appear to put this enigmatic Viennese in the ascendancy for any further reflections on twentieth-century art. But there is a dimension to Wittgenstein's presence that cannot be so tidily accommodated to modernism, even so elastic a modernism as Perloff espouses. By confining her historical scope to the twentieth century, instructive precedents are omitted, not least of which is the uncannily Wittgensteinian milieu of the Jena Romantics and their adamant "unphilosophy." The point is not that Wittgenstein rehashes German Romanticism; rather, a liability of Perloff's twentieth-century focus is the misleading assumption that modernist problems are modernist inventions. Even Wittgenstein's aphoristic mode replicates the favored practice of Schlegel and Novalis.

The salutary provocations of Wittgenstein, in Perloff's reading, involve: (1) a validation of the ordinary, (2) a renewed concern with the status of that exemplary common phenomenon which is language, and with it an awareness of (3) the menace of grammar, or system, and (4) the formal solution of a nonsystematic praxis, which in modern poetics includes serial composition, indeterminacy, and open form. If we set

aside Wittgenstein, this list encapsulates the very prospects that tanta-
lized the German Romantics. What Perloff celebrates in Wittgenstein is
the way he worked himself out of philosophy and, in effect, into art, by
developing an ethical instinct—"instinct" being the operative term, since
"however impossible it may be to formulate ethical principles, it *is* possible to engage in ethical actions" (21)—hence the need of "a form of
discipline that trains one to extract value from whatever situation one
happens to be in" (31). Perloff finds in Wittgenstein a guide to the union
of art and ethics, and thanks to her skillful exposition, it is possible to
discern the symbiosis in a broader historical field than she herself provides. But it *is* a field that is necessary in order to resist an effect helplessly precipitated by *Wittgenstein's Ladder,* which is to hypostatize the philosopher himself as determinate exemplar, an effect consolidated not
only by Perloff's appreciative biographical account, but by the oracular
effect his aphorisms have—especially when repeated several times, as
Perloff is prone to do.

Ever since the German Romantics, thought about the ground of value
has sought an intermediary between the subjective aspiration to autonomy and the objective condition of mediation. The pre-Romantic solution was revealed religion, an option attractive even to such contemporaries of the Romantics as F. H. Jacobi and J. G. G. Hamann, for whom
the simple givenness of the world as such was taken as revelation. The
theocentric supposition of such a solution has been untenable for most
post-Enlightenment thinkers and artists, however, so the principle of
revelation has been retained in a deferred or concealed manner, associated less with the world as given and more with the world as conceived
(or, from the viewpoint of utopian politics, as it is remade according to
a desirable conception). From the Hegelian intricacies of the quest of self
through encounters with the Other, to the modernist mobilization of discrete elements in constructivism, artists and writers of the past two centuries have had in common the prospect of an exploratory, dynamic art,
an art that does not so much rival religious revelation as replace it, as
Oscar Wilde predicted. The only difference between religion and art, but
such a crucial one, is that revelation is given in the former and sought in
the latter. Another way of putting it: religion provides a ground, where

art seeks one. Art is therefore inevitably experimental, essaying or attempting its result, researching an outcome that is unpredictable and un-
secured but, despite this perpetual openness, aspires to be as *consequential*
as revelation, as *grounded* as a first principle (albeit one that is lived,
not proved). Jacobi's sense was that absolute truth is unknowable, or
if known unprovable, and that "We can only demonstrate similarities
(*agreements, relatively necessary truths*), progressing in statements of identity. Every proof supposes something which has already been proved,
whose principle is *revelation*" (Bowie 39). For Jacobi, the final goal of the
"researcher"—a judicious term, admitting not only the philosopher, but
anyone embarked on a path of exploration—is not an elaboration of self-
sufficient theoretical integrities in the mode of explanation, but rather to
apprehend "that which cannot be explained: that which cannot be dissolved, the immediate, the simple" (Bowie 38). Unlikely as such an alliance may seem, it is instructive to place next to Jacobi Wittgenstein's
profession of faith at the end of the *Tractatus*: "There is indeed the in-
expressible. This *shows* itself; it is the mystical" (Perloff, *Ladder* 45). Like
Jacobi, Wittgenstein affirms the immediate, the commonplace, as the in-
expressible given. "The aspects of things that are most important for
us are hidden because of their simplicity and familiarity" (*Ladder* 106)—
indeed, beneath notice right before our eyes, in the path as the Latin
ob-viam attests, obvious.

When Perloff surmises that "the pursuit of the ordinary may well be
the most interesting game in town" (80), her vocabulary stimulates an
arresting thought, which is why the common, the immediate, the available, needs *pursuing* at all. She does not take into account Charles Olson's
adaptation of Heraclitus's adage that we are estranged from that which is
most familiar,[9] but Olson's project in *The Maximus Poems* does provide

---

9. It is hardly necessary to single out Olson in order to evoke the colonization of the
lifeworld. But to do so is to take issue with Perloff's procedure. The topic being of such
obvious extensiveness, her discussion is pragmatically limited to paradigmatic figures; but
because her analyses make careful if selective use of historical and biographical detail, the
book assumes an air of comprehension that is misleading (and surely not even intended).
By appending her representative sample to the motivating figure of Wittgenstein, of course,
Perloff circumvents much of the problem of selection. But the manner of relation is itself

a sense of *pursuit* inasmuch as the poet's declared affiliation with the "simple" proves notoriously difficult to sustain in practice. This is not only because Olson's concern for reclaiming the familiar entails both a domestic and a cosmological reckoning, but also because the public realm (the "polis") is itself a false commonplace, its communitas having been usurped for the special interests of advertising and political demagoguery, so that even the instinct of "common sense" is thoroughly habituated to the esoteric formulations of an ideological voice-over. When commodity culture is naturalized, the social cost is high, because the very ground of the given, the immediate, is saturated with the logic of the marketplace, seeming to be "given" along with water and air.

The ordinary, it seems, is apprehended as such only with extraordinary effort. ("Possible / To use / Words provided one treat them / As enemies. / Not enemies—Ghosts" [Oppen 97].) "But suppose one scraps the notion that the ordinary must be defined in relation to its opposite, the extraordinary, or indeed in relation to anything outside it. Wittgenstein's *ordinary* is best understood as quite simply *that which is,* the language we do actually use when we communicate with one another. In this sense, the ordinary need not be literal, denotative, propositional. . . . On the contrary, our actual language may well be connotative, metaphoric, fantastic" (*Ladder* 57).[10] This is a refreshing take on the

underdefined, as she goes from a discussion of Beckett's *Watt* as "Wittgensteinian novel" (133) to the "Wittgenstein fictions" of Thomas Bernhard (145); the distinction may be minor, but it might be major, and if so, it troubles the constellation.

10. Philip Fisher has recently undertaken a comprehensive aesthetics of the ordinary along lines similar to those set out by Perloff. In contrast to the sublime, which he calls "the aestheticization of fear," Fisher espouses *wonder,* "the most neglected of primary aesthetic experiences within modernity, involv[ing] the aestheticization of delight, or of the pleasure principle rather than the death principle" (2). If the sublime is an exceptional condition, wonder is normal, pedestrian (as in "I wonder how that got there"; or the exclamation of wonder in the presence of a familiar marvel like a rainbow) even as it confronts something out of the ordinary. Wonder is therefore a concomitant of everyday practice: "Wonder drives and sustains the defective rationality that gives us intelligibility under conditions where we will not even know that we have reached certain knowledge when and if we have" (9). Daniel Tiffany draws a similar conclusion in *Toy Medium: Materialism and Modern Lyric:* "For as long as materialism sees fit to maintain the pose of realism and, at the same time, insist that material substance is invisible, then the ingenuity and 'thickness' of lyric

ordinary, not least because it retains the extraordinary as a necessary dimension of the ordinary. Perloff herself tends to find the extraordinary as a hidden fruit, a concealed supplement, of the ordinary rather than the other way around, as in the case of magic realism. For the Romantics, of course, *both* options were simultaneously affirmed. As Schlegel put it, "All of the highest truths of every kind are altogether trivial; and for this very reason nothing is more necessary than to express them ever anew, and if possible ever more paradoxically, so that it will not be forgotten that they are still there and that they can never really be entirely expressed" ("On Incomprehensibility" 122); and Novalis defined Romanticism by the twofold operation whereby the commonplace is given a higher sense—"the known the dignity of the unknown, the finite an infinite appearance"—while "the unknown, the mystical, the infinite . . . is logorhythmized" and thereby "gains an everyday expression" (Bowie 80).

The everyday expression is not, of course, what has traditionally been associated with art. This association introduces a paradox into aesthetic thought, which is to render the everyday poignant, and in doing so to exalt the normal by means of the exceptional, to render the normal abnormally fine. The distance from the Romantic declaration of faith in the everyday and its actual integration into artistic praxis is nothing less

'culture' (of reality as poetry inscribes it) must serve as the unattainable standard of representational practice for science" (292). Modern science, like epicurean materialist philosophy, attests to a universe incommensurate with our senses, so in order to make sense of it we invariably draw upon the imaginative resources sustained by poetry (or in Fisher's terms, *wonder*).

Fisher draws on Wittgenstein's remark that we can't take note of the ordinary, for the ordinary is precisely what we don't notice. But awareness of the ordinary is not merely an inference made in the face of the extraordinary. This is where wonder comes in, as an experience of what cannot be experienced. "The ordinary can not or does not turn itself into experiences. The ordinary is what is there when there are no experiences going on. It is the necessary optics within which there can be such a thing as an experience, but which cannot itself be seen" (20–21). But wonder is not a practice in Certeau's sense (and Fisher takes pains to extricate wonder from modernist tactics of estrangement, or perceptual renewal: "Wonder is not one more episode in the aesthetic history of boredom" [28]). For Fisher, the ultimate value of wonder is its ability to solicit from an ordinary human response to events a sense not of their transcendence but their simple exigency: "Instead of a conversation with the tradition, we find a kind of intertextuality with everyday life" (150).

than the history of modernism. But well before anything as decisive as, say, "the futurist moment," somewhere between *The Prelude* and *Madame Bovary* a tension is noticed and then actively developed—a tension between the thought of the ordinary and the ordinary thought. The difference is one between the sophisticated apprehension of the commonplace and the studious replication of the banal. After two centuries of a deliberate retrieval and vindication of the everyday, it is now theoretically enlightened to revel in "the strangeness of the ordinary"; but it is also the case that few have a real taste for the ordinary as such, the ordinary unredeemed by the halo of the strange. A Brillo box by Andy Warhol seems to mark some verifiable threshold, and even the most diehard minimalists would not, I suspect, be enthralled by a systematic silkscreen inventory of every item in the supermarket aisle. So the problem of the common, initiated in Romanticism, continues to be hashed out at the boundary between quantity and quality.

A continuum of banal episodes can be conceptually gratifying but unendurable to watch. The common vindication of banality in modern art has been formal, an indifferent content packaged in the most sophisticated presentation. That this verges on a commodification of the aesthetic is naturally the great danger, which is why Perloff is so concerned to introduce the question of ethics into what otherwise seems mere aestheticism. In addition, the artists she favors are open to eruptions of the extraordinary in unlikely places. Most instructive are those formal procedures whereby the routine of the form is subverted by the very content it would neutralize—an exemplary instance in *Wittgenstein's Philosophy* being Ron Silliman's "Sunset Debris," composed entirely of questions. The rudimentary formal device makes for breathtaking results, as Silliman's poem forces the reader to acknowledge the potential equivalence of every "unit" in the text—each question being formally indistinguishable from any other—while at the same time recognizing the imponderable variety within such constraints. Not all constraints are as fertile; and as Perloff says of the common assumption that Gertrude Stein slings words about more or less randomly, "not all 'dislocations' are of equal value" (*Ladder* 105). Perloff is an expert guide to questions of value in the context of formalist art, sometimes through sheer ingenuity (the cleverness with which she pits Stein's "Mary Nettie" against Marinetti, turning him into a buffoon or "marionette" (109) of his own theories, is really something to behold) but mainly due to her careful balancing of text and context. That Beckett wrote *Watt* during his time in the French Resistance is, in Perloff's reading, instructive about the "resistance" that his language games demonstrate. The elevation of banality has probably not had a more predisposing practitioner than Beckett, but Perloff illuminates *Watt* in a way that preserves its aura of metaphysical enigma against the contextual ground of war, a milieu in which "life and death" polarities too easily obscure enigmatic taunts.

A problem endemic to the text/context dialectic is a unilateral reflex, whereby one provides the necessary ground for, and sufficient cause of, the other. This is hardly exclusive to doctrinaire criticism; it informs even the most offhand remarks, providing the unreflective backdrop against which a predictable pantomime of "Romanticism" or "Modernism" is conjured up in the classroom or the museum tour. It is a problem that will persist as long as any "art object" is objectified as such, detachable *as text* from a context and subject to adoration. The importance, then, of such insistently formalist works as "Sunset Debris" is their material resistance to the equally materializing idealism of a text/context aesthetics. The ethical imperative motivating such works—and clearly Perloff wants such an imperative—is that the reification imposed on art by commodity fetishism can be resisted or forestalled only in an assiduous *praxis* that disables its own market potential (at forty pages, Silliman's work disqualifies itself from anthologies—although it is equally the case that his method is legible in shorter, if not short, extracts). The emergent problem, however, as has long been evident in the art world, is that such artistic revoking of the object status of the work leaves the critic or explicator in a position of unwarranted power. Perloff's is an honorable exercise of such power, but the danger now is not that critics delegate rewards (which they've always done), but that critical discourse itself becomes the sine qua non of all activity in the arts. And by "critical discourse" I don't mean talk or exchange, but the legitimation procedures of delegated experts, idea brokers. Perloff has herself been active in establishing the marketability of "language poetry"; and while it is refreshing to find in *Wittgenstein's Ladder* that she does not evoke that rubric as the precondition for reading Silliman or Hejinian, it is sobering to reflect that she *needn't,* simply because that market is now secure. The pertinent question, then: Is a market a context? The context for all of Perloff's work is "Modernism," one of the most marketable configurations of the twentieth century, and it's to her credit that she has refused to accede to the given terms of intellectual exchange when trading in its market.

It is with particular poignance, then, that Perloff emphasizes—indeed, makes doctrinaire—Wittgenstein's passage from philosophy to art. "Philosophy ought really to be written only as a *form of poetry,*" he famously claimed (*Ladder* 51, repeated 65). Before Wittgenstein, Schlegel: "The whole history of modern poetry is a running commentary on the following brief philosophical text: all art should become science and all science art; poetry and philosophy should be made one" (*Fragments* 14, #115). Andrew Bowie summarizes this resistance to "the world of determinate knowledge," which for the German Romantics was "no longer the final locus of truth, because the determinacy of the particular only emerges via its continually being related to other things, which is a process of no necessary conclusion. . . . The world thus constituted is not a realm of fixed objects, but rather a world in which 'truths' arise by combining differing *articulations* of what there is" (Bowie 68, 69). Such a view dignifies the plastic imagination; but in the context of commodity reification it also dangerously extends to "Poesie" or art a saving grace—a problematic outcome that has yet to be addressed by those like Richard Rorty who advocate literature as a tactical attempt to outflank the onerous circumscriptions of universalist and foundationalist philosophies. The danger of such a position is that in fetishizing the literary object, it reifies "literature" *as category,* converting it into a mimic philosophy by virtue of the scope of its categorical claims, thereby replicating *the theory-death of the avant-garde* all over again, albeit in another register.

Beckett's famous phrase "I can't go on I'll go on" assumes a different aspect in the context of *Wittgenstein's Ladder,* in which Wittgenstein's open-ended notebook compilations are taken as salutary instances of a perpetually self-renewable process increasingly embraced by poets and artists for whom it is not the end product that counts but the " 'veritable continuous creation'" (Bourdieu, in *Ladder* 80). Such a claim is necessarily a tightrope performance, for how does one not cite approvingly—which is to say, make exemplary—those figures who make the case for the non-exemplary? How brandish "Sunset Debris" as a salutary instance of the de-fetishized text without, in effect, making an example (a fetish) of it? The teeter-totter precipitated by such a question is a perpetual motion machine, and brings on either the vertigo of infinite regress or the nihilistic conclusion that nothing ever changes. Wittgenstein understood this as a grammatical problem: "Distrust of grammar is the first requisite of philosophizing" (*Ladder* 17). The bewitchment of grammar is that it initiates us into a compromising model of completeness—the very model that is then surreptitiously imposed on the "freestanding" artwork, which is then recuperated to the grammatical requirements of a system, whether that be philosophical foundationalism or an aesthetic canon.

Perloff cites a poignant passage from Terry Eagleton's novel *Saints and Scholars* in which Wittgenstein repudiates revolution as a delusion of metaphysics: "[T]he idea of a total break in human life is an illusion. There's nothing *total* to be broken. As though all we know could stop, and something entirely different start" (*Ladder* 4). The inducement to revolution, the aspiration to revoke one world and put in its place a new one, is a theoretical fantasy harbored within the system-building of the philosophers. From Wittgenstein's viewpoint, the notion of a total break is an explanatory tactic within the claims of a theoretical system, confined to the logical requirements of intellect to which he opposed the pragmatic exigencies of "instinct." The total break is a delusional thought, along with the dream of shaking free of systems and theories and coercive foundations. "You cannot justify grammar," says Wittgenstein, to which Perloff adds, "it merely *is*" (58). Her forcible (italicized) conclusion: "*Description thus replaces explanation.*" Description here serves the same role as Rorty's "redescription," with a loss of the sense of repetition, beginning again. Admittedly, Perloff derives the term from Wittgenstein himself: "We must do away with all *explanation* and description alone must take its place" (*Ladder* 135). Wittgenstein's preference for description is explicitly grounded in aesthetics: "Aesthetics is descriptive.

What it does is to *draw one's attention* to certain features, to place things side by side so as to exhibit these features" (*Ladder* 61).

The labor of "drawing attention" to things is endless and wearisome, but it also provides texture to life as such. Wittgenstein abjures the aspiration to *get it right* as far as living is concerned; life is not the execution of grammatical requirements. The corollary for philosophy *and* for life is that "nothing we could ever think or say should be *the* thing" (*Ladder* 2). This has methodological consequences, as Wittgenstein comes to practice a lapidary mode of "sudden change, jumping from one topic to another" in a series of "philosophical remarks" rather than conceptual exposition. He noted that "my thoughts were soon crippled if I tried to force them on in any single direction against their natural inclination.— And this was, of course, connected with the very nature of the investigation." Perloff links this capacity for "sudden change" to Gertrude Stein's "beginning again and again" (*Ladder* 65); but it can as usefully be related to Schlegel's insistence that "Philosophy must begin with infinitely many propositions, according to its genesis (not with One proposition)" (Bowie 83). And further: "philosophy, like epic poetry, always begins in medias res" (*Fragments* 28, #84). One might also note an allied model in Deleuze and Guattari's admiration for the mobile rhizome. They regard the rhizome as American in much the way Schlegel associated poetic freedom with the French revolution: "Poetry is republican speech: a speech which is its own law and end unto itself, and in which all the parts are free citizens and have the right to vote" (*Fragments* 8, #65). Wittgenstein's comparable inclination to "travel over a wide field of thought criss-cross in every direction" is for Perloff proof that his work constitutes "Not an overarching theory . . . but a *method* for 'going on'" (*Ladder* 66). She cites a delicious formulation by Herman Rapaport, characterizing Wittgenstein's parataxis of presentation as "negative serialization": "In each sentence there is compulsory connectivity. But in thinking of the sentences serially, the question of reciprocity becomes vexed. In short, despite appearances, they are Other to one another" (*Ladder* 67). Such an internally refractory strategy, in Perloff's reading, means that "there need be no metalanguage, for each of us has access to the 'language full-blown (not some sort of preparatory, provisional one'), the language that is given to us" (71). But who gives it to us? Who (or what) authorizes such a convenient gift?

Circumventing the problem of metalanguages is not as easy as all that. A metalanguage is inseparable from social power, and as long as there are hierarchies of authority and status there will be metalanguages.[11] To say, as Perloff does, that "there need be no metalanguage" is in principle no different than saying there need be no social inequality, but the propositional form here is itself a victim of its grammar. The grammar of social relations *needs* neither metalanguages nor inequality; but as Wittgenstein famously puts it in the opening of the *Tractatus*, "The world is everything that is the case"—the *case* being not the logical requirement but the manifest given, the commonality of things, the exigent occasion—the "way it is," as Walter Cronkite used to say on the evening news telecast. The appeal to what there need or need not be, as I have suggested, is an appeal to grammar, an appeal to the requirements of a *system*. Wittgenstein's own tactical openness to the systemless makes a different sort of appeal, which Perloff finds in language as such, not as a hierarchy of determinate relations (grammar) but "full-blown," language as "given."

---

11. Schlegel's famous dictum, "Poetry can only be criticized by way of poetry," might be construed as a comparable denial of metalanguages. But his proposition goes on to acknowledge a political dimension within the sphere of art. If the only legitimate critique of poetry comes from poetry itself, this is because "A critical judgment of an artistic production has no civil rights in the realm of art if it isn't itself a work of art" (*Fragments* 14, #117). Schlegel and his associates aspired to envision a total Mischgedicht or mixed genre, an artistic form so capacious that it would fuse philosophy and religion, prose and poetry, fragment and totality. The merger of criticism and poetry was intrinsic to the destiny of poetry, Schlegel felt: "poetry should describe itself, and always be simultaneously poetry and the poetry of poetry" (51, #238). His vision is the very paradigm of restless self-overcoming in a Nietzschean sense. In the end, Schlegel celebrates sheer process as the telos of Romanticism: "Romantic poetry is in the arts what wit is in philosophy, and what society and sociability, friendship and love are in life. Other kinds of poetry are finished and are now capable of being fully analyzed. The romantic kind of poetry is still in the state of becoming: that, in fact, is its real essence: that it should forever be becoming and never be perfected" (32, #116). The implications of this and other aspects of German Romantic theory are concisely addressed in *The Literary Absolute* by Philippe Lacoue-Labarthe and Jean-Luc Nancy.

The problem with Perloff's enthusiasm is directly attributable to Wittgenstein himself; they share a euphoric embrace of language in its non-specialized, supposedly unintimidating everydayness, but they concede —problematically in my view—to its *givenness*. Who gives it? How is language bestowed "all at once"? (This is where some attention to Bruce Andrews is relevant, to compel reflection on the volatility of what seems freely given.) To imagine language *given* in its entirety is not only to be heedless of language as social code, but can even amount to quietism. I do an injustice to Perloff, for she has in fact acknowledged the dilemma by way of Beckett, Bachmann, and Bernhard, writers who begin with a wariness about how the totality of a language is "given" and what might be involved in accepting such an ambiguous gift. As for Wittgenstein's own practice, Perloff is content to remark that "increasingly the urgency of *not* saying what *cannot be said* came to dominate Wittgenstein's thinking" (*Ladder* 40).

From what position does one intuit what cannot be said? Perloff implies, and I would agree, that Wittgenstein's silence on certain matters is political. He remains a salutary if perplexing example of the problem of communication in the twentieth century: how we are compromised by the grammatical requirements of the systems and organizations to which we belong; how we furtively go about our business and pursue our passions anyway; and how, seeking integrity in artistic practice, we take the extraordinary risk of having our own words, thoughts, and precepts used against us or in spite of us—but we adhere to the art anyway, because it nourishes the greatest potential of all, which is that we might change our own minds.

8

Experiment as a Claim of the Book

Twenty Different Fruits on One Different Tree

Prefacing his selection of poets for the 1986 anthology *In the American Tree,* Ron Silliman observed that "the resources available to this moment in writing have been remarkably abundant." This reflection follows immediately upon a list of over eighty poets not included, but from whom a "volume of absolutely comparable worth could be constructed" (xxi, xx). Silliman's list was prescient, including numerous poets likely to be on an informed list for a prospective anthology today: Ken Irby, Beverly Dahlen, Rosmarie Waldrop, Alice Notley, Kathleen Fraser, Keith Waldrop, Craig Watson, Norman Fischer, John Taggart, Joan Rettalack, Leslie Scalapino, Rachel Blau DuPlessis, Maureen Owen, Mei-Mei Berssenbrugge, Lorenzo Thomas, and Aaron Shurin, to cite a generous baker's dozen.[1] Needless to add, Silliman's more concrete act of anthologizing thirty-eight poets established a canon of "language poetry" that has proven nearly intractable, at least as an object of reference, reverence, or

1. Most of these poets, along with several others on Silliman's list, have in fact been included in the most recent round of important anthologies edited by Paul Hoover, Douglas Messerli, and Eliot Weinberger. Of poets continuing to fall between the anthological cracks—to restrict myself to Silliman's list—I would want to draw attention to Johanna Drucker, Gerrit Lansing, Charles Stein, and Don Byrd.

derision. But his was hardly a peremptory or self-aggrandizing gesture. *In the American Tree* remains an exemplary assembly (in every sense of the word: as a book, *it works*); and what's more, a lion's share of significant books of American poetry since 1986 has been authored by Silliman's picks. The cynical view is that the phenomenon of language poetry has proven, like Surrealism, to be a grand enterprise in publicity, a platform hoisting a legion of minor talents into major prominence. I think, however, that the polemical value of language poetry as an issue is past—which is to say, the cheap shots are less and less viable as serious objections. By the same token, a superficial enthusiasm for sheer surface discontinuity may also have run its course. Finally, the careful placement of language writing in broader poetic and discursive contexts in Marjorie Perloff's *Radical Artifice,* Charles Bernstein's *A Poetics,* Bob Perelman's *The Marginalization of Poetry,* Hank Lazer's *Opposing Poetries,* and my *The American Poetry Wax Museum* should invalidate any further blanket dismissals like those common in the past.

This is a roundabout way of declaring that the issue of language poetry is *aufgehoben*—to use that peculiar word Hegel makes much of, a verb (*aufheben;* noun = *Aufhebung*) meaning *to preserve, to raise up,* and *to cancel.* In other words, I assume language poetry as a necessary given of the contemporary American poetic landscape, but I also assume this givenness in the mode of dissolution and absorption. Many of the most interesting demonstrations of the insistence of language writing are no longer to be found exclusively in the work of Silliman's core group; the lessons have migrated; the emphasis on the signifier climbed down from the tree and rhizomatically infused the grassy horizon. In turn, it is increasingly untenable to think of the language writers themselves as merely executing further proofs or demonstrations of first principles, comporting within the boundaries of groupthink. It's timely to consider the beneficial legacy of language poetry as a phenomenon not confined to its practitioners and theorists, but disseminated now into the environment of poetic innovation at large. Considered "at large," one might plausibly suggest that between Zukofsky's "*A*" and early Ashbery, Olson in the later *Maximus Poems,* Jack Spicer and Armand Schwerner, certain lesser-known experiments by Robert Kelly, Jackson Mac Low's procedural strategies, and Rothenberg's performative ethnopoetics, everything commonly attributed to language poetry was already accomplished in advance. But such a claim would be like saying T. S. Eliot's poetry is made redundant by Laforgue. Literary history is not really about priority, but about agency; not who did it first, but who coordinated doing with knowing, poetry with poetics. The terms of succession are contingent upon the fact that the known has limits, and going beyond the apparent limits (even if only to rediscover something previously known but obscured by the more recently and prominently known) is what constitutes "experiment." Experiment is whatever arises when the consequences are not self-evident.

The kind of experimentation associated with language poetry involves "method."[2] Method, however, can too easily forfeit agency to the experimental platform of an institutional provider. The difference between subservience to method and the stimulus of method is immense (and demonstrable in the developing oeuvre of individual language poets). *Experiment* in poetry now has more copious resources at its disposal, as method sheds some of the glamour of the new but is retained as everpresent generative potential. Even the use of rhymed couplets can seize an experimental moment if it's disencumbered of reactionary disavowal (glamorized as a restoration of "craft" to verse practice). The point is not tradition versus experimentation, but the accreditation of a *tradition of experimentation* as well as a further acknowledgment that every tradition is an experiment in temporality. As soon as the sense of experiment declines, tradition itself dwindles into routinized iteration.

The most pertinent consequence of language poetry is its erosion of the complacency with which the lyrical ego hoists its banner.[3] The lyrical

2. The *locus classicus* for language writing is Charles Bernstein's dictum, "All writing is a demonstration of method; it can assume a method or investigate it" (in Silliman, *American Tree* 590).

3. Because *ego* has tainted lyric in American poetry from confessionalism to the less dramatic lyric personalism of MFA programs, some anxiety is apparent about the status of lyric as such. Juliana Spahr takes pains to retain the lyric, often ingeniously, as in her assertion that "the desire to articulate those moments where meaning is slipping away is lyric's great tradition" (Introduction to Rankine and Spahr, *American Women Poets in the Twenty-First Century* 2). Many would dispute Spahr's claim that "Lyric is by definition innovative. When it stops being innovative it is no longer lyric" (13); though her point is less sweeping in light

ego has by no means been deposed as such (and in any case, a wholesale attunement of poetic activity to chronicling *language itself* would suggest nothing so much as a return of the repressed, in which ego fortification would be immunized from direct scrutiny by its artful displacement onto resistant surfaces);[4] but the diversification of poetic means and strategies have opened up sites of "agency" that require different sorts of validation and do not serve as vigilant fortifications of identity. As Alice Notley insists, "*Someone,* at this point, must take in hand the task of being everyone, & no one, as the first poets did. Someone must pay attention to the real spiritual needs of both her neighbors (not her poetic peers) & the future" (*Scarlet Cabinet* vi)—a demand magisterially met by her own book *Disobedience,* with its adamant declaration:

This is not the Whitman Intersection.

I see quietly

not walking out through the eye

---

of a further deliberation: "lyrics . . . reveal how our private intimacies have public obligations and ramifications, how intimacy has a social bond with shared meaning" (11).

4. This is the "waning of affect" Fredric Jameson takes to be symptomatic of the postmodern. "The shift in the dynamics of cultural pathology," he writes, "can be characterized as one in which the alienation of the subject is displaced by the latter's fragmentation" (*Postmodernism* 14). While Jameson is not really a booster of postmodernism, he acknowledges that fragmentation is no longer a choice but an objective circumstance, a "new and historically original dilemma, one that involves our insertion as individual subjects into a multidimensional set of radically discontinuous realities" (413). What's interesting is his assumption that "The literary value that emerges from this new formal practice is called 'irony'" (412). Romantic irony as a way of sketching provisional continuity across a discontinuous spectrum of experience here makes its return—and while it's reductive to associate language poetry exclusively with irony, it is plausible to regard the return of irony as a demonstrable (if unintended) contribution of language writing to current American poetry. As for the issue of discontinuity, I would simply note the pertinence of William Everdell's demonstration in *The First Moderns* that the revelation of the discontinuous is indistinguishable from modernism in the sciences as well as in art; so, while Jameson's diagnosis of the postmodern condition is persuasive, it involves a certain terminological equivocation.

into the blazing light of the Mystics
mingling with all

I am absolutely not You. (77)

To undertake the task of being everyone and no one, as Notley puts it, is a sublime instance of the experimental wager.

Ann Lauterbach makes the intriguing observation that "to be experimental is often taken to mean you have an aversion to form, rather than an aversion to conformity" (187). "Form" should be heard here as verb; *to form* means *to make,* and poetry is a making that may aspire to more than conformity. Such aspiration is risky. "To experiment means you must put what you know at risk to what you do not yet know" (189). Lauterbach rightly includes in her salutary definition the prospect not only of risk, but also of failure: "the experiment may fail."

> This willingness to risk failure seems essential.
> To risk failure one needs a sense of unfettered play, the play that would allow a failure to become useful for the next attempt, that would in a sense recycle the disaster.
> Nuclear waste cannot be recycled. It is the result of an experiment that should not have been undertaken. (188)

Conformist trends have been so pervasive in American poetry that experiment itself is often abjured as if it were radioactive waste. By advocating a recycling of the disaster, Lauterbach stands in tacit opposition to a masculine compulsion to repeat the disaster. *That* sort of disaster—the proper name for which is Apocalypse—is the eschatological event that validates all the tiny premonitions at its disposal, honorifically assimilating the martial ego (precipitated throughout history in the form of war) to divine fiat. We know how to "make war"; making peace remains experimental. As experimentation goes, I am reluctant to assign experiment a gender.[5] But historically, for reasons suggested in chapter 1, the

---

5. Adrienne Rich makes the following point about experiment and gender: "Even an 'experimental' solution can be conventional if it merely repeats an old experiment, doesn't

tide of innovation is now distinctly associated with women writers. In 1989 Susan Howe lamented the tendency for anthologists to "eliminate the work of women who have used or are using language in an experimental way" (171).[6] For my purposes, the point is not anthologies, but "experiment," and that has increasingly meant deliberating on work by women.

Because even the most "formalist" poem is admittedly an experiment during composition (after which its risks are not so evident), we need to imagine "experiment" in another register, or on another plane, as a claim of the *book* rather than the individual poem. The vast bulk of poetry fails to take up the challenge of the book as medium. (The verb "fail" is prejudicial; my concern here is not to criticize writers for simply gathering poems together, but to draw attention to those for whom gathering reveals a complexity not readily resolved by the judgment of taste or picking and choosing.) The book need not be an empty receptacle conveniently to hand, mere binder for a sheaf of poems that have no more claim to belonging together than the episodic momentum of a life or the ambitions of an imperial self. The actual pressure exerted by Whitman and Dickinson is precisely in their insistence on principles of poetic organization, a balance of discrete instances with the adhesiveness of a propositional order and a performative form.[7] The quality or urgency of a given group of poems can, of course, make a book like Ginsberg's *Howl* or Ashbery's *Self-Portrait in a Convex Mirror* seem compositional wholes.

---

recognize it has to struggle with a different problem—or with an old problem in a different way. A male poet who is frozen into conventional entitlements can only be conventional however 'experimental' his use of language" (137). Cogent as this sounds, in the first cited sentence Rich resorts to the formula touted by the New Critics after World War II in their dismissal of experimental modernism. What is an "old experiment"? The term is itself preemptively dismissive.

6. Howe's point is most recently proved, awkwardly enough, by Susan Aizenberg and Erin Belieu in their anthology *The Extraordinary Tide: New Poetry by American Women,* in which they offer the cavalier excuse for excluding so-called experimental poetry by suggesting it's readily available elsewhere.

7. *Leaves of Grass* in its perpetual revision until Whitman's death is familiar, of course; but recent investigations of Dickinson's "packets" reveal her as no less adamant about the adaptive schema available to the poet as continuance of poetic vision beyond the lyric occasion.

There is a wondrous profusion of recent books that have this kind of integrity, even though they are clearly compendia rather than composed books—for example, *Musca Domestica* by Christine Hume, *Torn Awake* by Forrest Gander, or *The Downstream Extremity of the Isle of Swans* by Mary Jo Bang—and I may be wrong in my estimation of what's composed and what's gathered; so, rather than attempt theoretical refinement, a series of examples will be more useful. Looking for signs of vitality and provocations of book potential, I offer the following (culled from a decade, in chronological order) as indicative and accomplished instances of an ongoing experimental tradition.

Oxota: A Short Russian Novel by Lyn Hejinian (1991). As everybody keeps saying about this book, it's not a novel; but the denials generate their own interest, an interest solicited by the subtitle in the first place, and I would advise readers of *Oxota* to recall the German Romantics' sense of the novel ("Roman" *auf deutsch*) as the culminating mode of poetry. This "short Russian novel" is also a long American poem at nearly three hundred pages, although the numbered sections are strictly fourteen lines apiece. The linear structure, however, resonates less with the sonnet than it does with the striated pattern of venetian blinds, particularly in that Hejinian's lines are paratactic; that is, "continuity" is to be discovered not from line to line, but in the larger rhythmic dimension of the narration (not so much story as *telling,* over the long haul). Parataxis in this case turns out to be an exemplary medium for tracking cross-cultural awakenings. It's as if between parallel lines bent on discovering "Russia," an unknown but gradually ascertainable set of other lines is directing an explorative pulsation back to an "America" that is harbored precariously in the American poet, who finds herself in the multiple site of sexual politics and cultural transaction—*translated,* in short, all the way there and back. Her own writing, in turn, dilates on itself as if it were a translation as well.

Iovis: All Is Full of Love by Anne Waldman (1993). *Iovis* is a savorful pot of mythopoeisis in which Waldman swishes around a concoction of American vernaculars in an exploration of masculinity. This is also an anthology of sorts, and Waldman's inclusion of so many personal statements begs the issue of "permissions" (over two dozen men are credited), but launches her well-developed riffing style into an expansive antiphonal dimension. The large page format is handsomely scored ("score" because Waldman's baseline *is* performance), and the graphic variability accentuates the multitude of voices, postures, and reckonings. The dance of genders is a real choreography here, and Waldman's vision—which is not a "version," not an argument—makes the old august presences of mythopoeisis seem plangently immediate, not numinous perhaps, but familiar and *breathing.* A second volume (1997) extends and consolidates the first, confirming the justice in Waldman's concluding affirmation: "*I had a lung / I sung him down*" (II: 311).

Materialism by Jorie Graham (1993). Graham has clearly emerged as successor to the Stevens-Ashbery lineage of high lyric meditation, which fits conventional expectations of "accomplishment" (registered symptomatically by Helen Vendler).[8] What's intriguing about *Materialism* is Graham's incorporation of fourteen sizeable extracts from a variety of sources, ranging from Plato and Bacon to Whorf and Wittgenstein, that introduce a welcome contrapuntal texture to her own poems. The extracts insinuate an anthology into the collection as a bifocal euphoria, dispossessing lyric authority just where it seems most assured. It's a telling effect, which reverberates its *alieniloquiam* back and forth through the rest of Graham's oeuvre, transforming *Materialism* from collection to conception. (Regrettably, the conception is effaced in Graham's selected poems, *The Dream of the Unified Field,* which includes none of the found materials.)

A Key into the Language of America by Rosmarie Waldrop (1994). Like Lucie Brock-Broido's *The Master Letters,* this is a work of cultivated ventriloquism. The title and the chapter sequence follow Roger Williams's 1643

8. Two Vendler books conclude with chapters on Graham: *The Given and the Made: Strategies of Poetic Redefinition* and *The Breaking of Style* (both Harvard University Press, 1995).

guidebook to the language of the Narragansett people of Rhode Island. The author makes a point of the numerological link between herself and her double: Waldrop was born in 1935, the year Williams's three-hundred-year banishment from Massachusetts expired. There are thirty-two chapters, all following a particular format: title, prose ethnography (with boldface indicating direct usage of Williams's original), a short list of words or phrases, then an italicized prose reverie (personal, female), concluding with a short verse. The supple resonances between these five elements evoke the conceptual aura of minimalist composers like Steve Reich or Philip Glass (though the historical orientation is closer to that of John Adams). It also preserves the feel of a reference book (with wacky entries). The writing is carefully positioned at the interface of cultural difference, intuited with appreciative wonder, while retaining a tinge of Eurocentric suppositions (Waldrop's German origin plays a most effective role here). Another interface is that between past and present: "Discrepancy of law pins **little aprons** on their females right from birth, the hairless genitive of price, to frighten off imagination. **Their second nakednesse** unsheathes a lack of foliage, but a few plant names cannot disturb the general conclusion as velvet can with us" (41).

Plainwater (1995) and *Glass, Irony, and God* (1995) by Anne Carson. Either book by itself would be notable, but their simultaneous publication enlivened them with the mark of Janus. Carson, like Alice Notley, is intrepid enough to adopt the claim of being everyone and no one. But Carson, by profession a classicist, has enviable resources at her disposal. For instance, the figure of Mimnermos—in the "Brainsex Paintings" sequence of poems, essay, and interviews that opens *Plainwater*—seems an altogether zany invention, but in fact such a poet existed, and Carson obtains momentum by means of her inspired translations. Scholastic conceits abound as Carson absorbs the travel narrative of Bashō (in "The Anthropology of Water"), spoofs a conference of phenomenologists (in "Canicula di Anna"), and in "Short Talks" (unfortunately edited somewhat from a previous chapbook version) produces a fascinating revelation of the parataxis implicit in scholarly lectures. *Plainwater*'s generic mix is less evident in *Glass, Irony, and God,* which, apart from its culminating essay on "The Gender of Sound," is a collection of five poem sequences. Yet even there "The Glass Essay" actually does engage essayistic compulsions, and "Book of Isaiah" is so powerful an act of biblical ventriloquism that reading it makes one feel witness to a nascent religion. Carson is a fierce ironist, and her title deliberately ticks off three of the most depleted tropes of conventional poetic yearning. But the fertility of formal invention does not obscure a passionate nature—which in fact stands better revealed. "I wonder if there might not be another idea of human order than repression," she writes at the end of *Glass, Irony, and God,* "another notion of human virtue than self-control, another kind of human self than one based on dissociation of inside and outside. Or indeed, another human essence than self" (136–37). With these books Carson is clearly inventing and practicing what she purports to merely wonder about.

Afterrimages by Joan Retallack (1995). "Gift" and "whimsy" are cover-blurb words that in this case ring true (the extra *r* in the utopian title is itself a whimsical gift that propagates expansively in the title "Amer-rata"). Retallack's book is unrelentingly composed, page by page, from beginning to end; *looking* prompts and subtends reading. Yet invitations to orality, animating spirits of enunciation, resound throughout, reminders of a cultural environment that indiscriminately weds sound to print in astonishing misalliances. We are attuned to the misalliances, as they constitute the media matrix of the daily real; but a poet like Retallack, subtly unthreading the same fibers, discloses another sensorium in her submersible hilarity. The power of the book is *hands-on* here, bearing a superficial resemblance to Susan Howe's painterly concoctions, but with a buoyant philosophical animation.[9]

9. Equally notable is Retallack's next book, *How to Do Things with Words* (1998), which also pursues "a new dispersal of the subject / or that there shall be a complete fragment" (63). In a surprising but well-deserved congestion, there are two articles about Retallack's work in the special issue of *Contemporary Literature* edited by Thomas Gardner on poetry of the 1990s: "Joan Retallack, A Philosopher Among the Poets, and Poet among the Philosophers" by Burton Hatlen, and " 'Fields of Pattern-Bounded Unpredictability': Recent Palimptexts by Rosmarie Waldrop and Joan Retallack" by Lynn Keller.

Muse and Drudge by Harryette Mullen (1995). First by the button-down tweed jacket ivy leaguers of the 1950s, later by the textualism of language poetry, the resources of song and chant and riddle have long been maligned in American poetry, despite such champions as Langston Hughes, Allen Ginsberg, and Gary Snyder. If these elements have always been central to black vernacular, they have never been so peppily integrated into a comprehensive poetic style as in *Muse and Drudge*. Eighty pages of quatrains (1,280 lines), at once playful and rueful, traverse a Möbius strip of topological stations in African American culture, an *imprinting* of orality that champions the crossroads where quick ear and close reading chance on each other and do their dance.

The Unbearable Heart by Kimiko Hahn (1995). Sex and death are often thematically intertwined, especially in opera—think of *La Bohème* or *Tristan and Isolde*—but in a lament for a mother? If mortality reveals organic form, how does one absorb accident (Hahn's mother died in a car crash) into the form? Hahn's book makes use of several formal strategies, undertaking the deep reckoning of grief in a way that discloses form helplessly bound to the isomorphic taunt of formlessness. "Form" is misleading in that Hahn uses *formats* as staging grounds for lament, *working through* trauma in the Freudian sense. A sequence of unabashedly personal poems is followed by a collage of vignettes; then the book takes a radical detour into erotica with "Cruising Barthes," after which a series of folktales serve as masks of domestic distress; then *The Unbreakable Heart* culminates in a sustained multivoiced rumination on orientalism, autobiography, and desire. "The Story and the Daughters" serves as a kind of coda, revisiting the obligation to find closure in grief by transmitting it and, in the process, transforming it into the continuum of generations, into the very fever of *generation* itself, performing once again the *mysterium tremendum* of sex and death.

The Master Letters by Lucie Brock-Broido (1995). The use of masks is a notable legacy of Browning, Yeats, and Pound, but it has been marginalized during the past fifty years. Pamela Hadas's *By Herself* (1983) is one of the most successful recent feats of transcorporeal innuendo, animating

a whole ancestry of plucky feminists. Brock-Broido's venture into mimicry is at once more delicate and more perilous, as she models her idiom
on the unique phraseology of Emily Dickinson's unmailed letters addressed "Dear Master." Brock-Broido adds a dozen letters to the count,
interspersed amid forty poems that, while maintaining the odd slant of
her Amherst diction, make no attempt to mimic Dickinson's poems.
"My voice thrown, my Other littler self on my own knee, practicing a
sleight of hand, the tongue of the Inventor wagging the tongue of the
Invented. It is true that each self keeps a secret self which cannot speak
when spoken to" (6). *The Master Letters* manifests this peculiar condition,
though the bravura of its eloquence confounds my urge to call it *voiced
speechlessness*.

Search Procedures by Erin Mouré (1996). This book marks the full plunge
of a prizewinning Canadian poet into an experiment in deconstruct-
ing her instinctive lyricism. The terms of the experiment are openly registered in periodic citations from language poets. Mouré contests the
space of the lyric by a series of procedures that truncate, abort, disband,
defile, and otherwise derange the unilateral momentum of the lyric impulse. Footnotes, hanging lines and phrases, countertexts, cross-outs,
and seriality dominate the book; the poems are forced into melodramatic
postures that cast a garish light on the emergent "person" one might (and
maybe should) mistake for an author; and Mouré heightens the internalized tension with periodic raids on legislated bilingualism (she lives in
Montreal): "Obelisk nature but we're wowed, eh. To touch / ce beau
monde. Malaise conduisant par-dessus / in granitic lesion, deposited in-
equally on terrain / mal interpreté" . . . "Mots anglais bien compris /
'outa here'" (53). There's nothing tepid about Mouré's embrace of poetic
experiment, which is continued and expanded in her follow-up volumes
A Frame of the Book (1999) and *O Cidadán* (2002). Like Jorie Graham,
Mouré is a prodigious writer, and both poets somewhat helplessly inhabit
their prodigality with a "voice" beholden ultimately to their preexperi-
mental roots. Mouré's "search procedures" resemble Graham's attempt
in *Swarm* to disband continuity. In both cases it's a bit like watching the
aristocrat go slumming (think Joel McCrea in Preston Sturges's film *Sul-*

livan's Travels). The great thing that leavens Mouré's attempt and sets it apart from Graham is her spirited sense of humor and play. It's a platitude to observe that most American comedy is actually made by Canadians; maybe the same holds true for infectious good cheer in poetry (e.g. Steve McCaffery, Christian Bök, Darren Wershler-Henry, Lisa Robertson, and even Anne Carson).

Some Other Kind of Mission by Lisa Jarnot (1996). So much effort has been directed at approximating the look of the printed page on the computer screen that it's nice to see its polymathic obverse in this other kind of mission. There are some two dozen photographs of collages (mainly text, not image) scattered throughout this hundred-page book, many of which approximate the hypertextual milieu of on-screen writing while returning it to its pragmatic precomputer labor of cut and paste. The sense of tide-pool gazing makes these pages a marvelous echo of Kurt Schwitters's collage boxes. The writing in the rest of the book is abstract (and/or concrete: "the fir terns rock pile. at a bank" [69]), careening off a spectrum of compositional procedures lending a fractal dimension to a limited series of narrative (and some dream) events and episodic set pieces. It's Jarnot's practical insight here to have realized a unique visual counterpoint (counterpunch) to such writing strategies.

The Front Matter, Dead Souls by Leslie Scalapino (1996). Scalapino's early work had a consistently unique tonality—a way of shaving and peeling perceptions into a bumpy continuum, like a film with a certain number of frames removed. In longer projects like *Way* (1988), *The Return of Painting, The Pearl, and Orion* (1991), and *The Front Matter, Dead Souls,* what had formerly seemed "technique" was newly revealed as virginal wonder, as if learning to talk and learning to write had occurred simultaneously. *Front Matter* deftly intercalates differing generic elements and impulses, commenting on its procedures as it goes. "I'm taking the outer now current culture *to be* the inner self drawing it in as one's core or manifestation—which it isn't. Then, it is externalized as oneself and is projected outward again as one's sense of real. That actually *is* one's inner self by acting upon its projection" (5). Scalapino cleaves enticingly near the spooky idiom of Opal Whiteley, the child diarist of 1920 whose lumber-camp universe largely consisted of animals like Lucian Horace Ovid Virgil, the toad, and the twin bats Plato and Pliny. But with Scalapino, what might seem childlike is actually the aperture (and fresh wound) of an ever-expanding chronicle of social inequity, human loss, and disorientation, exposure of discrepant lifestyles in the contested "public realm" that seems very much like a drainage ditch. It drains, it pours, and a manic/comic spectrum of moral hypertension is Scalapino's ineluctable result, as unique and spellbinding as the Eidophusikon (meaning "image of nature") of Philippe-Jacques Loutherbourg that took London by storm at the end of the eighteenth century.[10]

Debbie: An Epic by Lisa Robertson (1997). Everything about this book from Vancouver radiates cunning and style. (That old epic hero Odysseus was also evidence of his author's compositional guile.) The author's name and title on the cover typographically resemble an acrostic, against a deep blue background dark enough to obscure the photo of a ferocious barking dog. Throughout, the typography choreographs an "epic" display of mutations. The lines of text variously jump from one to twelve picas, and much of the book is composed in two-page spreads of display type. Despite the presentational grandeur, this is a diminutive epic that spans the book in eighteen episodes and a four-part interlude. The epic periodically spills over into verse footnotes, which themselves run hibernating beneath the text for a few pages ("ripe anthems in the clefts of prose / break in doubled utterance"—which is itself doubled by this footnote: "A ground will come, where persistence translates / those monuments, as follies of our fate" [lines 364–65]).[11] Profusion and precision abound. Typographic marvel though it is, *Debbie: An Epic* is a resoundingly delightful poem. Its epic provenance is legible not only in the diction, which effortlessly blends the archaic with current slang and reference, but also in the (re)appearance of "I" as a grammatically third-

10. On the Eidophusikon, see Stephan Oettermann, *The Panorama* 71–74, and Richard Altick, *The Shows of London* 117–27.

11. There are no page numbers, so all the display pages have to be referenced by proximity to the epic proper, which is provided throughout with line numbers (739 lines in all).

person character (an homage to Dorn's *Gunslinger?*): "I was a partici-
pant thespian / against knowledge authority decays / shall we take I
out close it up re / photograph it as soothing counting in / the dark
and the privacies we should be / fighting like we said we would" (lines
597–602).

Loose Sugar by Brenda Hillman (1997). Consider this gnostic proposition:
you will not "write" the poem; you will submit to a process—alchemy;
transmutation of the metals, the invincibles—and you yourself will become *prima materia,* your very being made raw (on the page, in the alem-
bic), remade in sufferance, kindled and smeared and leavened into a dis-
tillate: "your parents can't always help while the ruins assemble you"
(106). Meaning and being are sundered, and art appears to address the
rift, to adopt the seam as orphan other, twin vibrato of a "speaking self"
that hums with dark alliances. "The source of life is not life / but rebellion toward meaning" (75). Exactly. *Loose Sugar* is pitched at that exhilarating moment of release when an original and accomplished poet breaks
through to another medium. Hillman's *Death Tractates* (1992) and *Bright
Existence* (1993) had convened the poems around thematic axes, but here
the entire book is structurally dedicated in advance. The groupings have
in-binding integrity; the loose scatter of notes, headers, snag of antiphonal voicings, all serve as public notice of a new nourishment. *Loose Sugar*
is as deftly composed a book as Spicer's *Heads of the Town,* suffering its
descent with the same courage and ingenuity. And what a marvel to find
a new appropriation of alchemy (last glimpsed on such sustained scale in
The Loom by Robert Kelly), not as theme, but as mission and submission.

Deepstep Come Shining by C. D. Wright (1998). Idiomatic character is
also a prominent feature of this book-length poem, though the idiom
is clearly regional (Ozarks) and is vernacular rather than literary. But
Wright's procedure is distinctly experimental, as she splices voices and
images in an ongoing melody of attentions, banked and layered in different type sizes and changing principles of lineation. *Deepstep* is an archipelago of southern Americana (shockingly unattended, despite Jonathan
Williams's salutary provocations), with a quicksilver resonance likely to

evoke hillbilly blues one moment and Bakhtin the next. Wright's métier is the sound of colloquialism, and her homespun expressions combined with arcana embody Kenneth Burke's notion of poetry as the dancing of attitudes. American culture has long been too comfortable with its stereotypes of the Deep South; *Deepstep Come Shining* is a singular (and singularly unvexed) repudiation of such presumptions. Wright's work has always been peppy, with a zip best suited to the diminutive (e.g. *Tremble*). Here the spunk suffices for a hundred-page escapade, a buoyant homage to territorial footsteps tracking the open heart back home and beyond ("Make a left just beyond Pulltight Road" [8]; "We lunch on Onion River. Stop by Cloud's Fly Shop" [83]). To top it off, the cover design is utterly magnetizing.

The Character by Jena Osman (1999). Everybody knows what a puppet is, at least in the three-dimensional terms given by a two-dimensional proscenium in the theater. The complexity of *that* equation is what's on show in the cascade of operational scenarios Osman invents. Her explorations here embody a clear understanding of the residual invitations of representation, particularly if the space of the poem is reconceived as thespian enterprise. *The Character* has the cumulative effect of a long tour behind the scenes of a highly sophisticated opera house, but with this proviso: you will never see a performance. Seats sold out in perpetuity; access restricted; time run out—whatever. After inspecting the wizardry of the stage gadgets in *The Character,* however, it seems no great loss not to have the usual show, the expiring consumptive in the garret, the crowd of wailing suitors, the routine bohemian arias. Osman's "character(s)" have more affinity with the geomorphic assemblages of Oskar Schlemmer for his Triadic Ballet at the Bauhaus. When they do occasionally acquire names, the effect resurrects the spirit the Surrealists searched for in sundry objects from the flea market (see the found poem based on Supreme Court transcripts); and like the Surrealists, Osman recognizes that the question of social justice is most vividly posed in the form of the puppet (marionette, doll, character, and even *book* or *poem*). "According to Kleist the moment when all have attained the perfect grace of the dead text, the un-self-consciousness of the puppet, is the end of the world. He does not account for a time where a man is forced to be dead text and the others remain not so. He does not imagine a time where grace is the stance of the beaten. The relation between action and life depends on this" (108)—the last words of the book, and first principle for the savory labor of rereading that it artfully calls for.

Then, Suddenly— by Lynn Emanuel (1999). A casual glance might give a misleading impression, inasmuch as any page in this book incarnates characteristic faults of workshop verse: cavalier gestures of intimacy, ventured by prominent first-person singular, in familiar domestic settings. But then, *Suddenly*—it's all pastiche; the entire book is a meticulously orchestrated dollhouse of lyric gestures, deploying all the skills of simile, narrative incident, and frank avowal that have been routinized in free verse practice, but here bent on contesting the supposed virtues of immediacy and feeling. Emanuel is explicit about her aims in an interview: "*Then, Suddenly*— is a book of rebellions: the characters are in rebellion against the author, and the author both participates in and rebels against the literary conventions that make her an author. . . . I did not want this book to be the object of a reader's regard. I wanted to make the reader the object of the book's and author's regard. And yet, I too, as the author, play the role of the oppressor" (Interview 29). Emanuel certainly has the measure of her enterprise. To read this book is to be mercilessly exposed to the pump of lyric expectation implanted in readers weaned on late-twentieth-century poetry. Emanuel knows the voice-over of our moment and pins it wriggling on the wall, daring the reader to eat *that* peach and like it too. As different as they are in sensibility and orientation, Emanuel shares something crucial with Jena Osman. "I wanted to assert that a poem on a page is itself also a performance," Emanuel declares, adding, "there are many different ways of 'performing poetry'" (Interview 29).

A Point Is That Which Has No Part by Liz Waldner (2000). Waldner's first book, *Homing Devices,* was a fabulously inventive potpourri held together primarily by the device of phonic overlap. Where others might collage by abrupt discontinuity, Waldner uses single words as the banana peels of slippery synecdoche (*"comme on dit,* come up" [17], "if you herded ant feet through a sheen of beet, their traces could line faces or efface plans to meet destiny in later places" [67]). The result was a sensation of continuity through cacophony. *A Point* uses the same devices, but it is meticulously organized in terms provided by Euclid (point, line, circle, square, triangle). The flagrant artifice (and inner logic) of this arrangement curiously serves to accentuate Waldner's unique "voice" (which inimitably combines colloquialism with the semantic neutrality of machine-generated translations) in ways that *Homing Devices* buried in its undifferentiated onrush. In these two books Waldner has forged the most distinctive poetic idiom in English since Irish poet Paul Muldoon.

Plot by Claudia Rankine (2001). "The hidden solid in the shift of our experience is a child" (85), writes Rankine in what sounds descriptive but is actually propositional, for the child here is not what it seems. On one level *Plot* rehearses (in nine sections, how could it not?) a pregnancy undergone by Liv and husband Erland (the germinating infant is called Ersatz). But *Plot* is fictive at the core, where, fittingly, the reader encounters Lily Briscoe from *To the Lighthouse* struggling with her unfinished painting, followed by Virginia Woolf herself, loading her pockets with rocks on her final day. Rankine's compositional strategies vary with each section, disclosing the emplotment that lurks between every apparently innocuous gesture of mere presentation. That such emplotment masquerades as natural is highlighted (I want to say *backlit* to stress the *noir* aspect of what turns out to be a very dark vision) by the *natal* theme, which Rankine sustains with nautical poise. *Plot* renews Pound's periplum in a truly new world, shedding all the cultural baggage associated with his Homeric and Dantesque voyaging, while retaining "a hurt progeny to a live evil living hymn within" (44).

Disobedience by Alice Notley (2001). As Notley enthuses in "Homer's Art," "What a service to poetry it might be to steal story away from the novel & give it back to rhythm & sound, give it back to the line" (402). That's just what she managed to do in the long poem *The Descent of Alette* (1996), with its oneiric heraldry and unique application of quotation marks as prosodic cues. The venturesome sense of theft Notley claims for story is more audaciously pursued in *Disobedience,* which establishes a precarious reciprocity between the continuum of a dream life and the cultural displacement of the author's relocation to Paris. The mediumistic labor of culling dreams is exercised here on a scale to rival Yeats's séances. Notley deftly enfolds her oneiric *prima materia* in an idiom dispensing with all traces of reportage; the dreams here assume the dimensionality of historical events, numinous provocations endured in a spirit of whimsical desperation. The casual daybook notational style sustains a multilateral ventilation, so that memory, fantasy, imagist observation, political rage, and psychological disarray easily cohabit the same space, and the *amor fati* one associates with dreams leaks out into the circumambient medium of the real world, with all its desperations and elations intact.

In the examples enumerated here, inspiration does not consecrate the autonomous will of a creator; rather, it initiates writer and reader into a mutual habitat. Experiment, considered as a claim of the book, overcomes the lingering bifurcation of poetic praxis into rival camps (progressive versus conservative, experimental versus formalist). Except in rare instances, experiment is not an absolute; nor is any real risk involved in broad social terms. The book, however, is a precise locale in which risk can become productive, and the experiment is precipitated rather than anticipated by its author.

Susan Wheeler complains, of dissident gestures, that "To step outside is, also, a well-worn trope, and is absorbed just as readily" (325). True enough, and the point has been made definitively by Paul Mann in *The Theory-Death of the Avant-Garde.* After a century of overfamiliarization, "avant-garde" became the predictable site of dissidence. But what if we disencumber the value of experiment from avant-garde? What if the avant-garde was once an expedient means of making experiment visible but also historically delimited? What if we overcome the historical fetish that makes the urge to experiment seem "avant-garde" and therefore retrograde? To do so would enable us to recognize a differently configured avant-garde, one no longer preassigned a place in the banquet of indignity, but making selective use of its occasions, not all of which need be confrontational. To do so would also liberate "experiment" from agonistic overtones. Besides, when defiance is absolutely necessary, you don't want to add to the risk a further burden of experimentation. (*Howl* was written in biblical cadences, for good reason.) "The ambition to find language combinations, structures, methods of composition, that remain *unassimilable* in the broad banality of the cultural market should not be faulted, should not be construed as 'digging our own hole'" (Wheeler 324). The present vitality and variety of poetry would appear to confirm Paul Fry's sense, in his *Defense of Poetry,* that "the very intensity of our need for answers spins itself into a frenzy, a self-defeating compulsion generating cloned signifiers like a computer virus, a burnout or meltdown of reason that reveals, in its turn, an opposite need to which poetry responds" (4–5). Confronting such burnout, *response* is necessarily the fruit of experiment.

9

To Moisten the Atmosphere

Notes on Clayton Eshleman

The following notes make local points about the work. My strategy was to consciously avoid being swept along in the mode of commentary, exegesis, and hermeneutic probing, because I sensed that Eshleman's poetry compels, lavalike, an inevitable duplication if one tries to stay with it, reporting on it as it goes by. Many readers, I suspect, find themselves confused by Eshleman's work. I have always found it commendably direct in laying out its motives; but the imaginal texture is congested, thick, tactile. It requires not so much reading as digestion. *Gerere:* Indo-European root providing a basis for the words CONGEST, DIGEST, INGEST, SUGGEST, REGISTER, GESTURE, and JEST. Like Walter Benjamin's unfinished *Passagenwerk* on the arcades of Baudelaire's Paris, I feel as though the process of gesturing toward, digesting, and registering Eshleman's suggestive congestions and jests is an interminable project. What follows are episodes.

∾

In a 1977 article in *Boundary 2,* I identified Jack Spicer's Hades in terms of his Orphic emancipation of pronouns. The way in which *I, you, he, she, it, we,* and *they* in Spicer's book cycles get activated as phonemic particles extends not only to pronouns (spear points of identity) in Eshleman's

Hades, but to quantitative sections of language as biopsy, contusion, se-
cretion, no longer even "speech act" in the

> dear unframed minds of poets each
> clutching their pieces of hemispheric
> erection with its crocodile basis, the fear of
> drying verb, of doors whose nouns will not turn,
> of wee wee tethered kneenuts, alleyoops of traceyfire,
> of nail notwiches mouthed by Gertrude, of garbage.
>
> (*Hades* 50)

It is possible to read Eshleman's work in terms of its periodic swings between the manifest, embodied "garbage" (the pure menacing play of language), and its opposite, most evident in the earnest diagrammatic ex-
positions of what such play means. This latter pole is represented by
those poems that pursue such concepts as "therio-expulsion" and "the
separation continuum" and that are dominated by a rhetoric of the image
("Visions of the Fathers of Lascaux" and "Hades in Manganese"). The former mode, a supple embodiment of language play (not only in the ludic
sense, but as in the slack of a rope, excess *give,* Derridean supplement in
his account of Plato's pharmacy) is most evident throughout *Hades in
Manganese,* especially in "Sound Grottos," "Dot," "Hermes Butts In," and
"Silence Raving." Although *Hades* and *Fracture* overlap, both temporally
and thematically, they are clearly distinguishable in terms of the former's
playfulness and seriality (note the many pieces sectioned by asterisks,
pauses, and punning perturbations) and of the latter's relative sobriety of
purpose. In the selected poems, *The Name Encanyoned River,* there is a bias
for the expository retrospection of *Fracture,* but in the final section (suitably titled "Antiphonal Swing") there's a return to infant burbling, mul-
tiphasic identities rising up through the textured voicings of the poems
like so much laughing gas. In "Deeds Done and Suffered by Light" a further degree of hilarious solemnity is attained when the poet's dead parents start sputtering in their adjacent coffins, trying to get Clayton Jr.
(then fifty) to stop staying out late at night, while the father's "GLADYS

WHAT DO YOU WANT?" percolates up through the text over and over until it blurs to "GRADDISROTDRUDRURUNT" (*Name Encanyoned River* 232).

Eshleman's *antiphonal swing* (skimmed off the final line of Hart Crane's *The Bridge*—"Whispers antiphonal in azure swing") is literally what makes the poetry work. If it's serious, it must, somehow, get silly; if it's overcome with levity, it must submit to a sobering scene of instruction. This rhetorical oscillation keeps the language in view as event and obstacle both; it sustains wife Caryl, parents Gladys and Clayton Sr., along with many others as active eruptions rather than references; and most significantly, it gives the reader a place apart, a momentary sanctuary from the poem's inevitable compulsions, because there's always another mood, another bend in the road. When the air of the explanatory sarcophagus gets stale, there is bound to be some refreshment like "Eunice Wilson, over in Plot #52541" (*Name Encanyoned River* 232). Eshleman's is a work in which "mature transformations / intermingled with the immature," in which

> Words were walls worth boring through, worth
> turning into combs, words were livable
>
> hives whose centers, or voids,
> sounded the honey of emptiness dense
> with the greyish yellow light nature becomes
> to the soul for whom every thing is a cave
> (*Name Encanyoned River* 233)

The first grotto of the Eshleman grotesque is the cave of being bound by birth to Indianapolis (which Kurt Vonnegut, as I recall, dubbed the asshole of the universe) in a characteristically middle-American family romance, epitomized in the image of twelve-year-old Clayton stuck in the laundry chute, chatting with his mother, who prefers this arrangement that puts the Bakhtinian lower body out of sight (*Name Encanyoned River* 231). The second grotto is pledge week in Bloomington, Indiana, Tenth and Morton Streets, Phi Delta Theta, where "What is virgin or just beginning to be experienced / is destroyed before it is fully there" (*What She Means* 63). This is followed by the recuperative grotesquerie of

Reichian therapy, lying naked in fetal position "under the searching eye of a clothed adult" (*Hades* 107). Subsequent postures in the grotto resonate with Bud Powell sipping "lunch on all fours" in a "rudimentary turning, crawling / chorus after chorus" (*Name Encanyoned River* 139).[1] The informing image is Blake's engraving of Nebuchadnezzar with clawed hands and feet, his dripping torso breaking out in spots of animal pelt. Possibly the theme of therio-expulsion originates here; it recurs continually in images that duplicate Nebuchadnezzar "crawling in place on a leash" (see "Sound Grottos" and "Tartaros" in *Hades* for a start). In this posture, the animal body contaminates the human, and vice versa, as the separation of one from the other becomes a traumatic continuum. A singular fifth eidolon of this apparition is that of the doppelgänger in "The Dragon Rat Tail," who turns out to be Robert Kelly blurting instructions for dealing with the parents ("Find them in the grass!" [*Name Encanyoned River* 99]). The moment that Kelly speaks here, the terms of ventriloquial companionship stand revealed: Eshleman is in the grotto of *The Loom,* sliding through another man's entrails, vomiting prophetic axioms of a helpless parasitology.

～

Paul Blackburn enters Eshleman's work as the guardian angel of his own rebirth as a poet (the first birth being not as a poet, but as an Indianapolis WASP pursuing a literary career against all odds). Blackburn died in September 1971; in October, Kelly began writing *The Loom* while living in the Los Angeles area. The Kelly/Eshleman companionship during this time was integral to both men. The knot of fused intelligibility, then, is a "covering cherub" of Paul impacting Clayton and Robert into coauthors of a Nachlass, an afterbirth of his death in their own work.

   Much like Pound's surgical role in extracting *The Waste Land* out of "He Do the Police in Different Voices," Eshleman's maturation as a poet can be precisely dated from his role in guiding *The Loom* through inception, revision, to final publication. *The Gull Wall* is saturated with the reward, the privilege of the transference: stirrings of a third-person narration, an

---

   1. This poem, "The American Sublime" in *Hades in Manganese,* was retitled "Un Poco Loco" after Bud Powell's tune in *The Name Encanyoned River.* In general I cite from the latter volume because of its revisions (Eshleman is an immaculate, and fanatic, reviser).

enhanced clarity of first-person avowal, and the downward-spiraling, convulsive tug of the shorter line ("Realignment," "Creation," "Portrait of Francis Bacon") that tightens the focus and speeds the delivery. It's intriguing to note how much it has been Eshleman, rather than Kelly, who has delivered on the promise of *The Loom*.

Eshleman's focus as a poet is deeply indebted to others, in ways so explicit as to make a mockery of Harold Bloom's "family romance" of traumatic lineage and the psychic distress of stylistic appropriation. (On the other hand, Bloom's psychotropic model is exactly to the point with respect to Eshleman's literal family romance.) It's because of this indebtedness/embeddedness that his immersion in Kelly's *Loom* became Eshleman's own polar maelstrom, through which the spirit of Blackburn descends, corkscrews in, and makes the rounds as if it were a cherubic physician attending the legion of damaged souls in a personal-history clinic, patching them up so Eshleman can ventriloquize his own recovery through animated puppets (for puppets, think Hans Bellmer). It sounds like a hideous process—and it is. But I would suggest that it's just this grotesque commitment, unflinchingly faced at the time, that provided Eshleman with a mountain of useful debris to burrow through. What's more, because he was so assiduously burrowing, on all fours, subjected to the intertextual harrowing of Kelly-Blackburn-Vallejo, he was in the right position to feel the full impact of Paleolithic cave art during his first exposure to it in 1974.

This particular history I toss out as a challenge to anybody who would read Eshleman's work in conventional ontogenetic fashion, seeing a slow rise to maturity followed by a plateau of "major work." Such a canon-haunted perspective can never recognize what is most frightening about *Indiana, Altars,* or *Coils;* this is the work of a man so desperate to become a poet that if left unguided he will ruin his own life just to have suitable material (i.e., the conventional bourgeois romance of self-destruction for art's sake). The work of the 1970s–80s is the result of honoring the guides, the *daimons,* and attending to them when they came along.

～

Imagine Blake's image of Nebuchadnezzar as a portrait of Eshleman; those pelt drips off his flank are adhesive tentacles. Having carried so much of other people's writing on his back (as translator), some of it stuck and has come off in chunks. The Vallejo phrase "the name encanyoned river"—swollen with sixteen years' translation of Vallejo's work —became a dense six-page poem. The elegy for Holan in *Fracture* is uncannily given over to the Czech poet's voice (Eshleman having cotranslated his extraordinary long poem "A Night with Hamlet"). Comparable but smaller tatters of others' works and voices swirl about in eddies at the margins of poems, but they are generally submerged in the vortex. Eshleman's style is monolithic in its onward surge, so that the contributing elements glimpsed in the flood appear as bits of human flesh borne downstream after a catastrophe. The force of the flow is emblematic of the larger, overriding disaster humankind has made of the world; compulsion is not strictly individualized, and in fact the sense of personal identity is always clotted with others (like Whitman in "Song of Myself" #31: "I find I incorporate gneiss, coal, long-threaded moss, fruits, grains, esculent roots, / And am stucco'd with quadrupeds and birds all over"). At its most distressing, otherness is laminated as a mask, directly onto the face—too close to see, too restricting even to properly breathe through. "The Dragon Rat Tail" thus becomes a most peculiar flare, an *ars poetica* (*ars* rhyming in bodily *grottesca* with *arse*), the plasmic interiority of his poetics accidentally revealed within the poem. In the presence of this disclosed procedural turbulence, this autopoiesis, he can only be

>   hideously embarrassed by
> the closeness of the thing,
> whatever it was, to my
> own organs, that I was pulling
> myself inside out, that the poem
> I sought was my own menstrual
> lining.
>   (*Name Encanyoned River* 99)

Eshleman has not only translated, but in his choice of originals has also managed to constellate a pantheon of uncannily related figures in Césaire, Vallejo, Artaud, and Holan. The French, Spanish, and Czech texts are gnarled, full of glottal impediment, ungainly, chunky, even difficult to pronounce—which is to say, much like the English of Eshleman's own poems. It cannot be overemphasized that the material intractability of his work is intimately related to the experience of translating seemingly "untranslatable" figures. It has enabled him to forge an idiom that speaks to virtually inaccessible sensations of personal agony, and this in turn facilitates an acute registration of tortures and deprivations going on around the world, entering his work (most notably with "The Tomb of Donald Duck") as part of an ongoing texture of privacy where the public can begin to hurt in a familiar voice.

To read Eshleman is to an encounter a claim that prohibits browsing. You can't dip in casually; his is not a poetry of easy diversions. This demand has severely curtailed an adequate public reception of Eshleman, more perhaps than that of his contemporaries. Is it because most poets offer some ready-made cue, some starter kit for generating more poems, idiomatic plugs, or electrical sockets that can be tapped into for current? It is surely the case that Eshleman's work doesn't yield itself to this kind of poaching. His poetry provokes reflection, engagement, eliciting a bodily compulsion to either keep reading or else go on to something altogether different. It's exhausting to read, because it doesn't pander to any formulaic intimacy of disclosure. Nor does it conform to vanguard models, which can also provide the reader with an escape hatch (spot the method and move on). There is no pretense that it is habitable, in its concreteness, by anybody else than its author, its survivor.

Bob Perelman's taproot to César Vallejo in "The Unruly Child" (in *To the Reader*) provides a link with Eshleman as translator and, if followed out, affords one of the few glimpses of something like an Eshleman "influence" in a younger (and nonallied) poet. Where have we seen the mode of the political grotesque of Perelman's *The First World* before?

Let language, that sports page of being
mystify its appearance in all speech writing thought tonight

so that the thing, that object of burnished flirtation
can smuggle out of the self, that drill bit

(First World 46)

Having taken off our corsets and 19th century
headgear, how perplexing it is, to feel media
slipping the power out of language as one might debone
a chicken before the remaining flesh is roasted, eaten,
done with

(What She Means 68)

This is not an isolated example, but a demonstrable precedent; which is not to deny Perelman's particular skills, his unique acrobatic contortions, but to breathe a sigh of relief that somewhere, somehow, the cauterizing precisions of the Eshleman *grottesca politica* have acquired a life of their own, a functionality not indebted to the quirks of his temperament and particulars of his own life.

～

The *New York Times Book Review* assertion that Eshleman is a poet who "will not cooperate with taste, judgment, aesthetic standards" is possibly the most useful statement on his work to have appeared thus far (October 11, 1981). What it unwittingly says is that Eshleman is not one of those who *do* cooperate in every way they can, whose work settles benignly into a workmanlike poise, a determined but subservient professionalism. These "cooperative" poets resemble the legion of German artists who carried on during the Third Reich as if all those *others* who had fled the homeland were shirkers, misfits, or degenerates. In the *Times* formulation, "taste" is the watchdog of political hegemony. In literary politics, aesthetic "standards" are to the practice of poetry what bipartisan squabbles are to politics; both are masquerades, prosthetic compensations for something missing. Eshleman's noncooperation is exemplary, a much needed sensation of alarm on the phantom limb of the body politic.

～

How can you tell whether an Eshleman poem is "uncooperative"? Take "Junk Mail," for instance; to all conventional purposes, the poem replicates a familiar model: Poet as Tourist of Self-Authenticating Experience. Like any workshop poet, Eshleman sports with the provocation, spoofs it, takes it seriously, agonizes over it, but then, flagrantly uncooperative, turns himself into both spectator and spectacle. He schizzes. The poem bifurcates, and we're left with a self-diddling creature called Me unzipping his pants on the basement floor.

> Nothing, charmed from its nickel dungeon,
> eyes this little fellow like we frat rats used to eye
> a frightened, unsure, slightly ugly, clearly needy girl.
>   (*Name Encanyoned River* 198)

Nothing, I might add, can compare with the abrupt and utter rudeness of this change of face, the slipperiness of aspect in which the convention of a unifying perspective is abandoned and a hideously partial aspect ("we frat rats") is taken on without irony. Or if it is, it's catachresis, a "mis-use" (uncooperativeness) of image or figure by being a *full use* of it. In the fullness of the time of "Junk Mail," we frat rats are all eyeing an unsure, frightened, needy girl. The rest is up to the reader, that newfound *she,* that oasis of migratory pronouns.

~

A book by Geoffrey Harpham, *On the Grotesque: Strategies of Contradiction in Art and Literature,* usefully focuses the notion of the "grotesque" not only as a tradition, but also with application to the "grotesque realism" of Bakhtin (important to Eshleman since the early 1970s), with its riotous intrusions of the "lower body stratum" into the patrolled estate of Apollonian clarity. The following passages have immediate relevance for reading Eshleman.

(1) "[T]he grotesque, and those who indulge in it, frequently encounter a backlash that takes the form of genealogical abuse with accusations of illegitimacy, bastardy or hybridization, terms that indicate structural confusion, reproductive irregularity, or typological incoherence. *Genre, genus* and *genitals* are linked in language as in our subconscious" (Harpham 5). Not only does the *Times* critic reproach Eshleman for his uncooperative untidiness, blurring the categorical certainties of aesthetics

and the well-made poem (like a well-made bed, spit-shined shoes, and a clean rifle); but also I recall a comparably wild claim by another critic who accused Eshleman of printing his own photo on the cover of the 1968 Grove Press translation of Vallejo. A patent absurdity (the visage was recognizably Vallejo's to anybody who knew), this could only happen to someone like Eshleman, whose immersion in the grotesque incites a boundary delirium in others.

(2) "These figures can best be described as images of instantaneous process, time rendered into space, narrative compressed into image" (Harpham 11). Think of "Tiresias Drinking," with its image of "mouths forever frozen / at the roller coaster's summit in wild hello" (*Name Encanyoned River* 155). The poem collapses successive images of the underworld until it hits this freeze-frame greeting. In *Hades* and *Fracture* the continual brooding on the underworld is an attempt to spatialize the Paleolithic, make it visible now. Or to make the cave-wall images—all that *is* visible now—a potent compression of the natural history of early humans, the narration of origins disclosed in a glance (and not just any glance, but one given by the flash of a nuclear bomb).

(3) "The grotesque is a naive experience, largely contained within the context of representational art, art in which, however temporarily and provisionally, we believe" (Harpham 18). Eshleman's work is abidingly representational, but its means of representation are constantly destabilized by the matrix of the grotesque. Eshleman's pledge: to submit to the metamorphosis, but aspire to the coherence, of selfhood; to honor love and marriage as a functional resolution of two independent identities; to accede to reasonable statement and cultivated, nurtured images as being in themselves sufficient for communication and social bonding. Such notions are not naive; no, they are grotesque. "The Color Rake of Time" is their anthem.

(4) "[T]he grotesque consists of the manifest, visible, or unmediated presence of mythic or primitive elements in a nonmythic or modern context. It is a formula capable of nearly infinite variation, and one which, rightly understood, illuminates the entire vast field of grotesquerie" (Harpham 51). Eshleman's heraldic figures, like Tiresias or Ariadne, are calculated incubations, "unmediated" presences, because they

so saturate the poems with their insistently primitive nature. They are not classical statuary, but grotesque harbingers who reach up, pawing and fingering the present, contaminating it with the glow of *grottesca* as well. The mythic elements in Eshleman are diffused, not figurally specific so much as auras of an unfocusable aurora borealis of the imaginal. Despite his preoccupation with spiders (his heralds), Eshleman's is really a bovine, ruminating imagination, feeding perennially on the same turf. Maybe he sees the spiders so clearly because in the Nebuchadnezzar/Bud Powell posture they happen to be local centaurs in the bovine gaze, up to its ears in sacred nutritive filth. As Harpham says, "meaning, which must go somewhere, migrates to the low or marginal" (74).

(5) Harpham, like Eshleman, is drawn to Blake's rendering of the shaggy Nebuchadnezzar. Such emblematic figures of the grotesque "are in a state of anarchy, producing an impression of atrocious and inappropriate vitality" (Harpham 6). This is a useful description of Eshleman's poems, in which all forms of life are raffishly prolific and uncontainable; the dead parents won't stay dead, the frat rats' escapades from decades ago keep staining the present with their "aborted ooze," the daily count of animals going extinct asserts itself in the desperate cycle of food-to-fecality and the semen-menses continuum. Anything organic, in fact, if given a suitably grotesque space—a tunnel, an intestine, a cave— blurts out indelicate promptings from the deep carnal appetite, the implacable gargoyle that howls, over and over, the permeability of any hydrocarbon-based form of life, gnawing at "The Seeds of Narrative":

> at 15,000 BC our torso is already
>
> a slack empty loop, a kind of lariat falling
> nowhere, at the top of which is the bird head we've
> desperately put on to stop
>
> conformity to ourselves—already we are a mask
> atop a watery loop, heartless, organless
> but not sexless for, like a gash in motion,

our penis is out, without terminal, out on brown rock,
blackness-bathing, pronged up as if it could match
the uterine hunger of

Who is that hovering above this little tentacle,
this little only thing we are putting forth?

(Fracture 57–58)

Eshleman's fraternity scenes are as graphic as Robert Capa's war photos. But as language, they are more thoroughly self-portraits than a photo can ever be. The grotesquerie is thus comparable to the work of Diane Arbus, all of whose compositions seem self-portraits, hideously parasitical on the visages of others. What is most disturbing in Arbus, as in Eshleman, is the uncanny saturation of the whole world with the specificity of personal experience and idiosyncratic taste, as though everything—every extraneous detail, any disaster however distant, and the most abhorrent urges—were all in the family. The outer limit of this mode might be marked by the photos of Joel Peter Witkin, whose cadaverous tableaux raise the model of family and kinship to an unpalatable extreme.

∽

In light of its research orientation, Eshleman's is a scholarly poetry, improbably tethered to a churning language and a "fecality that wants to be born" (see "The Seeds of Narrative" in *Fracture*). *Fracture* and *Hades in Manganese* contain between them two dozen pages of prose contextualization. This procedure of self-exegesis then escalates: *Hotel Cro-Magnon* (1989), *Under World Arrest* (1994), and *From Scratch* (1998) add another sixty pages, much of it in the form of detailed notes to the poems. Such gestures are not self-important claims to seriousness, but a manifest care that the text be a worksite, a research center, not a performance space where the gladiatorial poetic ego struts. A ground of seriousness is provided for the reader at the poet's expense.

∽

Many of Eshleman's poems function like sanctuaries, safe houses for eye-witnesses on the lam, on the run, forced to change name and residence and even identity, simply to stay alive after giving testimony. But the poems are sanctuaries also in the religious sense of the confessional. To consider the integrity of this space, this sanctuary, note how many Eshleman poems undergo a healing toward the end, a sobering up after the Bacchanal, a suturing of exposed parts. The act of closure is rarely elegant in Eshleman; this is not because (as it may seem) he is a poet of middles—which after all would be entirely appropriate to his gastronomic poetics—but because the spatial organization of a sanctuary is strict; inside is kept strictly separate from outside, and the transition is abrupt, instantaneous, like coming out of a cave. In the lines that conclude "The Loaded Sleeve of Hades,"

> you are closed and opened
> in the multiple ambivalences of your fracture,
> and no resolution is sincere.
>
> (*Name Encanyoned River* 151)

In the preface to *Hades in Manganese,* Eshleman confesses an urge to divide the book into sections, "one for poems dealing more or less directly with paleolithic imagery and one for poems which do not. Then I realized that such a division would be against the way I try to write. I have no interest whatsoever in writing poems 'about' the caves, or even doing poems that can be identified as 'poems with the paleolithic as the subject.' It is the present itself, with all its loop backs and dead-end meanders, that is precious to establish" (12). However, this has not kept Eshleman from aligning himself with a procedural method all too easily mistaken for the genre poem of tourism, set theme, direct treatment of the "thing itself," and so forth. Some of his most eloquent poems are textbook topical in just this way, from "Hearing Betty Carter" in *What She Means* to "Permanent Shadow" and "The Lich Gate" in *Hades in Manganese,* "Magdalenian" and "The Inn of the Empty Egg" in *Fracture* and "The Man with a Beard of Roses" in *The Name Encanyoned River,* to cite a few. Not to mention the ongoing series of "portraits," "still-life" framings, or the travel poems (location given, date attached). For a reader inclined to the Brooks and Warren or Ciardi version of the poem as self-regulating and

well-behaved cultural artifact, Eshleman's work glitters with many exemplary pieces that could be lifted out of context, slapped together into
a book that even *The New York Times* might find compliant with its standards of taste and judgment. Impeccably crafted and envisioned pieces
such as "Ira," "The Crone," and "The Color Rake of Time" come to mind.
But these are really sleights of hand within the larger panorama, which
incline to process, image-based rhetoric, and an angular associative logic
rooted in the "weird" chords for which bebop was legendary. I trust the
tangible, marked progressions most in *Hades in Manganese,* its many poems in sections like oranges, opening out on the hinges of their asterisks
concentric, sweet, segmented, partial. By contrast, a monstrosity like
"Visions of the Fathers of Lascaux" abandons this formal integrity and
simply gushes, on and on, almost to no purpose (or rather, for the purpose of invigorating its author's imagination—a legitimate end, if less
rewarding for a reader).

∼

One of the signals of a new level of rigor in Eshleman's work of the early
1970s is a commitment to personal integrity (rather than aesthetic con-
straint) within the poems. "The Cogollo" is a prime example. The poem
sustains an acute vision of orgasm commercialized as the Big O (c.f., the
self-help industry Stephen Heath exposes in *The Sexual Fix*). Eshleman's
"orgasm as gargoyle" is profusely illuminated with grotesqueries, but
rather than rising in summation to a final, overpowering image, there is
instead an ebbing of the disturbance, the poem ending:

> love, made, keeps me living in the poem and the poem,
> to remain pregnant in birth, tumbles me out on the shore
> to illuminate, with Caryl again, antiphonal.
>
> (*Name Encanyoned River* 107)

This is not an aesthetically attractive or even cogent ending. It doesn't
begin to fulfill any of the literary establishment criteria for closure. But
the personal integrity it abides by is a singular model for a renewed aesthetic attention, where the old saw of the separation of life and work is
broken down, overcome, cast aside. Caryl's presence here is as necessary

as the many dedicatory prose notes explaining her role as auditor, mate, companion, insistent ever on "what she means."

What She Means is a terribly forthright title for a book of poetry, uniquely responsible to its ground, background, fact and act, motives and motifs. For in every book since *The Gull Wall,* Eshleman has done more than dedicate the work to his wife, Caryl (in *Under World Arrest* the concluding section of notes is titled "Gratitude and Annotation"); he has pointed insistently to the work as consecration of the marriage. The nature of what is said in the text is conditioned by, seasoned by, someone besides the author. This is properly *what she means.*

As a title, *What She Means* also reflects on the heredity of male poetry, exposing an unclaimed veil of companionship that is most assuredly there, but too often mystified by talk of the muse. There is much to be gained by looking beyond the traditional specter of literary continuity as a coterie of male bonding (and not only to discover the obvious neglected resource of the female writer). *What She Means* is a sure-footed contribution here, opening the male poet to an order altogether different from Phi Delta Theta. The antiphonal engagement with Caryl makes of the marriage a literary event, and makes the poet a "pledge" or initiate of something worthier than brotherhood.

⁓

Since the preceding notes were published in 1987, Eshleman has published three more books, big ones (another 550 pages), constituting not only a body of work, but a salutary model of what investigative poetry can be. His encounter with the Paleolithic has been sustained in ongoing visits to the Dordogne caves (the title *Hotel Cro-Magnon* honors his principal residence in the region, in Les Eyzies). The work continues to be involved with imaginative precursors, and increasingly preoccupied with painting (in the twenty-page poem "Soutine's Lapis," in *From Scratch,* Eshleman has found the perfect complement to his own imaginal contortions, resulting in one of his most enthralling pieces). It now seems clear that the studio environment of a visual artist is somehow germane to Eshleman's working habitat, and that his body of work may intimidate some because its tactility is borrowed from another medium. To read Eshleman, think Rodin (via Rilke's first-hand observations). Eshleman's aptitude at translation made a furtive leap into wholesale invention in the 1970s as he began writing and publishing poems under the name Horrah Pornoff. While I never doubted that it was his work, he always denied it. But he finally relented and included the Pornoff corpus in *Under World Arrest*. These poems have a character apart and make a convincing case for Eshleman as a partial author of heteronymy on the model of Valery Larbaud or Fernando Pessoa. His work has often been involved with masks, not in the sense of impersonation, but as a ritual gesture of the carnivalesque. (Eshleman's *hibernaculum:* squatting studiously in the excavated carcass, feasting on the glow of burning fat that provides warmth, light, and nourishment.)

The work in *Hotel Cro-Magnon, Under World Arrest,* and *From Scratch* is dedicated to examining (while continuing to occupy) the masks of investigative countenance. This has meant a humbling exposure to critical reflection (" 'You're pigging out on underworld hooey' " [*Hotel* 146]), which has had an enlivening effect on the work, making it more humorous and accessibly at ease. This is not to say that Eshleman's insistence on exposing himself to political horrors ("the monster composed of daily news" [*From Scratch* 163]) is compromised in any way—the very title *Under World Arrest* speaks to a decidedly fin-de-millennium condition—but the poems are less cocksure (to use a term associated with D. H. Lawrence), more open to starting *from scratch*. There is even a kind of pledge undertaken in "The Sprouting Skull": "I knew that poetry now was more a prisoner of this world / than an alternative to it—and this is why / I have drilled holes in my poems" (*Hotel* 156).

The holes themselves are variable. The recent books pointedly include poems resembling drafts, abandoned worksheets; and their presence helps ventilate the suffocating intensity of neighboring poems. But Eshleman's self-exegesis in accompanying notes and annotations amplify the ins and outs, the conduits through which the reader is led *and* in which the reader is read. In "Postentry," Eshleman is haunted by a dream of reading to an audience concerned only with listening to themselves, which he construes at first to reflect his "inability to have the book I thought I had written" (*From Scratch* 188). The resulting vision is an extraordinary reckoning with the interface between author and reader. The encounter is charged with a mute plea reminiscent of Robert Duncan's punning remark that *responsibility* means the ability to respond:

> Many in the audience had copies of things that looked like mine, a booked audience that shows up as all authors to hand to the bookless speaker volumes that appear to be his but turn out to be their own prayers. I'd call this blizzard weather, or books as flakes, a gyre in flail: who has come to hear who? Should I stand by the podium and listen to the three hundred read from books with my covers but books whose pages are more attached to the audience than to me? Plasmic pages, like loose skin pulled forth, a stomach furl gripped, held forth, and read? Why not? *Read the sun,* I once heard, becoming a poet is the process of learning to read into, around, and through, anything. To read the moon is to imagine the moon. To imagine the moon is to speak as moon. To be a mooner! So the audience is exposing various parts of their flesh which they read hearing me, or hearing my rustling looking for my book. I read, and they hear me as themselves. Shouldn't that be an occasion of great appreciation, even joy? They experience what I read as part of their own flesh. I am the man I suffered I was *theirs.* But it doesn't work this way anymore, does it? Holding forth a leaf of skin they fail to realize that the words are not theirs, these translators, they hear me as themselves and my presence translated into their pulled-forth selves is, upon translation, simultaneously erased. (*From Scratch* 188–89)

Ecce homo: to read is to be read, and to be read is to undergo translation—that is, dismemberment. Eshleman, among the most adept and dedicated translators, teases out the implications of his art only to find, like Orpheus before him, his head on a plate, wearing the cap of mortality. But his question remains, and remains most pertinent to readers: Shouldn't this work, this great labor, be an occasion of joy?

So the holes are consequential. In *Under World Arrest* Eshleman finally assimilates himself to an elegiac consistency. Previously, the prospect of elegy had been attenuated by obligation, hesitation, or most often by be-

ing rerouted toward the heroic insistence of self-making (writing as res-
cue). Here it's as though elegy arises, weirdly vigorous, from a source
close to fatigue; not malaise, but a forgetfulness hatched by indifference
to the distinction between poem and note, poetic line and genreless
jot. One consequence is that the political shock references stand out as
somehow inept (Indianapolis insisting on its Protestant indignity, oblivious to the baroque Catholic sprawl of the underworld). More moving is
the sense of simple vacancy—nothing to do, nothing to say—that begins
edging into the work, having no place (no set themes, no objective cor-
relatives), but by virtue of that condition deflects the elegiac potential of
the poems from headline atrocity to the less flamboyant, but no less immediate, drama of homelessness—by which I mean the dislodged condition that is the very ground of poetry for Celan, Vallejo, and others. A
life in poetry constitutes itself *as* dwelling, and poetry too has to submit
to its ends beyond that particular habitation.

> Watch out for unity as you age,
>   it's in cahoots with reduction

> Be as these rocks not deluged,
> just gleamy in their lenten instant

>   Myriad-glimmered
> reason surfing the tectonics of dream,

> Mallarmé's "throw" still tumbling in the air,

> poetry as shipwreck,   oceanic page,
> "a throw of the dice"   the gamble of alchemical research
> "will never abolish chance"   no way
>   to predetermine reception—

> Unless a work of art is its own shipwreck
> a master is proposed outside the maelstrom

Surf looks more perfect than I can imagine a god,
perfection that if not seen through
    dwarfs imagination—
seen through,   nature *is* imagination,
      roving tooth breast
      on which I row
    60 years a second

                                          (*From Scratch* 72–73)

CODA

Serendipitously, *Jupiter Fuse* was published just as I was proofreading this chapter. Subtitled "Upper Paleolithic Imagination & the Construction of the Underworld," *Jupiter Fuse* instantaneously infuses thirty years of Eshleman's work with a precipitous destiny. Decades spent visiting and revisiting caves largely in southwestern France; assimilating the archaeological scholarship; writing poems to and through the cave experience; but, above all, anchoring his life's work to the deepest (temporally most remote) grottos of human experience, Eshleman has wagered himself in the lines and specks on fissured walls with a sapience poised somewhere between Mallarmé's astral shipwreck and the tumbling dice of the blues. Even Wallace Stevens comes to hand with canny assurance in an epigraph: "The poetic act . . . is an illumination of a surface, the movement of a self in the rock." Although undertaken with different motives than the public service role envisaged by Ed Sanders in *Investigative Poetry,* Eshleman fully realizes the potential of such investigation in *Jupiter Fuse.* Inasmuch as *Jupiter Fuse* includes some forty poems, most of which have appeared in earlier books, it might be misconstrued as a topical culling, a sort of "selected poems on the theme of." Given Eshleman's incessant drive to revision, they might even be seen as *new and improved* versions. But to do so would belittle the project, which is a genuine fusion of diverse modes of investigation (including, besides the poems, 130 pages of prose, 40 pages of notes, more than 60 illustrations in color and black and white, along with a detailed index, all of which transfigure the apparition of a "poetry book" altogether). *Jupiter Fuse* makes an implacable claim for poetry as a necessary investigative prerogative. The shift in emphasis here is decisive: Paleolithic cave art, in *Jupiter Fuse,* is clearly not a "theme" capable of generating poems, but a challenge to poems to justify their existence in the face of insuperable pressures from outside—not an easy preposition where the caves are concerned, for they involve an *inside* that's *outside* historical reckoning, possibly qualifying the poet as the most reliable technician of these (pre-) "sacred" spaces. Not for nothing does Eshleman cite Rothenberg's stance, contra Adorno, that "After Auschwitz there is only poetry" (xiv). Literally, or metaphorically? For Eshleman, such a choice is a smokescreen, for "to be human is to realize that one is a metaphor, and to be a metaphor is to be grotesque (initially of the grotto)" (xxiv–xxv). Grappling with "the grotesque archetype" (166), *Jupiter Fuse* enlarges the scope of metaphor rendered enigmatically concrete in rock, "this wall" that "can sustain our marks / and send them back into our bodies / vibrations of the end beginning anew in us?" (148). The question mark—like *Jupiter Fuse* as a whole—is a jaw, gnawing on the future of the past, greeting us all "at the roller coaster's summit in wild hello" (67).

10

"Riddle Iota Sublime"

Ronald Johnson's *ARK*

In another world in which books would solicit their own readers in personal ads, we might find something like this: "A microparliament of minute particulars seeks alliance with discerning biomass, to synchronize liturgical summations on *randonées,* finger the plenitude, heave mutual sublunary satisfactions into orbit." Ronald Johnson's unabashedly joyous poetry, which often seems less written than pieced together with the resources of a Renaissance *Wunderkammer* (cabinet of wonders), has been out of circulation for so long now that to merely know of it is to be a harvester of esoterica. Unlikely as it seems, two major books of Johnson's poetry were published by Norton in the 1960s, *The Valley of the Many-Colored Grasses* and *Book of the Green Man.* Meanwhile, the long poem *ARK* is at hand, its puzzling glories at last available in a Living Batch edition (the publisher's name sounds just right).[1] "Long poem," however, is an inept and compromised term with which to refer to this book, the strength of which is that it is an assembly kit, a cabinet of curiosities in

---

1. Needless to say, Johnson's earlier books are decades out of print. A carefully considered selection by Peter O'Leary from the entire corpus, including *ARK,* is now available: *To Do As Adam Did: Selected Poems of Ronald Johnson.* There is a considerable portfolio of further writings by and about Johnson in *Facture* 1 (2000), edited by Lindsay Hill and Paul Naylor.

its own right. Regardless of terminology, *ARK*'s publication is a major event, a salience unique in the world of American poetry.

ARK labors inwardly and outwardly. That is to say, it is at times a stable object, a text, which can be read as such; open to interpretive latitude, of course, but objectively manifest in words on the page. There is also an interior labor not so easily scrutinized: "shrouded in accuracy" (section #77) in its effort to "riddle iota sublime" (#76). Johnson quotes an uncredited author's hope "that the inwardes of my head / be like the sun" (#35). A state of beatitude is not necessarily evident to, or easily grasped by, others. Likewise, *ARK* wavers between the objective status of language event and the subjective fertility of vision. It is the reader's share to trace the reciprocal involutions: "as lined snake slide side to side / neverrest / pulse's smelter, smith, and alchemist" (#39). "Everywhere you glance webs glisten to inner spider" (#29). If at times this leads the author to "compose sonorities / past sense / as compass new" (#54), the promise of the poem is that, like the Facteur Cheval's wheelbarrow of tools preserved in its own captioned sanctuary in his Palais Ideal west of Grenoble, the compass, quadrant, and other measures are somewhere on site.

The opening section of thirty-three "Beams" is indeed such a tool chest, and its prose summations of the organs of seeing and hearing (#4, #7) seem specifically designed to provoke reflection on the fragile yet robust resources with which the reader enters the maze, and the organism enters a world. (These are, of course, reciprocal conditions; as world enters organism, so maze slips cleanly into the reader of *ARK*.) Combining scientific data with observational felicity, *ARK*'s proprioceptive metaphysics propose an intimate conductivity between body and galaxy, as though Gala's milk were immediate incessant nourishment: "The Mind & Eye, the solar system, galaxy / are spirals coiled from periphery" (#11). And in acknowledgement of proportional complexity: "the inner regions, tangled along polarized / garland, turn faster than the outer" (#3).

> plus ringed by minus
> quickened in interlocking octaves
> into a daffodil
> (intricately fluted)

atop a hill
upon an ochre, blue, and white swirled world below
How to inquire
within the fire?
What thinnest spoke-infolded core
of farthest star
invoke, in what we are?

(#11)

In a reprise near the end of the book: "Unfolding worlds before us, / atom become unto flesh / branched pitchfork" (#91).

Johnson's minimalist inclinations participate, with the prairie resource of the big sky, in a maximal poetics. There is a point of conversion that is instructive; tiny pinpricks of starry light in the nocturnal sky are nothing less than worlds. *ARK* may qualify as a *Scipio's Dream* for the late twentieth century, not only in its adherence to this reciprocal proportionality between large and small, world and grain, but also in its alchemical insistence that to go up is to go down, to go in is to go out. A hurtled panoply, like earth, drawn to Whitman's bulking orb ("weighing billions of tons"), but intimate with Dickinson's dangling basket of worlds cradled in bunches.[2] It is planetary—acutely so. Its star chart is at once animate lettrism and proprioceptive distillation.

Aldebaran, Orion far, or Pleiades

shall we gather at the River Inner,
pouring from a cup
four corners of the earth

(#72)

2. "For Earths, grow thick as / Berries, in my native town," Dickinson writes. "My Basket holds — just — Firmaments — / Those — dangle easy — on my arm, / But smaller bundles — Cram" (#352). In "Democratic Vistas" Whitman argues the need for "a new Literature, perhaps a new Metaphysics, certainly a new Poetry," indicating that he does not mean "the smooth walks, trimmed hedges, poseys and nightingales of the English poets, but the whole orb, with its geological history, the cosmos, carrying fire and snow, that rolls through the illimitable areas, light as a feather, though weighing billions of tons" (984).

Here, where "each cell array galactic vertebrae" (#73)—as in those cunning transparencies and shifts of scale in Pavel Tchetlichev's paintings—there are "worlds in a drop of water, / Eden hid an eyeblink" (#92). The evident credo (one might imagine it in Latin, unfurled on an heraldic banner): "I tread the stars / in perilous anatomy" (#96). The method is the means, and the physician is everywhere preoccupied with curing himself:

Linkings, inklings,
around the stem & branchings of the nervetree—
shudder and shutterings, sensings.

SENSE *sings.*
"A world where chaos and cosmos are interlaced and superimposed,
where anything may happen,
but nothing happens twice"

—perceive! perceive! Reality is 'make' believe.

(that everything happens at once is the form of The Dance)

:THAT EAR IS FIRMAMENT TO CRICKET
THUMBPRINT FLOOR TO GALAXY:

I am alive as long as there is fire in my head

and sing for my supper, out of the mouth of the dead.

(#8)

ARK's semiotic rudder is wiggled by "some wilder parley from atom to star" (#39), seeking harbor in the curriculum of signals linking star to chromosome ("huge imaginings to whet the miniscule" [#29]). The convergence of prosodic richness with stellar thematizing is auspiciously convened in Hart Crane; I think particularly of "Cape Hatteras" and the passage beginning "The nasal whine of power whips a new universe . . . / Where spouting pillars spoor the evening sky"; where

Power's script,—wound, bobbin-bound, refined—
Is stropped to the slap of belts on booming spools, spurred
Into the bulging bouillon, harnessed jelly of the stars.

Such Swinburnian corruscations of prosody are not characteristic of
ARK's "intricate vernacular // wrestling the abstract" (#92), but the vision is comparably elastic.

At the juncture of abstract and concrete, in a realm of constant motion
and energy transformation, it's useful to remember that "Ratio is all" (#25):

> . . . great gold sunflowerhead of photons
> sum of sun and moon
> in array the flicker of diamond-lattice pattern
> against a complex dappled back-
> ground also moving.

> Ratio is all.

The task of the poem—and cause of its considerable difficulty—is to
sustain an equation ("here, / everywhirr" [#36]) without belaboring the
obvious. The result is a kind of alchemical filibuster, in which the apparent simplicity of its mantralike dicta (as above, so below) is laboriously
magnified and refracted in a kaleidoscopic fury of the Opus Magnum.

> cellophane in cellophane of Salamander slid within a flame

> (to pin to the shimmer a name)

> Beauty is easy.

> It is the Beast that is the secret.

> (#14)

The atomic nucleus of matter is often sought here as an inmost wizardry
of the word as such. Like the swapping of carbon and hydrogen atoms in

terrestrial forms, *ARK* seeks its resolutions in an artistry of minute transpositions:

> Daedal, the seamless seen—the screen of seem:
> Lave & Weave
> Wave & Leave
>
> (#9)

> The Murmurer herself overspills space.
> New hushes through the polyhedral push and crux.
>
> In exquisite garble
> . . . .
> particulars evolve.
>
> no where
> now here
> no where
> now here
>
> (#29)

An even more recessed intricacy of homophones occasionally comes
to light as deft but oblique accreditation of resources: Priapus and Mozart slip along just under the surface in "pry up us" (#43) and "mote's
art" (#72), and the guiding spirits of Linnaeus and Noah Webster are
carnivally masked in "Line eye us. / Web stir us" (#8). Such glimpses
provoke a readerly paranoia: How much of my incomprehension needs
the enlightening resolution to a focal plane that can render such clues
legible, or even make them apparent in the first place? What do I need
to know to read this text that the text isn't telling me, or is so obliquely
told as to elude grasp? Beginning with Mallarmé, these might be considered the defining questions of modern poetry. But they also propose, as
Paul Valéry discerned, the inauguration of new literary constellations.
Regarding the new world of *Un Coup de dés,* Valéry reflected of the poet,
"*He has undertaken finally to raise a printed page to the power of the midnight
sky*" ("Introduction" 312).

Imagine this—letters meet and consort inside a sonnet by Shake-speare. Joining hands, they spin a rotation in *terza rima* in a canto of Dante. Their ecstasy clings to them like a faint odor of garden herbs until it eventually dissipates as they are dispersed through the airless conduits of newspapers, billboards, minutes of meetings. The savor is gone, so a new poetic initiation is called for. Like the distant memories aroused by Proust's madeleine, the letters in a poetic environment sense ancestral precedent and begin summoning to one another in lettristic animation. This is where *ARK* begins, in this subaudible hum of preternatural alli-ance, the erotic complicity of which every word is composed and is one more embellishment. It is a prospect majestically realized in *Finnegans Wake,* when Joyce heaved English (and scores of other tongues) back into the cauldron of material constellation. Since then, a few others have sought out this filigree of minute joyance, taking care to awaken the syl-lables one by one, tingling each consonant to sentience with a stroke of cunning fidelity. *Fidele d'amour:* a heretic ardor of the blazoned world of words. A new congregation named in this deliberation of consonants, this ostentation of vowels and collaboration of diphthongs (as one says of multiples of animals, convened in #83, "a pedelyng of ducks, a skein of / geese, muster of / peacocks, bevy of quails").

ARK's is a world of microscopic dalliance. As in the old practice of the *sortes virgilianae,* confident that the flexing of a single copy text might suffice for the world to renew itself just by scrambling the letters, feeling itself anew in the folds and unfoldings, the interpenetrations, of "the seim anew" (Joyce), everything is appointed ambassador of ecstasy. As if a poet might pen vectors of DNA, pondering the elegant simplicity of transpositions in "form from form from form from form" (#5), or the synaptic firing of the Purkinje cells in "f lux f lux f lux f lux" (#13), or the dangling mobile of geometric forms in "Beam 29," portents of un-supposed reanimation from lettristic alloys:

rec

tangle

ova

l

sp

here

squ

are

In "Beam 24" a six-line block of larger type repeats in adamant concreteness "earthearthearth"—which is sufficient to arrest the gaze, draw it
down into the folds and recesses of "earth" where "the art" and "hearth"
jostle for recognition in the heart. Rereading *ARK* in autumn in Pro-
vence, I reflected that the industry of cicadas, crickets, and grasshoppers
constitute the flying needles of a diagram by which the living earth is
composed, denizens of a textual anatomy made lucent by *ARK*'s beams
and spires and arches.

" 'GO INTO THE WORDS TO EXPAND THEM' The Voices said" (#28). The
lineage behind this provocation is extensive, and includes not only an array of modern poets (F. T. Marinetti, Alexei Kruchenykh, Velimir Khlebnikov, I. K. Bonset, Hugo Ball, Raoul Hausmann, Vicente Huidobro, Kurt
Schwitters, Robert Desnos, bp Nichol, to cite a few) but also a veritable
heterodoxy of lettristic beguilement, from the familiar (François Rabelais and Jonathan Swift) to the arcane (Juan Caramuel de Lobkowitz
and Francis Lodwick), encompassing along the way gematria, kabbalah,
speculative linguistics, and more.[3] These are not the accredited resources
of *ARK*—Johnson operates within a conventional lineage of modernist
American poetics—but they do propose a web of filiations that are more
useful than such anemic terms as "postmodern." Ostensibly a homespun
work of Americana—like Charles Ives's music, Simon Rodia's Watts Tow-
ers, or James Hampton's "Throne of the Third Heaven of the Nations
Millennium General Assembly"[4]—*ARK* is a book bristling with affinities

3. A considerable portfolio is available in Jed Rasula and Steve McCaffery, *Imagining
Language*.

4. Ives, Rodia, and Hampton are Johnson's references. One could also cite Tyree Guyton's "Heidelberg Project" in Detroit (see Clayton Eshleman's "Guyton Place" in *UnderWorld
Arrest*) as well as the "Concrete Garden of Eden" in Salina, Kansas—to mention one closer
to the poet's home. (There is now a tribe of poets who register in the evidence of their

for Europe. The doors of the Baptistery in Florence offer reciprocal schemes of miniaturization, and of course the postman Cheval's Palais Ideal in Hauterives is credited as a major resource and guide (see figure 2). Cheval, Hampton, and Rodia compose a triumvirate of amateur audacity that is misleading with respect to *ARK*. In its idiosyncrasy it shares the bricolage aptitude of these autodidact artists, but in its fastidious prosody *ARK* rivals nothing less than the most artful precedent of Pound and Zukofsky (particularly *"A"22–23*). If it aspires to the condition of music, the analogy with Palais Ideal suggests that the words are still a kind of cement, obdurate and intractable, "intimate into the inanimate" (#50).

The riprap sensibility is truly a builder's prerogative, and if at times the semantic dimension seems opaque, there is always the reassuring tactility of a solid wall of words (however slender their spires appear on the page). There are long stretches where the words can be as intelligibly read in reverse order (which seems congruent, after all, with Johnson's insistent center alignment of the lines); in fact, as the poet notes, #47 does indeed incorporate phrases in reverse from Henry James. Such practices, sometimes fiendishly coy and recessed, do end up emphasizing the structural elasticity of *ARK,* which consistently (almost superstitiously) spurns the servility of the poem-as-semantic-trowel. There is a certain kind of work, rarely predominant but found in every art, that is not constructed to human proportions, not given to the scale of human perception. So each such work incarnates its own focal plane and tactics of attention. "If my confreres wanted to write a work with all history in its maw," Johnson concedes, "I wished, from the beginning, to start all over again, attempting to know nothing but a will to create, and matter at hand."[5] While it does not "include history," as Pound said of his *Cantos,*

---

personal enigmas a place called Kansas. Simply to cite Ken Irby, Michael McClure, Ronald Johnson, and Ed Sanders is to render "Kansas" a realm of incommensurable enchantments; but quite apart from this, Johnson somehow makes Kansas appear inconceivable, which is to say miraculous. "Kansas Aweigh" [#65]!) All of these gardens and projects, along with numerous others, are handsomely documented in John Beardsley, *Gardens of Revelation.*

5. This is from Johnson's "Note" at the end of the unpaginated volume of *ARK.*

Figure 2. Adam and Eve, detail from *Palais Ideal* by Ferdinand Cheval, Hauterives, France. (Photo by author)

ARK does "include" biology, astronomy, crystallography, and (predominantly) *words*—an obvious scale, but not idly assumed. Rather, language in *ARK* is attained in a memorable combination of exactitude and hunch, its materials discovered and extracted. Despite the divergence over the question of history, no poet after Pound (except Zukofsky, Johnson's acknowledged mentor) has taken the credo "*Dichtung* = *condensare*" more to heart, and hand, than Ronald Johnson (and I recall Robert Kelly's remark many years ago that if you turn away from the clock, Creeley's poem "The Door" becomes an epic). His "style" forces agonies of compaction on the perceptual scale of the (bewildered) reader. The pace is distinct; the images are as specific and strange as those seen through a scanning electron microscope; revelations of a dense, confounding world in minutiae of expression that require careful unfolding, like the exquisite and exemplary Beam 10, a mere two lines—

> *daimon* diamond Monad I
> Adam Kadmon in the sky

—which, like Olson's "veda edda upanishad than", is a veritable *Summa* of the man's poetic Borealis.

Sometimes *ARK*'s condensation yields sheer unassimilable density (#79):

> Kindling anew line lifted of sea,
> perfect in messenger
> table spread ember hid vow

—the last line in particular reading like a crib from which to work up a translation of Chinese ideograms;[6] but more often the concision encompasses a world of observation in a Netsuke apparition (#60):

6. Johnson's poems are ideograms without the moral fetishism of Pound, but also without the substantiating guidance of mythic leitmotif. *ARK* rehearses a certain Orphism, but only as a pastel grace note reinforcing a posture of descent.

> exploded sod
> plowed to
> cornstalk plume

Or consider the exactitude of observation in "pool all a mareshiver / of lights" (#34). The enviable imagism of such moments, dispersed amid lines offering nothing as recognizable, suggests not that the "images" are intermittent, but that the scale of observation fluctuates, following contours of its own exactitude. To pursue a vision of "life itself / telescoped out of the recesses of essence" (#26), it is essential that the telescope actually *include* the recesses, and its "bliss abut abyss" (#43).

ARK is a poem that dilates with the determination to write paradise, its "Eden, glossolalia of light" (#14) a "Maelstrom itself prolonged // riddled into gospel" (#95). The adamant ecstasies of *ARK* forego the "trapeze of paraphrase" (#34), and one encounters in the poem a disconcerting mixture of scrupulousness and haze, as Johnson forgoes the dogmatic rubble of late Pound (in which the glimmers are breathtaking for that reason), as well as the piety of Dante (whose religiosity is doctrinally explicit if embellished by surreptitious soundings of dissident arcana). The words are impeccably balanced, selected, it seems, with a goldsmith's exactitude, and when they fail to converge on a recognizable focal plain, it's best to recall the poet's declaration, "Literally an architecture, ARK is fitted together with shards of language, in a kind of cement of music" ("Note").

ARK's logological dimension is deceptive; words are here as grit and spackle, mosaic particle. *ARK* is artifact, not argument. It consistently resists the closures of syntax—resists, that is, the binge-and-purge cycle of proposition and conclusion—which should be sufficient warning to the reader not to persist in reading for adage or message.[7] Johnson may aspire to be "Exact as Ezekiel" (#35), but as the biblical reference implies,

---

7. *ARK* could be taken as a thoroughly unapologetic example of language poetry. That would be a mistake, but it would highlight the divergent provocations of Zukofsky. Still, *ARK* may be a work that makes the most impacted zones of language poetry seem paragons of plain statement.

such exactitude eludes lazy habits of expectation—habits that *ARK*'s "Laocoön of cocoon" (#14) openly defies. In the author's note, it is not merely an incidental aside that compels his confession of deriving from "stout pioneer stock, grandson of prairie settlers come to Kansas in a covered wagon, I grew up in no concert with ideas whatsoever." Nor are there ideas here. There are, instead, strata of pertinence, ineluctable contours of enigma and gratification in equal measure, in a poem content to invest its semantics in weight and mass, gravity and velocity.

But how to achieve, in words, a wordless summation? The indications given in "The Foundations" favor diversity of means. In this opening— first published in 1980 in an impeccable edition by North Point—the thirty-three sections are called Beams, an architectural reference substantiating the Spires of the second part and the Arches of the third. Until the present edition, I had savored the ambiguity of beams as cross-timbers and as beams of light, an ambiguity that heightened my pleasure in the sensory manifold with which Beams 1-33 substantiated "foundation." Some eight of these initial beams are predominantly prose, giving a welcome antithetical sensibility to the architectonic cross-weave; there are visual illustrations (a Priapus in #16; a sequence illustrating cell division in #25; and a full handprint, serving as the entire text of #18); and the overall design makes handsome use of variable spacing, proportionate leading and kerning, bold caps, and judicious variation of point size. *Ark, The Foundations* was one of the most thoughtfully and beautifully prepared typographic editions of poetry since Mallarmé's *Un Coup de dés*—and, like that predecessor, conceived as such, not merely embellished in production. The fastidious design appears to have been an intention limited to the first book, however. "The Spires" (#34–66) incorporate little typographic variation, and "The Ramparts" (#67–99) none at all (although, in this case the conservative design accentuates the consistency of compositional unit; each Arch—which is what the Ramparts are individually called—consists of eighteen three-lined stanzas). The unity (one might at times be tempted to say monotony) of "The Ramparts" is conspicuously antithetical to the buoyant inventiveness and variety of "The Foundations," and thus enhances the sense of overall design. The discrepancy, for me, lies with the middle "Spires," which fail to mediate between such explicit contraries, meandering instead along their own winsome way, less concerned about structural integrity: a collection of bagatelles. It is a damaging charge, of course, to say of a book insistent on its architectural plan that it increasingly voids its own foundations and ends up offering words and more words in place of the word-transforming visual and concrete cornucopia of "The Foundations." So I retract the charge, mindful of my own culpability. Not that I know how to proceed to rectify the bewilderment I repeatedly feel in attempting to read some of those Spires and Arches that fail to gratify or inform my sense of overall design (which is not at all to deny the bewitchment of prosody and vision attending my reading of them). But the author's studious preparation of the text, and his instructively concise note at the end of the book, suggest that these limits of insight and orientation are mine, not his. *ARK*'s apparent discrepancy of end and means is one of which this reader hopes someday to be cured.

Meanwhile, the poem surveys my quibbles with an instructive haughtiness and undeniable grandeur, a reminder (notwithstanding Johnson's reversal in Beam 14, cited above) of Beardsley's dictum and Pound's solace, "Beauty is difficult." In light of the astonishing lucidity of condensation everywhere evident in *ARK*, I should have the grace to let the poet have the last word. And how not assent to the thrill with which *ARK*'s "pinwheel unzip the deeps" (#72)? "From the ape at my shoulderblade I see angels. Our embryo dreamt the fishes' sleep, became a ripple, leapfrogged itself, and later a mammal: perception is a slingshot drawn back to first plasm" (#12).

Taking Out the Tracks

Robin Blaser's Syncopation

The queen of rhythm, syncope is also the mother of *dissonance;* it is the source, in short, of a harmonious and productive discord. The process allows some limping before the harmony, however: it is sometimes said that syncope "attacks" the weak beat, like an enzyme, a wildcat, or a virus; and yet the last beat is the saving one. Attack and haven, collision; a fragment of the beat disappears, and of this disappearance, rhythm is born.

Catherine Clément, Syncope

Robin Blaser has long incorporated these interruptions as a rapture of his work. The syncope, its syncopation, involves the risk of letting in some arrhythmia, some inspiring fatality (duende resounds here), and the trick is to survive this creative prostration. To make of its arrest a restorative bewilderment (and I hear *arrest* here as the final word of Robert Duncan's last poem, as well as Clayton Eshleman's *Under World Arrest*). Arrested: somehow spasm back into play.

The spasm concurs with the *randonée,* or sporadic syncopation of the hunt, the sudden natality of spoor. Eruptive sigillation.[1] When these

---

1. "Sigillation" is a term I take from Walter Charleton's *Physiologia* (1654), by which he means the natural imprint of signs in objects of nature (Patey 37). Charleton went on to consider the temporal erosion of such natural sigils, in dismayed consideration of the elusive unity of nature owing to its invariable reversion to entropic illegibility. But this ruination still spelled out the rudiments of a script—for Charleton, an admonitory utterance like the Sybilline leaves or the gnomic pronouncements of the Delphic oracle ("a hole in the wind / it is an alphabetic wind rises" [Blaser, *Holy Forest* 131]). In *Chorea Gigantum* (1663, 3rd ed. 1725), he argued that Stonehenge was an ancient monument, linking *monumentum* etymologically to *moneo* and *memoria,* so that this "inanimate remembrancer" served as "ad-

things occur, we become part of the place, pieces of The Place, a "place-meant," in which the disabling de-composition composes itself with uncanny complacency. To simultaneously say and unsay; to find in citation a site, a place to work *in audition.* The music of Monteverdi may become "an achievement at the turn / of the next room" (Blaser, *Holy Forest* 211). Common sense interposes centuries between the Italian composer and West Vancouver, between original and copy. But the experiences we have are real to us. When Walter Benjamin laments the decline of the aura, he overlooks the recombinant prospect; so the mechanical reproduction of Monteverdi, lacking a cathedral, is given the chance to grow a new aura in a place where "the december tomatoes shine on the top of the refrigerator," where *also* "the *shattered marble* of my unwalled / thought enters the Rondanini Pietà / silently—*shaking hands of the substance / melt away*" (*Holy Forest* 211). A fluid interpenetration of distinct spaces and discrete modes of being, joined by syncopation's stutter, sutured in tantalizing indiscretion.

This is why Aristotle subordinated history to poetry. History is the record of what happened only once, he said, but poetry is what happens all the time. Our thoughts and wishes *do* penetrate silently the objects of our desires; we *do* couple with the phantasm. It's simple, *sim-plex,* "once pleated" or folded over as Giorgio Agamben has it in *Stanzas* (156). The irrevocable dissemination by which the simple is doubled is the ache and savor of creation. To create, Gilles Deleuze says in a lovely formulation, "*is to reach that point where the associative chain breaks, leaps over the constituted individual, is transferred to the birth of an individuating world*" (*Proust* 99).[2]

---

monition by putting in remembrance." The ruin, in Charleton's view, was also a rune. (Walter Benjamin, too, makes much of this phonetic convergence, ruin/rune, in *Trauerspiel,* his study of German baroque tragedy.)

2. Deleuze regards the amplitude of Proust's work inhering in the (Jamesian) principle of point of view. But he carefully defines point of view as "not individual, but on the contrary a principle of individuation" (*Proust* 98), or a site admitting of further occupancy, eventually even a sanctuary. Essence is thus contingent on nontotalized segmentation. Deleuze's theory in *Proust and Signs* is more amply worked out in *The Fold,* his book on Leibniz and the Baroque. In the Baroque countenance, a whole is only ever a part, a part provisionally folded over other parts (a dual pretension which Hegel will later call "*Aufhebung,*" a semantic equivocation happily to hand in the German language, meaning both *cancellation*

Blaser offers a parable about such occasions: Opal Whiteley has a cow called Elizabeth Barrett Browning. "Her mooings now are very musical, and there is poetry in her tracks. She does make such dainty ones. When they dry up in the lane, I dig up her tracks, and I save them. There is much poetry in them" (*Holy Forest* 204).[3] Tracks make a plausible double for writing. Both are traces of a passage (symptoms of Deleuze's "leap"). Opal Whitely saves cow tracks; Robin Blaser salvages tracks of others' writing. Writing as tracking:

> The work is always the passage of a wildness. The suddenness of the man I watch is both visible and invisibly continuous. At an edge. ("Stadium of the Mirror" 55)

> . . . The whole culture has brought him there at the edge of himself. ("Stadium" 56)

> I speak entering what is speaking—at an edge. I enter many directions, the synchron or coming together of time, in order to find words which are not alone. ("Stadium" 56)

To quote is to create company around the words, to convene companionship ("break bread" in an etymology Blaser delights in) there at the edge, the flicker. To incubate the words. Blaser's poems are ventilators as well as incubators, choreographed to make of space a syncopation. These ups and downs (cups and hiccups) are the nests of syncope.

To nourish words as eggs, to take them as fragmentary aspirations to

---

and *preservation*). For more, see Steve McCaffery's intricate explication "Blaser's Deleuzian Folds" in *Prior to Meaning: The Protosemantic and Poetics.*

3. There is much poetry in Opal Whiteley herself, with her charming world of animals bearing names like Felix Mendelssohn, Thomas Chatterton Jupiter Zeus, and Nannerl Mozart. Here's her piquant report of the death of a workhorse named after The Bard: "The man that wears grey neckties and is kind to mice did go with us to see William Shakespeare having his long sleep there in the field. My dear William Shakespeare will no more have wake-ups again. Rob Ryder cannot give him whippings no more" (Bradburne 194).

growth, morphogenesis. The poetics of the palimpsest: inklings from the dream world in the poem dated 6 November 1982:

so. . . . . .prize
. . . .
. . . .
surprise
(Holy Forest 216)

This is the look of the incubator, ellipses or dots as rows and rows of embryos punning their way into life.

People started to take an interest in fragments in the eighteenth century, when such fragments were deeply implicated in the development of the historical sense. So much of antiquity is fragmentary, like Heraclitus and Sappho. The vogue for ruins became an architectural fad. The German Romantics in the Jena circle (Hölderlin, the brothers Schlegel, Novalis, Schelling) were interested in fragments: "as a fragment, the incomplete appears in its most bearable form" (Novalis, in Seyhan 72). They recognized that conversation, the discursive Socratic exchange, is "a chain or garland of fragments" (Schlegel, *Philosophical Fragments,* #77). A voice is significant not as expression of a self, but as a momentary attribute of a growing form, the verge when the conversation folds back on itself en route to another voice.

the voice is recognizable
as fragments
of a greater language,
a live and changing
face
(Holy Forest 116)

A fragment is not only ruin or wreckage, but also the trace of a passage, the site of a creative deformation, a decomposition with new tracks through it.

'If there's one thing Harry learned
to love more than the sacred, it was
the sacred in ruins.'

(*Holy Forest* 261)

The provocation of ruin is manifested in what I take to be a typo in "The Stadium of the Mirror": "The wreckage of prenouns [*sic?*] is a great deal of fun" (57). No longer *pronouns,* we (you, me, her, him) are pre- or before nouns; and as Robert Duncan posited his final book, "Before the War," as before a mirror, we are both in front of—fronting the wave of—and temporally preceding the nouns of the known. We are *pre*-nouns becoming nouns in the process. Pronounced. "A noise" Spicer puns: "It annoys me" (213). A pun is an error savored, held over. The error is an invention. Blaser quotes Hölderlin's translator: "the modern imagination invents itself (and thereby reinvents antiquity) out of the evidence of wreckage, . . . for to scrutinize a fragment is to move from the presence of a part to the absence of the whole, to seize upon the sign as a witness of something that is forever elsewhere" (*Holy Forest* 299).

The god of fragments might be the two-faced god, Janus. Resident genius of partitions; presiding over transits; guardian of exits and entrances, internal and external, above and below, before and after.[4] Janus

---

4. Janus is not a deity with a particularly focused iconography. A Latin solar god (although L. A. MacKay argues for a lunar affiliation) with no Hellenistic precedent, Janus was most commonly associated with doorways and beginnings. Macrobius sees his iconic paraphernalia, the scepter and the key, as proof of his solar identity. Virgil traces his duplex nature to his sheltering of Saturn, who purportedly taught him husbandry and monetary calculation, in gratitude for which Janus deeded him half his kingdom. The sixteenth-century mythographer Natale Conti cites the Plutarchian identification of Janus as god of the double life of humans in transition from barbarity to civility. The *bifrons* feature of Janus has proven the most durable over time. For Pico della Mirandola, the celestial souls "'were signified by the double-headed Janus, because, being supplied like him with eyes in front and behind, they can at the same time see the spiritual things and provide for the material'" (Wind 201). Edgar Wind, reviewing the Renaissance enigma of the bifold Pan/Proteus, finds a consistently esoteric compound at work in such hermetic conjunctions (quoting W. H. Auden's lines, "For through the Janus of a joke / The candid psychopompos spoke" [200]). George Wither, in *Emblems* (1635), regards Janus as the god of mysteries in general, providing the epithet, "He that concealèd things will find / Must look before him and be-

might also be a patron of collage, that kinship system of debris. But it's too easy to get distracted by the modernity of collage. We need to reflect on the historical foreground of the fragment, like the fact that the respect accorded the fragment in the eighteenth century challenged the classical criteria of formal unity. The vogue for Chinoiserie and the Islamic design sense—from which the word "arabesque" derives—suggests an aesthetic apprehension of fragments of the culturally remote, the principles of unity of which are inscrutable but, it turned out, no impediment to appreciation of them as fragments, or as the objects corresponding to a fragmentary understanding. A fragment is a question (suggested by the proximity of the German words *Frage* and *Fragment*). And for Blaser (as Valéry said of Leonardo), "His desire to probe utterly the slightest fragment, the merest shard, of the world renews the force and cohesion of his being" (Valéry, "Method" 36).

There is another eighteenth-century reconfiguration having to do with "nature." Where nature had formerly signified grand design, the fledgling sciences of mineralogy, geology, and vulcanism discovered the earth itself to be a protean challenge to Vitruvian and Pythagorean harmonies. The book of nature, *liber naturae,* turned out to be *libertine,* busily composing a secret perishable script, "stammering the illimitable dialects of an incessantly fabricating earth" (Stafford 32). So the fragment, as both natural and cultural species of erasure, marks a transition from signifying form to signifying force.

Once libertine nature is honored for its signifying propensity, and the link is forged between geological and linguistic ruin, it's possible for Henry Thoreau to watch thawing sand on a railway embankment and fancy that he has stumbled into the primal workshop of a natural alphabet ("as if in a peculiar sense I stood in the laboratory of the Artist who made

hind" (Wind 230). In 1648 Alexander Ross ventures a curious etymological hinge by which Janus, via Hebrew *jain* (wine) is assimilated to Noah, becoming god of the two worlds—before and after the Flood (A. Ross 197). The most ambitious recent evocation is by Arthur Koestler, who uses Janus as the figure for his autopoetic theory of "holons": "self-regulating entities which manifest both the independent properties of wholes and the dependent properties of parts" (34). Janus embodies for Koestler the precarious equilibrium of whole and part, while the holon exemplifies the balance of integration and self-assertion.

the world and me,——had come to where he was still at work, sporting on this bank, and with excess of energy strewing his fresh designs about")—— to which I hear Blaser's lines (in his poem for bp Nichol, "the universe is part of ourselves") as illuminating coda:

> the ferns dream as they return
> to green   the efformation, the
> dis-creation, the kindness of fragments
>   (*Holy Forest* 234)

Ralph Waldo Emerson has a passage about fragments in his essay on "Experience":

> Illusion, Temperament, Succession, Surface, Surprise, Reality, Sub-jectiveness——these are threads on the loom of time, these are the lords of life. I dare not assume to give their order, but I name them as I find them in my way. I know better than to claim any complete-ness for my picture. I am a fragment, and this is a fragment of me. (490–91)

To be a fragment is to be borne along, as we all are by virtue of being born. At each encounter with one of the lords of life, the figure of Janus, the two-faced god, arises to mark the passage above or below, left or right, in or out. It is Janus to whom Ashbery's line might be pledged: "We get lost in life, but life knows where we are" (*Wave* 16). People complain of Emerson's disorienting prose, his pugnacious pell-mell aphoristic en-ergy. But he is aware of what he does. His work, like Blaser's, moves by implication and explication; folding and unfolding. For instance, in the passage from "Experience" he claims to name the "lords of life" "as I find them in my way." This formulation is itself an elaboration or unfolding of the Latin behind the English word "obvious"——*ob-viam,* or literally "in the way." On the road. Emerson is always saying something like *I'm going to help you lose your way, then help you find you never lost it.*

Robin Blaser does not shy away from such perplexing formulations either, as in "The Art of Combinations":

nothing simpler than what I have said because
I didn't say it, nothing simpler than what
I have said, because I said it—
                              (*Holy Forest* 258)

Blaser, like Emerson, understands the doctrine of signatures as a gregarious application of the principle of the speaker to the open world of utterance—endless, copious, and common. Commonly lost in finding; un-
commonly so.

There is always a saying or telling, oblivious to the speaker's identity.
"One may offer another only a world, not oneself" ("Stadium" 61). So this
is a seismic transaction—there's the rub—a *frictive* certainty.

I am not whole   not one   but, as Montaigne
said in his essay on friendship, divided
                              (*Holy Forest* 304)

—fractured, but also ventilated, and syncopated. Division is imminent—and immanent—kinship. At odds, we divine a dividend in our divided ends.

All poetry is translation (or a work on and in division) insofar as it
takes words from one place and deposits them in another. The language
is seamed with striations of a geophysical transposition. Poetry names the
unaccustomed new surroundings in which transported words find themselves and are translated out of themselves. A familiar estrangement. An
estrangement made even stranger by that other practice of the outside,
quotation (and I would append here Paul Valéry's remark that "We should
speak of 'the Strange' as we speak of Space and Time" [*Analects* 291]).
What quotation reveals is that even as the words themselves remain the
same, the mind transporting or transposing them changes, erodes.

Blaser's most insistent conviction is that "It is within language that the
world speaks to us with a voice that is not our own" ("Practice" 278), "a
speaking that *lodges within my own speech*" ("Stadium" 58). This is the operational "duplicity [of] the poetic job"—to credit "a speech along side
my speech, which allows a double-speech. A placement" (59). These are

figurative propositions made literal in *Syntax,* the poaching zone of *The Holy Forest,* the sanctuary at the heart of Blaser's grand design, a collage portfolio of graffiti (like "Artists are the deodorant pucks in the urinals of life" from the men's room at Leo's Fish House, Gastown [*Holy Forest* 191]). *Syntax* is an apparition of joints and junctures, boundaries and edges, the coordination of discrepancies and dependencies as its title suggests. In the notes to the first edition of *Image-Nations 1–12,* Blaser defines the author as "a composition of bound and unbound, visible-invisible, thought and unthought,—ultimately double" (*Image-Nations* 66). The title "Image-Nations" is not a pun, but a hinge, a fold; a recovery and reanimation of the fragments incubating in the common word.

Blaser's citations fracture, while *egging on,* continuity. Often the only mark of difference is the use of italics. Italics are commonly used for emphasis, so I glean from Blaser's use of italics to indicate citation a sense that the quote is emphatic in its blow to the text. A quote is a typological thump, that "universal thump" Ishmael refers to as the whale's gift of *storytailing* in *Moby-Dick.* A force that blows in, creasing the letters like prairie grass. Blaser's spaces are exhalations, fissures or crevices venting oracular moans. To read the poems too insistently as continuous arguments is to miss or ignore the force of this boreal scattering of the Sybilline leaves in the arboreal lens of the Holy Forest. (There is almost a Janus principle of reversal in the lines, making it undecidable whether to read backward or forward, up or down—as in the passage from Ezekiel, "word by word, right to left—myth resuming" [*Holy Forest* 322].)

Blaser's work is positioned *with care* at that interface of visible and invisible, thought and unthought, original and derivative. Its doubling is conjugal: "Every existence has its idiom, every thing has an idiom and tongue . . . he is the joiner, he sees how they join" (Whitman, "Song of the Answerer" #1). Philo speaks of "Logos as cutter," producing "creation by dichotomy" but also serving as "joiner of the universe" (Wind 202). There is a conjugal accent in Blaser's access of others' words—as if the poems were always on the verge of saying "in other words." "I was once another man's heart" he says in *Image-Nation #9* "(half and half" —paraphrasing Empedocles—and at the "*flowing boundary . . . /* at the

point of the heart" is "a continual / division of halves" that produce
tantalizing heterogeneous duplications of the Different Same, the "seim
anew" as Joyce has it in *Finnegans Wake*. So "language itself can be experienced as other" [Blaser, "Poetry and Positivisms" 23]).

As introjected remnants—revenants—of the other, words are uncanny. Blaser defines imagination as "more a power to take in and hold
than it is a power of making up" ("Fire" 239). To "take in" is to reposition
the world, or its fragments, in that interior pocket or imaginal fold
"haunted by a sense of the invisibility of everything that comes into me"
("Fire" 235). Conversely, "I wish to let the reader loose in the invisibility
where the text leads him" ("Stadium" 57).

The imagination "holds" what cannot be held in the hands.

> when he lifted up his cup,   he let the sky
> go free   out of his hands
> > > > *(Holy Forest* 125)

> the words do not end   but come back
> from the adventure
> > > > the body is at the edge
> of their commotion
> > > > the nonsense
> the marvellous clarity
> > > > in the pool of the
> heart
> > > > > *(Holy Forest* 113)

In Blaser's poetics of ventilation, attuned to the porousness of boundaries, selfhood is a play of partitions. In the Romantic imagination up to
Rimbaud and extending through Surrealism, this was a project of dislo-
cation and self-estrangement, countering the alienation effects of history
with a strategic swerve or Lucretian *clinamen*.[5] But Blaser, inclined more

---

5. My contrast here of Lucretius and Mallarmé is a momentary sophistry, Lucretius
being, of course, an agent of Democritan and Epicurean atomism that admitted a void or

to Mallarmé, adheres instead to *kenosis* or emptying as the primary respiratory thesis of selfhood. The self, in this figuration, is what is empathically released to the world in calculated abandonment; and this evacuation creates a zero or blank into which the countercurrent washes its tidal offerings.

---

boundlessness, which in turn posited an infinity of worlds. This is not the occasion for adumbrating the various accounts of a fecund blankness (which would need to include Peirce and Heidegger, not to mention Buddhism), but with reference to Lucretius, some genealogical clarification is in order.

Montaigne is a major presence, a steady force, in Blaser's work. Emerson, in *Representative Men,* finds in Montaigne the solution to his need for a philosophy of "fluxions and mobility." "Every fact is related on one side to sensation, and on the other to morals," the essay begins, as Emerson outlines a Janus philosophy of the pitch-penny. "We never tire of this game, because there is still a slight shudder of astonishment at the exhibition of the other face, at the contrast of the two faces" (690). The faces (as if in homage to Emerson's friend Carlyle) take a sartorial cast, sporting the variable wardrobes of Identity and Difference, Finite and Infinite, Relative and Absolute, Apparent and Real. The skeptic stands in the middle, aspiring "to be the beam of the balance" amid these flipping coins. Montaigne was one of those Renaissance authors who were much taken by the reappearance of Epicurus and Lucretius after the vast blackout of Church opprobrium, and his *Essays* are plentifully stocked with Epicurean quotations. Of course, skeptics and epicureans are not the same, but Emerson's formulation suggests a convergence; both are adepts in the science of the balance. The tranquil life was the gist of Epicurus's Garden School training (to be attained by a nonattachment strikingly similar to that in Buddhism). The Epicurean principle of self-guided moderation aroused the ire of those who would live by rules, and so the adjective "epicurean" came to be synonymous with *libertine.* But the double meaning of "libertine" puts a check to the abuse, because in addition to meaning "sensualist" it also bears a political connotation somewhere between *libertarian* and *iconoclast.* It all comes together in Blaser's "Even on Sunday" after he cites Hans Mayer's recognition that, for outsiders, *"one's existence itself becomes a breaking of boundaries"*: "we can thereby return to ourselves a *measure of freedom,* and take form— / the work of a lifetime—in this breaking of boundaries" (*Holy Forest* 349).

To achieve form by breaking boundaries is to deviate from the predestined course, to become oneself the rupture of that inertia, "the work of a lifetime." It is to swerve, and in swerving *become.* The *clinamen* or *parenklisis* is the most famous of Epicurus's concepts— most famously as transmitted by Lucretius. The *clinamen* is the sudden swerve of a falling atom, and each such swerve creates a pocket of turbulence, which is how material forms are generated. Now, these pockets are the very folds and pleats of the manifold, the creases through which nature increases—paradigms, in other words, of *poiesis* or production. As I have been elaborating in this essay, Blaser's work advances by means of an articulation of

This is not the New England sensibility of Puritanism in which every citation of self is canceled by a ritual denial of self, in a language that renders the personal pronoun incessant and central; nor is it D. H. Lawrence's wind tunnel of the romantic ego verified by inversion ("not I but the wind that blows through me"). "What had been imaginings of the whole . . . now become an imagination of holes" (Blaser, "Poetry and Positivisms" 23)—conduits, which Duncan named Passages. Deliberately leaky buckets; a form of ready emptiness, empty mind:

> if I think 'I' unifies
>
>   I lose,
> and the feeling overflows the bucket
>
> if I think the aggregate of large numbers of us,
> massified, unifies,
>
>   our hunger
> unifies without justice
>
>   (*Holy Forest* 302)

The bucket (consciousness, culture) organizes, but it does not unify. Unity achieves integrity not in monuments, but in heartbeats, synco-

---

space, an inclination of acknowledgement (citation as tactility, as in the old locution for *concerning:* "touching upon"), and a complication of address. It's in the *pli* of complication, explication, application, that we feel the pleat or fold of the atomic pocket, the bump of the swerve or *clinamen* where it issues in a clump or clot. A clinimized coagulate. An "unfolded fold" in the language of the poem that follows "Even on Sunday" in *The Holy Forest*, and further elaborated in the grand conclusions of "Exody," as Blaser brings Lucretius explicitly into the fold of his concerns (*Holy Forest* 370).

Deleuze is, not surprisingly, an Epicurean adept (proving, in the tour de force of *The Logic of Sense,* a stoic expositor as well); and the following summary might well be taken to apply to Blaser's poetics: "Nature is not attributive, but rather conjunctive: it expresses itself through 'and,' and not through 'is.' This *and* that—alternations and entwinings, resemblances and differences, attractions and distractions, nuance and abruptness. Nature is Harlequin's cloak, made entirely of solid patches and empty spaces. . . . Nature is indeed a sum, but not a whole. With Epicurus and Lucretius the real noble acts of philosophical pluralism begin" (Deleuze, *Logic* 267).

pated polyrhythms, or in the vibratory dazzle of light prism'd into rainbow. Between glimpses of unity we live in the cracks—or maybe *are* the cracks.

Splits, pleats, faults, furrows, mouths, pockets. Tracks. Cows make tracks; spontaneously, fortuitously, certain tracks suddenly excite attention and a girl digs them up. This *suddenness* is the aesthetic event, the *pleat* that, as it joins, divides, making many out of one, and "the soul becomes a fracture in the old paint—like the surface of a moonlit Ryder painting—running joyous and jagged—here and there" (*Holy Forest* 365–66); "*a greedy flowering of amorous play*" (*Holy Forest* 369) with "*no entrance, only interpretative delirium, fragments of a language*" (*Holy Forest* 368); in other words, a Holy Forest. Implication, complication, explication: the neoplatonic *omnia complicans*,[6] the preparatory congestion of impending blankness.

6. Edgar Wind is pertinent again:

But however irregular and unfamiliar to the outward view, the hybrid gods of Orphic theology consistently follow a logic of their own, which is the logic of concealment. And by that logic their meaning can be "unfolded" or made more explicit, provided the rule of "infolding" has been mastered first, which Cusanus distinguished from *explicatio* by the quaint but fitting name of *complicatio*. When the Venus-Virgo becomes 'unfolded' in the three Graces . . . each Grace represents a less "complicated" state of mind than the "infolded" Venus from whom they descend. Theoretically, the process of explication could be continued indefinitely; and the farther it proceeds, the plainer are the elements obtained. But so long as the elements remain interdependent, they all partake of each other's nature, and pure externality is never reached. Absolute plainness is therefore an illusion produced by a severance of that universal link through which even the most "explicit" members of this expanding series retain an inherent "complication" (204–05).

And as a reminder, the medium of this "severance" is *Janus bifrons,* cutter and joiner. Wind elaborates the neoplatonic aspect further: "When Pico wrote that 'the unity of Venus is unfolded in the trinity of the Graces', he added that he who understands that operation clearly and fully holds the key to the whole of Orphic theology. Indeed, the unfolding of a divine unit into a triad is but an inverse expression of the Neoplatonic law that 'the contraries coincide in the One'" (192). The Orphic mysteries have been misconstrued as harboring some grand ineffable secret; but as Wind's exposition makes clear, it is the earthly condition of mutability as "secret gate" (218) that proliferates concealment/disclosure in a continuum of folds. Just as there is always something plain, there always remains something

Blaser's is the art of *drawing a blank*. It is a deliberate withdrawal from the voluble givens of chatter that would fill in the blanks. His is an art of spacing and release. An unretentive poetics opening out on a different order of attentions. ("And it was from the human mind that even the gods received their gift of *creation*, because that mind, being periodic and abstract, can expand any of its conceptions to the point at which they are no longer conceivable" [Valéry, "Method" 41].) Blaser describes how, "back of the first *Image-Nations* was the old comfort—a discourse which I could have substituted for the holes in intelligence, and thus, have closed the poems inside a formality of what my mind constituted,—an anthropomorphism in tatters" ("Stadium" 58). We get instead something moving in the direction of, but not as severe as, Ronald Johnson's poem RADI OS, in which he admits to using Milton's text (*Paradise Lost*), but says that he composed the holes.

But Blaser's porosities are not holier than thou: "the word soul what a haughty   standing alone that is" (*Holy Forest* 129). It is an art of humility—from *humus*, close to earth, grounded. Llewelyn Powys reports his brother John (author of *Wolf Solent* and *Glastonbury Romance*) saying people "are no better equipped for comprehending the unfathomable mysteries that surround us than is a tadpole in that dew-pond of envisaging earth-life from the squinnying glimpse it gets of the animal's cloven hoof" (73). Let's go back in conclusion to the cloven view.

Think again of Opal Whitely's portable tracks. Those tracks are signs of her cow, hapless designs of Elizabeth Barrett Browning's hooves pressed into wet soil. For Opal they are medallions, icons, which is why she collects them and shelters them in the kitchen drawer. She can see her cow in the tracks; which is to say, her tracks are lenses. They magnify the cow insofar as they are separable from the cow. To cut off a bit of cowhide, or a few hairs from the tail, would mean being satisfied with a mere indexical relation. Opal's tracks are far more circuitous, devious, extravagant;

---

yet to be explained. Having come into appearance or into the light of understanding, however, experience is folded back in the convolutions of memory, reverting to the arcanum or shadow world. In the end there is no secrecy, only temporality. Or time is that which secrets (and secretions) reveal—the revelation of which leaves an open secret, or secret *as openness*, "*das Offene*" of Rilke's eighth Duino Elegy—the open, the gap, the blank: full of awe.

her cow is signified exclusively by something that is *not cow.* But the signification does not stop there. The tracks are not souvenirs. For her, the numinous quality of the tracks is not that they refer to the cow, but that *her cow referred to the tracks,* as it were, by making them.[7]

"Always a 'matter' of form reopening, like footsteps" (Blaser, *Bach's Belief* 12). The tracks are contagious; they're *symptoms.* In the terms given by the Delphic oracle, the symptom neither speaks nor conceals, but bestows itself as sign, creating a "semantic space . . . excavated by the force of a desire which the mathematician Plato called 'eros,' the biologist Aristotle 'orge,' and the Latin Stoics 'libido' " (Baer 58). "The archaic may be understood as a pre-rational language of being in love with the earth and the heavens" (Blaser, "Violets" 90). Pre-rational: before the ratio, the stipulated address. To be in love with the world without positing a limit, or limits, of either love or world. Love precedes measure, but in this precedence love excites or stimulates measure. The primal measure of sexual conduct is cosmology. Sex is cosmological symptom. A magic word, an enigma (like that given by the Sphinx), the symptom is the "*destiny of full signification,* pregnant thick/sick with meaning" (Baer 45). "It produces the form it talks about; it per-forms what it announces, creates the world it presents, does what it says" (60). A symptom is not index or reference, but propagation, explication, invitation.

Robin, thank you for the invitation. R.S.V.P.—Reader So Very Pleased (for work so very pleated).

---

7. That cow tracks are an esoteric resource of writing is made explicit in Geoffroy Tory's *Champ Fleury* (1528), a treatise on orthography. Tory proposes that all the letters of the Roman alphabet are derived from *I* and *O,* and that the exclamation "Io" "came into use as a proverb signifying exaltation and triumph . . . show[ing] the joy which the ancient Ionians felt in having invented & designed these said Attic letters" (23). As further evidence Tory recounts, by way of Ovid (*Metamorphoses* Book I) and Boccaccio (*De Genealogia Deorum*), the tale of Io, the girl turned into a cow by Jupiter's lust, whose identity is revealed to her father by the hoof prints she leaves in the mud, spelling her name.

12

Syncope, Cupola, Pulse

for Nate Mackey's
"cardiognostic need"
"as though song were a leg"
"as though the heart were a ventriloquist"

To *re-make* the mistake. Seize the flaw. Flow.

"The queen of rhythm, syncope, is also the mother of *dissonance;* it is the source, in short, of a harmonious and productive discord. The process allows some limping before the harmony, however: it is sometimes said that syncope 'attacks' the weak beat, like an enzyme, a wildcat, or a virus; and yet the last beat is the saving one. Attack and haven, collision; a fragment of the beat disappears and of this disappearance, rhythm is born." Catherine Clément, *Syncope*

Obatala (the "unblemished god . . . the serene womb of chthonic reflections . . . a passive strength awaiting and celebrating each act of vicarious restoration of his primordial being" [Wole Soyinka]) leads the deities in soaking up the human broth. In Sanskrit poetics, *rasa* is the savor, the aesthetic presentiment of divine nutrition; art as sublime altruism, from mortals to the immortals—this nudge of flavorful necessity.

A "physics of bliss, the groove, the inscription, the syncope: what is hollowed out, tamped down, or what explodes, detonates." (Roland Barthes)

Speck or scar; striations of the fold, creasing the text.
Stains, blurs, corruptions.
Bracketed dust of Sappho, Archilochus . . .

Mistake as revelation.

Interpretations often want to heal the text of some mistake, its *petit mal,* its tiny seizure. Its coughs, sneezes, stutters. Its limp.

Limp: limbp. Legba's legs—one foot in each world, heaven and earth —make a discordant sound when he walks.

Legba's genius: each leg makes its own sound. (Two does not exist: every pair is one + one. "Double consciousness": feel the *verb* in it!— *double time.*)

. (((((Polyrhythm)))) .

Legba: god of gates and doors, fences and boundaries, also patronizes roads and paths; blesses not only the block, but the break. A paradox. Pledging uncanny junctions, spooked transitions of empowerment. (Robert Johnson at the crossroads.) Enabler of agile transgressions. "Legba is the divine linguist," master of a "unique dialectic, the copula in each sentence. . . . He has sexual relations with any woman he chooses because these boundaries—physical, social, religious, and even metaphysical—dissolve and reform in his presence" (Robert D. Pelton). He's a reformer.

In Haiti, Legba is associated with St. Peter because the saint holds the keys to the kingdom. There (as well as for the Fon of West Africa— and in European alchemical lore[1]) Legba's an old man in rags, with a crutch: *pied cassé* or broken-foot.

---

1. Figure 3 shows Emblem XLII of Michael Maier's *Atalanta Fugiens* (1618), with its accompanying epigram: "Let Nature be your guide, and with your Art / Follow keenly her lead, without which you go astray. / With sapience as staff, seasoned experience vivifies sight. / Let learning be your lamp, dispelling dark / That throngs of things and words may not disarm you." The term "alchemy" comes from several Sanskrit roots concentrated on blackness, *nigredo.* **Au I** = down, and is rooted in "avatar" (*au ter* = cross over). Vishnu's avatars include Rama and Krishna, both of which mean *black* in Sanskrit. (Krishna is **kers II,** black.) In Egypt the Nile's black effluvial flood is *khem.* **Gheu** = pour, in Greek *khein.* Juice is *khulos* and *khumos.* Chemistry's chums, the black patron gods. Flooders.

Oedipus, too (with prophecies said to "flutter about his head" like birds) hobbles—as his name indicates: "Swellfoot."

It's as if those feet were swollen with eyes, overcompensating for some other mutilation. Emerson: "I become a transparent eyeball" . . . — . . . "we are lined with eyes; we see with our feet." The eyes continue Ezekiel's vision (1:18) of the heavenly chariot, its inter-revolving wheels "full of eyes round about." And in Zachariah 4:10 the "eyes of the Lord run to and fro through the whole earth." Blake: "The Chariot Wheels filled with Eyes rage along the howling Valley."

Jung finds such symbols "multiple luminosities of the unconscious," suggesting that "complexes possess a kind of consciousness, a luminosity of their own, which, I conjecture, expresses itself in the symbol of the soul-spark, multiple eyes (*polyophthalmia*), and the starry heaven."

Eyes are multiplied in the blind; into seeing and seen or present and past, seeing and sensing or knowing otherwise, outer and inner, knower and

Figure 3. Emblem XLII from Michael Maier, *Atalanta Fugiens* (1618)

known, singer and song. Blind Lemon Jefferson. Blind Blake. Blind Willie Johnson. Blind Boy Fuller. Blind Willie McTell.

Certain Dahomey & Yoruba gods reappear as *loas* in vodun; roadside heavy breathers in Delta blues (Legba, Ogun, Djamballah) resonate with Orpheus, the sacrificed singer.

To be weighted down with lightness: the emancipating bruise.

("*If it wasn't for bad luck, I wouldn't have no luck at all.*")

To lighten. Make light of. Arouse elation, buoyant ascension. Legba, Esu Elegbara, god of the crossroads, "loosens knowledge" (Henry Louis Gates). *Get loose, lighten up.*

Resolution as laughter. The goal of interpretation is *to air out,* ventilate, expend stale accumulations with a laughing snort. Not ascertain meaning, nor place or fix or determine it, but *uncork it.*

Laughter is the sneeze of the soul.

"Procreation and sneezing appear to be the distinctive manifestations of the *psyche.* Here, then, strange as it may seem, must be sought the origin of the name, if its nearest kin be ψύχειν, 'to blow'" (Richard Broxton Onians).

Bird (Charlie Parker) could even blow on the nod.

("Rapids to baptism
In one blue river." [Lawon Fusao Inada])

When you read and find yourself nodding off, Hermes is on his way to guide you to an underworld, a crepuscular subtext.

For the Greeks, a contractual arrangement was signed by a nod, pledged in the name of Psyche. "A sneeze is also a nod, a nod not expected or controlled by the conscious self but an apparently spontaneous expression of the life in the head" (Onians).

The sanctity of the sneeze: prophecy. Nodding acknowledges prophecy. Or: a nod acknowledges the prophetic, the kerygmatic annunciation.

Al-chymia's chimera—from *nigredo* to *rubedo* and into the clarified *calci-natio* or *albedo.*

    The ointments, the facilitators. Regulators. In the *Koran* the angelic beings are

"those who repulse"   "those who recite"

      "those who distribute"

              "those who are sent"

"those who disperse"

        "those who seize"   "those who extract gently"

    "those who precede"

      "those who float"   "those who deliver the word"

"those who conduct the cosmic tasks"

             "those arrayed in order"

Everything written on the sacrosanct Tablet needs these angels for its actualization. In the mystical alphabet of the Dhauqi branch of the Chishtiyya Sabiriyya the enunciated letters are lunar mansions.

"Man's heart is between two of God's fingers, and He turns it as He pleases," a Muslim adage has it. What is written takes many forms. So "one has to cultivate, first of all, the eye to see the selfsame reality of ink in all letters, and then to see the letters as so many intrinsic modifications of the ink." (Haydar-i Amuli [d. 1385])

Figure 4. Medieval Arabic Calligraphy

"As long as Oedipus is the protagonist on the stage, we are not Oedipus. Let his terrible secret be exposed to the whole world, provided we can leave the theater with our secret intact. Myth is a powerful hypnotic, in which cultures inscribe their own ideology, and the mythologist's task is certainly to discover the little secrets that one ideology or another hides away in the folds of myth.

But myth also reveals that which was to be concealed. Like our dreams, which seem to disguise our secrets to protect our sleep, myth keeps confessing the very secrets that it was constructed to conceal. With a chorus of signifiers it circles around the traumatic rupture, where the subject vanished into the field of the Other" (Norman Austin).

One correction: The mythologist's true "task" is not to discover but to dislodge the secrets (the more unintentionally the better) which flutter up, buoyant, like moths.

Moth to mouth to myth.

The numinous is creaturely presence. Secrets are creatures. Little secrets "hidden away in the folds of myth": Myths are the genitals of the collective unconscious.

Is "collective unconscious" an oxymoron? Unconscious is *uncollected consciousness.* Consciousness in its *menstruum universale* and its *dissemination* is endlessly dispersed, "un-concealed," but scattered, lost, bereft (the paradigmatic phallic disorder: postcoitum tristum, yearning for "full presence").

Myth is tumescence and flow, the waxing and waning of cosmogenesis, fecundating psyche.

"No sooner have you grabbed hold of it than myth opens out into a fan of a thousand segments. Here the variant is the origin." (Roberto Calasso)

Myth, says Detienne, invents what is memorable.

In the *Aitareya Upanishad* (1.4): "The Self heated 'Man.' When it was heated, its mouth broke off, like an egg. From the mouth, there was speech; from speech, fire. Its nostrils peeled away. From the eyes, there was vision; from vision, the sun. Its ears broke off. From the ears, there was hearing; from hearing, the cardinal directions. Its skin peeled off. From the skin, there was bodily hair; from the bodily hair, plants and trees. Its heart sloughed off. From the heart, there was mind; from mind, the moon. Its navel peeled off. From the navel, there was breath of anal grit; from gritty breath, death. Its penis broke off. From the penis, there was semen; from semen, the waters."

Ananse, Ashanti trickster, sets his children to scheme against a rival:

• *Father broke his penis in seven places, and went to a blacksmith for repairs.*
• Then where's your momma?
• *She went to the river to fetch water, and her pot would have been broken but she caught it just in time. But she didn't quite, so she's gone back to finish catching it.*

«Creation seemed a mighty Crack
To make me visible.» (Emily Dickinson)

The path you search for appears only in proportion as you disappear.

> Blunt the sharpness;
> Untangle the knots;
> Soften the glare;
> The way is empty; yet use will not drain it.

(The translator [Lao Tzu, *Tao Te Ching*, #4] comments: "The word in the text meaning 'full' has been emended to one meaning 'empty.'")

> Like the stretching of a bow
> the exalted's brought low
> the debased is raised up
> the excessive is deficient
> & the meagre abounds in gratuity. (*Tao Te Ching*, #72)

The bow and the lyre illustrate for Heraclitus (fr. 51) that "that which is at variance with itself agrees with itself." And there is another bow that gives life in the pun (gives life *to* the pun): "its name is life, its work is death": τῷ τόξῳ ὄνομα βίος, ἔργον δὲ θάνατος. (fr. 48) The pun of *bíos* and *biós* conflates bow/life, the difference being exclusively in the placement of the accent. Application of a dollop.

Illumination: something burns so brightly that what it illuminates is actually obscured: the eye is "blinded" by the light, by its *incandescence*.

There is also *sonorescence*. "In our sonorescence, nature and artifice compose each other's excesses and their excesses" (Stephen David Ross). This "reciprocal excess" is a habitation in doubling—a mark of mind, a notch in matter.

Like Mercury's counsel aglow in Dolphy's alto.

In music, "The note began as something which was pulling and stretching, but does it want to go on like this?" (Ernst Bloch). The function of time in music is as undertow, to make the instantaneous felt as re-iteration, the doing as done again in undoing; the instrument itself a timer, a plasm-Geiger taking the pulse of the place. (Note is tone.)

Pulsional appetite: music deploys humans in productive consort with waves ("play it like a waterfall," Duke Ellington told his reed men), consecrated in bop as a punctiform *via regia* (Kenny Clarke, Max Roach, Art Blakey, Roy Haynes).

Before bop, Betty Boop was the *look* of hot jazz, its bubble, its droops and dips, its *azz*. Wriggling the *as if* off with her hip shake.

Valéry: "By the indirect route of musical stimuli I am, in some strange fashion, *combined with myself.*"

"I *seem* to experience all this,
for actually I cannot tell whether I am subject or object . . . "

Senses awaken; stretch, rouse. Aroused, they multiply.
Each sense exercising its autonomy, gnawing, gnowing.

"I 'thought' and desired in my fingers.
If I had made a man, I should certainly have put the brain and soul in his fingertips" (Helen Keller).

Excursus on Monk

THELONIOUS MONK made the piano a theatrical space, a theater endowed with volume, depth, shadow, vanishing perspectival points, and wings. In the wings you hear ("Brilliant Corners") heavy furniture being moved, yet oddly as if airborne.

Monk: someone grumbling aloud in his sleep, turning over. Gymnastic somnambulation.

Monk gave Coltrane pause. The acoustic residuum of tact.

Monk fit his hands to the ivories like a surveyor placing the tripod. Distance, span, plane, and incline. *Inclination.*

With Monk, as in Anton Webern, you never know the exact measure being applied, so you don't see the size of the object that, in a system of representation, would figure into the calculus of a ground. With some of his pieces you don't know whether "tune" is skin or bone; whether it holds up and constitutes the internal structural horizon, or whether instead (as in Roland Barthes's erotic principle of hermeneutics, interpretation is like peeling layers off an onion: there's no core, no seed, no bottom, just a never-ending *end to onion*—like the one about the world perched on the back of an elephant . . . and what's the elephant standing on? A turtle. And the turtle? Well, it's *turtles all the way down*) every figural motif is an excursion not distinct in principle from a series of steps, bends, twists, none of which are ever done with any sort of calculation of their place in a finite series. Every gesture is the infinitude compacted into the moment of its release.

With Monk, it's all denotation, no connotation. A plectrum of the cogito: fingers drumming the metal rim of a Formica table. Or the edge of a seat during a lecture, hearing not the analytical persuasion of the talk, but the budgeting of sidesteps, tones, the largo of the drawl, the crunch of its release. The size of the footprint, hand span.

Each rhythmic cell, harmonic phrase: prismatic alliances. So no embellishments: the grace notes are all down there, nose to the ground, canine. Reticular activating stem, perched with insistence, then dealt.

Monk's tunes are the propositional counterparts of a labyrinth. Getting in and getting out again are what it's all about. Crossing a tricky crevasse. Monk's pianistic applications disclose survival tools. He plays not according to predetermined rhythms, but as someone crossing a river, stone by stone. There is the hesitation, the creative preparation, the foresight—followed by a contagion of leaps, clustered, bippety-bip-bip, bop, budobbopp. Learning to roll with the fall. A metronome coming undone or unwound. Being "wound up"—tense or nervous—is the antithesis of everything Monk's about. Cool chops, a cool that smolders, and goes.

In pop-song format the "bridge" of the AABA 32-bar framework is also called the *release,* the *inside,* or the *channel.* Think of a floodgate, listening to Monk: a volume of liquid pressed against a restraint, then suddenly released. Monk's gambit: *to compose the release.*

Rotundity. Bell of the horn. Dome of the rock. The sonorescent cupola of a solo driven by duende darkens the listener's pulse, even as it "consults" the wind (as García Lorca says of *cante jondo*). The pregnant pause; and the billowing skirt on the line in the wind (Art Ensemble: *Full Force* photo). The inflated vibrating garment becomes, at a distance, an eye. Even sound pays a silent visit to *Polyophthalmia.*

The halo: "an absolutely inessential supplement" — "matter that does not remain beneath the form, but surrounds it with a halo" (Giorgio Agamben).

Atilt in the ease of otherwise, the tiny budge of apocalyptic ellipse, where "everything will be as it is now, just a little different" (say the Hassidim).

Spiritual correspondences seek equilibrium as attunement to— rather than cessation or cancellation of—opposites. So, in Islamic alchemy, "without the idea of the *balance,* there can be no worlds in correspondence with each other." "The science of the Balance spatializes the succession of time by substituting for the order of succession the order of simultaneity, the unity of the 'cupolas'" (Henry Corbin).

"Having reached the *interior,* one finds oneself paradoxically on the *outside.* . . . Yet, strange as it may seem, once the journey is completed the reality which has hitherto been an inner and hidden one turns out to envelop, surround, or contain that which at first was outer and visible" (Corbin).

{"To lower oneself is to rise in the domain of moral gravity. Moral gravity makes us fall toward the heights" (Simone Weil).}

"Spiritual reality can therefore not be found *'in the where.'* The *'where'* is in it."

"After we realize the emptiness of things, everything becomes real—not substantial." — {where "nothing is clear; everything is significant" [Heidegger]} — "When we have emptiness we are always prepared for watching the flashing." "Every existence is a flashing into the vast phenomenal world." (Shunryu Suzuki)

> As Lightning on a Landscape
> Exhibits Sheets of Place —
> Not yet suspected — but for Flash —
> And Click — and Suddenness. (Emily Dickinson)

In *Etidorhpa* (1895) by John Uri Lloyd (Cincinnati pharmacist):

> "As the tip of the whip-lash passes with the lash, so through life the soul of man proceeds with the body. As there is a point just when the tip of the whip-lash is on the edge of its return, where all motion of the line that bounds the tip ends, so there is a motionless point when the soul starts onward from the body of man. As the tip of the whip-lash sends its cry through space, not while it is in motion either way, but from the point where motion ceases, the spaceless, timeless point that lies between the backward and the forward, so the soul of man leaves a cry (eternity) at the critical point. It is the death echo, and thus each snap of the life-thread throws an eternity, its own eternity, into eternity's seas, and each eternity is made up of the entities thus cast from the critical point."

It could even be called a *diacritical* point. G. Spencer Brown's "distinction" or "mark."

Desire encases language in the duplexity of conscious / unconscious.
Symbol cements this bifurcation into the enigma of incarnation.
Desire says "one," to which symbol adds "two," together making three.
　　—The sum does not cancel and supersede the two, but preserves them in its harbor or shelter. *Aufhebung.*

A symbol is a door, an opening, a passageway.
Mouth : tongue : vulva : urethra : nested frames, limits, *tao.*

～

Pascal: "I had a thought. I have forgotten it. In its place I write that I've forgotten it."
　　What if the notion you thought you'd never remember returned to you in all its fullness, integrity, coherence, and it was:
　　"What if closure, coherence, and mastery kept on repeating itself, insinuating its finality to us, not in narrative form or eschatological vision, but as a logic of the sentence, the paradigm of grammar itself?"

　　"If water boils in a kettle, steam comes out of the kettle and also depicted steam comes out of the sketched kettle. But what if one insisted on saying that there must also be something boiling in the sketch of the kettle?" (Ludwig Wittgenstein)

And if you didn't need to insist?

What if words themselves were sparrows pecking Zeuxis's grapes?

　　So all the animals peeled themselves and turned into drums, stretching their skins for the heads of the drums, and each of these heads could think. Think *dunk.*

　　"Life is an ecstasy." (Ralph Waldo Emerson)

　　"Thought is a permanent orgasm." (René Thom)

Works Cited

Adams, Hazard, ed. *Critical Theory Since Plato*. Rev. ed. San Diego: Harcourt, 1992.

Adorno, Theodor. *Aesthetic Theory*. Ed. Gretel Adorno and Rolf Tiedemann. Trans. C. Lenhardt. London: Routledge, 1984.

Agamben, Giorgio. *The Coming Community*. Trans. Michael Hardt. Minneapolis: U of Minnesota P, 1993.

———. *Stanzas: Word and Phantasm in Western Culture*. Trans. Ronald L. Martinez. Minneapolis: U of Minnesota P, 1993.

Aizenberg, Susan, and Erin Belieu, eds. *The Extraordinary Tide: New Poetry by American Women*. New York: Columbia UP, 2001.

Algarín, Miguel, and Bob Holman, eds. *Aloud: Voices from the Nuyorican Poets Cafe*. New York: Henry Holt, 1994.

Altick, Richard D. *The Shows of London*. Cambridge: Harvard UP, 1978.

Altieri, Charles. "Avant-Garde or Arrière-Garde in Recent American Poetry." *Poetics Today* 20.4 (1999): 629–53.

Ammons, A. R. *Collected Poems, 1951–1971*. New York: W. W. Norton, 1972.

Andrews, Bruce. *Edge*. Washington, D.C.: Some of Us, 1973.

———. *Give Em Enough Rope*. Los Angeles: Sun and Moon, 1987.

———. *I Don't Have Any Paper So Shut Up (Or, Social Romanticism)*. Los Angeles: Sun and Moon, 1992.

———. *Paradise and Method: Poetics and Praxis*. Evanston: Northwestern UP, 1996.

———, and Charles Bernstein, eds. *The L=A=N=G=U=A=G=E Book*. Carbondale: Southern Illinois UP, 1984.

Antin, David. *Talking at the Boundaries.* New York: New Directions, 1976.

———. *Tuning.* New York: New Directions, 1984.

Arnold, Matthew. *Culture and Anarchy. Selected Prose.* Ed. P. J. Keating. New York: Penguin, 1980.

———. "The Function of Criticism at the Present Time." *Critical Theory Since Plato.* Ed. Hazard Adams. Rev. ed. San Diego: Harcourt, 1992. 592–603.

Aronowitz, Stanley. *False Promises: The Shaping of American Working-Class Consciousness.* New York: McGraw-Hill, 1973.

Ashbery, John. *Houseboat Days.* New York: Penguin, 1977.

———. "The Impossible." *Poetry* 90.4 (1957): 250–54.

———. *A Wave.* New York: Viking, 1984.

Athenäum, Eine Zeitschrift von August Wilhelm Schlegel, und Friedrich Schlegel. 1798. Ed. Gerda Heinrich. Leipzig, Germany: Reclam, 1984.

Attali, Jacques. *Noise: The Political Economy of Music.* Trans. Brian Massumi. Minneapolis: U of Minnesota P, 1985.

Austin, Norman. *Meaning and Being in Myth.* University Park: Penn State UP, 1990.

Baer, Eugen. "A Semiotic History of Symptomatology." *History of Semiotics.* Ed. Achim Eschbach and Jürgen Trabant. Amsterdam: John Benjamins, 1983. 41–66.

Baker, Houston A., Jr. *Modernism and the Harlem Renaissance.* Chicago: U of Chicago P, 1987.

Bakhtin, M. M. *The Dialogic Imagination: Four Essays.* Ed. Michael Holquist. Trans. Caryl Emerson and Michael Holquist. Austin: U of Texas P, 1981.

———. *Problems of Dostoevsky's Poetics.* Ed. and trans. Caryl Emerson. Minneapolis: U of Minnesota P, 1984.

———. *Speech Genres and Other Late Essays.* Ed. Caryl Emerson and Michael Holquist. Trans. Vern W. McGee. Austin: U of Texas P, 1986.

Bartelik, Marek. *To Invent a Garden: The Life and Art of Adja Yunkers.* New York: Hudson Hills, 2000.

Barthes, Roland. *The Pleasure of the Text.* Trans. Richard Miller. New York: Hill and Wang, 1975.

———. *The Rustle of Language.* Trans. Richard Howard. New York: Hill and Wang, 1986.

———. *S/Z.* Trans. Richard Miller. New York: Hill and Wang, 1974.

Baudrillard, Jean. *Forget Foucault.* Trans. Nicole Dufresne. New York: Semiotext(e), 1987.

———. *In the Shadow of Silent Majorities; or, The End of the Social, and Other Essays.* Trans. Paul Foss, John Johnston, and Paul Patton. New York: Semiotext(e), 1983.

———. *Simulations.* Trans. Paul Foss, Paul Patton, and Philip Beitchman. New York: Semiotext(e), 1983.

Bayley, John. "Richly Flows Contingency." *New York Times Book Review,* 15 August 1991, 3–4.

Beach, Christopher. *ABC of Influence: Ezra Pound and the Remaking of American Poetic Tradition*. Berkeley: U of California P, 1992.

Beardsley, John. *Gardens of Revelation: Environments by Visual Artists*. New York: Abbeville, 1995.

Bernstein, Charles. *A Poetics*. Cambridge: Harvard UP, 1992.

———. *The Sophist*. Los Angeles: Sun and Moon, 1987.

Blaser, Robin. *Bach's Belief*. Canton, N.Y.: Institute of Further Studies, 1995.

———. "The Fire." *The Poetics of the New American Poetry*. Ed. Donald M. Allen and Warren Tallman. New York: Grove, 1973. 235–46.

———. *The Holy Forest*. Toronto: Coach House, 1993.

———. *Image-Nations 1–12 and The Stadium of the Mirror*. London: Ferry, 1974.

———. "Poetry and Positivisms: High-Muck-A-Muck or 'Spiritual Ketchup.'" *Silence, the Word and the Sacred: Essays*. Ed. E. D. Blodgett and H. G. Coward. Waterloo, Ont.: Wilfrid Laurier UP for the Calgary Institute for the Humanities, 1989. 21–50.

———. "The Practice of Outside." *The Collected Books of Jack Spicer*. Ed. Robin Blaser. Los Angeles: Black Sparrow, 1975. 271–329.

———. "The Stadium of the Mirror." *Image-Nations 1–2 and The Stadium of the Mirror*. London: Ferry, 1974. 53–64.

———. "The Violets: Charles Olson and Alfred North Whitehead." *Line* 2 (fall 1983): 61–103.

Bloch, Ernst. *Essays on the Philosophy of Music*. Trans. Peter Palmer. New York: Cambridge UP, 1985.

Bowie, Andrew. *From Romanticism to Critical Theory: The Philosophy of German Literary Theory*. New York: Routledge 1997.

Bradburne, E. S. *Opal Whiteley, the Unsolved Mystery; Together with Opal Whiteley's Diary, "The Journal of an Understanding Heart."* London: Putnam, 1962.

Brathwaite, Edward Kamau. "English in the Caribbean: Notes on Nation Language and Poetry." *English Literature: Opening Up the Canon*. Ed. Leslie A. Fiedler and Houston A. Baker Jr. Baltimore: Johns Hopkins UP, 1981. 15–53.

Brock-Broido, Lucie. *The Master Letters*. New York: Knopf, 1995.

Brown, G. Spencer. *Laws of Form*. New York: Bantam, 1973.

Brown, Norman O. "Homage to Robert Duncan." *Sulfur* 19 (spring 1987): 11–23.

———. *Love's Body*. New York: Random House, 1966.

Byrd, Don. *The Great Dimestore Centennial*. Barrytown, N.Y.: Station Hill, 1986.

Cabico, Regie, and Todd Swift, eds. *Poetry Nation: The North American Anthology of Fusion Poetry*. Montreal: Véhicule, 1998.

Cabri, Louis. *The Mood Embosser*. Toronto: Coach House, 2001.

Calasso, Roberto. *Literature and the Gods*. Trans. Tim Parks. New York: Knopf, 2001.

———. *The Marriage of Cadmus and Harmony*. Trans. Tim Parks. New York: Knopf, 1993.

Carson, Anne. *Glass, Irony, and God*. New York: New Directions, 1995.

———. *Plainwater: Essays and Poetry*. New York: Knopf, 1995.

Cendrars, Blaise. *Complete Poems.* Trans. Ron Padgett. Berkeley: U of California P, 1992.

Certeau, Michel de. *Heterologies: Discourse on the Other.* Trans. Brian Massumi. Minneapolis: U of Minnesota P, 1986.

———. *The Practice of Everyday Life.* Trans. Steven Rendall. Berkeley: U of California P, 1984.

Césaire, Aimé. *Aimé Césaire, the Collected Poetry.* Trans. Clayton Eshleman and Annette Smith. Berkeley: U of California P, 1983.

Char, René. *Leaves of Hypnos.* Trans. Cid Corman. New York: Grossman, 1973.

Clément, Catherine. *Syncope: The Philosophy of Rapture.* Trans. Sally O'Driscoll and Deirdre M. Mahoney. Minneapolis: U of Minnesota P, 1994.

Collins, Christopher. *Reading the Written Image: Verbal Play, Interpretation, and the Roots of Iconophobia.* University Park: Penn State UP, 1986.

Collins, Wilkie. *My Miscellanies.* Vol. 1. London: Sampson Low, 1863.

Conrad, Joseph. *Nostromo: A Tale of the Seaboard.* Ed. Keith Carabine. New York: Oxford UP, 1984.

Coolidge, Clark. "From Notebooks (1976–1982)." *Code of Signals: Recent Writings in Poetics.* Ed. Michael Palmer. Berkeley: North Atlantic, 1983. 172–84.

———. *Now It's Jazz: Writings on Kerouac and the Sounds.* Albuquerque: Living Batch, 1999.

———. *Solution Passage: Poems, 1978–1981.* Los Angeles: Sun and Moon, 1986.

———. *Space.* New York: Harper and Row, 1970.

Corbin, Henry. "*Mundus Imaginalis;* or, The Imaginary and the Imaginal." *Spring: An Annual of Archetypal Psychology and Jungian Thought* (1972): 1–19.

———. *Spiritual Body and Celestial Earth: From Mazdean Iran to Shi'ite Iran.* Trans. Nancy Pearson. Princeton: Princeton UP, 1977.

———. *Temple and Contemplation.* Trans. Philip Sherrard. London: Islamic, 1986.

Costello, Bonnie. "John Ashbery and the Idea of the Reader." *Contemporary Literature* 23.4 (1982): 491–514.

Cottom, Daniel. *Ravishing Tradition: Cultural Forces and Literary History.* Ithaca: Cornell UP, 1996.

Creeley, Robert. *The Collected Poems, 1945–1975.* Berkeley: U of California P, 1982.

Daumal, René. *Rasa; or, Knowledge of the Self: Essays on Indian Aesthetics and Selected Sanskrit Studies.* Trans. Louise Landes Levi. New York: New Directions, 1982.

Davidson, Michael. "Discourse in Poetry: Bakhtin and Extensions of the Dialogical." *Code of Signals: Recent Writings in Poetics.* Ed. Michael Palmer. Berkeley: North Atlantic, 1983. 143–50.

Deleuze, Gilles. *Essays Critical and Clinical.* Trans. Daniel W. Smith and Michael A. Greco. Minneapolis: U of Minnesota P, 1997.

———. *The Logic of Sense.* Trans. Mark Lester with Charles Stivale. New York: Columbia UP, 1990.

———. *Proust and Signs.* Trans. Richard Howard. New York: Braziller, 1972.

Desmangles, Leslie G. *The Faces of the Gods: Vodou and Roman Catholicism in Haiti.* Chapel Hill: U of North Carolina P, 1992.

Detienne, Marcel. *The Creation of Mythology.* Trans. Margaret Cook. Chicago: U of Chicago P, 1986.

Dickinson, Emily. *The Complete Poems.* Ed. Thomas H. Johnson. Boston: Little, Brown, 1960.

Dogen. *Moon in a Dewdrop: Writings of Zen Master Dogen.* Ed. Kazuaki Tanahashi. San Francisco: North Point, 1985.

Dorn, Edward. *Hello, La Jolla.* Berkeley: Wingbow, 1978.

Dretske, Fred I. *Knowledge and the Flow of Information.* Cambridge: MIT P, 1981.

Duncan, Robert. *The Opening of the Field.* New York: Grove, 1960.

Dussel, Enrique. *Philosophy of Liberation.* Trans. Aquilina Martinez and Christine Morkovsky. Maryknoll, N.Y.: Orbis, 1985.

Eliot, T. S. *Selected Essays.* 3rd ed. London: Faber, 1958.

———. "Ulysses, Order, and Myth." *Modernism: An Anthology of Sources and Documents.* Ed. Vassiliki Kolocotroni, Jane Goldman, and Olga Taxidou. Chicago: U of Chicago P, 1998. 371–73.

Emanuel, Lynn. Interview with Lynn Emanuel by Eliot K. Wilson. *American Poetry Review* 29.3 (2000): 29–31.

———. "Language Poets, New Formalists, and the Techniquization of Poetry." *Poetry after Modernism.* Ed. Robert McDowell. Brownsville, Ore.: Story Line, 1998. 199–221.

———. *Then, Suddenly——.* Pittsburgh: U of Pittsburgh P, 1999.

Emerson, Ralph Waldo. *Essays and Lectures.* New York: Library of America, 1983.

Equi, Elaine. *Decoy.* Minneapolis: Coffee House, 1994.

Eshleman, Clayton. *Fracture.* Santa Barbara: Black Sparrow, 1983.

———. *From Scratch.* Santa Rosa: Black Sparrow, 1998.

———. *Hades in Manganese.* Santa Barbara: Black Sparrow, 1981.

———. *Hotel Cro-Magnon.* Santa Rosa: Black Sparrow, 1989.

———. *Jupiter Fuse: Upper Paleolithic Imagination & the Construction of the Underworld.* Middletown, Conn.: Wesleyan UP, 2003.

———. *The Name Encanyoned River: Selected Poems 1960–1985.* Santa Barbara: Black Sparrow, 1986.

———. *Under World Arrest.* Santa Rosa: Black Sparrow, 1994.

———. *What She Means.* Santa Barbara: Black Sparrow, 1978.

Evans, Steve. "After Patriarchal Poetry: Feminism and the Contemporary Avant-Garde." *Differences* 12.2 (2001): i–iii.

Everdell, William. *The First Moderns: Profiles in the Origins of Twentieth-Century Thought.* Chicago: U of Chicago P, 1997.

Fenollosa, Ernest. *The Chinese Written Character as a Medium for Poetry.* Ed. Ezra Pound. San Francisco: City Lights, [1936].

Fisher, Philip. *Wonder, the Rainbow, and the Aesthetics of Rare Experiences.* Cambridge: Harvard UP, 1998.

Foster, Edward, ed. *Poetry and Poetics in a New Millennium: Interviews with Clark Coolidge, Theodore Enslin, Michael Heller, Eileen Myles, Alice Notley, Maureen Owen, Ron Padgett, Armand Schwerner, Anne Waldman, and Lewis Warsh.* Jersey City, N.J.: Talisman House, 2000.

———, ed. *Postmodern Poetry: The Talisman Interviews.* Hoboken, N.J.: Talisman House, 1994.

Fraser, Kathleen. *Translating the Unspeakable: Poetry and the Innovative Necessity.* Tuscaloosa: U of Alabama P, 2000.

Freud, Sigmund. *The Interpretation of Dreams.* Trans. James Strachey. New York: Basic, [1955].

Frost, Robert. *Collected Poems, Prose, and Plays.* New York: Library of America, 1995.

Fry, Paul H. *A Defense of Poetry: Reflections on the Occasion of Writing.* Stanford: Stanford UP, 1995.

Gandelman, Claude. *Reading Pictures, Viewing Texts.* Bloomington: Indiana UP, 1991.

Gates, Henry Louis, Jr. *The Signifying Monkey: A Theory of Afro-American Literary Criticism.* New York: Oxford UP, 1988.

Glück, Louise. *Proofs and Theories: Essays on Poetry.* Hopewell, N.J.: Ecco, 1994.

Godzich, Wlad, and Jeffrey Kittay. *Emergence of Prose: An Essay in Prosaics.* Minneapolis: U of Minnesota P, 1987.

Goldbarth, Albert. *Across the Layers: Poems Old and New.* Athens: U of Georgia P, 1993.

———. *Adventures in Ancient Egypt.* Columbus: Ohio State UP, 1996.

———. *Arts and Sciences.* Princeton: Ontario Review, 1986.

———. *Beyond.* Boston: Godine, 1998.

———. *Comings Back: A Sequence of Poems.* Garden City, N.Y.: Doubleday, 1976.

———. *The Gods.* Columbus: Ohio State UP, 1993.

———. *Heaven and Earth: A Cosmology.* Athens: U of Georgia P, 1991.

———. *Marriage and Other Science Fiction.* Columbus: Ohio State UP, 1994.

———. *Original Light: New and Selected Poems, 1973–1983.* Princeton: Ontario Review, 1983.

———. *Popular Culture.* Columbus: Ohio State UP, 1990.

Goux, Jean-Joseph. *Symbolic Economies after Marx and Freud.* Trans. Jennifer Curtiss Gage. Ithaca: Cornell UP, 1990.

Graham, Jorie. *Materialism.* Hopewell, N.J.: Ecco, 1993.

Grossman, Allen R. *The Long Schoolroom: Lessons in the Bitter Logic of the Poetic Principle.* Ann Arbor: U of Michigan P, 1997.

Guillory, John. "Canonical and Non-Canonical: A Critique of the Current Debate." *ELH* 54.3 (1987): 483–527.

Hacking, Ian. "Biopower and the Avalanche of Printed Numbers." *Humanities in Society* 5.3/4 (1982): 279–95.

Hahn, Kimiko. *The Unbearable Heart*. New York: Kaya Production, 1995.

Halliday, Mark. *Selfwolf*. Chicago: U of Chicago P, 1999.

Haraway, Donna. "A Manifesto for Cyborgs: Science, Technology, and Socialist Feminism in the 1980s." *Socialist Review* 80 (1985): 65–107.

Harpham, Geoffrey Galt. *On the Grotesque: Strategies of Contradiction in Art and Literature*. Princeton: Princeton UP, 1982.

Harrison, Jane Ellen. *Themis: A Study of the Social Origins of Greek Religion*. 2nd ed. rev. Cambridge: Cambridge UP, 1927.

Hartman, Geoffrey. *Beyond Formalism: Literary Essays 1958–1970*. New Haven: Yale UP, 1970.

Hatlen, Burton. "Joan Retallack, A Philosopher among the Poets, and Poet among the Philosophers." *Contemporary Literature* 42.2 (2001): 347–75.

Hegel, G. W. F. "The Philosophy of Fine Art." *Critical Theory Since Plato*. Rev. ed. Ed. Hazard Adams. San Diego: Harcourt, 1992. 534–45.

———. *Science of Logic,* Vol. 1. Trans. W. H. Johnston and L. G. Struthers. London: Allen and Unwin, 1929. 119–20.

Hejinian, Lyn. *A Border Comedy*. New York: Granary, 2001.

———. *The Language of Inquiry*. Berkeley: U of California P, 2000.

———. *Oxota: A Short Russian Novel*. New York: The Figures, 1991.

Hillman, Brenda. *Loose Sugar*. Middletown, Conn.: Wesleyan UP, 1997.

Homer. *The Odyssey*. Trans. Robert Fitzgerald. Garden City, N.J.: Anchor, 1963.

Hooke, Robert. *Micrographia; or, Some physiological descriptions of minute bodies made by magnifying glasses, with observations and inquiries*. London: Martyn and Allestry, 1665.

Howe, Susan. *The Birth-mark: Unsettling the Wilderness in American Literary History*. Middletown, Conn.: Wesleyan UP, 1993.

Inada, Lawson Fusao. *Legends from Camp*. Minneapolis: Coffee House, 1993.

Ivask, Ivar, ed. *Odysseus Elytis: Analogies of Light*. Norman: U of Oklahoma P, 1981.

Jameson, Fredric. *The Ideologies of Theory: Essays 1971–1986; Vol. 1: Situations of Theory*. Minneapolis: U of Minnesota P, 1988.

———. *Postmodernism; or, The Cultural Logic of Late Capitalism*. Durham: Duke UP, 1991.

Jarnot, Lisa. *Some Other Kind of Mission*. Providence, R.I.: Burning Deck, 1996.

———, Leonard Schwartz, and Chris Stroffolino, eds. *An Anthology of New (American) Poets*. Jersey City, N.J.: Talisman House, 1998.

Johnson, Ronald. *Ark: The Foundations: 1–33*. San Francisco: North Point, 1980.

———. *ARK*. Albuquerque: Living Batch, 1996.

———. *To Do as Adam Did: Selected Poems of Ronald Johnson*. Ed. Peter O'Leary. Jersey City, N.J.: Talisman House, 2000.

Jones, David. *The Dying Gaul and Other Writings*. Ed. Harman Grisewood. London: Faber, 1978.

Joyce, James. *Finnegans Wake*. New York: Viking, 1957.

———. *Ulysses*. New York: Vintage, 1990.

Jung, C. G. *Aion: Researches into the Phenomenology of the Self.* 2nd ed. Trans. R. F. C. Hull. Princeton: Princeton UP, 1968.

Kang, Eyvind. "Music Suffers." John Zorn, ed. *Arcana: Musicians on Music.* New York: Granary Books, 2000. 167–69.

Kaufman, Alan, ed. *The Outlaw Bible of American Poetry.* New York: Thunder's Mouth, 1999.

Keller, Helen. *The World I Live In.* Chicago: Century, 1908.

Keller, Lynn. " 'Fields of Pattern-Bounded Unpredictability': Recent Palimptexts by Rosmarie Waldrop and Joan Retallack." *Contemporary Literature* 42.2 (2001): 376–412.

Kermode, Frank. *The Sense of an Ending: Studies in the Theory of Fiction.* New York: Oxford UP, 1967.

Kevorkian, Martin. "John Ashbery's Flow Chart: John Ashbery and The Theorists on John Ashbery against the Critics against John Ashbery." *New Literary History* 25.2 (1994): 459–76.

Koestler, Arthur. *Janus, A Summing Up.* London: Hutchinson, 1978.

Koethe, John. *Poetry at One Remove: Essays.* Ann Arbor: U of Michigan P, 2000.

Krauss, Rosalind. "The Originality of the Avant-Garde: A Postmodernist Repetition." *October* 18 (fall 1981): 47–66.

Krell, David Farrell. *Of Memory, Reminiscence, and Writing: On the Verge.* Bloomington: Indiana UP, 1990.

LaBarre, Weston. *Muelos: A Stone Age Superstition about Sexuality.* New York: Columbia UP, 1984.

Lacan, Jacques. *Ecrits: A Selection.* Trans. Alan Sheridan. New York: W. W. Norton, 1977.

———. *Four Fundamental Concepts of Psycho-Analysis.* Trans. Alan Sheridan. New York: W. W. Norton, 1978.

Lacoue-Labarthe, Philippe, and Jean-Luc Nancy. *The Literary Absolute: The Theory of Literature in German Romanticism.* Trans. Philip Barnard and Cheryl Lester. Albany: State U of New York P, 1988.

Lao Tzu. *Tao Te Ching.* Trans. D. C. Lau. [Baltimore]: Penguin, 1963.

Latour, Bruno. "Give Me a Laboratory and I Will Raise the World." *Science Observed: Perspectives on the Social Study of Science.* Ed. Karin Knorr-Cetina and Michael Mulkay. Los Angeles: Sage, 1983. 141–70.

Lauterbach, Ann. "Use This Word in a Sentence: Experimental." *By Herself: Women Reclaim Poetry.* Ed. Molly McQuade. Saint Paul: Graywolf, 2000. 187–91.

Lecercle, Jean-Jacques. *Philosophy through the Looking-Glass: Language, Nonsense, Desire.* La Salle, Ill.: Open Court, 1985.

Lehman, David. *The Daily Mirror: A Journal in Poetry.* New York: Scribner, 2000.

Lew, Walter K., ed. *Premonitions: The Kaya Anthology of New Asian North American Poetry.* New York: Kaya Production, 1995.

Lloyd, John Uri. *Etidorhpa; or, The End of Earth.* New York: Pocket Books, 1978.

Logan, William. *Reputations of the Tongue: On Poets and Poetry.* Gainesville: UP of Florida, 1999.

———. *Night Battle.* New York: Penguin, 1999.

Lorca, Federico García. *Deep Song and Other Prose.* Ed. and trans. Christopher Maurer. New York: New Directions, 1980.

Luhmann, Niklas. *Art as a Social System.* Trans. Eva M. Knodt. Stanford: Stanford UP, 2000.

MacKay, L. A. *Janus.* Berkeley: U of California P, 1956.

Mackey, Nathaniel. *Discrepant Engagement: Dissonance, Cross-Culturality, and Experimental Writing.* New York: Cambridge UP, 1993.

Maier, Michael. *Atalanta Fugiens: An Edition of the Fugues, Emblems, and Epigrams.* Trans. Joscelyn Godwin. Grand Rapids, Mich.: Phanes, 1989.

Mann, Paul. "A Poetics of Its Own Occasion," *Contemporary Literature* 35 (1994): 171–81.

———. *The Theory-Death of the Avant-Garde.* Bloomington: Indiana UP, 1991.

McCaffery, Steve. *Prior to Meaning: The Protosemantic and Poetics.* Evanston: Northwestern UP, 2001.

———. *Seven Pages Missing, Vol. 1: Selected Texts 1969–1999.* Toronto: Coach House, 2000.

McGann, Jerome. *Dante Gabriel Rossetti and the Game That Must Be Lost.* New Haven: Yale UP, 2000.

McGuirk, Kevin. "Poetry and 'Stupidity': Beats to L=A=N=G=U=A=G=E." *Open Letter* Eleventh Series, no. 1 (spring 2001): 96–112.

McHugh, Heather. *Broken English: Poetry and Partiality.* Middletown, Conn.: Wesleyan UP, 1993.

McLuhan, Marshall. *From Cliché to Archetype.* New York: Viking, 1970.

Meltzer, David, *No Eyes: Lester Young.* Santa Rosa: Black Sparrow, 2000.

———, ed. *San Francisco Beat: Talking with the Poets.* San Francisco: City Lights, 2001.

Melville, Herman. *Pierre, Israel Potter, The Piazza Tales, The Confidence-Man, Uncollected Prose, Billy Budd, Sailor.* New York: Library of America, 1984.

Merleau-Ponty, Maurice. *The Visible and the Invisible.* Trans. Alphonso Lingis. Evanston: Northwestern UP, 1968.

Meyer, Donald B. *The Positive Thinkers: Religion as Pop Psychology, from Mary Baker Eddy to Oral Roberts.* New York: Pantheon, 1980.

Mill, John Stuart. "What Is Poetry?" *Critical Theory Since Plato.* Ed. Hazard Adams. San Diego: Harcourt, 1971. 537–43.

Milton, John. *The Poems of John Milton.* Ed. Helen Darbshire. London: Oxford UP, 1958.

Mitchell, W. J. T. *Iconology: Image, Text, Ideology.* Chicago: U of Chicago P, 1986.

Mouré, Erin. *Search Procedures.* Concord, Ont.: Anansi, 1996.

Mullen, Harryette. *Muse and Drudge.* Philadelphia: Singing Horse, 1995.

Nelson, Cary. *Revolutionary Memory: Recovering the Poetry of the American Left.* New York: Routledge, 2001.

Notley, Alice. *Disobedience*. New York: Penguin, 2001.

———, and Douglas Oliver. *The Scarlet Cabinet: A Compendium of Books*. New York: Scarlet Editions, 1992.

Novarina, Valère. *The Theater of the Ears*. Trans. and ed. Allen S. Weiss. Los Angeles: Sun and Moon, 1996.

Oettermann, Stephan. *The Panorama: History of a Mass Medium*. Trans. Deborah Lucas Schneider. New York: Zone, 1997.

O'Flaherty, Wendy Doniger. *Dreams, Illusions, and Other Realities*. Chicago: U of Chicago P, 1984.

O'Neill, John. *Five Bodies*. Ithaca: Cornell UP, 1985.

Olsen, William. *Vision of a Storm Cloud*. Evanston: TriQuarterly, 1996.

Olson, Charles. *The Maximus Poems*. Ed. George Butterick. Berkeley: U of California P, 1983.

Onians, Richard Broxton. *The Origins of European Thought about the Body, the Mind, the Soul, the World, Time, and Fate: New Interpretations of Greek, Roman, and Kindred Evidence, Also of Some Basic Jewish and Christian Beliefs*. Cambridge: Cambridge UP, 1951.

Oppen, George. *Collected Poems of George Oppen*. New York: New Directions, 1975.

Osman, Jena. *The Character*. Boston: Beacon, 1999.

Palmer, Michael. *Sun*. San Francisco: North Point, 1988.

Patey, Douglas Lane. *Probability and Literary Form: Philosophic Theory and Literary Practice in the Augustan Age*. New York: Cambridge UP, 1984.

Paulson, William R. *The Noise of Culture: Literary Texts in a World of Information*. Ithaca: Cornell UP, 1988.

Paz, Octavio. *Alternating Current*. Trans. Helen R. Lane. New York: Viking, 1973.

Pearce, Roy Harvey. "Introduction." *Leaves of Grass by Walt Whitman: Facsimile Edition of the 1860 Text*. Ithaca: Cornell UP, 1961.

Peirce, C. S. *Collected Papers, Vol. 6: Scientific Metaphysics*. Ed. Charles Hartshorne and Paul Weiss. Cambridge: Harvard UP, 1935.

Pelton, Robert D. *The Trickster in West Africa: A Study of Mythic Irony and Sacred Delight*. Berkeley: U of California P, 1980.

Perelman, Bob. *The First World*. Great Barrington, Mass.: Figures, 1986.

———. *The Marginalization of Poetry: Language Writing and Literary History*. Princeton: Princeton UP, 1996.

Perkins, David. *A History of Modern Poetry: Modernism and After*. Cambridge: Harvard UP, 1987.

Perloff, Marjorie. *Poetic License: Essays on Modernist and Postmodernist Lyric*. Evanston: Northwestern UP, 1990.

———. *Wittgenstein's Ladder: Poetic Language and the Strangeness of the Ordinary*. Chicago: U of Chicago P, 1996.

Poirier, Richard. *Poetry and Pragmatism*. Cambridge: Harvard UP, 1992.

———. *The Renewal of Literature: Emersonian Reflections*. New York: Random House, 1987.

Powys, Llewelyn. *Swiss Essays*. London: John Lane, 1947.

Prufer, Kevin, ed. *The New Young American Poets: An Anthology*. Carbondale: Southern Illinois UP, 2000.

Pynchon, Thomas. *The Crying of Lot 49*. New York: Perennial, 1986.

Radin, Paul. *The Trickster: A Study in American Indian Mythology*. New York: Bell, 1956.

Rankine, Claudia. *Plot*. New York: Grove, 2001.

——, and Juliana Spahr, eds. *American Women Poets in the Twenty-First Century: Where Lyric Meets Language*. Middletown, Conn.: Wesleyan UP, 2002.

Rasula, Jed. *The American Poetry Wax Museum: Reality Effects, 1940–1990*. Urbana, Ill.: National Council of Teachers of English, 1996.

——. "Poetry's Voice-Over." *Sound States: Innovative Poetics and Acoustical Technologies*. Ed. Adalaide Morris. Chapel Hill: U of North Carolina P, 1997. 274–316.

——. "Spicer's Orpheus and the Emancipation of Pronouns," *Boundary 2* VI.1 (1977): 51–102.

——, and Steve McCaffery, eds. *Imagining Language: An Anthology*. Cambridge: MIT P, 1998.

Rehak, Melanie. "Things Fall Together." *New York Times Magazine*, 26 March 2000, 37–39.

Retallack, Joan. *Afterrimages*. Middletown, Conn.: Wesleyan UP, 1995.

——. *How to Do Things with Words*. Los Angeles: Sun and Moon, 1998.

Rich, Adrienne. *Arts of the Possible: Essays and Conversations*. New York: W. W. Norton, 2001.

Ricoeur, Paul. *From Text to Action: Essays in Hermeneutics, II*. Trans. Kathleen Blamey and John B. Thompson. Evanston: Northwestern UP, 1991.

Rilke, Rainer Maria. *Where Silence Reigns: Selected Prose*. Trans. G. Craig Houston. New York: New Directions, 1978.

Robertson, Lisa. *Debbie: An Epic*. Vancouver, B.C.: New Star, 1997.

Rosenfeld, Alvin. *A Double Dying: Reflections on Holocaust Literature*. Bloomington: Indiana UP, 1980.

Ross, Alexander. *Mystagogus Poeticus; or, The Muses Interpreter*. 1648. New York: Garland, 1976.

Ross, Stephen David. *The Ring of Representation*. Albany: State U of New York P, 1992.

Rothenberg, Jerome, ed. *Technicians of the Sacred: A Range of Poetries from Africa, America, Asia and Oceania*. 2nd ed. Berkeley: U of California P, 1985.

——, and Pierre Joris, eds. *Poems for the Millennium, Vol. 1: From Fin-de-Siècle to Negritude*. Berkeley: U of California P, 1995.

——, and Diane Rothenberg, eds. *Symposium of the Whole: A Range of Discourse toward an Ethnopoetics*. Berkeley: U of California P, 1983.

Rukeyser, Muriel. *The Life of Poetry*. New York: Current, 1949.

Scalapino, Leslie. *The Front Matter, Dead Souls*. Middletown, Conn.: Wesleyan UP, 1996.

——. *The Public World / Syntactically Impermanence*. Middletown, Conn.: Wesleyan UP, 1999.

Schiller, Friedrich. "On Naïve and Sentimental Poetry." *Essays.* Ed. Walter Hinderer and Daniel O. Dahlstrom. Trans. Daniel O. Dahlstrom. New York: Continuum, 1993. 179–260.

Schimmel, Annemarie. *Calligraphy and Islamic Culture.* New York UP, 1984.

Schlegel, Friedrich. "Dialogue on Poesy." *Theory as Practice: A Critical Anthology of Early German Romantic Writings.* Ed. and trans. Jochen Schulte-Sasse et al. Minneapolis: U of Minnesota P, 1997. 180–94.

———. "On Incomprehensibility." *Theory as Practice: A Critical Anthology of Early German Romantic Writings.* Ed. and trans. Jochen Schulte-Sasse et al. Minneapolis: U of Minnesota P, 1997. 118–28.

———. *Philosophical Fragments.* Trans. Peter Firchow. Minneapolis: U of Minnesota P, 1991.

Schwitters, Kurt. *pppppp: Poems, Performance Pieces, Proses, Plays, Poetics.* Ed. and trans. Jerome Rothenberg and Pierre Joris. Philadelphia: Temple UP, 1993.

Scobie, Stephen, et al. "Present Tense: The Closing Panel." *Future Indicative: Literary Theory and Canadian Literature.* Ed. John Moss. Ottawa: U of Ottawa P, 1987. 239–45.

Seyhan, Azade. *Representation and Its Discontents: The Critical Legacy of German Romanticism.* Berkeley: U of California P, 1992.

Shannon, Claude, and Warren Weaver. *The Mathematical Theory of Communication.* Urbana: U of Illinois P, 1949.

Silliman, Ron. "Afterword." *The Art of Practice: Forty-Five Contemporary Poets.* Ed. Dennis Barone and Peter Ganick. Elmwood, Conn.: Potes and Poets, 1994. 371–82.

———. *The Age of Huts.* New York: Roof, 1986.

———, ed. *In the American Tree.* Orono, Me.: National Poetry Foundation, 1986.

Sloan, Mary Margaret, ed. *Moving Borders: Three Decades of Innovative Writing by Women.* Jersey City, N.J.: Talisman House, 1998.

Sloterdijk, Peter. *Critique of Cynical Philosophy.* Trans. Michael Eldred. Minneapolis: U of Minnesota P, 1987.

Sollers, Philippe. *Writing and the Experience of Limits.* Ed. David Hayman. Trans. Philip Barnard and David Hayman. New York: Columbia UP, 1983.

Soyinka, Wole. *Art, Dialogue, and Outrage: Essays on Literature and Culture.* New York: Pantheon, 1993.

Spicer, Jack. *The Collected Books.* Ed. Robin Blaser. Los Angeles: Black Sparrow, 1975.

Stafford, Barbara. " 'Illiterate Monuments': The Ruin as Dialect or Broken Classic." *The Age of Johnson: A Scholarly Annual* 1. Ed. Paul J. Korshin. New York: AMS, 1987. 1–34.

Stein, Gertrude. *What Are Masterpieces?* New York: Pitman, 1970.

Stevens, Wallace. *Collected Poems.* London: Faber, 1955.

———. *The Palm at the End of the Mind.* Ed. Holly Stevens. New York: Knopf, 1971.

Stewart, Garrett. *Reading Voices: Literature and the Phonotext.* Berkeley: U of California P, 1990.

Suzuki, Shunryu. *Zen Mind, Beginner's Mind.* Ed. Trudy Dixon. New York: Walker/ Weatherhill, 1970.

Thom, René. "Animal Psychism vs. Human Psychism." *Glossogenetics: The Origin and Evolution of Language.* Ed. Eric de Grolier. Chur, Switzerland: Harwood Academic, 1983. 3–13.

Thompson, Michael. *Rubbish Theory: The Creation and Destruction of Value.* New York: Oxford UP, 1984.

Tiffany, Daniel. *Toy Medium: Materialism and Modern Lyric.* Berkeley: U of California P, 2000.

Todorov, Tzvetan. *Mikhail Bakhtin: The Dialogical Principle.* Trans. Wlad Godzich. Minneapolis: U of Minnesota P, 1984.

Tory, Geoffroy. *Champ Fleury.* 1528. Trans. George B. Ives. New York: Grolier, 1927.

Trilling, Lionel. *Mathew Arnold.* New York: W. W. Norton, 1939.

Turner, Frederick. *Natural Classicism: Essays on Literature and Science.* New York: Paragon House, 1985.

Valéry, Paul. *Analects (Collected Works, Vol. 14).* Trans. Stuart Gilbert. Princeton: Princeton UP, 1970.

———. "Introduction to the Method of Leonardo da Vinci," *Leonardo, Poe, Mallarmé (Collected Works, Vol. 8).* Trans. Malcolm Cowley and James R. Lawler. Princeton: Princeton UP, 1972. 3–63.

Virgil. *The Aeneid.* Trans. Robert Fitzgerald. New York: Random House, 1983.

Virilio, Paul, and Sylvère Lotringer. *Pure War.* Trans. Mark Polizotti. New York: Semiotext(e), 1983.

Waddington, C. H. *Tools for Thought.* London: Cape, 1977.

Waldman, Anne. *Iovis: All Is Full of Jove.* Two vol. Minneapolis: Coffee House Press, 1993 and 1997.

Waldner, Liz. *A Point Is That Which Has No Part.* Iowa City: U of Iowa P, 2000.

Waldrop, Rosmarie. *A Key into the Language of America.* New York: New Directions, 1995.

Wallace, Ronald. *The Uses of Adversity.* Pittsburgh: U of Pittsburgh P, 1998.

Watten, Barrett. *Total Syntax.* Carbondale: Southern Illinois UP, 1985.

Weil, Simone. *Gravity and Grace.* Trans. Arthur Wills. New York: Putnam, 1952.

Weinberger, Eliot, ed. *American Poetry Since 1950: Innovators and Outsiders: An Anthology.* New York: Marsilio, 1993.

———. "*Sunrise* by Frederick Seidel." *Sulfur* 1 (1981): 221–25.

Weiss, Allen S. *Shattered Forms: Art Brut, Phantasms, Modernism.* Albany: State U of New York P, 1992.

Wheeler, Susan. "Poetry, Mattering?" *By Herself: Women Reclaim Poetry.* Ed. Molly McQuade. Saint Paul: Graywolf, 2000. 317–27.

Whitman, Walt. *Poetry and Prose.* Ed. Justin Kaplan. New York: Library of America, 1982.

Williams, William Carlos. *The Collected Poems, Vol. II: 1939–1962.* Ed. Christopher MacGowan. New York: New Directions, 1988.

———. "The Great American Novel," in *Imaginations.* Ed. Webster Schott. New York: New Directions, 1970. 158–227.

Wind, Edgar. *Pagan Mysteries in the Renaissance*. Rev. ed. New York: W. W. Norton, 1968.

Wittgenstein, Ludwig. *Philosophical Investigations*. Trans. G. E. M. Anscombe. New York: Macmillan, 1953.

Woolf, Virginia. *A Room of One's Own*. New York: Harcourt, 1929.

Wright, C. D. *Deepstep Come Shining*. Port Townsend, Wash.: Copper Canyon, 1998.

Zaehner, R. C., trans. *Hindu Scriptures*. London: Dent, 1966.

Index